Windows PowerShell Desired State Configuration Revealed

Ravikanth Chaganti

Apress®

Windows PowerShell Desired State Configuration Revealed

ISBN-13 (pbk): 978-1-4842-0017-9

ISBN-13 (electronic): 978-1-4842-0016-2

Publisher: Heinz Weinheimer
Lead Editor: Gwenan Spearing
Development Editor: Chris Nelson
Technical Reviewer: Shay Levy
Editorial Board: Steve Anglin, Mark Beckner, Ewan Buckingham, Gary Cornell, Louise Corrigan, Jim DeWolf, Jonathan Gennick, Robert Hutchinson, Michelle Lowman, James Markham, Matthew Moodie, Jeff Olson, Jeffrey Pepper, Douglas Pundick, Ben Renow-Clarke, Dominic Shakeshaft, Gwenan Spearing, Matt Wade, Steve Weiss
Coordinating Editor: Christine Ricketts
Copy Editor: Michael G. Laraque
Compositor: SPi Global
Indexer: SPi Global
Artist: SPi Global
Cover Designer: Anna Ishchenko

Distributed to the book trade worldwide by Springer Science+Business Media New York, 233 Spring Street, 6th Floor, New York, NY 10013. Phone 1-800-SPRINGER, fax (201) 348-4505, e-mail orders-ny@springer-sbm.com, or visit www.springeronline.com. Apress Media, LLC is a California LLC and the sole member (owner) is Springer Science + Business Media Finance Inc (SSBM Finance Inc). SSBM Finance Inc is a Delaware corporation.

For information on translations, please e-mail rights@apress.com, or visit www.apress.com.

Apress and friends of ED books may be purchased in bulk for academic, corporate, or promotional use. eBook versions and licenses are also available for most titles. For more information, reference our Special Bulk Sales–eBook Licensing web page at www.apress.com/bulk-sales.

Any source code or other supplementary material referenced by the author in this text is available to readers at www.apress.com. For detailed information about how to locate your book's source code, go to www.apress.com/source-code/.

Without a second thought, this book is dedicated to my loving wife, Silpa, and my son, Kaustubh. Words can't express how much I love you both!

Contents at a Glance

About the Author xv

About the Technical Reviewer xvii

Acknowledgments xix

Introduction xxi

■Part I: Introduction to Windows PowerShell 1

■Chapter 1: Beginning Windows PowerShell 3

■Chapter 2: Introducing Windows Remote Management and CIM 43

■Part II: Desired State Configuration Essentials 75

■Chapter 3: Introducing Desired State Configuration 77

■Chapter 4: Getting Started with DSC...91

■Chapter 5: Using Built-in DSC Resources 113

■Chapter 6: Building Advanced DSC Configurations 151

■Part III: Advanced DSC Concepts and Tips 177

■Chapter 7: DSC Configuration Delivery Modes...179

■Chapter 8: Monitoring, Correcting, and Reporting Configuration 207

■Chapter 9: Building Custom DSC Resources...223

■Chapter 10: Troubleshooting Common DSC Issues 247

■Chapter 11: DSC—From the Field 257

■Appendix A: DSC Community Resources 269

■Appendix B: WMF 5.0 and DSC for Linux 277

Index 285

Contents

About the Author xv

About the Technical Reviewer xvii

Acknowledgments xix

Introduction xxi

■Part I: Introduction to Windows PowerShell... 1

■Chapter 1: Beginning Windows PowerShell 3

What Is Windows PowerShell? 3

Object-Based Shell 4

Distributed Automation Engine 5

Scripting Language.. 5

Installing Windows PowerShell 5

Downloading and Installing WMF 4.0 6

Verifying PowerShell 4.0 Install 6

Exploring PowerShell Console and PowerShell ISE...7

PowerShell Console.. 7

PowerShell Integrated Scripting Environment (ISE) 9

Exploring PowerShell 10

Exploring PowerShell Commands... 11

Getting Help.. 12

Exploring Objects.. 13

Cmdlet Parameters... 14

Language Semantics 16

    Variables 16

    Operators 21

    Arrays and Hash Tables 26

    Custom Objects in PowerShell 28

    Flow Control in PowerShell 28

    Aliases 33

Understanding the PowerShell Pipeline 33

PowerShell Scripts 34

    Execution Policies 34

    Writing and Executing Scripts 35

PowerShell Functions 37

PowerShell Modules 38

    Discovering Modules 38

    Importing Modules 39

    Writing Modules 39

Customizing the PowerShell Environment 40

Summary 41

■Chapter 2: Introducing Windows Remote Management and CIM 43

Windows Remote Management (WinRM) 43

    WS-Management Cmdlets 44

Common Information Model (CIM) 51

    Introduction to CIM Cmdlets 52

    Understanding MOF 69

Summary 74

■Part II: Desired State Configuration Essentials 75

■Chapter 3: Introducing Desired State Configuration 77

The Configuration Management Challenge 77

The Continuous Delivery Challenge 80

Understanding Desired State Configuration 81

Imperative vs. Declarative Syntax 81

Enabling Desired State Configuration 83

Configuring Your Environment for Desired State Configuration 84

Summary 90

■Chapter 4: Getting Started with DSC 91

DSC Configuration Management Architecture 91

Configuration Authoring and Staging 92

Authoring 93

Staging and Delivery 103

Configuration Enactment 105

Local Configuration Manager 105

Configuration Enactment in Push Mode 109

Configuration Enactment in Pull Mode 110

Summary 111

■Chapter 5: Using Built-in DSC Resources 113

Exploring Built-in Resources 113

Archive Resource 115

Environment Resource 120

File Resource 122

Group Resource 126

Log Resource 128

Package Resource 130

WindowsProcess Resource 133

Registry Resource 136

Script Resource 137

Service Resource 142

User Resource 144

WindowsFeature Resource 146

Using the DependsOn Property 148

Summary 150

■**Chapter 6: Building Advanced DSC Configurations** **151**

Reusable Configurations 151

Understanding Configuration Data 154

  Introduction 155

  Separating Configuration Data 157

  Extended Configuration Data 159

Using Credentials in Configuration 163

  Using Plain-Text Credentials... 163

  Encrypting Credentials 166

Creating Nested Configurations 170

Summary 175

■**Part III: Advanced DSC Concepts and Tips... 177**

■**Chapter 7: DSC Configuration Delivery Modes..179**

Push Mode 179

  Using Start-DscConfiguration Parameters.. 180

  Limitations of the Push Mode 186

Pull Mode 186

  OData-Based (HTTP/HTTPS) Pull Service.. 187

  SMB-Based Pull Server 194

  Configuring Pull Clients 194

  Enacting Configuration in Pull Mode... 203

Summary...205

■**Chapter 8: Monitoring, Correcting, and Reporting Configuration** **207**

Configuration Enactment..207

  Target System Configuration 207

  Target System Meta-Configuration 210

Configuration Monitoring and Correction 210

DSC Consistency Checks...210

DSC Event Logs 212

Configuration Reporting 214

Using DSC PowerShell Cmdlets...215

Conformance Endpoint for Pull Clients 217

Summary...222

■Chapter 9: Building Custom DSC Resources..223

Introduction to DSC Resource Development 223

DSC Resource Schema..224

DSC Resource PowerShell Module 226

DSC Resource Execution Flow...226

Resource Module Manifest..227

Packaging DSC Resource Modules..228

Writing Our First DSC Resource...229

Test-TargetResource..230

Set-TargetResource...232

Get-TargetResource...233

Custom DSC Resource Patterns 237

Inducing Reboot After a Configuration Change..237

Localizing Verbose and Debug Messages...238

Adding Help Content..241

Granularity in DSC Resources...242

Composite Resources..242

Creating Composite Resources..242

InstanceName Parameter of the Configuration Command 245

Summary...246

■**Chapter 10: Troubleshooting Common DSC Issues** **247**

All Systems Must Be at Least at WMF 4.0 247

Custom DSC Resources Not Available 249

WinRM Issues 249

Errors with Pending Configuration 251

DSC Engine Cache 252

Summary 255

■**Chapter 11: DSC—From the Field** **257**

DSC for Cross-Domain Configuration Management 257

Using Credentials 258

Using Domain Trusts 258

Configuration Management As API 259

Configuration MOF to Byte Array 259

GetConfiguration 260

SendConfiguration 261

ApplyConfiguration 262

SendApplyConfiguration 262

TestConfiguration 263

RollBack 263

PerformRequiredConfigurationChecks 264

Expert Tips 264

PowerShell Profile and Customization 265

Avoid Multiple Configuration Scripts 266

Version Control and Backups 266

Automatic and Environment Variables in Configuration Script 267

Summary 268

■Appendix A: DSC Community Resources 269

The DSC Community 269

Windows PowerShell DSC Resource Kit...270

  DSC Resource Designer..270

  DSC Diagnostics 272

  DSC Service Resource 274

Summary..276

■Appendix B: WMF 5.0 and DSC for Linux 277

Windows Management Framework 5.0...277

  Credential Property of Archive Resource 277

  Multiple Attributes in the File Resource...278

  Installing Packages from an HTTPS Location 279

  Changes to Test-DscConfiguration 279

  DebugMode in Meta-configuration...279

DSC for Linux...280

  Installing and Configuring DSC for Linux 280

  DSC Resources for Linux 281

  Enacting Configuration 282

  Linux Configuration Store and Logs...282

Summary..283

Index..285

About the Author

Ravikanth Chaganti is a well-known blogger and a member of the Windows PowerShell community. He has been a Windows PowerShell MVP since 2010 and works at Dell Inc. as an architect for Microsoft solutions. He is passionate about automation and works in his free time writing scripts and tools to help automate management tasks for Windows OS and applications on Windows OS. Ravikanth has more than 13 years of industry experience and a broad set of skills in the IT infrastructure domain, ranging from servers to storage to networking. He started scripting in early 2000 and continued to hone his skills from that point. In 2006, he fell in love with an early release of Windows PowerShell and has been evangelizing PowerShell ever since.

About the Technical Reviewer

Shay Levy works as a senior systems engineer for a government institute in Israel. He has more than 20 years of experience, focusing on Microsoft server platforms, especially on Exchange and Active Directory. He is an internationally recognized knowledgeable figure in the PowerShell scripting arena.

He is the cofounder and editor of the PowerShell Magazine web site (www.powershellmagazine.com). He often covers PowerShell-related topics on his blog at http://PowerShay.com, and you can also follow him on Twitter at http://twitter.com/ShayLevy.

Shay is a Microsoft Certified Trainer (MCT) at the John Bryce Training center, and for his contribution to the community, he has been named a Microsoft Most Valuable Professional (MVP) for seven consecutive years.

Acknowledgments

It is never an easy task to write a book, especially when it is on a technology that is still in its infancy. While I am the sole author of this book's content, this work would not have been possible without the help of numerous people. First and foremost, I am grateful to the Almighty and my parents for what I am today.

This book wouldn't have been possible without a lot of support from Hemant Mahawar, Narayanan Lakshmanan (Nana), Abhik Chatterjee, Travis Plunk, Narine Mossikyan, and everyone else on the Windows PowerShell team. You guys are just amazing and super-helpful. I owe a lot of my learning to my friend and fellow MVP Steven Murawski. He was one of the early adopters of DSC and the first person I reached out to almost every time I had a question about DSC.

Huge thanks to my technical reviewer, Shay Levy, a good friend and my partner at PowerShell Magazine. Shay's feedback really shaped this book. Last but not the least, my thanks to the folks at Apress. This book wouldn't have been possible without their constant support. Thank you everyone!

Introduction

About the beginning of this year, Gwenan Spearing (at Apress) approached me to see if I was interested in writing a book on Desired State Configuration (DSC). I couldn't say no, because after Windows PowerShell remoting and WMI/CIM, DSC has been my favorite subject. I have been writing and speaking about DSC since the first preview came out in 2013, and there is no better way to capture that experience than in a book such as this.

Over last few years, IT service processes at various organizations, small and large, have been gearing up to support the Agile development and release cycles. It is no longer about how many features a product gains with every release cycle, but it is about how fast those features are delivered. As system administrators, developers, and DevOps engineers, you must have been experiencing this already. There are several tools and/or frameworks developed to support continuous delivery and configuration management in a data center. This is not a new subject, but it is certainly an area that is still evolving. There is no standard way of achieving your goals through these frameworks.

Microsoft, with its Cloud OS vision, has been focusing on building tools that enable developers and IT professionals alike to build and manage cloud infrastructure. One such initiative is Desired State Configuration. DSC is a configuration standards-based management platform rather than a tool. DSC supports both Windows and Linux platforms. By *management platform*, we mean that the Application Programming Interfaces (API) provided by DSC can be used within any programming language, to manage configuration of devices and applications in a data center. This book provides an example of how these interfaces are used within PowerShell. While this book focuses on DSC with PowerShell, the concepts that you learn here can easily be leveraged in any programming or scripting language that has support for accessing DSC API. I have included several examples in each chapter, to build a greater understanding of the concepts. These examples do not require any special infrastructure. All that's required is just a couple of virtual machines.

An Overview of This Book

Windows PowerShell Desired State Configuration Revealed is divided into three distinct parts. Each part contains related chapters that help you to understand thoroughly the concepts that are covered.

Part I: Introduction to Windows PowerShell

Part I provides an overview of Windows PowerShell as an automation engine and scripting language. It also includes a survey of Windows Remote Management (WinRM) and the Common Information Model (CIM).

Chapter 1: Beginning Windows PowerShell

This chapter introduces Windows PowerShell to beginners. The examples featured in this book require that you understand PowerShell, and it is necessary that you know the key PowerShell concepts, to make good use of the content of this book. For beginners, this chapter provides an overview that explains what PowerShell is, the need for PowerShell, the semantics of the PowerShell scripting language, and writing scripts, functions, and modules. Readers experienced with the key concepts of Windows PowerShell may choose to skip this chapter.

Chapter 2: Introducing Windows Remote Management and CIM

Desired State Configuration (DSC) is built on Windows Remote Management (WinRM) and Common Information Model (CIM). The most common DSC issues—discussed in Chapter 10—that you will face relate mostly to WinRM configuration or understanding CIM. This chapter builds a foundation for understanding these technologies. This knowledge is necessary to build the environment-use DSC for configuration management.

Part II: Desired State Configuration Essentials

This part of the book focuses on explaining DSC basics and general concepts. Using the knowledge you gain from Part I, you will learn in Part II how it can be applied to DSC.

Chapter 3: Introducing Desired State Configuration

Before delving into the DSC concepts, it is important that you understand the need for continuous delivery and configuration management and the challenges in employing these methodologies. Continuous delivery and configuration management are critical parts of almost every IT manager's plan to ensure that data center service-level agreements are met. Microsoft invested in adding the infrastructure required to enable continuous configuration management and automation of the related tasks. This chapter describes how DSC fits the bill here and provides an introduction to configuring your environment for DSC. You will learn the difference between imperative and declarative syntax and how the declarative nature of DSC helps in simplifying configuration management tasks.

Chapter 4: Getting Started with DSC

Once you understand the need for configuration management and DSC itself, it is time to look at the basics of DSC. This chapter takes you through the architecture and components of DSC. While discussing the architecture, this chapter provides an overview of different phases in the DSC configuration management process and describes how each DSC component plays a role in one or more of these configuration management phases. Understanding these different phases in DSC configuration management, and how the components are used at each phase, is essential both for making DSC work for you and extending it as needed. By the end of this chapter, you will be able to create a DSC configuration script and apply the configuration, using DSC PowerShell cmdlets.

Chapter 5: Using Built-in DSC Resources

In any configuration management framework, an entity that is getting configured is called a configuration item. The management of these configuration items does not occur automatically. There has to be some code that understands how to configure the entity and perform it for you. This is implemented as resources in DSC. These resources are nothing but PowerShell modules or MI providers. DSC has a few built-in resource modules that help you configure such entities as Files and Folders, Registry, Windows features, Windows services, Windows processes, and so on. This chapter provides an overview of these built-in resources and demonstrates their use.

Chapter 6: Building Advanced DSC Configurations

In Chapters 4 and 5, you learn the basics of DSC configuration authoring and how to use built-in resources for writing configuration scripts. DSC offers patterns for making these configuration scripts reusable. This chapter explores parameterizing DSC configuration scripts, using configuration data, and creating nested configuration scripts. It also helps in understanding how credentials are used with DSC and what is needed to pass credentials as a part of configuration authoring.

Part III: Advanced DSC Concepts and Tips

While Part I and Part II of the book focus on the fundamentals of Windows PowerShell and Desired State Configuration, Part III builds on what you've learned to that point and describes the advanced concepts of DSC.

Chapter 7: DSC Configuration Delivery Modes

DSC supports two modes of configuration delivery: Push and Pull. Each of these modes has both advantages and disadvantages. This chapter provides in-depth information on how the configuration enactment process works in each of these delivery modes. You will learn how to use the Push mode of configuration delivery, its limitations, and the need for the Pull mode. You will learn how to configure DSC pull servers and clients and to deliver configuration and resource modules to the target systems.

Chapter 8: Monitoring, Correcting, and Reporting Configuration

Chapter 3 provides an overview of different phases in the configuration life cycle, describing that monitoring and correcting configuration drift is an essential step in configuration management. This chapter describes how DSC helps administrators in controlling configuration drift. To make complete use of these DSC features, it is essential that you understand what goes on behind the scenes when enacting configuration, using DSC. This chapter helps you gain this knowledge and provides examples on how to use DSC PowerShell cmdlets and Conformance server endpoint to monitor configuration. You will also see how the DSC Local Configuration Manager can be configured to detect and auto-correct configuration drift.

Chapter 9: Building Custom DSC Resources

Chapter 5 provides an overview of built-in DSC resources. These resources are either binary or script PowerShell modules or MI providers. This chapter provides in-depth information about authoring PowerShell script modules as custom DSC resources. This chapter provides an overview of the semantics and walks you through building a complete custom DSC resource for managing hosts file entries. In this chapter, you will also learn how to add help content for custom resources and how to localize messages from the custom DSC resources.

Chapter 10: Troubleshooting Common DSC Issues

In this chapter, you will discover some of the most common problems you may come across when using DSC and the solutions to them. This list of common issues was compiled based on my own experiences and from what I've learned helping others resolve issues in their own DSC deployment. The concepts and knowledge gained from earlier chapters is used here to understand and resolve a problem. There is no structured learning from this chapter, but it is a useful reference, should you encounter a problem using DSC.

Chapter 11: DSC—From the Field

This chapter provides an assorted collection of real-world scenarios, such as cross-domain configuration management with DSC, tips that make better use of DSC API, and best practices to follow when writing custom DSC resources and configuration scripts. The sections in this chapter are unrelated, and as in the case of Chapter 10, you can use this chapter as a reference for different topics that are covered in the book.

Appendix A: DSC Community Resources

Chapter 9 provides an in-depth look into how custom DSC resources are created. While you can write PowerShell script modules as custom DSC resources for configuring almost anything you want, remember that there are also other people who are trying to solve the very same problem. To this extent, Microsoft has released several waves of a DSC resource kit that contains close to 50 custom DSC resources and helper utilities. This appendix provides an overview of some of the custom DSC resources that are a part of the resource kit and demonstrates how to use DSC resource designer, the DSC diagnostics module, and so on.

Appendix B: WMF 5.0 and DSC for Linux

This appendix explores some of the changes and enhancements to DSC on Windows through the WMF 5.0 preview release and looks at how to deploy and use DSC for Linux. These two components are still in the early stages of development, and the content in this chapter may or may not be applicable upon the final release. This is provided as an early guide, and I recommend that you consult any updated documentation from the preview releases, for more information.

PART I

Introduction to Windows PowerShell

This part introduces you to Windows PowerShell and the foundational building blocks for Desired State Configuration (DSC).

Chapter 1 takes you on a quick journey through PowerShell. We will look at the history of PowerShell, what the need for PowerShell is, and how PowerShell is different from the good old command shell and scripting languages of the past. You will learn how to explore PowerShell, using the cmdlets and interfaces provided by Windows PowerShell. You will also learn language semantics, such as data types, variables, operators, and flow control statements. Toward the end of Chapter 1, you will see how to create reusable PowerShell code, by writing functions, scripts, and modules.

Chapter 2 takes you through the foundational building blocks of DSC—Windows Remote Management (WinRM) and Common Information Model (CIM). You will learn how WinRM is configured and used. After you gain a thorough understanding of WinRM, we will look at what CIM is and how your acquired knowledge of WinRM can be used with CIM cmdlets in Windows PowerShell.

CHAPTER 1

Beginning Windows PowerShell

For a Windows administrator, until early last decade, the options available for automation of administrative tasks were very limited. I started my career with the Windows NT platform and worked my way through limited scripting technologies, such as DOS batch scripts, VBScripts, JScripts, and so on. I had written several scripts to automate my daily tasks, and each of those scripts was tens to hundreds of lines in length. It was not easy and/or possible to integrate them with other automation technologies or scripting languages. For example, using VBScript, it was—and still is—impossible to access the functionality provided by .NET assemblies or Win32 native API. The Windows shell provided command-line tools to automate a few tasks, but the output generated by these tools is always text, which requires complex parsing, using regular expression techniques that generally intimidate any person getting started with scripting. While the technologies were great during that time, they had certain limitations, and compared to where we are today, they were not all that productive. One big reason for this was the lack of focus on command-line scripting within the Windows OS. Microsoft, to a large extent, focused on making an end user's life easy, by providing excellent graphical user interfaces (GUIs). However, the lack of proper scripting tools and languages was certainly a shortcoming for the enterprise IT administrator.

Microsoft realized this toward the beginning of the last decade and started investing in developing a better automation and scripting framework for the Windows OS. This was when **Monad** was born and later renamed to **Windows PowerShell**. The first version of PowerShell was released in 2006, and the most recent version, 4.0, in 2013. Every release added features to the scripting language and shell offered by PowerShell. Today, PowerShell is called an *object-based command-line shell, distributed automation engine*, and *scripting language.* True to its description, PowerShell is the most versatile and feature-rich automation platform on the market today, and it is endorsed by thousands of IT professionals and organizations worldwide. PowerShell is a critical part of Microsoft's **Common Engineering Criteria (CEC)** and is adapted by many other partners and companies as the automation platform for their products.

In this chapter, we look at some key concepts in Windows PowerShell that are important for any beginner. If you are already familiar with Windows PowerShell, you can skip to Chapter 2 and continue reading about Windows Management Instrumentation. However, if you are just getting started with PowerShell, this chapter offers an introduction to several concepts and provides examples to help you understand these concepts more clearly.

What Is Windows PowerShell?

This is the first question I get asked in a formal PowerShell training session for beginners or in an informal discussion with people who know virtually nothing about PowerShell. I like answering it by saying that PowerShell is an object-based command-line shell, distributed automation engine, and scripting language. Yes, I said that already! Let us start by looking at the specifics of this statement, to understand what PowerShell is.

Object-Based Shell

Before I begin to explain what an object-based shell is, take a minute to understand the following code and try to infer what it is doing.

```
@echo off
For /F "tokens=*" %%a IN ('"dir /s /-c /a | find "bytes" | find /v "free""') do Set xsummary=%%a
For /f "tokens=1,2 delims=)" %%a in ("%xsummary%") do set xfiles=%%a&set xsize=%%b
Set xsize=%xsize:bytes=%
Set xsize=%xsize: =%
Echo Size is: %xsize% Bytes
```

So, what do you think the preceding DOS batch script is doing? If you thought that it is finding the size of the current working folder, you are absolutely right. You just graduated in DOS batch scripting. If you could not infer the script, don't worry. You may never have to write something like it. So, in this batch script, we are working with raw text, generated by `dir /s /-c /a`, arranged in columns, parsing it for a specific column that contains the size of each file and then summing it up. This may not work if the number of columns in the output changes.

Now, take a look at how the same thing can be done in PowerShell.

```
Get-ChildItem -Recurse | Measure-Object -Property Length -Sum
```

The PowerShell command looks much simpler and cleaner. Okay, only if you understand what it is doing. This is where the object-based nature comes into the picture. Windows PowerShell is built on top of Microsoft .NET, where everything is represented as an object.

■ **Note**   An object is a self-describing entity that has properties and methods. For example, if you consider a computer as an object, it will have properties such as the model, manufacturer, CPU speed, memory, and so on. The methods or actions on a computer object will be powering on a computer or shutting it down, etc. Now, relate this analogy to a folder or a file. Each of these entities will have a name, size, full path, and so on, which are the properties of the file or folder object. You can move a file or folders and create new files or folders using the methods of the objects. There are many such methods supported by the file or folder objects. In other words, properties hold the data representing the characteristics of an object, and the methods represent the actions that can be performed on the object. In PowerShell, an object is an instance of a .NET class.

Coming back to our PowerShell example, the `Get-ChildItem` cmdlet retrieves these properties of a file or folder object. We will discuss cmdlets in detail in a later section in this chapter. For now, think that cmdlets are a type of command in PowerShell. The `-Recurse` parameter tells the cmdlet to perform a recursive search for files and folders. Now, each file and folder object retrieved by the `Get-ChildItem` cmdlet gets passed to the `Measure-Object` cmdlet through a pipeline that is represented using a | symbol. We will discuss the PowerShell pipeline concept in detail later. For now, just think of it as an assembly line where a component gets passed from one place to another, and at the end, you see a finished product. In simple terms, a PowerShell pipeline is a collection of commands connected together. So, once the `Measure-Object` cmdlet receives the objects, it sums up the `Length` property. If you closely follow that, we are not parsing any text. We don't have to convert between data types. We just deal with objects and their properties. This is what defines the object-based nature of PowerShell. We will continue to see such examples and learn more about it.

Distributed Automation Engine

IT automation in an enterprise is not just about how we automate tasks on a single system but also about how we manage a set of systems that are used to achieve a common goal and how these management tasks can be automated. This is where we need the capability to distribute and orchestrate automation tasks to multiple devices in the data center. And, at the same time, we need the capability of performing these tasks in a sequential or parallel method, as required. In PowerShell 2.0, Microsoft added a feature called Remoting with which we can execute commands and scripts on remote systems. PowerShell remoting is built on the premise that if a script or a command executes locally, it should run on a remote system, without requiring any modification. This is called the Universal Code Execution Model (UCEM). I will discuss remoting in detail in Chapter 3.

PowerShell remoting is a foundation for other features, such as Workflows. Using workflows helps automate the distribution, orchestration, and parallel or sequential execution of multi-device tasks, and this defines the distributed nature of PowerShell. PowerShell workflows are built on top of the .NET Workflow Foundation (WF) and support almost every aspect of .NET workflows. PowerShell workflows are a bigger subject and not in the scope of this book.

Scripting Language

Scripting languages, unlike compiled programming languages, provide a quick way to "script" a task or activity. The scripting languages, similar to programming languages, offer different data types, variables, arrays and hash tables, flow control statements, and so on. Windows PowerShell, while providing all the facilities offered by a command-line shell, is a great scripting language. Apart from the basic aspects of any scripting language, PowerShell offers interfaces to access .NET and Win32 native APIs. This makes PowerShell the most powerful scripting and automation platform available for Windows OS. Also, the other features, such as Remoting, Workflows, and Desired State Configuration, give administrators a complete tool set to automate the data center management tasks, using PowerShell.

Installing Windows PowerShell

The most recent release of Windows PowerShell is 4.0. This version of PowerShell comes integrated with the Windows Server 2012 R2 and Windows 8.1 operating systems. So, if you are using these versions of the OS, don't worry about installing PowerShell 4.0. You can skip this section. If not, continue reading.

Windows PowerShell 4.0 is also available as a part of the Windows Management Framework (WMF) 4.0 package. This package includes updates to the following:

- PowerShell automation engine
- Windows PowerShell Integrated Scripting Environment (ISE)
- PowerShell Web Services
- Windows Remote Management (WinRM)
- Windows Management Instrumentation (WMI)

WMF 4.0 includes a new feature called Windows PowerShell Desired State Configuration (DSC)—the main subject of this book. The components of the WMF 4.0 package form the basis of several management functions using Windows PowerShell, and that is one of the reasons why all these components are packaged together.

Downloading and Installing WMF 4.0

You can locate the WMF 4.0 package download on the Microsoft download center by searching for WMF 4.0 or by simply pointing your browser to bit.ly/wmf40. The WMF 4.0 package is available as a Windows update package for the down-level operating systems, and the name of the MSU package differs for each OS. Here is a list of supported OS and the update package file names:

- Windows 7 SPI
  - x86 version: Windows6.1-KB2819745-x86.msu
  - x64 version: Windows6.1-KB2819745-x64-MultiPkg.msu
- Windows Server 2008 R2 SP1
  - x64 version: Windows6.1-KB2819745-x64-MultiPkg.msu
- Windows Server 2012
  - x64 version: Windows8-RT-KB2799888-x64.msu

■ **Note**   There is no WMF 4.0 download for Windows 8 operating system. You have to upgrade Windows 8 OS to 8.1 to get Windows PowerShell 4.0. The WMF 4.0 package for Windows Server 2012 cannot be installed on Windows 8 OS.

WMF 4.0 requires .NET Framework 4.5.1 as a prerequisite. This must be installed before attempting a WMF 4.0 install. Note that the WMF 4.0 install does not complain about the missing prerequisite. Instead, it will silently complete, but none of the components gets updated. You can download the .NET Framework 4.5.1 offline installer package by navigating to bit.ly/dnet451.

Once you have installed .NET Framework 4.5.1, WMF 4.0 can be installed by double-clicking the package or using the command prompt, taking the following steps:

1. Open cmd.exe and navigate to the folder where you stored the WMF 4.0 package.
2. Run packagename.msu /quiet (replace *packagename* with the name of the MSU package, as described earlier in this section).
3. Reboot the computer.

Verifying PowerShell 4.0 Install

It is important to verify whether PowerShell 4.0 install completed successfully. We can do this by looking at the PowerShell version table. To check the version table, do the following:

1. Open the Windows PowerShell Console (powershell.exe or powershell_ise.exe).
2. Type $PSVersionTable and press Enter.

The $PSVersionTable.PSVerion shown in Figure 1-1 is the PowerShell engine version we just installed.

```
PS C:\> $PSVersionTable

Name                           Value
----                           -----
PSVersion                      4.0
WSManStackVersion              3.0
SerializationVersion           1.1.0.1
CLRVersion                     4.0.30319.18444
BuildVersion                   6.3.9600.16406
PSCompatibleVersions           {1.0, 2.0, 3.0, 4.0}
PSRemotingProtocolVersion      2.2
```

Figure 1-1. PowerShell version table information after WMF 4.0 install

Exploring PowerShell Console and PowerShell ISE

When I speak to beginners, I tell them that whatever runs at the PowerShell console runs in a script as well. So, before getting started with PowerShell scripting, I recommend that users master the console. The binaries for the PowerShell console (powershell.exe) and PowerShell ISE (powershell_ise) are located at C:\Windows\System32\ WindowsPowerShell\v1.0. Both console and ISE are PowerShell hosts. In Windows PowerShell, a host is the runtime environment for the PowerShell engine. It is possible to create your own host, if you know how to write one in a programming language like C#.

PowerShell Console

The PowerShell console (see Figure 1-2) host looks similar to cmd.exe. Many beginners think that powershell.exe is just a wrapper around cmd.exe. This is not true. This console is a host written in .NET and enables us to run all existing Windows OS commands.

Figure 1-2. *PowerShell Console*

■ **Note** The default colors for foreground text and background used in the PowerShell console are different from what is shown in Figure 1-2. For better readability, the images with PowerShell output use dark text on a white background.

All navigation features supported in cmd.exe are supported at the PowerShell console too. For example, you can use the arrow keys to navigate through the history of commands run at the PowerShell console. You can use the Tab key to auto-complete file paths, cmdlet names, cmdlet parameters, and parameter arguments.

Table 1-1 shows a subset of PowerShell console keyboard shortcuts. For a complete list of keyboard shortcuts you can use at the PowerShell console, refer to http://technet.microsoft.com/en-us/magazine/ff678293.aspx.

Table 1-1. *Subset of PowerShell Console Keyboard Shortcuts*

Keyboard Shortcut	Purpose
Left / Right arrow keys	Move the cursor left or right on the current line
Up / Down arrow keys	Move forward or backward through your command history
Page Up / Page Down	Access the first or last command in the command history
Tab / Shift+Tab	Access the tab expansion function
F7	Displays a pop-up window with your command history and allows you to select a command
Alt+F7	Clear command history
Ctrl+Left arrow / Ctrl+Right arrow	Move left or right one word at a time

PowerShell Integrated Scripting Environment (ISE)

For any developer or for an administrator writing scripts, it is critical, when writing code, to use a development environment that supports features such as syntax highlighting, debugging, code folding and formatting, and so on. These features are very important for ensuring productivity when developing scripts. With the release of Windows PowerShell 2.0, Microsoft added a script editor, called the Integrated Scripting Environment (ISE), to Windows PowerShell. The script pane is where you can write scripts, and the command pane is similar to the PowerShell console and is used to show all script output (see Figure 1-3).

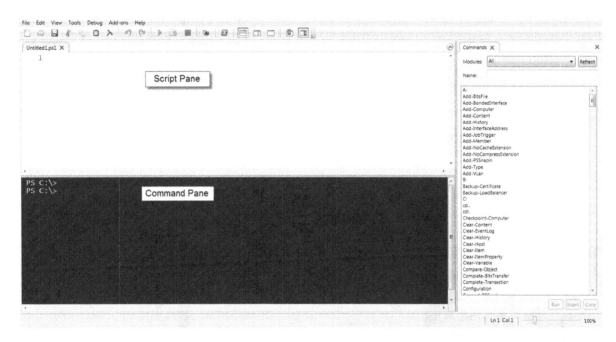

Figure 1-3. *PowerShell Integrated Scripting Environment*

The ISE supports Intellisense similar to Visual Studio and allows for writing and debugging scripts. Using the Intellisense features, as we start typing the cmdlet name in the script pane or command pane, ISE displays a drop-down menu with all relevant cmdlet names.

After the initial 2.0 release, the ISE got several new features in the PowerShell 3.0 release. For all my scripting purposes, I use ISE as my primary editor. My favorite part of ISE is its extensibility features. The PowerShell ISE exposes its internal scripting model as an object, $psISE. Using this and the methods available underneath, it is easy to create your own add-ons and extensions over and above what ISE offers. For example, the following code adds a new menu item called "Copy Current Line" under the Add-ons menu.

```
$ScriptBlock = {
 $psISE.CurrentFile.Editor.SelectCaretLine()
 $psISE.CurrentFile.Editor.SelectedText | clip
}

$psISE.CurrentPowerShellTab.AddOnsMenu.Submenus.Add("Copy _Current Line", $ScriptBlock, "Alt+C")
```

You can copy and paste the preceding code into the ISE script pane and press F5 to execute the code. This adds the menu entry, as discussed earlier, and also assigns the Alt+C keyboard shortcut. Now, if you press the Alt+C keyboard shortcut or select the menu entry from the Add-ons menu, the current line, where the cursor is placed, will be selected and copied to the clipboard.

Apart from these types of add-ons, the ISE also supports binary add-ons. These are nothing but Windows Presentation Foundation (WPF) controls that can be used to extend the ISE functionality. For example, in Figure 1-3, the right-most pane with the "Commands" title is a binary add-on. These add-ons are written using .NET and WPF and require a good knowledge of C#.

Similar to the PowerShell console, ISE, too, supports keyboard shortcuts to enable faster access to different features of the host. One of my favorite shortcuts is the use of Ctrl+J when writing scripts. This brings up a drop-down menu from which to select the code snippets available in ISE (see Figure 1-4). In this drop-down, we can select a snippet and press Enter, to add it to the script editor.

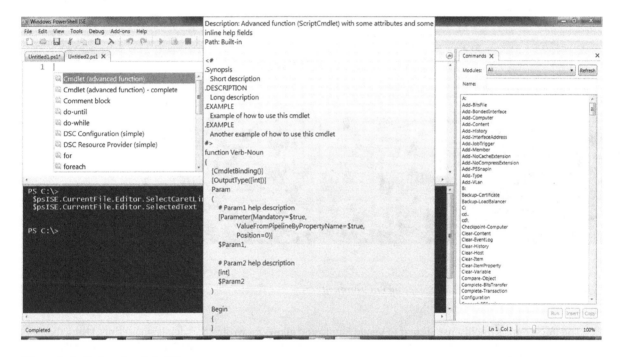

Figure 1-4. *Code snippets in ISE*

What's even better is that you can extend this functionality by adding your own code snippets, by using the New-IseSnippet cmdlet. The Get-IseSnippet cmdlet gets a list of all custom ISE snippets. Also, ISE lets you change the look and feel. You can change the syntax highlighting colors, using the Options item in the Tools menu or based on your preferences, and ISE automatically remembers these changes.

Exploring PowerShell

So far in this chapter, I have mentioned the word *cmdlet* more than once. A cmdlet, pronounced "command-let," is one of the command types in PowerShell. The other types of commands include functions, scripts, and native commands. I will discuss these other types of commands in greater detail a little later. So, for now, I will focus on cmdlets.

A cmdlet in PowerShell is implemented as a .NET class and always has the form verb-noun. Take, for example, the Get-ChildItem cmdlet we used in an earlier example. The Get part is the verb, and ChildItem represents the noun part. In PowerShell, there are a set of approved verbs, and this list can be retrieved using the Get-Verb cmdlet. The approved verbs provide guidelines on naming your cmdlets. Before I discuss cmdlets further, you have to know how to explore PowerShell. This is the most basic requirement for any beginner in PowerShell. So, I will stop discussing cmdlets and come back to them after you learn how to explore PowerShell.

Exploring PowerShell Commands

We have seen, so far, three cmdlets: Get-ChildItem, Measure-Object, and Get-Verb. How do I know that these cmdlets exist? There is a cmdlet for that! The Get-Command cmdlet helps us to explore the commands available. If we execute Get-Command without any parameters, it will return a full list of cmdlets and supported commands (see Figure 1-5).

```
PS C:\> Get-Command

CommandType    Name                                             ModuleName
-----------    ----                                             ----------
Alias          Add-WAPackEnvironment
Alias          Disable-WAPackWebsiteApplicationDiagnostic
Alias          Enable-WAPackWebsiteApplicationDiagnositc
Alias          Get-AzureStorageContainerAcl
Alias          Get-WAPackEnvironment
Alias          Get-WAPackPublishSettingsFile
Alias          Get-WAPackSBLocation
Alias          Get-WAPackSBNamespace
Alias          Get-WAPackSubscription
Alias          Get-WAPackWebsite
Alias          Get-WAPackWebsiteDeployment
Alias          Get-WAPackWebsiteLocation
Alias          Get-WAPackWebsiteLog
Alias          Import-WAPackPublishSettingsFile
Alias          Invoke-Hive
Alias          New-WAPackSBNamespace
```

Figure 1-5. *Partial output from Get-Command cmdlet*

If you observe the output in Figure 1-5, it shows the CommandType, Name, and ModuleName. There are many more PowerShell commands. What is shown in Figure 1-5 represents only a partial list. I briefly touched upon the command type earlier. There are four primary command types: cmdlets, functions, scripts, and native commands. The Get-Command cmdlet tells us what type of a command it is retrieving. The ModuleName property tells us to which module the command belongs.

■ **Note**   In PowerShell, a module can be considered as a library of commands or functions. We will discuss modules toward the end of this chapter.

The output that we see in Figure 1-5 is the same as if running Get-Command -CommandType Function, command. So, we can get a complete list of commands by using All as the argument for the CommandType parameter.

■ **Tip** If you want to see what all possible argument values to the -CommandType parameter are, simply type the command Get-Command -CommandType and hit the Tab key several times. This shows all the possible values for the CommandType parameter.

If we want to retrieve commands in a specific PowerShell module, we can use the -Module parameter. But, what if we don't know the module name itself? The Get-Module cmdlet is our friend here.

```
Get-Module -ListAvailable
```

Getting Help

We have seen the Get-Command cmdlet that helps us in exploring different types of commands available on a system. In PowerShell, help for any of the cmdlets can be seen by the Get-Help cmdlet. This help includes different types of parameters for the cmdlets, explanation about each parameter, and examples on how to use parameters.

■ **Note** Some of the cmdlets in modules that you may have downloaded from the Internet or copied from someone else may not include detailed help for the cmdlets. This is because the help information has to be authored as a part of the module, and the author of the module or cmdlet may not have included this.

The Get-Help cmdlet has several parameters to help users explore PowerShell. For example, you can use this cmdlet to get help information on it too. As a beginner, you should take time to read through the detailed help information for each cmdlet. You can use the -Detailed and -Full parameters or the -Examples parameter to access information on how to use the cmdlet and its parameters. Partial output from the Get-Help cmdlet is shown in Figure 1-6.

```
PS C:\> Get-Help Get-Help

NAME
    Get-Help

SYNOPSIS
    Displays information about Windows PowerShell commands and concepts.

SYNTAX
    Get-Help [[-Name] <String>] [-Category <String[]>] [-Component <String[]>] [-Full] [-Functionality <String[]>] [-Path
    <String>] [-Role <String[]>] [<CommonParameters>]

    Get-Help [[-Name] <String>] [-Category <String[]>] [-Component <String[]>] [-Functionality <String[]>] [-Path <String>]
    [-Role <String[]>] -Detailed [<CommonParameters>]

    Get-Help [[-Name] <String>] [-Category <String[]>] [-Component <String[]>] [-Functionality <String[]>] [-Path <String>]
    [-Role <String[]>] -Examples [<CommonParameters>]

    Get-Help [[-Name] <String>] [-Category <String[]>] [-Component <String[]>] [-Functionality <String[]>] [-Path <String>]
    [-Role <String[]>] -Online [<CommonParameters>]

    Get-Help [[-Name] <String>] [-Category <String[]>] [-Component <String[]>] [-Functionality <String[]>] [-Path <String>]
    [-Role <String[]>] -Parameter <String> [<CommonParameters>]

    Get-Help [[-Name] <String>] [-Category <String[]>] [-Component <String[]>] [-Functionality <String[]>] [-Path <String>]
    [-Role <String[]>] -ShowWindow [<CommonParameters>]
```

Figure 1-6. *Partial output of the Get-Help cmdlet*

Another very useful feature of the PowerShell help subsystem is the about help topics. These topics are plain text files located in the WindowsPowerShell directory under the C:\Windows\System32 folder. They range from the very basics of PowerShell to such complex topics as using remoting and workflows. You can access these topics using the Get-Help cmdlet.

```
Get-Help -Name about_*
```

The preceding command will list all the about topics on the system. I suggest that you take a look at each of these topics. For example, if you are looking for the help topic on Functions, you can simply run Get-Help about_Functions.

On systems with PowerShell 3.0 and above, when you run the Get-Help cmdlet for the first time, you will see a message to update the help content on your system. This is because, starting with PowerShell 3.0, there is no inbox help content. All the help content related to PowerShell modules packaged with the Windows operating system roles and features has to be downloaded from the Microsoft Download Center. So, to do this, PowerShell has two cmdlets: Update-Help and Save-Help. The Update-Help cmdlet analyzes the local system for PowerShell modules and the help content location for each module. It then downloads the content from the Internet and installs it on the local system. The Save-Help cmdlet helps you save the help content downloaded from the Internet at a specified location. You can use the -SourcePath parameter of the Update-Help cmdlet to install help content from a local folder. For systems with no Internet connectivity, this method can be useful to directly download the content, using the Update-Help cmdlet. The Update-Help cmdlet requires administrative privileges, as the downloaded help files are written to the WindowsPowerShell folder under the C:\Windows\System32 folder.

UPDATE POWERSHELL HELP

- Use the Get-Help Update-Help -Online command to understand the parameters available.

- Run the Update-Help cmdlet to update help on your system.

You have to check for updated help content once in a while, to ensure that you have the most recent copy of help content on your system. You can also use the -Online parameter of the Get-Help cmdlet to open help content in a browser, instead of downloading the content to a local system.

Exploring Objects

We have seen earlier what an object is and the object-based nature of PowerShell. I also mentioned previously that objects have properties and methods. But, how do we explore all the properties and methods an object has? There is a cmdlet for that too. It is called Get-Member. This cmdlet can be used to examine the objects. Let us start with an example.

```
Get-Item C:\Scripts | Get-Member
```

In the preceding command, the Get-Item cmdlet is used to obtain information about the C:\scripts folder. We are passing the output, which is an object, to the Get-Member cmdlet. As you see in Figure 1-7, the first line of the output generated by the Get-Member cmdlet tells us that the type of object we are examining is System.IO.DirectoryInfo. If you recall the earlier discussion, an object in PowerShell is an instance of a .NET class, and the object that we see here is an instance of System.IO.DirectoryInfo class in the .NET Framework. The MemberType column in the output tells us what type of object members—property, method, event, and so on—is available.

```
PS C:\> Get-Item -Path C:\Scripts | Get-Member


    TypeName: System.IO.DirectoryInfo

Name                        MemberType      Definition
----                        ----------      ----------
Mode                        CodeProperty    System.String Mode{get=Mode;}
Create                      Method          void Create(), void Create(System.Security./
CreateObjRef                Method          System.Runtime.Remoting.ObjRef CreateObjRef(
CreateSubdirectory          Method          System.IO.DirectoryInfo CreateSubdirectory(s
Delete                      Method          void Delete(), void Delete(bool recursive)
EnumerateDirectories        Method          System.Collections.Generic.IEnumerable[Syste
EnumerateFiles              Method          System.Collections.Generic.IEnumerable[Syste
EnumerateFileSystemInfos    Method          System.Collections.Generic.IEnumerable[Syste
Equals                      Method          bool Equals(System.Object obj)
```

Figure 1-7. *Get-Member cmdlet output*

For example, in Figure 1-7, we see a partial output from the above command that shows us methods available on a directory object.

To filter the output to see only one type of member, we can use the -MemberType parameter. This parameter takes several arguments, and you can use the tab completion feature of PowerShell to explore what valid values are for this parameter.

```
Get-Item C:\Scripts | Get-Member -MemberType Property
```

In general, because of PowerShell output formatting, you may not see all available properties of an object. So, knowing how to use the Get-Member cmdlet helps in exploring different properties available on an object.

What we have seen so far in exploring PowerShell is one of the first things a beginner must learn. Once you know how to use these three cmdlets—Get-Command, Get-Help, and Get-Member—it becomes easy for you to explore PowerShell.

In each of the examples we have seen so far, we used parameters. In some instances—for example, when talking about exploring objects—we did not use a parameter name; instead, we used an argument. So, what are these parameters? And, what are different types of parameters in PowerShell? Let us explore that.

Cmdlet Parameters

Each cmdlet takes zero or more parameters, and a parameter may take an argument, depending on the type of parameter. It is important to understand the different types of parameters and how they are used. There are mainly three types of parameters in PowerShell.

Named Parameters

The named parameters in PowerShell take the parameter name, followed by an argument. For example:

```
Get-ChildItem -Path C:\Scripts
```

In the preceding example, -Path is a named parameter. When we execute this command, the value C:\Scripts (the argument) gets assigned to the -Path parameter. This is an explicit binding of a value to a parameter name.

Positional Parameters

When using PowerShell cmdlets, it is not always necessary to specify the name of the parameter. For example, the preceding example can be simply written without the -Path parameter name and still achieve the same result.

```
Get-ChildItem C:\Scripts
```

This is possible because PowerShell tries to bind an argument to a parameter, based on the argument's position in the command line. We need to examine the -Path parameter of the Get-ChildItem cmdlet to understand this better (see Figure 1-8). This is where we use what you just learned in the earlier sections about exploring PowerShell. The Get-Help cmdlet with -Parameter can help us examine the details of parameters.

```
Get-Help Get-ChildItem -Parameter Path
```

```
PS C:\> Get-Help Get-ChildItem -Parameter Path

-Path <String[]>
    Specifies a path to one or more locations. Wildcards are permitted. The default location is the current directory (.).

    Required?                 false
    Position?                 1
    Default value             Current directory
    Accept pipeline input?    true (ByValue, ByPropertyName)
    Accept wildcard characters?  true
```

Figure 1-8. *Get-ChildItem positional parameters*

If you look at the the output in Figure 1-8, you see that the Path parameter of Get-ChildItem has a position of 1. This means that it is not necessary to specify the -Path parameter, if a valid value for that parameter is placed at position 1 in the command line. And that is what we did in our example. Now, to really understand this, let us consider another example.

```
Get-ChildItem *.ps1 C:\scripts
```

Take a minute to try this and determine what the output is. We see an error here, because the Get-ChildItem cmdlet was expecting a valid path value at position 1. Instead, we provided a wildcard string that cannot be bound to the -Path parameter. How do you fix this? Try it yourself.

Switch Parameters

Another type of parameter in PowerShell is a switch parameter. The switch parameter in a command line is either present or not present. These parameters do not take an argument.

```
Get-ChildItem C:\Scripts -Recurse
```

In the preceding example, -Recurse is a switch parameter. It tells the Get-ChildItem cmdlet to perform a recursive search for any items in all the subfolders. So, how do I know that -Recurse is a switch parameter? Well, I understand how to explore PowerShell! You remember the three cmdlets discussed in the previous section? We can use the Get-Help cmdlet to understand more about the –Recurse parameter. This is shown in Figure 1-9.

```
PS C:\> Get-Help Get-ChildItem -Parameter Recurse

-Recurse [<SwitchParameter>]
    Gets the items in the specified locations and in all child items of the locations.

    In Windows PowerShell 2.0 and earlier versions of Windows PowerShell, the Recurse parameter works only when the value
    of the Path parameter is a container that has child items, such as C:\Windows or C:\Windows\*, and not when it is an
    item does not have child items, such as C:\Windows\*.exe.

    Required?                   false
    Position?                   named
    Default value               False
    Accept pipeline input?      false
    Accept wildcard characters? false
```

Figure 1-9. -Recurse switch parameter

Using the same method, can you find out what other parameters of Get-ChildItem are switch parameters?

Language Semantics

When talking about scripting languages, I mentioned that PowerShell is a scripting language and that it supports almost every language feature that is in a programming or scripting language. In this section, we will examine some of the language semantics required to get started with PowerShell scripting. I recommend that, once you learn these basics, you use the about help topics in PowerShell to learn the advanced concepts of the PowerShell language.

Variables

Variables, as in any other language, represent a unit of memory for storing data. In PowerShell, the variable names are represented with strings starting with a dollar ($) sign. Variable names in PowerShell are not case sensitive, which means $name is the same as $Name. The variables in PowerShell are not strongly typed. This means, there is no data type associated when you initially assign a value to a variable. PowerShell converts the data type of the variable based on the type of the value assigned to the variable. The following example in Figure 1-10 demonstrates this behavior.

```
PS C:\> $name = "PowerShell"

PS C:\> $name.GetType()

IsPublic IsSerial Name                                     BaseType
-------- -------- ----                                     --------
True     True     String                                   System.Object


PS C:\> $name = 4.0

PS C:\> $name.GetType()

IsPublic IsSerial Name                                     BaseType
-------- -------- ----                                     --------
True     True     Double                                   System.ValueType
```

Figure 1-10. PowerShell variables are not strongly typed

We can, however, change the default behavior of variables, by using a method called type casting. Type casting makes variables strongly typed.

■ **Note** PowerShell, similar to .NET, offers multiple data types. If you have ever used any other programming language, you might find String, Int, Double, and so on familiar. PowerShell, too, offers all these data types and many more. For more information on how to use type casting in PowerShell, refer to the about_Variables help topic.

For using the type notation, we enclose the name of the data type in square brackets, followed by the variable name. Let us look at an example to understand this better. Once we execute this, we create a strongly typed string variable. Now, assigning a floating type value, in the case of default PowerShell behavior and as seen in Figure 1-10, would have changed the type of the variable to *double*. However, in the case of strongly typed variables, PowerShell tries to convert the value being assigned to the type of the variable. In this example, the value gets converted to string representation. Therefore, even after the assignment, the type of the variable $name remains as String (see Figure 1-11).

```
PS C:\> [String] $name = "PowerShell"

PS C:\> $name.GetType()

IsPublic IsSerial Name                                    BaseType
-------- -------- ----                                    --------
True     True     String                                  System.Object


PS C:\> $name = 4.0

PS C:\> $name.GetType()

IsPublic IsSerial Name                                    BaseType
-------- -------- ----                                    --------
True     True     String                                  System.Object
```

Figure 1-11. *Creating strongly typed variables in PowerShell*

■ **Tip** We already know that PowerShell is object-based, and most of the code we write deals with objects. Each object is an instance of a .NET class, and the methods available in the .NET class will be available on the object as well. As you see in Figure 1-11, the GetType() is one such method available on all objects, to inspect the type of the object.

So, what happens when we have a strongly typed integer variable and we try assigning a string to it as a value? Here is a hint: you can make a variable a strongly typed integer by using the type notation *[int]*.

In PowerShell, variables' names can include spaces, and the variable name can start with a number too. When a variable name includes a space, it has to be enclosed in curly braces.

```
PS C:\> ${Version Number} = 4.0
PS C:\> ${Version Number}
4.0
```

However, you should avoid creating variables with spaces in their names. This introduces complexity and can be confusing to others reading your scripts. Creating a new variable is as simple as shown in the preceding example. We decide on a variable name and assign it a value. That is it. However, PowerShell offers cmdlets to create and manage variables. We can use the Get-Command cmdlet to retrieve this list of cmdlets for managing variables (see Figure 1-12).

```
PS C:\> Get-Command -Noun Variable

CommandType     Name                                          ModuleName
-----------     ----                                          ----------
Cmdlet          Clear-Variable                                Microsoft.PowerShell.Utility
Cmdlet          Get-Variable                                  Microsoft.PowerShell.Utility
Cmdlet          New-Variable                                  Microsoft.PowerShell.Utility
Cmdlet          Remove-Variable                               Microsoft.PowerShell.Utility
Cmdlet          Set-Variable                                  Microsoft.PowerShell.Utility
```

Figure 1-12. *Cmdlets to manage variables*

The New-Variable cmdlet is used to create variables. The -Name parameter of this cmdlet becomes the variable name, and the argument you specify for the -Value parameter gets assigned to the variable.

```
New-Variable -Name ShellVersion -Value 4.0
```

Note that, in the preceding example, we don't prefix the name of the variable with a dollar sign. In fact, the cmdlet will generate an error if we use a dollar sign as a part of the name, and such a variable doesn't already exist in the PowerShell session. If a variable with that specified name already exists, the value of that variable will be used as the name of the new variable. This behavior is demonstrated in Figure 1-13.

```
PS C:\> New-Variable -Name $age -Value 78
New-Variable : Cannot bind argument to parameter 'Name' because it is null.
At line:1 char:20
+ New-Variable -Name $age -Value 78
+                    ~~~~~
    + CategoryInfo          : InvalidData: (:) [New-Variable], ParameterBindingValidationException
    + FullyQualifiedErrorId : ParameterArgumentValidationErrorNullNotAllowed,Microsoft.PowerShell.Commands.NewVariableComma
   nd

PS C:\> $age = 78

PS C:\> $age
78

PS C:\> New-Variable -Name $age -Value 100

PS C:\> $78
100
```

Figure 1-13. *Using a variable name with $ prefix*

In the example shown in Figure 1-13, we first try to create a variable by passing $age as the argument to the –Name parameter. Because the $age variable does not exist, PowerShell complains that the argument value is null. Next, we explicitly create a variable named $age and assign it a value 78. We repeat step 1 with an argument 100 assigned to the parameter –Value. Because the $age variable is present in the session, its value gets assigned to the –Name parameter, and a variable named $78 is created.

The Get-Variable cmdlet lists all the variables in the PowerShell session. The other cmdlets, such as Clear-Variable and Remove-Variable, are used to clear the value assigned to a variable and delete the variable. The Set-Variable cmdlet can be used to assign a value to a variable. There are other aspects, such as scope and visibility of the variables, in PowerShell. We will see these after you learn how to write scripts. This is the key difference between a simple variable assignment vs. using a New-Variable cmdlet to create variables. For example, we can use the –Option parameter of the New-Variable cmdlet to create constants. As an exercise, explore further these cmdlets and how they are used.

Types of Variables

Windows PowerShell offers different types of variables. The variables in the previous section are all user-defined variables. These variables live only in the existing session, which means that you create a variable and assign it a value. The variable will be available as long as the PowerShell console or ISE is open. Once you close and reopen the PowerShell console or ISE, the variable you created earlier won't be available.

The other types of variables are automatic, preference, and environment variables. Following is a brief explanation of these variables.

Automatic Variables

Automatic variables are created by Windows PowerShell to store the state of PowerShell. For example, $pwd is an automatic variable in PowerShell. $pwd represents the current directory and changes when you navigate from one directory to another. This is demonstrated in Figure 1-14.

```
PS C:\> $pwd

Path
----
C:\


PS C:\> cd .\Windows

PS C:\Windows> $pwd

Path
----
C:\Windows
```

Figure 1-14. *Automatic variables in PowerShell*

There are several such automatic variables in PowerShell. For example, $PID tells us the process ID of the PowerShell host, and $PSHOME gives us the path to the installation directory for Windows PowerShell.

In an earlier section, we looked at how to verify if PowerShell 4.0 is installed. We used the $PSVersionTable variable to examine the version of Windows PowerShell. The $PSVersionTable is an automatic variable.

For more information and a complete list of automatic variables in Windows PowerShell, read the about_Automatic_Variables help content. If you have updated the help content on your system, you can use the following command to read this help topic:

```
Help about_Automatic_Variables
```

Preference Variables

Similar to automatic variables, preference variables are created and used by Windows PowerShell. These variables are used to customize the behavior of PowerShell. The PowerShell cmdlets, too, use the preference variables to change the behavior of the cmdlet. Let us see an example.

In PowerShell, the -Verbose parameter is used to display verbose log messages during the cmdlet execution. The $VerbosePreference variable is used to define this behavior in PowerShell. By default, this is set to SilentlyContinue, which means that the cmdlets won't produce verbose loggings, unless the -Verbose switch parameter is explicitly specified. With $VerbosePreference set to Continue, the cmdlet with verbose logging produces the verbose messages automatically. This is evident from what is shown in Figure 1-15.

```
PS C:\> $VerbosePreference
SilentlyContinue

PS C:\> Write-Verbose "Testing Verbse Preference"

PS C:\> Write-Verbose "Testing Verbse Preference" -Verbose
VERBOSE: Testing Verbse Preference

PS C:\> $VerbosePreference = "Continue"

PS C:\> Write-Verbose "Testing Verbse Preference"
VERBOSE: Testing Verbse Preference
```

Figure 1-15. *$VerbosePreference in PowerShell*

There are several such preference variables in PowerShell. Using these, you can set the behavior of PowerShell cmdlets and customize the PowerShell configuration. I recommend that you read the about_Preference_Variables help content to explore more on this topic. An understanding of these variables is a must for advancing your knowledge of PowerShell to writing scripts and modules.

Environment Variables

Environment variables store information related to the operating system environment. Environment variables exist in other types of command shells, such as cmd.exe. PowerShell lets us view and modify these variables like any other variable in PowerShell. The PowerShell environment provider lets you access Windows environment variables as Env: drive. The Env: drive behaves like any other file system drive. The $env: prefix is required to access the values of environment variables. For example, $env:Path gives the value of Path environment variable. Similarly, $env:COMPUTERNAME gives the hostname of the local system.

As mentioned earlier, we can also access the Env: drive like a file system drive. This is shown in Figure 1-16. Note that this is only a partial list from the Env: drive. There are many environment variables.

```
PS C:\> cd env:

PS Env:\> dir

Name                            Value
----                            -----
ALLUSERSPROFILE                 C:\ProgramData
APPDATA                         C:\Users\Ravikanth\AppData\Roaming
CLIENTNAME                      WN7X64-G9WGYX1
CommonProgramFiles              C:\Program Files\Common Files
CommonProgramFiles(x86)         C:\Program Files (x86)\Common Files
CommonProgramW6432              C:\Program Files\Common Files
COMPUTERNAME                    WSR2-1
ComSpec                         C:\Windows\system32\cmd.exe
FP_NO_HOST_CHECK                NO
HOMEDRIVE                       C:
HOMEPATH                        \Users\Ravikanth
LOCALAPPDATA                    C:\Users\Ravikanth\AppData\Local
LOGONSERVER                     \\WSR2-1
NUMBER_OF_PROCESSORS            1
OS                              Windows_NT
```

Figure 1-16. *Env: drive in PowerShell*

The about_Environment_Variables help topic includes a complete description of environment variables and how to access and modify them in PowerShell.

Operators

For any scripting language, including PowerShell, operators are a part of the core language semantics. The standard set of operators includes arithmetic, assignment, comparison, and logical operators. In this section, we will take a brief look at some of these operator types and explore a few examples.

Arithmetic Operators

Arithmetic operators are the most basic form of operators we all know. At some point in time, either in another scripting language or elsewhere, you must have used the addition (+), subtraction (-), multiplication (*), and division (/) operators. PowerShell also supports the use of the modulus (%) operator, which can be used to calculate the remainder of a division.

The Windows PowerShell console host can be used to evaluate these calculations. Thus, it is not necessary to always write a script to use these operators. For example, if you type 2 + 2 at the PowerShell prompt, it returns 4. This is called *expression mode* in PowerShell. A few examples demonstrating the expression mode evaluation at the PowerShell console host are shown in Figure 1-17.

```
PS C:\> 2 + 2
4

PS C:\> 4 * 2
8

PS C:\> 4 / 2
2

PS C:\> 4 - 2
2

PS C:\> 7 % 2
1
```

Figure 1-17. *Expression mode evaluation at PowerShell prompt*

PowerShell supports using these operators with multiple data types and not just numbers. For example, you can concatenate two strings by using the addition operators. "Windows " + "PowerShell" returns "Windows PowerShell" as a single string.

We can also use some of the arithmetic operators with multiple data types in the same expression. For example, we can add the string "PowerShell" and 4 (see Figure 1-18). This is possible because PowerShell tries to convert the right-hand side (RHS) of the expression to the data type on the left-hand side (LHS). So, in this case, 4, which is an integer, gets converted to a string representing "4." However, the expression 4 + "PowerShell" results in an error. This is because the string "PowerShell" cannot be converted to an integer representation.

```
PS C:\> "PowerShell" + 4
PowerShell4

PS C:\> 4 + "PowerShell"
Cannot convert value "PowerShell" to type "System.Int32". Error: "Input string was not in a correct format."
At line:1 char:1
+ 4 + "PowerShell"
+ ~~~~~~~~~~~~~~~~~
    + CategoryInfo          : InvalidArgument: (:) [], RuntimeException
    + FullyQualifiedErrorId : InvalidCastFromStringToInteger


PS C:\> "PowerShell" * 4
PowerShellPowerShellPowerShellPowerShell

PS C:\> 4 * "PowerShell"
Cannot convert value "PowerShell" to type "System.Int32". Error: "Input string was not in a correct format."
At line:1 char:1
+ 4 * "PowerShell"
+ ~~~~~~~~~~~~~~~~~
    + CategoryInfo          : InvalidArgument: (:) [], RuntimeException
    + FullyQualifiedErrorId : InvalidCastFromStringToInteger
```

Figure 1-18. *Errors when using multiple data types with arithmetic operators*

In the case of multiplication, as shown in Figure 1-18, the string on the LHS gets printed four times. However, there is no way we can derive "PowerShell" multiples of a number, and that is the reason you see the expression 4 * "PowerShell" failing.

What happens when you try to execute an expression that has multiple data types and a division operator? What results do you see? The about_Arithmetic_Operators help topic provides complete information on how these operators can be used. I recommend reading this content.

Assignment Operators

We have seen some examples of using assignment operators in the "Variables" section earlier in this chapter. Assignment operators are used to assign one or more values to variables. The simplest example would be what we have already seen in Figure 1-10. An equal to sign (=) represents the most basic assignment operator. In the definition of assignment operators, I also said that we can use **one or more** values to a variable. So, what does that mean?

```
$name = "Windows", "PowerShell"
```

In this example, we are assigning two strings to a variable named $name. This is perfectly valid in PowerShell. In fact, what happens behind the scenes is that PowerShell converts $name into a string array (or a string collection). If you use the GetType() method on $name, you will see that its type is set to object[]. When an object type is followed by a pair of square brackets ([ ]), the type is called an *array* of the object. Arrays are a collection of objects. This is demonstrated in Figure 1-19.

```
PS C:\> $string = "Windows","PowerShell"

PS C:\> $string
Windows
PowerShell

PS C:\> $string.GetType()

IsPublic IsSerial Name                                     BaseType
-------- -------- ----                                     --------
True     True     Object[]                                 System.Array


PS C:\> $string[0]
Windows

PS C:\> $string[1]
PowerShell
```

Figure 1-19. Multiple assignment in PowerShell

Arrays in PowerShell, as in many other languages, have indexes, and the index starts at zero. We can use the array index to refer the value at the index.

■ **Note** For more details on how PowerShell arrays work, and other methods to create PowerShell arrays, refer to the about_Arrays help topic.

In PowerShell, we can also assign the same value to multiple variables at the same time.

```
$name = $ShellName = "Windows PowerShell"
```

Not only that, we can assign different values to multiple variables at the same time.

```
$name,$shellName = "PowerShell","Windows PowerShell"
```

The other assignment operators available in PowerShell, such as +=, -=, *=, /=, and %=, can be used to append values to variables.

```
$a = 10
$a += 10
```

When we execute the preceding code, the value of $a after the second command will be 20. So, in reality, the $a += 10 is nothing but $a = $a + 10. Now that you understand the assignment operator and its uses, experiment using these operators with multiple types of data and observe the results.

We can also assign the output of a cmdlet to a variable, using the assignment operators.

```
$files = Get-ChildItem -Path C:\Scripts *.ps1
```

The preceding command assigns the output generated by the Get-ChildItem cmdlet to the $files variable. In this case, the $files variable becomes an array of file objects returned by the Get-ChildItem cmdlet.

You can get more information on these operators by reading the about_Assignment_Operators help topic.

Comparison Operators

The comparison operators in PowerShell are used to compare values of two or more variables or expressions. These operators can either be used in an expression directly or as a part of a conditional or looping construct. We will see these branching constructs in the "Flow Control in PowerShell" section.

The way these operators are represented in PowerShell is different from other programming or scripting languages. This is shown in Table 1-2.

Table 1-2. *Comparison Operators in PowerShell*

Operator	Purpose
-eq	Equal to
-ne	Not equal to
-gt	Greater than
-ge	Greater than or equal to
-lt	Less than
-le	Less than or equal to
-Like	Match using wildcard
-NotLike	Does not match
-Match	Match using regular expressions

(continued)

Table 1-2. (*continued*)

Operator	Purpose
-NotMatch	Does not match using regular expressions
-Contains	Test if a collection of reference values includes a single test value
-NotContains	Test if a collection of reference values does not include a single test value
-In	Test if a single test value appears in a collection of reference values
-NotIn	Test if a single test value does not appear in a collection of reference values
-Replace	Changes the specified elements of a value

We won't be going through each and every operator and seeing examples. The about_Comparison_Operators help topic includes a very detailed discussion of each of these operators. Most beginners confuse these operators with the comparison operators they would have seen or used in other languages, for example, using '=' or '==' instead of -eq for equality tests. So, make sure you familiarize yourself with the usage of these operators.

One thing you must remember is that all these comparison operators usually return a Boolean value. That is, the return value is either True or False, depending on the condition. Some of the operators return the value when one or more values are identical. For completeness, let us see a few examples on how to use some of these operators.

A few examples demonstrating the use of PowerShell operators are shown in Figure 1-20.

```
PS C:\> 3 -eq 4
False

PS C:\> 3 -ne 4
True

PS C:\> 3 -lt 4
True

PS C:\> 1,3 -contains 1
True

PS C:\> 1 -in 1,3,4
True

PS C:\> 1,2,3 -eq 1
1
```

Figure 1-20. *Examples of comparison operators*

Observe the last example in Figure 1-20. The -eq operator returns the matching value when we use it with a collection of reference values.

Logical Operators

Logical operators are used to connect various conditional statements in PowerShell. For example, if you want to evaluate an expression based on the result of two different conditions, you can connect the two conditions together, using the logical operators. This includes -and, -or, -xor, -not, or !. The following examples provide a quick overview of how some of these operators can be used:

```
$a = 10
$b = 20
$a -lt 15 -and $b -gt 18
```

As you see in the preceding example, we can connect a couple of conditional statements using the -and logical operator. The -and logical operator returns True only when **both** the conditions specified in the expression evaluate to True. This method can be used to connect any number of such conditions and any combination of logical operators.

```
$a -lt 15 -and $b -gt 18 -or $a+$b -lt 30
```

What do you think is the output of the preceding code snippet? When you want to combine multiple conditions into a single check, you can do that by enclosing them in parentheses. For example, the following condition returns True even when only one of the conditions is true. This is because we are connecting them using the -or logical operator.

```
($a -lt 15 -and $b -gt 18) -or $a+$b -eq 30
```

The -not or ! operators are called the negation operators. They negate the result of a conditional statement. For example, if the condition $a -eq $b evaluates to True, using -not or ! negates it to False.

```
-not (10 -eq 10)
```

When comparing against Boolean values, you have to use $True and $False variables instead of 'True' or 'False' strings. For example, $a -eq $True represents a valid Boolean comparison.

For more details on how to use logical operators, refer to the about_Logical_Operators help topic.

Arrays and Hash Tables

The variables, in general, are scalar objects. This means we can only store a single variable. However, when there are situations for which we have to store more than one value in a variable, we require something more than a scalar variable. This is where vector variables such as arrays and hash tables help.

Arrays

We have briefly looked at arrays in a couple of examples in the previous section. If I have to formally introduce arrays, arrays are the data structures that store a collection of items. The best part of using arrays is that they can be used to store data of different types as the same collection.

The simplest way to create an array is to just assign multiple values to a variable. These values can be of the same data type or of multiple data types.

```
$a = "PowerShell",4.0,"Windows",2012
```

The preceding command creates an array of length 4. We can examine the length or count of items in an array by looking at the Count or Length property. We can add items to an array by using the append assignment operator.

```
$a += "Server",10
```

The preceding code will append the items "Server" and 10 toward the end of the array. We can retrieve the items in an array by specifying the location of the items index. The array index always starts at zero. Therefore, $a[2], for example, gives us the string "Windows", which is the third item in the array. Referring to an array with only the variable name will display all the items in an array.

If we know how many items are there prior to creating an array, we can use the method shown at the beginning of this section. However, when we just need an empty array so that we can add the items at a later point in time, we can use a special operator called the array operator. This is represented by the symbol @(). For example, $a = @() creates an empty array. We can add items to the empty array by using the append assignment. Also, we can create strongly typed arrays by using the method discussed in the "Variables" section. The help topic about_Arrays has a great deal of content on using arrays in PowerShell. A complete overview of the help topic gives a clear understanding of arrays.

Hash Tables

Similar to arrays, hash tables in PowerShell are used to store a collection of items. Other names for hash tables are *dictionaries* and *associate arrays*. Hash tables store a collection of key-value pairs. We can create a hash table using the @{} syntax.

```
$hash = @{}
```

The preceding example creates an empty hash table. We can create a new hash table with a predefined set of elements by using the following syntax:

```
$hash = @{"Name"="PowerShell";"Version"=4.0}
```

The Add() method on the hash table variable is used to add a new element to the hash table.

```
$hash.Add("Server","2012 R2")
```

As with arrays, we can use the append assignment with hash tables too.

```
$hash += @{"UserName"="Administrator"}
```

The Keys property on a hash table variable gives us all the keys of a hash table, and the Values property gives us all the values stored in the hash table. We can retrieve the value associated with a specific key, using the following syntax:

```
$hash["Name"]
```

If you want to change the value of a specific key in the hash table, you can do so by using the following:

```
$hash["Name"] = "Windows PowerShell"
```

For more information on PowerShell hash tables, read the help content described in about_Hashtables. A hash table is a very useful data structure for storing data used in PowerShell scripts. It provides a method with which to refer to elements by name rather than by index numbers, as in arrays. So, it is important that you understand how to use them.

Custom Objects in PowerShell

So far, we have seen how different types of objects are created and how the properties and methods of those objects can be used. Have you ever wondered how we can create our own custom objects? We can use the hash tables data structure that you just learned, to create custom objects in PowerShell. The custom objects are a very useful way to structure the output from a script or cmdlet into a meaningful form for users to understand. There are two main ways to create custom objects.

Using New-Object

The New-Object cmdlet allows us to create custom objects from a hash table. This cmdlet can be used to create objects from .NET classes and COM objects too. We will, however, focus only on custom object creation using the New-Object cmdlet.

Custom objects in PowerShell are represented by the PSCustomObject or PSObject type name. When creating a custom object using the New-Object cmdlet, we must specify PSCustomObject or PSObject as the argument for the -TypeName parameter. The properties of the custom object should be provided as a hash table to the -Property parameter.

```
$NewObject = New-Object -TypeName PSCustomObject -Property @{
    "Name"="PowerShell"
    "Version"=4.0
}
```

Once you execute this, you see a new object created, and the properties can be accessed by referencing to the properties. For example, $NewObject.Name gives us the value we assigned to the Name property in the hash table.

Using the [PSCustomObject] type

As with data types, custom objects can also be represented by their type name. This representation is usually called a type accelerator or shorthand notation. We can create a custom object by type casting a hash table to a PSCustomObject type. Let us see an example to understand this.

```
$NewObject = [PSCustomObject] @{
    "Name"="PowerShell"
    "Version"=4.0
}
```

This is it. If you observe closely, this is very similar to the way we used the New-Object cmdlet. In this case, by using the type accelerator, we don't use any cmdlet.

Flow Control in PowerShell

Sequential code execution is not always helpful. You might want to control the flow of execution based on predefined conditions, or you might want to perform the same command execution until a certain condition is met. This is made possible in PowerShell by using flow control features such as branching and looping constructs. In this section, we will see what keywords are used to create branching and looping in PowerShell.

Branching in PowerShell

Branching statements in PowerShell enable moving to a different path of execution, based on a condition. At the very basic level, this is enabled by using if and else keywords. The general syntax of an if statement is shown in the following example. Observe that the condition is followed by an opening curly brace and is closed after the code that has to be executed is specified. This is demonstrated in the following code and in the output shown in Figure 1-21.

```
if ($a -eq 10) {
    "Value is equal to 10"
}
else {
    "Value is not equal to 10"
}
```

```
PS C:\> if ($a -eq 10) {
    "Value is equal to 10"
}
else {
    "Value is not equal to 10"
}

Value is not equal to 10
```

Figure 1-21. *if and else statements in PowerShell*

What if we want to check for more than one condition and move to a different code path? This is where we can use the elseif statement.

```
if ($a -le 10) {
    "Value is less-than or equal to 10"
}
elseif ($a -ge 20) {
    "Value is greater-than or equal to 20"
} else {
    "Value is between 10 and 20"
}
```

And, you can keep adding such conditions and change the way execution changes from one code path to another. However, this becomes unmanageable once you have multiple such conditions. So, it is ideal to use a Switch statement when you have multiple conditions in the code path. The Switch statement provides another branching technique in PowerShell.

Let us see how we can convert the if - elseif - else example we just saw, by using the Switch statement. The basic Switch statement has the following format:

```
Switch ($a) {
    30 { "Equal to 30" }
    40 { "Equal to 40" }
    Default { "Value is not 30 or 40" }
}
```

Observe how the `Switch` statement is formatted. We enclosed within curly braces what needs to be checked. In PowerShell, this is generally called a script block. Each value we want to check is specified at the beginning of a line, followed by another script block that gets executed when a match is found. For example, if the value of $a is 30, we get an output "Equal to 30".

Now, this is not same as what we have seen in the example in which we used `if-elseif` statements. In the earlier example, we checked with the help of comparison operators. We can use those comparison operators inside a `Switch` statement too.

```
Switch ($a) {
    {$_ -le 10} { "Less-than 10" }
    {$_ -gt 20} { "Greater-than 20" }
    Default { "Value is between 20 and 30" }
}
```

The condition that we have to check is specified as another script block, followed by what must be executed when the condition evaluates to `True`. One thing I did not discuss in both these examples is the meaning and purpose of `Default` inside the `Switch` statement script block. The script block associated with the `Default` gets executed when no other match is found. For example, if the value of $a is 25, in the previous example, we would see the output as "Value is between 20 and 30".

The `about_Switch` help topic has tons of examples explaining how to use the `Switch` statement and different possibilities of checking conditions. I suggest that you read that topic.

Looping in PowerShell

The branching statements we have seen so far execute a script block based on the result of a condition, and the script block executes only once. But what if we want to execute the commands in the script block multiple times until a condition evaluates either to `True` or `False`? Windows PowerShell supports a variety of looping statements similar to other scripting languages.

For Statement

The `For` statement can be used to create a loop that runs commands in a script block until the condition specified evaluates to `True`.

```
For ($i=0;$i -lt 10;$i++) {
    "Value is $i"
}
```

In the preceding example, the value of $i gets initialized to 0 and then gets incremented by one after every iteration. Once the condition evaluates to `True`, in this case $i is 10, the loop is exited. The condition specified can be anything that uses the comparison operators discussed in an earlier section. You can either increment or decrement the value of the variable being checked.

ForEach Statement

The `ForEach` statement is used when there is a collection of items for each specified script block that has to be executed. The number of times the script block gets executed will be equal to the number of items in the collection. Let us illustrate this. In the following example, we take a list of processes from the `Get-Process` cmdlet and then filter the output for the process with a `Handles` property value greater than 500.

```
$processes = Get-Process
ForEach ($process in $processes) {
    if ($process.Handles -gt 500) {
        $process.Name
    }
}
```

Most of the code in the preceding example should not be new to you. We have looked at assigning cmdlet output to a variable. So, $processes is an array of process objects returned by the Get-Process cmdlet. Using the ForEach loop, we iterate over each object in this collection. In each iteration, we get the item in the collection assigned to the $process variable. We then examine the object referenced by the $process variable to check if the Handles property is greater than 500. When the condition evaluates to True, we simply display the name of the process.

With the ForEach loop, there is no need to increment any sort of variable. The body or the script block associated with the ForEach loop gets executed until the collection is exhausted.

While Statement

Using the While statement, we can create a looping construct that executes a script block until the condition is evaluated to False. When creating a looping construct with the While statement, we have to ensure that the variable used in the condition is already initialized. Using an uninitialized variable may not produce an error, but the output from such a command will not be accurate.

```
$i=0
While ($i -lt 10) {
    "Value is $i"
    $i += 1
}
```

The functionality of the preceding example is similar to that we have seen in the For statement and produces the same output. Can you describe what happens if we do not increment the value of $i in the script block? Try it yourself.

Do Statement

All of the looping constructs we have seen so far execute a script block associated with the loop only when the condition specified evaluates to True. This also means that there is a chance that the script block may not even execute at least once, if the condition evaluates to False. But what if we want to execute the loop at least once, irrespective of the outcome of the condition? This is where the Do statement helps. The loop created with the Do statement executes the script block associated with it at least once.

```
$i = 10
Do {
    "Value is $i"
    $i += 1
} While ($i -lt 10)
```

Execute the preceding code and observe the output. We are setting the value of $i to 10. However, look at the condition. We want to check if $i is less than 10. Because the condition is checked after the script block execution, the output from this loop will be "Value is 10".

There is another variation of a loop created using a Do statement. This uses the Until statement, instead of While, for checking the condition. The major difference, however, is that a loop created using Do-Until executes until the condition is False.

```
$i = 0
Do {
    "Value is $i"
    $i += 1
} Until ($i -gt 10)
```

Observe how we used the condition in the preceding example. Instead of saying $i -lt 10, which will evaluate to True, we used $i -gt 10. This condition evaluates to False, until the value of $i becomes 11.

Break Statement

The Break statement is not used for creating a looping construct, but this is something we must know when creating loops in PowerShell. Let us use an example to understand this better. In the preceding examples, we are initializing the value of $i to 0 and then executing the loop until the value of $i is less than 10. So, by this process, what if we want to exit the loop when the value of $i is something divisible by 5. This is where the Break statement helps.

```
$i = 0
While ($i -lt 10) {
    "Value is $i"
    $i += 1
    if ($i % 5 -eq 0) {
        Break
    }
}
```

When you execute this, you will see that the loop exits when the value of $i is 4, even though the outer condition we specified is looking for a value less than 10.

Continue Statement

As with the Break statement, we can use the Continue statement to change the behavior of the loop. The Continue statement, when used in a loop, shifts control back to the top of the loop, skipping the current iteration. If, for example, we wish to display only the odd numbers in a loop, we have to skip the values that are even numbers.

```
For ($i=1;$i -lt 10;$i++) {
    if ($i % 2 -eq 0) {
        Continue
    }
    "Value is $i"
}
```

During the execution of this example, whenever the condition $i % 2 -eq 0 evaluates to True, we change the control back to the top of the loop, using a Continue statement. We output the number only when it is an odd number.

Aliases

PowerShell supports what is known as aliases to enable elastic syntax. This allows us to use a short form for cmdlet names. For example, the alias for the Get-ChildItem cmdlet is gci. So, we can simply use gci C:\scripts, instead of its full form. This has been enabled to make sure we don't have to type longer commands at the PowerShell prompt. But when writing production scripts, and for clarity sake, we should use the full form of the cmdlets. We can use the built-in PowerShell cmdlets to work with aliases.

The Get-Alias cmdlet gives us a list of all aliases defined in the system. The New-Alias cmdlet helps us add new aliases, based on preference.

```
New-Alias -Name wo -Value Where-Object
```

Using your skills in exploring PowerShell, can you list the other cmdlets that are used to manage aliases?

Understanding the PowerShell Pipeline

The pipeline is central to understanding PowerShell. As discussed in the beginning of this chapter, the pipeline is used to combine commands. The operator that is used to combine commands is called a pipeline operator and represented by the | symbol.

When multiple commands are combined by a pipeline, the output of the first command gets passed on to the second command, the second command's output gets passed on to the third command, and so on. This also means that the pipeline is executed from left to right. The entire pipeline of commands is considered a single operation, and the output is displayed as it is generated by the last command in the pipeline. This behavior can be observed by looking at the output from the following command:

```
Get-ChildItem -Path C:\Windows\system32 -Recurse *.dll | Where-Object -FilterScript
{ $_.Length -gt 10MB }
```

▪ **Tip** In the preceding example, MB in 10MB is a size unit. PowerShell supports referring to size units, by using KB, MB, GB, TB, and PB suffixes. These automatically get converted to a bytes value.

When you execute the preceding script, you will see that output is getting displayed, one object at a time, even before the command completes execution. This is called the streaming behavior of the pipeline. The streaming behavior may not always work. For example, let us suppose that we want to retrieve all files that are bigger than 100MB and then sort them based on size. We can use the Get-ChildItem and the Sort-Object cmdlets for this task.

```
Get-ChildItem -Path C:\Windows\system32 -Recurse *.dll -ErrorAction SilentlyContinue | Where-Object
-FilterScript { $_.Length -gt 10MB } | Sort-Object -Property Length
```

This example is very much similar to the last example, in which we filtered a collection of objects for files bigger than 10MB. In this example, we added a third command to the pipeline, by which we are sorting the file objects based on size. By default, the Sort-Object cmdlet sorts in ascending order. When we execute this new pipeline of commands, we see that the result is returned as a whole. Sort-Object does not use the object streaming method, because to sort a collection based on a specific property, it is important that you have the entire collection handy. So, in this specific example, PowerShell waits for the objects to get generated and then sorts them, using the Sort-Object cmdlet. The output from the pipeline gets displayed only after the last command is run. In summary, the object streaming behavior depends on the type of commands used in the pipeline.

Now, what if you want to intentionally stop the object streaming behavior? You can do so by enclosing the commands in the pipeline in a pair of parentheses.

```
(Get-ChildItem -Path C:\Windows\system32 -Recurse *.dll -ErrorAction SilentlyContinue) | Where-
Object -FilterScript { $_.Length -gt 10MB }
```

By enclosing the command in parentheses, we are asking PowerShell to complete the execution of the command first and then move to the next command. This, essentially, stops the object streaming behavior.

Now that we understand the object streaming behavior, let us look one level deep into the previous pipeline example. In the preceding examples, the second command is the Where-Object cmdlet. This cmdlet is used to filter the objects from other cmdlets—Get-ChildItem, in our example. Now, if you look at the argument provided to the -FilterScript parameter, we are using a script block. Within the script block, we used a variable called $_.

In PowerShell, $_ is called an input variable, in the pipeline. This is an automatic variable that contains the current object in the pipeline. So, in our example, $_ within the Where-Object cmdlet is used as a reference for each File object that the Get-ChildItem cmdlet generates. Remember that $_ is not used only within the pipeline but wherever there is a script block and you must refer to a value coming from another command. In fact, we have already seen an example using $_ when discussing the Switch branching statement.

Now, using the knowledge you have gained so far, can you write a pipeline of commands that gets a list of processes and filters the list of processes for objects that have a HandlesCount of more than 400?

The Windows PowerShell pipeline, as I mentioned earlier, is the heart of PowerShell implementation. I encourage you to read the about_Pipelines help topic. The content of this help topic takes a deeper look at the working of a pipeline, and it is very important for advancing into PowerShell scripting. We shall stop our discussion of the pipeline here but revisit a few concepts, after we discuss how to start writing PowerShell scripts, functions, and modules.

PowerShell Scripts

Learning to use PowerShell and running commands is certainly the first step, but when you want to advance into automating larger tasks with Windows PowerShell, you need more than just the PowerShell console and the ability to run commands. You need to store the commands into a script file, so that you can reuse it at a later point in time. I always suggest that beginners start at the console or shell, as whatever runs at the shell will run in a script as well. So, once you master how to use the shell and the cmdlets in PowerShell, it is very easy to start putting that knowledge into writing complex scripts.

In PowerShell, script files have a .PS1 extension. This has nothing to do with the PowerShell version. Even with PowerShell 4.0, the same file name extension is identified as a PowerShell script. In addition, a PowerShell script is just a plain text file with a bunch of commands. Therefore, you can take any example we have seen so far, paste it into a text file, and save it as a .PS1 file. You have a PowerShell script there!

Execution Policies

Before I discuss how to run the PowerShell scripts, let us take a look at some groundwork we need to perform. Windows PowerShell is secure by design, which means the running of PowerShell scripts is not enabled by default. This is controlled by a PowerShell configuration feature called Execution Policy. There are cmdlets to manage the execution policy—Get-ExecutionPolicy and Set-ExecutionPolicy. The default execution policy setting is Restricted. This is the reason why we cannot run PowerShell scripts until we change the policy setting. The other possible execution policy settings are AllSigned, RemoteSigned, Unrestricted, ByPass, and Undefined.

The AllSigned policy setting enforces the usage of digital signing of PowerShell scripts. So, if a PowerShell script is written locally or received from elsewhere, it has to be signed with a digital signature from a trusted authority.

The RemoteSigned policy is similar to AllSigned, but it enforces digital signing only for scripts received from the Internet or elsewhere. For locally written scripts, there is no digital signature requirement.

The Unrestricted and Bypass policy settings enable execution of PowerShell scripts without any signing restrictions. For development purposes, use of Unrestricted and Bypass policy settings is allowed. However, in a production or data center environment, when possible, one must strive to ensure that only signed scripts are allowed to run.

Coming back to the discussion on cmdlets for managing execution policies, the Get-ExecutionPolicy cmdlet gets the effective policy setting within the PowerShell session. I have used the phrase *effective policy setting*, because there are multiple levels of execution policy. The PowerShell execution policies can be set at process, user, and machine levels, with precedence in the same order. This means the execution policy set at the process scope has higher priority than the other two.

We can use the Set-ExecutionPolicy cmdlet to set the execution policy at any scope just discussed. However, changing the execution policy at machine level requires administrative privileges. You can open PowerShell host as administrator and then use the Set-ExecutionPolicy cmdlet (see Figure 1-22).

```
PS C:\> Set-ExecutionPolicy -ExecutionPolicy AllSigned -Verbose
VERBOSE: Performing the operation "Set-ExecutionPolicy" on target "AllSigned".
```

Figure 1-22. *Execution policy in PowerShell*

■ **Note** In Windows Server 2012 R2 and above operating systems, the PowerShell execution policy is set to RemoteSigned by default.

Writing and Executing Scripts

As I mentioned, you can copy and paste any example we have seen so far into a text file and save it as .PS1 file. The code in the example generates odd numbers. So, let us name the script GetOddNumbers.ps1.

```
For ($i=1;$i -lt 10;$i++) {
    if ($i % 2 -eq 0) {
        Continue
    }
    "Value is $i"
}
```

If you are using PowerShell ISE to run the scripts (in general, I recommend using ISE for all PowerShell work), you can simply press F5, and you will see the output from this script. If you want to execute the script at the PowerShell console prompt or PowerShell ISE prompt, you can use the following method:

```
.\GetOddNumbers.ps1
```

■ **Note** The .\ notation is used to specify that the script file is at the same folder as the current working directory.

This script is too primitive. If you want to change the initial value of $i, you have to edit the script, and the same applies to the value we are checking in the While loop condition. PowerShell scripts support an automatic variable called $args. This variable is an array that contains all the arguments provided at the command line, along with the script name. Now, let us modify the script to use the arguments coming from the command line.

```
For ($i=$args[0];$i -lt $args[1];$i++) {
    if ($i % 2 -eq 0) {
        Continue
    }
    "Value is $i"
}
```

We have now added support for command-line arguments. The first argument on the command line will be used for the initial value of $i, and the second argument as the value to check in the While loop condition. These are represented by $args[0] and $args[1]. You have already learned about arrays, and this notation of using array indexes shouldn't be new to you. Now, we can use the following method to execute this script:

```
.\GetOddNumbers.ps1 7 18
```

■ **Tip** The comma and script arguments in PowerShell are separated by a space, which is different from how this is done in other languages. Using a comma (,) to separate arguments, makes them a single argument of an array type.

By using the $args variable, we have hard-coded that the first value from the command line is always the initial value of $i. Any change in this will break the script. This is where the named parameters discussed earlier will help us. You can add named parameters to a script by placing a param() block at the beginning of the script. Let us see an example.

```
param (
    $InitialValue,
    $ConditionValue
)

For ($i=$InitialValue;$i -lt $ConditionValue;$i++) {
    if ($i % 2 -eq 0) {
        Continue
    }
    "Value is $i"
}
```

Take a look at the way we used the `param ()` block. It is not necessary to give the line breaks within the parameter block, as in the example. You can have all parameter names in the same line, separated by commas. The way we define the parameter names is nothing but writing them as variable names. We then reference those variable names within the script, wherever we need to. Now, the order of arguments does not change the behavior of the script. This is much clearer than using `$args`.

```
.\GetOddNumbers.ps1 -InitialValue 10 -ConditionValue 56
```

The preceding example is the same as `.\GetOddNumbers.ps1 -ConditionValue 56 -InitialValue 10`.

Now that you understand how to write scripts and add parameters to the scripts, let us move on to writing functions within a script file and using the functions.

PowerShell Functions

As noted earlier, PowerShell has four types of commands: cmdlets, scripts, functions, and native commands. We have seen what scripts are and how to write and execute them. We shall now explore functions in PowerShell. Scripts, when executed, are always loaded for execution from the disk into memory. Functions, on the other hand, once loaded from a script, remain in memory. So, the subsequent execution of functions will be much faster than scripts.

```
Function TestFunction {
    param (
        $InitialValue,
        $ConditionValue
    )

    For ($i=$InitialValue;$i -lt $ConditionValue;$i++) {
        if ($i % 2 -eq 0) {
            Continue
        }
        "Value is $i"
    }
}
```

The preceding example shows the general syntax of functions in PowerShell. We use the `Function` keyword, followed by a script block that contains the function code. In the example, the body of the function is the same as the example in last section. To be able to use the function, we should load it into memory. We can do that either by dot-sourcing the script file or by selecting the code in the ISE script editor and pressing F8. The syntax for dot-sourcing is as follows:

```
. .\GetOddNumbers.ps1
```

Observe the syntax used to dot-source the script. This does not execute the script. Instead, it loads all the functions defined in the script into memory. Once the functions are loaded into memory, we can call the function like any other cmdlet, by using its name.

```
TestFunction -InitialValue 10 -ConditionValue 20
```

The syntax you see here is nothing different from what we have seen so far with the cmdlets. You can include any number of functions in a script file and load them using dot-sourcing. There are two help topics related to functions. I encourage you to read about_Functions and about_Functions_Advanced to get a deeper understanding of how to write PowerShell functions.

PowerShell Modules

You have seen how to write scripts and convert some of them to functions, so that we can reuse the code. Once we have a few functions, we can start organizing them as PowerShell modules. You can think of PowerShell modules as libraries in other languages. A module is a package that contains Windows PowerShell commands, such as cmdlets, providers, functions, workflows, variables, and aliases. There are a ton of modules that come with Windows Server 2012 and Windows 8, and there are cmdlets that can be used to discover and work with modules easily.

Discovering Modules

The Get-Module cmdlet can be used to discover PowerShell modules available on a system. This cmdlet, by default without any parameters, lists only the modules loaded into the PowerShell session. You can use the -ListAvailable switch parameter to list all modules available in the system. In Windows PowerShell, a module can be a plain text file with a file extension as .PSM1 or a DLL file that has the PowerShell cmdlets written in C# and .NET.

```
Get-Module -ListAvailable
```

If you observe the output of this command, you see a list of modules stored in different folders in the system. This is because the PowerShell modules can be placed at different locations, and the path of the modules is referenced using an environment variable called $env:PSModulePath. Because this is an environment variable, anyone—applications or users—with the requisite privileges can add new directories as a PowerShell modules path. For example, Figure 1-23 shows what I see on my system.

```
PS Env:\> $env:PSModulePath -split ";"
C:\Users\Ravikanth\Documents\WindowsPowerShell\Modules
C:\Program Files\WindowsPowerShell\Modules
C:\Windows\system32\WindowsPowerShell\v1.0\Modules\

PS Env:\>
```

Figure 1-23. *PowerShell modules path*

The Get-Module cmdlet looks at all the directories available in the $env:PSModulePath variable and then searches for any PowerShell modules. We can use the Get-Command cmdlet to discover the cmdlets in a module.

```
Get-Command -Module Storage
```

If you are running the command on a system with Windows Server 2012 and above, or a Windows 8 and above operating system, you will see a list of cmdlets that you can use to manage storage on a Windows system.

Importing Modules

Starting with PowerShell 3.0, there is no need to explicitly import a module into a PowerShell session. The module autoloading feature loads the module automatically upon referring to a cmdlet in that module. This is governed by a setting stored in a $PSModuleAutoLoadingPreference preference variable. If you don't want the module autoloading feature enabled, you can disable it by setting the relevant preference variable to "None."

```
$PSModuleAutoloadingPreference = 'None'
```

To explicitly load a PowerShell module—for example, when it is not in the module path described above—you can use the Import-Module cmdlet with a –Name parameter, to specify the path to the module PSM1 or PSD1 file.

```
Import-Module -Name MyModule.psm1
```

This will load all the cmdlets, functions, aliases, and so on. When calling a cmdlet or function within the module, you can simply refer to the name of the cmdlet or function. Note that the PowerShell execution policy has to be set to an appropriate level for running scripts. This is required for modules as well.

Writing Modules

We have already seen that functions are written and stored in PowerShell script files with the .PS1 extension. PowerShell module files written as scripts should be stored as .PSM1 files. Let us see an example, and then I will provide the details of how we can use the module we will be authoring.

```
Function Get-OddNumber {
    param (
        $InitialValue,
        $ConditionValue
    )

    For ($i=$InitialValue;$i -lt $ConditionValue;$i++) {
        if ($i % 2 -eq 0) {
            Continue
        }
        "Value is $i"
    }
}
```

Put this sample code in PowerShell ISE and save it as Numbers.psm1. Once we have the file, create a folder named Numbers under one of the directories shown in $env:PSModulePath. You can use the following PowerShell command to create this folder:

```
New-Item -Type Directory -Path $home\Documents\WindowsPowerShell\Modules\Numbers
```

Copy the module file, Numbers.psm1, to this newly created folder. It is important that the folder into which we are placing the .PSM1 file have the same name as the module file name. Without doing this, the module cannot be loaded.

```
Copy-Item -Path .\Numbers.psm1 -Destination $home\Documents\WindowsPowerShell\Modules\Numbers
```

Once the files are copied, we can simply call the Get-OddNumber function with appropriate input values. Congratulations! You have already written your first PowerShell module. Now, can you write another function to generate only even numbers, given the same input values as the Get-OddNumber function, and add it to our Numbers module? How would you name that function?

In PowerShell, all cmdlets are singular. This means that the noun part of the cmdlet should never contain plurals. Well, this is a guideline from Microsoft for people writing cmdlets and modules. It is good to follow, and certainly the reason why I named the odd numbers function Get-OddNumber instead of Get-OddNumbers.

Also, a module need not only contain functions. We learned about aliases earlier. You can even place aliases as a part of the module file. When the module is loaded, the aliases defined using the New-Alias cmdlet in the module file are automatically loaded into the session.

There is still a lot we need to learn about PowerShell modules. What we have covered so far should get you started with authoring simple modules. There are ways to create modules that can use predefined configuration data and define the module metadata. To learn these advanced concepts, I suggest that you read the about_Modules help topic.

Customizing the PowerShell Environment

Throughout the discussion of the basics of PowerShell and of how to use it, we have seen several features that help us customize the PowerShell environment. For example, we have seen examples of a few preference variables and have learned how to use aliases. However, one thing not discussed to this point is that these changes are valid only during the current session. So, what do we do to make these changes persistent? This is where PowerShell profiles come in.

PowerShell profiles are nothing but PowerShell scripts that are loaded every time a PowerShell host is opened. There are different types of profiles for different types of hosts. The location for these profile scripts is different, but the content can be the same. The $PROFILE automatic variable gives the path to the profile script for the current host (see Figure 1-24). You can see a list of all possible profile paths by using the following command:

```
$PROFILE.PSExtended.PSObject.Properties | Select-Object Name,Value | Format-Table -AutoSize
```

```
PS Env:\> $PROFILE.PSExtended.PSObject.Properties | Select-Object Name,Value | Format-Table -AutoSize

Name                   Value
----                   -----
AllUsersAllHosts       C:\Windows\System32\WindowsPowerShell\v1.0\profile.ps1
AllUsersCurrentHost    C:\Windows\System32\WindowsPowerShell\v1.0\Microsoft.PowerShellISE_profile.ps1
CurrentUserAllHosts    C:\Users\Ravikanth\Documents\WindowsPowerShell\profile.ps1
CurrentUserCurrentHost C:\Users\Ravikanth\Documents\WindowsPowerShell\Microsoft.PowerShellISE_profile.ps1
```

Figure 1-24. *PowerShell profile path*

As you can see in this example, there are four different types of profile scripts. The output in the preceding command does not mean that those script files already exist. We have to create them explicitly. You can put all the commands you want to execute every time you open the PowerShell console or ISE in a script file and save it at one of the paths shown in the preceding example. The file names with ISE are specific to the PowerShell ISE host. Those profile scripts won't be loaded for other PowerShell hosts in the system. The CurrentUserAllHosts profile is the profile script of my choice. This profile script gets executed for any PowerShell host you use and ensures that the environmental settings are the same across all PowerShell hosts you use.

Summary

This chapter provided a whirlwind tour of Windows PowerShell basics. While it did not cover all the concepts and features available in Windows PowerShell, it did, however, give a kick start in PowerShell scripting. The intention of this chapter is to provide a foundation for people who are interested in learning about the PowerShell Desired State Configuration (DSC). This is, by no means, a complete guide for PowerShell neophytes. For a beginner, the three most important cmdlets to remember are `Get-Help`, `Get-Command`, and `Get-Member`. These cmdlets help us explore PowerShell. Once we know how to discover the capabilities of cmdlets and PowerShell in general, we can begin to write commands and scripts. As with any other scripting language, PowerShell, too, supports flow control constructs that help execute different script blocks, based on conditions. The other language features, such as aliases, make PowerShell suitable for both console execution and scripts. You can choose your commands to be either concise or detailed. PowerShell scripts and modules help us create reusable code. This is useful for a task that has to be performed repeatedly or a script that must be shared with someone else.

And, as I mentioned, we have not even scratched the surface of PowerShell. For each of the concepts and features that I discussed, there is certainly an advanced level of expertise that can be acquired. As a beginner, you can start building your skills in PowerShell straight away, by using cmdlets and writing simple scripts to automate daily tasks. Also, remember that the help content available online and offline in your system as about topics is very useful. It provides more in-depth information than standard PowerShell-related books out there.

■ ■ ■

CHAPTER 2

Introducing Windows Remote Management and CIM

The Desired State Configuration (DSC) feature is built on the Common Information Model (CIM) standard developed by the Desktop Management Task Force (DMTF) and uses Windows Remote Management (WinRM) technology as a communication mechanism. Both these technologies are standards-based, and you will see more about these as you start learning about DSC in the later chapters. However, as a foundation, it is important to look at what these technologies offer and how PowerShell can be used to access the management data from CIM-compliant management objects using WinRM as a communication method. In this chapter, we will look at what Windows Remote Management is and how it is used in the Windows OS world to enable standards-based management. We will then extend our knowledge of WinRM to see how CIM cmdlets in PowerShell use WinRM to work with management data from remote systems.

Windows Remote Management (WinRM)

Windows Remote Management, or, simply, WinRM, is Microsoft's implementation of Web Services for Management (WS-Management) protocol specification. WS-Management specification is developed by DMTF and describes a protocol based on the Simple Object Access Protocol (SOAP) for exchanging control information and data between capable devices. These devices can be hardware, such as servers, network switches, and so on, software applications, or other manageable components. The main goal of WS-Management-based implementation is to provide a common way for these systems or components to access and exchange information.

■ **Note** Do not confuse Windows Remote Management with the Remote Management configuration option seen in Server Manager. Server Manager remote management (SM remoting) uses the WinRM service, but disabling SM remoting has no impact on WinRM service.

Remote management of Windows systems is enabled by a service called winrm. Except for the Active Directory domain-joined Windows Server 2012 and Windows Server 2012 R2 systems, this service is disabled by default. We can check the status of the WinRM service, using the Get-Service cmdlet. The -ComputerName parameter of this cmdlet helps us to get service information from a remote system.

```
Get-Service -ComputerName WC81-1 -Name WinRM
```

As you see in Figure 2-1, the WinRM service is in stopped state on the remote system. We can start the service and set it to automatic startup type, using the Set-Service cmdlet.

```
Set-Service -Name WinRM -ComputerName WC81-1 -StartupType Automatic -Status Running


Status    Name                DisplayName
------    ----                -----------
Stopped   WinRM               Windows Remote Management (WS-Manag...
```

Figure 2-1. *WinRM service status from a remote computer*

However, enabling the WinRM service does not create the required WinRM listeners for remote system communication. The WinRM listeners are the endpoints in the WS-Management-based architecture that authorize remote systems to connect and access management information. To access and manage remote systems using WinRM, we should create these listeners. Before Windows PowerShell 2.0, the only way to manage WinRM configuration on the Windows OS was to use the Windows Remote Management Command Line Tool (winrm.cmd). With the release of PowerShell 3.0, Microsoft included the PowerShell WS-Management module.

WS-Management Cmdlets

The WS-Management, or, simply, WSMan, cmdlets in PowerShell are a part of the Microsoft.WSMan.Management module (see Figure 2-2).

```
PS C:\> Get-Command -Module Microsoft.WSMan.Management

CommandType    Name                        ModuleName
-----------    ----                        ----------
Cmdlet         Connect-WSMan               Microsoft.WSMan.Management
Cmdlet         Disable-WSManCredSSP        Microsoft.WSMan.Management
Cmdlet         Disconnect-WSMan            Microsoft.WSMan.Management
Cmdlet         Enable-WSManCredSSP         Microsoft.WSMan.Management
Cmdlet         Get-WSManCredSSP            Microsoft.WSMan.Management
Cmdlet         Get-WSManInstance           Microsoft.WSMan.Management
Cmdlet         Invoke-WSManAction          Microsoft.WSMan.Management
Cmdlet         New-WSManInstance           Microsoft.WSMan.Management
Cmdlet         New-WSManSessionOption      Microsoft.WSMan.Management
Cmdlet         Remove-WSManInstance        Microsoft.WSMan.Management
Cmdlet         Set-WSManInstance           Microsoft.WSMan.Management
Cmdlet         Set-WSManQuickConfig        Microsoft.WSMan.Management
Cmdlet         Test-WSMan                  Microsoft.WSMan.Management
```

Figure 2-2. *WSMan cmdlets in PowerShell 4.0*

Let us take a look at some of these cmdlets and determine how we can access management information from remote systems. First and foremost, the Test-WSMan cmdlet tells us if the remote system has WinRM configured for allowing remote system communication.

```
Test-WSMan -ComputerName WC81-1
```

In the previous example, we enabled the WinRM service and started it, but we did not configure any WinRM listeners. Therefore, the Test-WSMan cmdlet results in an error, as shown in Figure 2-3.

```
Test-WSMan : <f:WSManFault xmlns:f="http://schemas.microsoft.com/wbem/wsman/1/wsmanfault" Code="2150858770"
Machine="DSC-Demo.MSCollab.lab"><f:Message>The client cannot connect to the destination specified in the request.
destination is running and is accepting requests. Consult the logs and documentation for the WS-Management service
commonly IIS or WinRM. If the destination is the WinRM service, run the following command on the destination to an
"winrm quickconfig". </f:Message></f:WSManFault>
At line:1 char:1
+ Test-WSMan -ComputerName WC81-1
+ ~~~~~~~~~~~~~~~~~~~~~~~~~~~~~~~~
    + CategoryInfo          : InvalidOperation: (WC81-1:String) [Test-WSMan], InvalidOperationException
    + FullyQualifiedErrorId : WsManError,Microsoft.WSMan.Management.TestWSManCommand
```

Figure 2-3. *WSMan communication error without listeners*

This shows that we need to enable the WinRM listeners and ensure that WinRM is ready to accept incoming requests for management information. There are two types of WinRM listeners we can create. These are based on HTTP or HTTPS protocols. The HTTP listener, by default, listens on port number 5985, and the HTTPS listener, on port 5896. The HTTPS listener requires SSL certificates to authenticate the remote system access requests.

Creating a WinRM HTTP Listener

We can use the Set-WSManQuickConfig cmdlet to create either HTTP (default) or HTTPS WinRM listeners. This cmdlet has no -ComputerName parameter and, therefore, needs to run on the system where we want to create the listeners. Using the -Force parameter, we can avoid any prompts that appear for confirmation before creating the WinRM listener. Also, note that this cmdlet configures the WinRM service startup type and status, if it is not already in the running state. This is shown in Figure 2-4.

```
PS C:\> Set-WSManQuickConfig -Force
WinRM is already set up to receive requests on this computer.
WinRM has been updated for remote management.
Created a WinRM listener on HTTP://* to accept WS-Man requests to any IP on this machine.
WinRM firewall exception enabled.
```

Figure 2-4. *WinRM HTTP listener creation*

■ **Note** DSC documentation indicates that PowerShell Remoting is a requirement for using DSC. This is not completely accurate and will be updated in subsequent releases. DSC depends on WinRM listeners and not remoting. This is detailed in my *PowerShell Magazine* article "Desired State Configuration and the remoting myth." You can read it at www.powershellmagazine.com/2014/04/01/desired-state-configuration-and-the-remoting-myth/.

As we see in the cmdlet output, the WinRM service is already running, and the WinRM HTTP listener is created to accept requests from any IP address. We can verify this by running the Test-WSMan cmdlet from a remote system again. The result of using this cmdlet is shown in Figure 2-5.

```
PS C:\> Test-WSMan -ComputerName WC81-1


wsmid           : http://schemas.dmtf.org/wbem/wsman/identity/1/wsmanidentity.xsd
ProtocolVersion : http://schemas.dmtf.org/wbem/wsman/1/wsman.xsd
ProductVendor   : Microsoft Corporation
ProductVersion  : OS: 0.0.0 SP: 0.0 Stack: 3.0
```

Figure 2-5. *Testing WinRM requests after creating listeners*

In PowerShell, after we enable the WinRM service, we can navigate to the WSMan: drive created by the WS-Management PowerShell provider. This provides a view of all WinRM related settings. We can use the Set-Location cmdlet, or cd alias, to change the current working directory to the WSMan: drive. The best part of PowerShell providers is that they work with the standard cmdlets we have already encountered in Chapter 1. For example, once you navigate to the WSMan: drive, you can execute Get-ChildItem, or the dir alias, to see a list of items in the drive.

■ **Note**   Reading and manipulating WSMan: drive settings requires administrative privileges.

The localhost entry in Figure 2-6 represents the local system, and we can navigate into that container to see the configuration of the WinRM service. The listener container inside the localhost container shows us the listener we just created.

```
PS C:\> Set-Location WSMan:

PS WSMan:\> dir


   WSManConfig:

ComputerName                          Type
------------                          ----
localhost                             Container
```

Figure 2-6. *Items in the WSMan: drive*

As with any other filesystem folder, we can navigate into the listener container to see the configuration, using the Set-Location cmdlet or the cd alias. As shown in Figure 2-7, the listener container on my system is named Listener_1084132640. The name will be different on your system, if you are following these examples.

```
PS WSMan:\> Get-ChildItem .\localhost\Listener


   WSManConfig: Microsoft.WSMan.Management\WSMan::localhost\Listener

Type            Keys                                   Name
----            ----                                   ----
Container       {Transport=HTTP, Address=*}            Listener_1084132640
```

Figure 2-7. *WinRM HTTP listener*

As you can see in Figure 2-8, and as discussed earlier, the HTTP listener is assigned a port number, 5985, by default. This can be changed, using the Set-Item cmdlet.

```
Set-Item -Path .\Port -Value 4444 -Force


PS WSMan:\> Set-Location .\localhost\Listener\Listener_1084132640

PS WSMan:\localhost\Listener\Listener_1084132640> dir


   WSManConfig: Microsoft.WSMan.Management\WSMan::localhost\Listener\Listener_1084132640

Type             Name                        SourceOfValue     Value
----             ----                        -------------     -----
System.String    Address                                       *
System.String    Transport                                     HTTP
System.String    Port                                          5985
System.String    Hostname
System.String    Enabled                                       true
System.String    URLPrefix                                     wsman
System.String    CertificateThumbprint
System.String    ListeningOn_862655728                         10.10.10.117
```

Figure 2-8. *WinRM HTTP listener configuration*

■ **Note** Changing a Listener property, as shown in the preceding example, changes the name assigned to the listener container item. For example, the Listener_1084132640 container in Figure 2-8 will not be valid anymore. This behavior is shown in Figure 2-9.

```
PS WSMan:\localhost\Listener\Listener_1084132640> dir
dir : Cannot find path 'localhost\Listener\Listener_1084132640' because it does not exist.
At line:1 char:1
+ dir
+ ~~~
    + CategoryInfo          : ObjectNotFound: (localhost\Listener\Listener_1084132640:String) [Get-ChildIte
   m], ItemNotFoundException
    + FullyQualifiedErrorId : PathNotFound,Microsoft.PowerShell.Commands.GetChildItemCommand
```

Figure 2-9. *Error with the listener container after changing Listener properties*

To fix this, we need to go back to the parent container and navigate to the updated listener container. Once again, we can use the standard PowerShell file system navigation cmdlets here, to navigate the WS-Management provider (see Figure 2-10).

```
PS WSMan:\localhost\Listener\Listener_1084132640> cd ..

PS WSMan:\localhost\Listener> cd .\Listener_64990557

PS WSMan:\localhost\Listener\Listener_64990557> dir


    WSManConfig: Microsoft.WSMan.Management\WSMan::localhost\Listener\Listener_64990557

Type                 Name                     SourceOfValue   Value
----                 ----                     -------------   -----
System.String        Address                                  *
System.String        Transport                                HTTP
System.String        Port                                     4444
System.String        Hostname
System.String        Enabled                                  true
System.String        URLPrefix                                wsman
System.String        CertificateThumbprint
System.String        ListeningOn_862655728                    10.10.10.117
```

Figure 2-10. *Updated WinRM listener port*

As you can see in Figure 2-10, the port number of the WinRM HTTP is set to 4444. Because this is a non-default port number for an HTTP WinRM listener, you have to specify the port number explicitly, with the WS-Management cmdlets. This can be done using the -Port parameter. An example of this is shown in Figure 2-11.

```
PS C:\> Test-WSMan -Port 4444 -ComputerName WC81-1


wsmid           : http://schemas.dmtf.org/wbem/wsman/identity/1/wsmanidentity.xsd
ProtocolVersion : http://schemas.dmtf.org/wbem/wsman/1/wsman.xsd
ProductVendor   : Microsoft Corporation
ProductVersion  : OS: 0.0.0 SP: 0.0 Stack: 3.0
```

Figure 2-11. *Using non-default port numbers with WSMan cmdlets*

Creating a WinRM HTTPS Listener

We have seen that the Set-WSManQuickConfig cmdlet creates the HTTP listener when the -UseSSL parameter is not specified. So, that was easy. However, creating a WinRM HTTPS listener requires an SSL certificate. For the purpose of learning, we will create a self-signed SSL certificate and use that for creating an HTTPS listener.

To create a self-signed SSL certificate, we can use the makecert.exe program, which is a part of Visual Studio tools.

■ **Note**   Read more about makecert.exe and the command-line switches on MSDN at http://msdn.microsoft.com/en-us/library/bfsktky3(v=vs.110).aspx.

Once you have the makecert.exe utility, you can run the following command at either cmd.exe or in the PowerShell console. Because we are adding the certificate to the local machine store, we have to elevate the console as administrator, to execute this command successfully.

```
makecert -r -pe -n "CN=WC81-1" -b 01/01/2014 -e 01/01/2050 -eku 1.3.6.1.5.5.7.3.1 -ss my -sr
localMachine -sky exchange -sp "Microsoft RSA SChannel Cryptographic Provider" -sy 12
```

This command creates and installs the certificate on the local system. To be able to create the WinRM HTTPS listener, we need the certificate thumbprint. We can use the PowerShell certificate provider to get this information. We can use the Set-Location cmdlet to navigate to the certificate provider and the place where the newly created certificate is stored. This is shown in Figure 2-12.

```
PS C:\> Set-Location Cert:\LocalMachine\My

PS Cert:\LocalMachine\My> dir


    Directory: Microsoft.PowerShell.Security\Certificate::LocalMachine\My


Thumbprint                                Subject
----------                                -------
2C64610BD8725FCF4077389756F4FDC8EA43C4D1  CN=WC81-1
```

Figure 2-12. *Retrieving certificate thumbprint*

We can use the New-WSManInstance cmdlet to create a new HTTPS listener (see Figure 2-13). You have to replace the certificate thumbprint value in the command with the value shown for your certificate. Once again, the following command has to be executed as administrator.

```
New-WSManInstance winrm/config/Listener -SelectorSet @{Transport='HTTPS';Address="*"} -ValueSet @
{Hostname="WC81-1";CertificateThumbprint="2C64610BD8725FCF4077389756F4FDC8EA43C4D1"}


wxf                  : http://schemas.xmlsoap.org/ws/2004/09/transfer
a                    : http://schemas.xmlsoap.org/ws/2004/08/addressing
w                    : http://schemas.dmtf.org/wbem/wsman/1/wsman.xsd
lang                 : en-US
Address              : http://schemas.xmlsoap.org/ws/2004/08/addressing/role/anonymous
ReferenceParameters  : ReferenceParameters
```

Figure 2-13. *Output from the New-WSManInstance command execution*

Once the HTTPS listener is created, we can verify the listeners available on the local system by getting a list of items under the listener container in the WSMan: drive. We can use the Get-ChildItem cmdlet to retrieve a list of all WinRM listeners. The result of this is shown in Figure 2-14.

```
Get-ChildItem -Path WSMan:\Localhost\Listener


   WSManConfig: Microsoft.WSMan.Management\WSMan::localhost\Listener

Type         Keys                              Name
----         ----                              ----
Container    {Transport=HTTPS, Address=*}      Listener_1305953032
Container    {Transport=HTTP, Address=*}       Listener_64990557
```

Figure 2-14. *Successful creation of the HTTPS listener*

We can verify the functionality of the newly created HTTPS listener by using the Connect-WSMan cmdlet. Because the certificate we created is a self-signed SSL certificate, we must ensure that PowerShell does not validate the certificate publisher details, and so on. For this, we can use the New-WSManSessionOption cmdlet.

```
$SessionOption = New-WSManSessionOption -SkipCACheck -SkipCNCheck -SkipRevocationCheck
Connect-WSMan -ComputerName WC81-1 -SessionOption $SessionOption -UseSSL
```

Once the Connect-WSMan cmdlet is executed, we can verify that the remote system, WC81-1 in this example, appears in the WS-Management provider drive.

As shown in Figure 2-15, the presence of the remote system in the WSMan: drive indicates that we are able to connect to the remote WinRM HTTPS listener we just created.

```
PS C:\> Get-ChildItem WSMan:\


   WSManConfig:

ComputerName                              Type
------------                              ----
localhost                                 Container
wc81-1                                    Container
```

Figure 2-15. *Connection to a remote system using the HTTPS listener*

Accessing Management Information

So far, we have seen how to enable the infrastructure required to connect to remote systems using the standards-based WS-Management protocol. Now, we will see some examples that use this infrastructure to access management information from the remote systems. To start with, we can use the Get-WSManInstance cmdlet to retrieve the management information. An example of this is shown in Figure 2-16.

```
Get-WSManInstance -ResourceUri WmiCimv2/Win32_Service -Selectorset @{Name="WinRM"} -ComputerName
WC81-1


xsi                : http://www.w3.org/2001/XMLSchema-instance
p                  : http://schemas.microsoft.com/wbem/wsman/1/wmi/root/cimv2/Win32_Service
cim                : http://schemas.dmtf.org/wbem/wscim/1/common
type               : p:Win32_Service_Type
lang               : en-US
AcceptPause        : false
AcceptStop         : true
Caption            : Windows Remote Management (WS-Management)
CheckPoint         : 0
CreationClassName  : Win32_Service
```

Figure 2-16. *Partial output from the Get-WSManInstance cmdlet*

The preceding command is similar to one we wrote at the beginning of this chapter with the Get-Service cmdlet. We use the -ResourceUri parameter to specify the resource for which we want to retrieve the management information. In this example, the resource we are interested in is the Windows Service named WinRM.

We can invoke methods of a remote resource, using the `Invoke-WSManAction` cmdlet.

```
Invoke-WSManAction -Action StopService -Resourceuri wmicimv2/win32_service -Selectorset @
{name="audiosrv"} -ComputerName WC81-1
```

In the preceding example, we use the `-Action` parameter to specify what action we want to perform on the remote resource, which is specified using the `-ResourceUri` parameter. The `ReturnValue` in the output, shown in Figure 2-17, indicates the success or failure of the action on the remote system. A value 0 indicates that the action was successfully executed.

```
xsi        : http://www.w3.org/2001/XMLSchema-instance
p          : http://schemas.microsoft.com/wbem/wsman/1/wmi/root/cimv2/Win32_Service
cim        : http://schemas.dmtf.org/wbem/wscim/1/common
lang       : en-US
ReturnValue : 0
```

Figure 2-17. *Invoking an action on a remote system using WSMan cmdlets*

If you have observed the commands used in the preceding examples, you will realize that the syntax of these commands is somewhat cryptic. How exactly do we specify what resource URI to use and what the valid values are? How do we specify additional properties in a selector set? The usage of WSMan cmdlets is certainly complex and not very well appreciated. However, Microsoft created another set of cmdlets, called CIM cmdlets, to access the management information from remote systems. These cmdlets support standards-based management over the WS-Management protocol. In the following sections, we will see what the Common Information Model (CIM) is and learn various language constructs used in writing CIM queries and how the CIM cmdlets can be used to access management information from remote systems.

Common Information Model (CIM)

The CIM standard is a part of Web-Based Enterprise Management (WBEM) technologies for systems management. The CIM standard defines how managed IT elements in the enterprise are represented as a common set and describes the relationships between them. Microsoft implemented the CIM standard as the Windows Management Instrumentation (WMI). WMI can be used to query management information from either local or remote systems. WMI represents management data for the OS and other related components as CIM-compliant objects.

Starting with Windows PowerShell 3.0, Microsoft introduced CIM cmdlets to work with devices that support standards-based management. In the earlier versions of PowerShell, WMI cmdlets were used to access the management information from WMI classes; however, the WMI cmdlets used legacy DCOM for Remote Procedure Calls (RPC). Therefore, these cmdlets could not be used to manage non-Windows systems and are not firewall-friendly. With CIM cmdlets, Microsoft added support for WS-Management-based communication. Using the CIM cmdlets, it is now possible to manage both Windows and non-Windows systems that are CIM-compliant, using PowerShell. Furthermore, the CIM cmdlets provide better discovery capabilities for CIM properties and methods.

In this section, we will look at the CIM cmdlets in PowerShell and see how they can be used. We will explore the CIM property and method-discovery capabilities, using examples spread across different subsections and in a more contextual way. Discussing both leads to confusion; therefore, it is better if that is avoided. We won't be focusing on the WMI cmdlets, as the new CIM cmdlets are down-level compatible, and where required, we can force CIM cmdlets to communicate over DCOM. There are subtle differences in the cmdlet parameters between CIM and WMI cmdlets. The knowledge gained from this chapter can be used to understand the internals of PowerShell DSC.

Introduction to CIM Cmdlets

The CIM cmdlets in PowerShell are a part of the CimCmdlets module. No surprises there! We can use the Get-Command cmdlet to obtain a list of cmdlets available in this module. A list of the CIM cmdlets is shown in Figure 2-18.

```
Get-Command -Module CimCmdlets
```

CommandType	Name	ModuleName
Cmdlet	Export-BinaryMiLog	CimCmdlets
Cmdlet	Get-CimAssociatedInstance	CimCmdlets
Cmdlet	Get-CimClass	CimCmdlets
Cmdlet	Get-CimInstance	CimCmdlets
Cmdlet	Get-CimSession	CimCmdlets
Cmdlet	Import-BinaryMiLog	CimCmdlets
Cmdlet	Invoke-CimMethod	CimCmdlets
Cmdlet	New-CimInstance	CimCmdlets
Cmdlet	New-CimSession	CimCmdlets
Cmdlet	New-CimSessionOption	CimCmdlets
Cmdlet	Register-CimIndicationEvent	CimCmdlets
Cmdlet	Remove-CimInstance	CimCmdlets
Cmdlet	Remove-CimSession	CimCmdlets
Cmdlet	Set-CimInstance	CimCmdlets

Figure 2-18. *Cmdlets in the CIM module*

The CimCmdlets module provides cmdlets to

- Retrieve information about CIM classes

- Create new, delete, and change properties of CIM instances and associations

- Create and manage CIM sessions to access management information on remote computers

- Invoke CIM methods

- Register and respond to CIM indication events

Let us dive into these cmdlets and see how they can help us explore CIM classes and work with the management data.

Exploring CIM Classes and Instances

The DMTF CIM standard has two important parts: the CIM schema and the CIM infrastructure specification. The infrastructure specification defines the conceptual view of the managed environment and defines the standards for integrating multiple management models, using object-oriented constructs and design. The CIM infrastructure specification does not provide any actual application programming interfaces (API) for the integration. The CIM schema, on the other hand, provides actual model descriptions. It provides a structured management environment that has a collection of classes with properties and methods. The classes, methods, and associations between various classes are used to organize the available information about the managed environment.

■ **Note**   A more extensive discussion of CIM and related concepts deserves a book of its own. You can read more about the CIM standard at dmtf.org/standards/cim.

Microsoft implemented the CIM standard and the models defined in the CIM schema as a set of Windows Management Instrumentation (WMI) classes. There are several tools to explore CIM models and WMI classes and objects in the Windows OS. We can use the CIM cmdlets to do the same. Within CIM, the managed elements are organized into namespaces. For example, the root\cimv2 namespace contains the Win32 WMI classes that describe the operating system, computers, and the related components. The root\cimv2 namespace is the default namespace for all the CIM cmdlets.

We use the Get-CimClass cmdlet to retrieve a list of CIM classes in a specific namespace. When we run the Get-CimClass cmdlet without any arguments, it lists all the classes within the root\cimv2 namespace. We can use the -Namespace parameter to get classes from a namespace other than the root\cimv2 namespace. This can further be filtered by using the -ClassName parameter. Output from this usage is shown in Figure 2-19.

```
Get-CimClass -Namespace root\wmi -ClassName Win32*
```

```
   NameSpace: ROOT/wmi

CimClassName                    CimClassMethods   CimClassProperties
------------                    ---------------   ------------------
Win32_Perf                      {}                {Caption, Description, Name, Frequency_Object...}
Win32_PerfRawData               {}                {Caption, Description, Name, Frequency_Object...}
Win32_PerfFormattedData         {}                {Caption, Description, Name, Frequency_Object...}
Win32_PrivilegesStatus          {}                {StatusCode, Description, Operation, ParameterInfo...}
```

Figure 2-19. *Listing of Win32 WMI classes in the* root\wmi *namespace*

■ **Tip**   With CIM cmdlets, you can tab-complete the arguments for the -Namespace and -ClassName parameters. For example, after typing "root" as an argument to the -Namespace parameter, you can hit the Tab key, to auto-complete the namespaces under the root namespace.

■ **Note**   Remember: Some of the CIM classes require administrative privileges. You may have to use the elevated PowerShell host for getting information from those classes.

What if we don't know the namespace identifier either? We can use the root namespace to get a list of CIM namespaces available on a computer.

```
Get-CimInstance -Class __NAMESPACE -Namespace root | select Name
```

Each CIM namespace is an instance of the __NAMESPACE class. In CIM and WMI, the classes that begin with "__" are called system classes. So, the preceding command gives us all the namespaces within the root namespace. We can use this method to get all CIM namespaces on a system. It requires a bit of recursion, and we can use functions to make this reusable.

```
Function Get-CimNamespace {
    Param (
        $Namespace='root'
    )
    Get-CimInstance -Namespace $Namespace -ClassName __NAMESPACE | ForEach-Object {
            ($ns = '{0}\{1}' -f $Namespace,$_.Name)
            Get-CimNamespace $ns
    }
}
```

■ **Note**   The command output for some of the examples is quite long and, therefore, deliberately not included. Try these examples yourself, to understand how they work.

In the preceding example, we recursively call the Get-CimNamespace function with the namespace as a parameter, to get a complete list of namespaces on the system. To get a list of namespaces within a namespace, we have used another CIM cmdlet called Get-CimInstance. The Get-CimInstance cmdlet retrieves the instances of a CIM class. We have seen that the __NAMESPACE is the parent class of all namespaces, and getting an instance of that class basically gives us all the namespaces. Let us consider some additional examples of this cmdlet, to understand different parameters and their purposes.

```
Get-CimInstance -ClassName Win32_Process
```

We have seen in the preceding example that the -ClassName parameter can be used to specify the name of the class. Unlike the Get-CimClass cmdlet, the Get-CimInstance cmdlet does not allow wildcards to be used in the argument. For example, specifying Win32* as the class name fails when using this cmdlet. We have to provide the complete and accurate class name. We have already seen an example of retrieving all classes within any given namespace. So, it should not be hard for you to explore the class names, if you don't know the complete name.

We can use the -Filter parameter of the Get-CimInstance cmdlet to get a list of instances that match specific criteria. To do this, we must know the name of the property we want to filter on. For example, to get a list of all Chrome.exe processes running on my system, I can write the following:

```
Get-CimInstance -ClassName Win32_Process -Filter "Name='chrome.exe'"
```

The output from the preceding example is shown in Figure 2-20. When using the equal to operator, the complete name of the process must be used for comparison. We won't see any output, if we use "Name='Chrome'" or "Name='Chrome*'" as an argument to the -Filter parameter. Also, note the quotes around the process name. They are important too. Without the quotes surrounding the process name, the cmdlet returns an invalid query error.

ProcessId	Name	HandleCount	WorkingSetSize	VirtualSize
1180	chrome.exe	1341	199090176	514330624
6152	chrome.exe	254	96579584	439959552
6320	chrome.exe	142	22048768	205910016
6768	chrome.exe	142	21245952	197586944
10120	chrome.exe	158	145469440	324407296

Figure 2-20. *Filtering the Win32_Process class instances for Chrome.exe*

After looking at some of the examples, you must have questioned why the "equal to operator" here is not -eq. Instead, it is '=', which we thought was the assignment operator. To understand this, we have to explore the WMI Query Language (WQL) a bit. Let's pause here briefly and investigate what WQL is and some of the differences between the WQL and PowerShell languages.

WMI Query Language

The WMI Query Language is a subset of the American National Standards Institute Structured Query Language (ANSI SQL)—with minor semantic changes. Like SQL, WQL has a set of keywords and operators and supports three types of queries: data, event, and schema queries. I will discuss these three types of queries shortly. First, let us take a look at the WQL keywords and operators. I will get back to using a few other CIM cmdlets, after you learn how to write WMI queries.

WQL Keywords

As with SQL, WQL queries use keywords to retrieve data from the management objects. WQL has nineteen keywords to perform these queries against WMI repositories. Even though there are nineteen WQL keywords, only a few of them can be used in all three possible query types. Table 2-1 lists all the WQL keywords and lists the query type in which they can be used.

Table 2-1. *Keywords in WQL*

Keyword	Query Type			Description
	Data	Schema	Event	
AND	X		X	Combines two Boolean expressions and returns TRUE when both expressions are TRUE
ASSOCIATORS OF	X	X		Retrieves all instances that are associated with a source instance. Use this statement with schema queries and data queries.
FROM	X	X	X	Specifies the class that contains the properties listed in a SELECT statement. Windows Management Instrumentation (WMI) supports data queries from only one class at a time.
GROUP			X	Causes WMI to generate one notification to represent a group of events
HAVING			X	Filters the events that are received during the grouping interval that is specified in the WITHIN clause
IS	X		X	Comparison operator used with NOT and NULL. The syntax for this statement is the following: IS [NOT] NULL (where NOT is optional)
ISA	X	X	X	Operator that applies a query to the subclasses of a specified class
KEYSONLY	X			Used in REFERENCES OF and ASSOCIATORS OF queries to ensure that the resulting instances are only populated with the keys of the instances. This reduces the overhead of the call.
LIKE	X			Operator that determines whether or not a given character string matches a specified pattern

(continued)

Table 2-1. (*continued*)

Keyword	Query Type			Description
	Data	Schema	Event	
NOT	X			Comparison operator used in a WQL SELECT query to negate the value of NULL
NULL	X			Indicates an object that does not have an explicitly assigned value. NULL is not equivalent to zero (0) or blank.
OR	X			Combines two conditions. When more than one logical operator is used in a statement, the OR operators are evaluated after the AND operators.
REFERENCES OF	X	X		Retrieves all association instances that refer to a specific source instance. The REFERENCES OF statement is similar to the ASSOCIATORS OF statement. However, it does not retrieve endpoint instances; it retrieves the association instances.
SELECT	X	X	X	Specifies the properties that are used in a query
TRUE	X	X	X	Boolean operator that evaluates to -1 (minus one)
WHERE	X	X	X	Narrows the scope of a data, event, or schema query
WITHIN			X	Specifies polling or grouping interval
FALSE	X	X	X	Boolean operator that evaluates to 0 (zero)
__CLASS	X	X		References the class of the object in a query

We will see examples of these keywords being used in WMI queries when we discuss types of queries a little later. If you are familiar with Transact-SQL, you may find keywords familiar.

WQL Operators

WQL operators cause a bit of confusion among people getting started with Windows PowerShell or already writing PowerShell scripts. This is because of the symbols used and the meaning or purpose of those operators. Take a look at the list of operators in Table 2-2. Some of them are similar to the PowerShell arithmetic operators, while others are similar to those you may have seen in other scripting languages, such as VBScript.

Table 2-2. *Operators in WQL*

Operator	Purpose
=	Equal to
<	Less than
>	Greater than
<=	Less than or equal to
>=	Greater than or equal to
!= or <>	Not equal to

A few WQL keywords, such as IS, ISA, NOT, and LIKE, can also be considered as operators. Of these keywords, IS and IS NOT operators are valid in the WHERE clause only if the constant is NULL.

Writing WQL Queries

Now that we have the list of WQL operators and keywords handy, let us explore more about creating the WQL queries. To start with, we will revisit one of the earlier examples and convert that to use a query to filter the properties.

```
Get-CimInstance -Query "SELECT * FROM Win32_Process WHERE Name='Chrome.exe'"
```

As you see in Figure 2-21, we use the -Query parameter and not -ClassName. Within the query, we use the SELECT keyword, followed by an asterisk (*). This specifies that we want all properties from the class specified in the query. In our example, we are getting all properties of the Win32_Process class.

ProcessId	Name	HandleCount	WorkingSetSize	VirtualSize
1180	chrome.exe	1344	198873088	514330624
6152	chrome.exe	254	96579584	439959552
6320	chrome.exe	142	22048768	205910016
6768	chrome.exe	142	21245952	197586944
10120	chrome.exe	158	148230144	326504448

Figure 2-21. *Filtering Windows process objects using WQL syntax*

If you need to get only a subset of properties, you can specify the names of those properties as a comma-separated list, instead of using an asterisk. This result from the following example is shown in Figure 2-22.

```
Get-CimInstance -Query "SELECT Name,HandleCount FROM Win32_Process WHERE Name='Chrome.exe'"
```

ProcessId	Name	HandleCount	WorkingSetSize	VirtualSize
	chrome.exe	1336		
	chrome.exe	254		
	chrome.exe	142		
	chrome.exe	142		
	chrome.exe	158		

Figure 2-22. *Selecting a subset of properties using WQL syntax*

We have a filter for listing the properties of a process, only if the process name is Chrome.exe. For specifying the filter condition, we use the WHERE keyword, followed by the condition. If you observe closely, the condition we specified in this example is similar to the one we discussed in the last section, except that, there, it was specified as an argument to the -Filter parameter. In fact, even when using the -Filter parameter, the Get-CimInstance cmdlet converts it into a WMI query, behind the scenes.

Now, what if you don't know the complete process name? As we saw in the keywords table and later described in the operators section, the LIKE keyword can be used when we have to use wildcards.

```
Get-CimInstance -Query "SELECT * FROM Win32_Process WHERE Name LIKE 'Chrome%'"
```

In this example, we used the LIKE keyword and partial name of the process. Make a note of the % symbol. In PowerShell language, the wildcards are described by an asterisk (*), while in WQL, they are denoted by %. If you are searching for a word that is in between some text, you can wrap the word between % symbols.

```
Get-CimInstance -Query "SELECT * FROM Win32_Process WHERE Name LIKE '%rome%'"
```

The % symbol is called a meta character in WQL. There are other meta characters, such as '[ ]', '_', and '^'. The square brackets can be used to specify a range.

```
Get-CimInstance -Query "SELECT * FROM Win32_Process WHERE Name LIKE '[A-C]hrome%'"
```

Similarly, you can use the other meta characters as well. The underscore (_) is used to specify a single character wildcard, and the caret (^) is used to negate the values. For example, a condition similar to "Name LIKE '^[A-C]%'" will return only processes with a name that doesn't start with the characters A, B, or C.

Let us move on to other examples and see how we can combine multiple conditions in a query. We can use the AND and OR operators to do this. The following example demonstrates this, and Figure 2-23 shows the output from the command.

```
Get-CimInstance -Query "SELECT * FROM Win32_Process WHERE Name='Chrome.exe' OR Name='iexplore.exe'"
```

ProcessId	Name	HandleCount	WorkingSetSize	VirtualSize
1180	chrome.exe	1378	200601600	514580480
6152	chrome.exe	251	88104960	429477888
6320	chrome.exe	142	22048768	205910016
6768	chrome.exe	142	21245952	197586944
8464	iexplore.exe	441	31465472	185937920
5300	iexplore.exe	955	177205248	677810176
10120	chrome.exe	150	132349952	309727232
11380	chrome.exe	148	49295360	231301120

Figure 2-23. *Filtering Windows processes for multiple processes using WQL*

The preceding query returns the output, if the name of a process is either Chrome.exe or iexplore.exe. Similarly, we can add other conditions to the same query string.

```
Get-CimInstance -Query "SELECT * FROM Win32_Process WHERE (Name='Chrome.exe' OR Name='iexplore.exe')
AND HandleCount > 150"
```

Figure 2-24 shows the preceding example in action. Just as we grouped conditions in a PowerShell IF statement, we can use parentheses to combine multiple conditions in a WQL query string too.

ProcessId	Name	HandleCount	WorkingSetSize	VirtualSize
1180	chrome.exe	1381	200556544	514646016
6152	chrome.exe	251	88104960	429477888
8464	iexplore.exe	441	31461376	185937920
5300	iexplore.exe	955	177205248	677810176

Figure 2-24. *Filtering the process output for processes with HandleCount more than 150*

What we have seen so far are all examples of **data queries**. CIM data queries are the simplest form of querying for CIM management data. CIM data queries are used to retrieve class instances and associations.

■ **Note**   CIM associations are used to describe the relationship between CIM classes. The subject of associations warrants further discussion. For more information on CIM associations, access `www.wbemsolutions.com/tutorials/` `CIM/meta-assoc.html`.

As I had mentioned earlier, there are three different types of queries. As we have already seen some examples of data queries, let us now examine event queries and how we can use them. While learning about event queries, we will also focus on learning some additional CIM cmdlets and CIM concepts.

In the CIM standard specification, events are represented as indications. In simple terms, an event or indication can be defined as change of state. For example, when you play music, you can pause, change the music track, and so on. Each of these changes in state represents an event. In the CIM world, there are events associated with different types of managed objects and instances. For example, you can subscribe to a process creation event or a process deletion or termination event. By subscribing to the events, we are notified whenever the event is triggered. It is then up to us to act upon that trigger.

The PowerShell CIM cmdlets support subscribing to the CIM indications. We can use the `Register-CimIndicationEvent` class to subscribe to the events from any supported CIM event class or otherwise. Let us consider an example, to understand this.

■ **Note**   You need administrative privileges to subscribe to CIM events. This means that the following examples should be executed within an elevated PowerShell host.

```
Register-CimIndicationEvent -ClassName Win32_ProcessStartTrace -Action {
    Write-Host "A new process started"
}
```

With PowerShell, it is as simple as the preceding example to subscribe to CIM events. To test whether this really works or not, just execute the command in the example and start an instance of `notepad.exe`. You should see a message at the console that a new process has started. This can be seen in Figure 2-25.

```
Id      Name            PSJobTypeName   State       HasMoreData   Location   Command
--      ----            -------------   -----       -----------   --------   -------
3       9f465ca2-9e0...                 NotStarted  False                    ...


PS C:\> A new process started
A new process started
```

Figure 2-25. *Event subscription and script block execution on receiving an event*

Now, let us dissect the command, to understand it thoroughly. I had already mentioned that `Register-CimIndicationEvent` is the cmdlet we have to use for event subscriptions. The `-ClassName` parameter isn't new to us. The `-Action` parameter is what we need to discuss in detail. The script block that is given as an argument to this parameter specifies what needs to be done when the event is triggered. In our example, we are not doing anything useful. We are just printing a simple message. But how do we know what process has started? This is where the `$Event` automatic variable helps us. This variable will be available only within the `-Action` script block. So, if we want to examine the `$Event` variable after an event is triggered, we have to set the global scope. I use a simple trick here.

■ **Tip** The CIM event subscriptions reside in memory until we close the PowerShell host. The event subscriptions created earlier will still be in the memory and may confuse you when you are running different examples in this section. I recommend that you run the `Get-EventSubscriber | Unregister-Event -Force` command to remove all event subscriptions. Alternatively, you can close and reopen the PowerShell host.

```
Register-CimIndicationEvent -ClassName Win32_ProcessStartTrace -Action {
    $Global:ProcessEvent = $Event
}
```

What we are doing in the preceding example is simple. Whenever the event is triggered, we assign the object available in `$Event` variable to `$ProcessEvent` in the global scope. The `-Action` script block runs in a completely different runspace, and the variables created within that won't be available in global scope, unless they are explicitly created in the global scope. The `$Global:` variable is what helps us do that. Figure 2-26 demonstrates accessing the global variable populated in an event action.

```
Id     Name          PSJobTypeName   State      HasMoreData   Location    Command
--     ----          -------------   -----      -----------   --------    -------
3      01ec2bf8-478...               NotStarted False                     ...


PS C:\> $ProcessEvent


ComputerName       :
RunspaceId         : 568a2208-14b0-46d9-b806-88431c55e138
EventIdentifier    : 3
Sender             : Microsoft.Management.Infrastructure.CimCmdlets.CimIndicationWatcher
SourceEventArgs    : Microsoft.Management.Infrastructure.CimCmdlets.CimIndicationEventInstanceEventArgs
SourceArgs         : {Microsoft.Management.Infrastructure.CimCmdlets.CimIndicationWatcher, }
SourceIdentifier   : 12cd5d9a-e373-4db9-9c5e-97e4b7448864
TimeGenerated      : 4/4/2014 2:08:35 PM
MessageData        :
```

Figure 2-26. *Exploring the $Event variable*

Now that we have a copy of the `$Event` automatic variable, let us examine it to see where we can find the name of the process. Every event in CIM has the `SourceEventArgs` property. This property contains the new event that is generated. So, in the global scope, `$ProcessEvent.SourceEventArgs.NewEvent` contains the details of the process that was created. This is shown in Figure 2-27.

```
PS C:\> $ProcessEvent.SourceEventArgs.NewEvent


SECURITY_DESCRIPTOR :
TIME_CREATED        : 130410744949824610
ParentProcessID     : 620
ProcessID           : 7472
ProcessName         : conhost.exe
SessionID           : 0
Sid                 : {1, 1, 0, 0...}
PSComputerName      :




PS C:\> $ProcessEvent.SourceEventArgs.NewEvent


SECURITY_DESCRIPTOR :
TIME_CREATED        : 130410745109750613
ParentProcessID     : 1176
ProcessID           : 8404
ProcessName         : notepad.exe
SessionID           : 1
Sid                 : {1, 5, 0, 0...}
PSComputerName      :
```

Figure 2-27. *Examining the $Event variable*

As you see here, we can use the ProcessName property to determine what process was created and use the ProcessID property to get the PID of the newly created process. But, if you execute this example, start a Notepad process, leave the console for a few minutes, and then try checking the $Event variable, you may see details about another process in the $Event variable. This is because on the Windows OS, many processes get created and terminated for various services at regular intervals. So, how do we subscribe to events that are triggered only when a specific process is created? For example, suppose you want to be notified only when a notepad.exe gets created.

With the Register-CimIndicationEvent cmdlet, there is no -Filter parameter, as we saw in the Get-CimInstance example. This is where we need the WQL knowledge.

```
Register-CimIndicationEvent -Query "SELECT * FROM Win32_ProcessStartTrace WHERE
ProcessName='notepad.exe'" -Action {
    Write-Host "A new notepad process created with PID: $($Event.SourceEventArgs.NewEvent.
ProcessID)"
}
```

Output from the preceding example is shown in Figure 2-28.

```
Id      Name            PSJobTypeName    State       HasMoreData    Location    Command
--      ----            -------------    -----       -----------    --------    -------
4       6cebb469-30f...                  NotStarted  False                      ...


PS C:\> A new notepad process created with PID: 6864
```

Figure 2-28. *Message from the event subscription*

The query string that we used is very similar to that we have seen earlier. This should not be difficult to understand. The -Action script block can have any arbitrary code. For example, every time a certain process is created, you might want to create a log entry in a text file, and so on.

Now, let us see if we can create a similar event subscription for Windows Services. The class that we are interested in is Win32_Service.

```
Register-CimIndicationEvent -Query "SELECT * FROM Win32_Service" -Action {
    $Global:ServiceEvent = $Event
}
```

Execute the code in preceding example and see what happens. Do you see an error, as shown in Figure 2-29?

```
Register-CimIndicationEvent : Class is not an event class.
At line:1 char:1
+ Register-CimIndicationEvent -Query "SELECT * FROM Win32_Service" -Action {
+ ~~~~~~~~~~~~~~~~~~~~~~~~~~~~~~~~~~~~~~~~~~~~~~~~~~~~~~~~~~~~~~~~~~~~~~~~~~~~~~
    + CategoryInfo          : NotSpecified: (:) [Register-CimIndicationEvent], CimException
    + FullyQualifiedErrorId : HRESULT 0x80041059,Microsoft.Management.Infrastructure.CimCmdlets.RegisterCimIndicationComman
   d
```

Figure 2-29. *Error when subscripting to a non-event class*

PowerShell tells us that Win32_Service is not an event class, and that is the truth! Unlike Win32_ProcessStartTrace, Win32_Service cannot be directly used in an event query. But, how do I know that it is not an event class? How do I get a list of CIM event classes? PowerShell and Get-CimInstance have an answer as shown in Figure 2-30.

```
Get-CimClass -ClassName * -QualifierName Indication
```

```
    NameSpace: ROOT/cimv2

CimClassName                CimClassMethods    CimClassProperties
------------                ---------------    ------------------
CIM_Indication              {}                 {CorrelatedIndications, IndicationFilterName, IndicationIdentifi...
CIM_ClassIndication         {}                 {CorrelatedIndications, IndicationFilterName, IndicationIdentifi...
CIM_ClassDeletion           {}                 {CorrelatedIndications, IndicationFilterName, IndicationIdentifi...
CIM_ClassCreation           {}                 {CorrelatedIndications, IndicationFilterName, IndicationIdentifi...
CIM_ClassModification       {}                 {CorrelatedIndications, IndicationFilterName, IndicationIdentifi...
CIM_InstIndication          {}                 {CorrelatedIndications, IndicationFilterName, IndicationIdentifi...
CIM_InstCreation            {}                 {CorrelatedIndications, IndicationFilterName, IndicationIdentifi...
CIM_InstModification        {}                 {CorrelatedIndications, IndicationFilterName, IndicationIdentifi...
CIM_InstDeletion            {}                 {CorrelatedIndications, IndicationFilterName, IndicationIdentifi...
CIM_Error                   {}                 {CIMStatusCode, CIMStatusCodeDescription, ErrorSource, ErrorSour...
MSFT_WmiError               {}                 {CIMStatusCode, CIMStatusCodeDescription, ErrorSource, ErrorSour...
MSFT_ExtendedStatus         {}                 {CIMStatusCode, CIMStatusCodeDescription, ErrorSource, ErrorSour...
```

Figure 2-30. *Event classes in root\cimv2 namespace*

So, how do we work with event subscriptions for CIM classes that are not event classes? We use special types of event queries to do this. For the non-event CIM classes, the WMI provider does all the heavy lifting of delivering notifications whenever a CIM class instance is created, modified, and deleted. We can subscribe to such events using the __InstanceCreationEvent, __InstanceModificationEvent, and __InstanceDeletionEvent system classes. These types of events are called intrinsic events. Let us see some examples.

```
Register-CimIndicationEvent -Query "SELECT * FROM __InstanceModificationEvent WITHIN 1 WHERE
TargetInstance ISA 'Win32_Service'" -Action {
    $Global:ServiceEvent = $Event
}
```

Take a minute to understand this example. The query string that we used is not new to us. We have seen it in the data queries and the earlier event query examples. We have used the __InstanceModificationEvent system class to subscribe to any changes happening to the Win32_Service class. Because these system classes can be used to represent any CIM class in the repository, we have to specify what our target class type is. We have specified this by using the TargetInstance property and comparing to a string using the ISA keyword. We are actually using the ISA keyword as an operator here. It is similar to saying TargetInstance is equal to Win32_Service. By using the WITHIN keyword, we are specifying the polling interval time in seconds. For intrinsic event queries, we have to specify a polling interval, as there might be too many changes to CIM classes at any given point in time.

We are using the technique we learned earlier to see what the $Event automatic variable contains when the event gets triggered. So, let us examine this further to understand it in greater detail. To test this and get the $ServiceEvent variable set in the global scope, run the preceding example and then stop any Windows service. For the sake of demonstration, stop the AudioSrv service. We won't lose much by stopping the music for a minute!

```
Stop-Service -Name AudioSrv
```

As seen in Figure 2-31, the contents of $ServiceEvent must be familiar by now. It also appears in an earlier example.

```
PS C:\> $ServiceEvent


ComputerName      :
RunspaceId        : 568a2208-14b0-46d9-b806-88431c55e138
EventIdentifier   : 98
Sender            : Microsoft.Management.Infrastructure.CimCmdlets.CimIndicationWatcher
SourceEventArgs   : Microsoft.Management.Infrastructure.CimCmdlets.CimIndicationEventInstanceEventArgs
SourceArgs        : {Microsoft.Management.Infrastructure.CimCmdlets.CimIndicationWatcher, }
SourceIdentifier  : 16e3850b-df89-4888-bcfb-f839700147cd
TimeGenerated     : 4/4/2014 2:24:29 PM
MessageData       :
```

Figure 2-31. *Intrinsic event for Win32_Service class*

So, let us access $ServiceEvent.SourceEventArgs.NewEvent to look more deeply into the event data. An example of this is shown in Figure 2-32.

```
PS C:\> $ServiceEvent.SourceEventArgs.NewEvent


SECURITY_DESCRIPTOR  :
TIME_CREATED         : 130410754927178096
TargetInstance       : Win32_Service: Windows Audio (Name = "AudioSrv")
PreviousInstance     : Win32_Service: Windows Audio (Name = "AudioSrv")
PSComputerName       :
```

Figure 2-32. *Event data from the intrinsic event*

This is where we see the difference from the earlier event example. Here, we see two more properties, called TargetInstance and PreviousInstance. This should ring some bells about why we used the TargetInstance property in the query string. The PreviousInstance property can also be used in the query string. The difference is simple. The TargetInstance property gives the state of the object after the event occurs, and PreviousInstance gives us the state before the event. We can use these properties to attach conditions to our query string.

```
Register-CimIndicationEvent -Query "SELECT * FROM __InstanceModificationEvent WITHIN 1 WHERE
TargetInstance ISA 'Win32_Service' AND TargetInstance.Name='AudioSrv'" -Action {
    $Global:ServiceEvent = $Event
}
```

You can see that we used the AND operator and then used TargetInstance.Name, to check if the name of the service is AudioSrv or not. By doing so, we are indicating that we want to deliver events only when the service whose state changed is AudioSrv. Now, let us indicate that we want to receive the notifications for changes to AudioSrv service only when the previous state of this service is running. This is where the PreviousInstance helps us.

```
Register-CimIndicationEvent -Query "SELECT * FROM __InstanceModificationEvent WITHIN 1 WHERE
TargetInstance ISA 'Win32_Service' AND (TargetInstance.Name='AudioSrv' AND PreviousInstance.
State='Running')" -Action {
    $Global:ServiceEvent = $Event
}
```

Observe how we are using the PreviousInstance.State property. To test this, start the AudioSrv service and execute the preceding code. To see whether or not the event is triggered, let us modify the service. The safest change will be to update the description of this service.

```
Set-Service -Name AudioSrv -Description "Testing event"
```

After this, you should see that $ServiceEvent becomes available in the global scope, and $ServiceEvent. SourceEventArgs.NewEvent.TargetInstance.Description should be "Testing event" (see Figure 2-33).

```
PS C:\> $ServiceEvent.SourceEventArgs.NewEvent.TargetInstance.Description
Testing event

PS C:\> |
```

Figure 2-33. *Verifying the change in service description*

We have not verified the condition we set with the `PreviousInstance` property. So, to verify that, let us stop the service, using the `Stop-Service` cmdlet. After the service is stopped, let us reset the description of the service to "Windows Audio Service." If everything worked as planned, you should not see any changes to the `$ServiceEvent` variable set in the global scope. This is because we wanted an event subscription only when the `State` in the `PreviousInstance` is set to "Running." However, in our example, we forcefully stopped the service (see Figure 2-34). So, the condition did not evaluate to `True`.

```
PS C:\> Stop-Service -Name AudioSrv

PS C:\> Set-Service -Name AudioSrv -Description "Windows Audio Service"

PS C:\> $ServiceEvent.SourceEventArgs.NewEvent.TargetInstance.Description
Testing event

PS C:\>
```

Figure 2-34. *Verifying the AND condition with* PreviousInstance

As an exercise, can you write an event query to subscribe to instance creation events of the `Win32_Volume` CIM class? Can you use this event subscription to find when a USB flash drive is inserted?

So far, we have seen CIM event queries with both event and non-event classes. We have seen how to use intrinsic events. There are other types of events, such as extrinsic events and timer events. The way we write the event queries does not change for these other types of events. So, you should be able to use the knowledge you gained so far to work with extrinsic events and timer events. For more information on these types of events, refer to http://msdn.microsoft.com/en-us/library/aa390355(v=vs.85).aspx.

■ **Tip**   The `about_WQL` help topic has complete information about using various WQL operators and keywords. Before you advance to the next section, take some time to read this help topic and understand the usage of WQL semantics.

Working with CIM Methods

We have looked at PowerShell objects and understand that objects have properties and methods. The CIM specification and the models described by the CIM schema are based on object-oriented methodologies. So, each of the CIM classes contains both properties and methods. We have already seen how to get an instance of a CIM class, which essentially gives us all the properties. We did that using the `Get-CimInstance` cmdlet. The `Invoke-CimMethod` cmdlet helps to invoke methods on a CIM instance.

In the earlier example, we looked at how we can get an instance of a `notepad.exe` process. Using the `Invoke-CimMethod` cmdlet, let us see how we can create a new `notepad.exe` process.

```
Invoke-CimMethod -ClassName Win32_Process -MethodName Create -Arguments @{ Path = "notepad.exe" }
```

We have to provide the arguments to the method as a hash table. To start a process, we must specify the path to the file, and that is what we have in the hash table. We can use the WQL query method to invoke methods when we have an existing instance.

```
Invoke-CimMethod -Query "SELECT * FROM Win32_Process WHERE Name='notepad.exe'" -MethodName Terminate
```

The preceding command closes all the open Notepad instances. We can also use the -Filter parameter, instead of the -Query, to filter the processes for notepad.exe.

```
Get-CimInstance Win32_Process -Filter "Name='notepad.exe'" |
Invoke-CimMethod -MethodName Terminate
```

In the preceding command, we use the -Filter parameter to specify the condition and then pipe the output from the Get-CimInstance cmdlet to the Invoke-CimMethod cmdlet.

Working with Remote Systems

In all our examples so far, we have only seen how to access CIM management data from the local system. Using the CIM cmdlets, we can access management data from remote systems as well. The CIM cmdlets, starting with Windows PowerShell version 3.0, use the WS-Management protocol to communicate with remote systems. The following list provides a set of requirements on the local and remote systems for the CIM cmdlets to work.

- Windows PowerShell 3.0 or above
- WinRM service enabled and running (on the remote systems only)
- WinRM listeners created for remote system communication (on the remote systems only)

We saw the methodology for creating WinRM listeners, at the beginning of this chapter. For the following examples, I assume that you have used the process described earlier to create the HTTP listeners.

Once these prerequisites are met, we can use the -ComputerName parameter to access CIM management information on the remote systems. The output in Figure 2-35 demonstrates this.

```
Get-CimClass -ComputerName WC81-1 -ClassName Win32_Process
```

```
   NameSpace: root/cimv2

CimClassName                    CimClassMethods      CimClassProperties
------------                    ---------------      ------------------
Win32_Process                   {Create, Terminat... {Caption, Description, InstallDate, Name...}
```

Figure 2-35. *List of processes from a remote system*

When we access the CIM management information from a remote system, an additional property gets added to the object output. This property is called PSComputerName, and it identifies the remote system name. This property can be used when working with multiple remote systems in the command. For example, take a look at following command. We are getting service state information from two different systems. If we don't have the PSComputerName property added to the object output, it can be quite confusing to differentiate between the objects we receive. This is shown in the preceding example and in Figure 2-36.

```
Get-CimInstance -Query "SELECT * FROM Win32_Service Where Name='Winrm'" -ComputerName WC81-1,DSC-Demo
```

ProcessId	Name	StartMode	State	Status	ExitCode	PSComputerName
496	WinRM	Auto	Running	OK	0	WC81-1
1948	WinRM	Auto	Running	OK	0	DSC-Demo

Figure 2-36. *The PSComputerName property in the Get-CimInstance output*

When using the -ComputerName parameter, a temporary CIM session is created. This is a client-side session, and it gets destroyed after the command execution is complete. So, there is an overhead of setting a session and destroying it after the execution. Imagine running a series of Get-CimInstance commands with the -ComputerName parameter? It will be slow. So, this is where the cmdlets to create CIM sessions are useful. Instead of the Get-CimInstance doing all the hard work, we can give the cmdlet a ready-made session, and all the CIM commands can run inside that session. This is useful, especially when more than one CIM command has to be executed on a remote system. Let us see how.

```
$CimSession = New-CimSession -ComputerName WC81-1,DSC-Demo
```

The -ComputerName parameter can take multiple computer names. When we specify more than one computer name, the resulting variable value, $CimSession in this example, will be an array of all CIM sessions. This is shown in Figure 2-37.

```
Id          : 1
Name        : CimSession1
InstanceId  : abeda214-e733-465d-b5b9-a56cea4b7604
ComputerName : DSC-Demo
Protocol    : WSMAN

Id          : 2
Name        : CimSession2
InstanceId  : b600e405-8e70-4be7-bcd1-a14092a48748
ComputerName : WC81-1
Protocol    : WSMAN
```

Figure 2-37. *CIM sessions in PowerShell*

Once we have a CIM session created, we can use the -CimSession parameter on the CIM cmdlets to retrieve CIM management information from the remote systems (see Figure 2-38).

```
Get-CimInstance -Query "SELECT * FROM Win32_Service Where Name='Winrm'" -CimSession $CimSession
```

ProcessId	Name	StartMode	State	Status	ExitCode	PSComputerName
1948	WinRM	Auto	Running	OK	0	DSC-Demo
496	WinRM	Auto	Running	OK	0	WC81-1

Figure 2-38. *WinRM service status on remote systems using CIM sessions*

The preceding example, shown in Figure 2-38, is similar to the example using the -ComputerName parameter. We just replace this parameter with -CimSession. The difference in execution speed when using a ready-made CIM session can be easily visualized by using the Measure-Command cmdlet. This cmdlet measures the time it takes to run a command.

```
Measure-Command -Expression {
    Get-CimInstance -Query "SELECT * FROM Win32_Service Where Name='Winrm'" -ComputerName WS12-R2-
1,DSC-Demo
} | Select-Object Milliseconds

Measure-Command -Expression {
    Get-CimInstance -Query "SELECT * FROM Win32_Service Where Name='Winrm'" -CimSession $CimSession
} | Select-Object Milliseconds
```

In the preceding example, we specified the command to run as an argument to the -Expression parameter and pipe the output of the Measure-Command cmdlet to the Select-Object cmdlet. Using the Select-Object cmdlet, we are selecting only a single property that we are interested in, which is Milliseconds. This is shown in Figure 2-39.

```
PS C:\> Measure-Command -Expression {
    Get-CimInstance -Query "SELECT * FROM Win32_Service Where Name='Winrm'" -ComputerName WC81-1,DSC-Demo
} | Select-Object Milliseconds


                                                                                    Milliseconds
                                                                                    ------------
                                                                                             172



PS C:\> Measure-Command -Expression {
    Get-CimInstance -Query "SELECT * FROM Win32_Service Where Name='Winrm'" -CimSession $CimSession
} | Select-Object Milliseconds


                                                                                    Milliseconds
                                                                                    ------------
                                                                                             143
```

Figure 2-39. *Difference in execution time when using CimSessions*

The difference in execution time in this example may not be significant. However, when you have multiple such commands to retrieve different sets of CIM data from remote systems, the execution time difference can be very significant.

Once we have the CIM sessions set up and the command execution is complete, we can remove the existing CIM sessions, by using the Remove-CimSession cmdlet. The Get-CimSession cmdlet gets all the CIM sessions, and this can be piped directly to Remove-CimSession, to delete all the CIM sessions.

```
Get-CimSession | Remove-CimSession
```

If you want to remove a specific CIM session and not all, you can get the ID of the session from the Get-CimSession cmdlet and use it with the Remove-CimSession cmdlet. This is shown in Figure 2-40.

```
Get-CimSession
Remove-CimSession -Id 2
```

```
PS C:\> Get-CimSession


Id          : 1
Name        : CimSession1
InstanceId  : abeda214-e733-465d-b5b9-a56cea4b7604
ComputerName : DSC-Demo
Protocol    : WSMAN

Id          : 2
Name        : CimSession2
InstanceId  : b600e405-8e70-4be7-bcd1-a14092a48748
ComputerName : WC81-1
Protocol    : WSMAN



PS C:\> Remove-CimSession -Id 2
```

Figure 2-40. *Removing a specific CIM session*

Understanding MOF

We understand that the CIM standard defines a conceptual information model for managed elements. The structure of this model is described using terminology that is specific to the model and uses object-oriented programming principles to describe the model. The language that the CIM standard uses to define managed elements is called Managed Object Format (MOF). In the Windows OS, the CIM or WMI providers implement the classes as MOF files. These files are compiled using mofcomp.exe into the WMI repository. An MOF file content defines the data and event classes for which the provider returns data. Usually, the code required for generating the data is packaged as a dynamic-link library (DLL) file.

You can use PowerShell to explore the MOF files for the existing classes. The output from this is shown in Figure 2-41.

```
([wmiclass]"Win32_CurrentTime").GetText("mof")
```

```
PS C:\> ([wmiclass]"Win32_CurrentTime").GetText("mof")
[Abstract, Singleton: DisableOverride ToInstance ToSubClass]
class Win32_CurrentTime
{
    [read] uint32 Year;
    [read] uint32 Month;
    [read] uint32 Day;
    [read] uint32 DayOfWeek;
    [read] uint32 WeekInMonth;
    [read] uint32 Quarter;
    [read] uint32 Hour;
    [read] uint32 Minute;
    [read] uint32 Second;
    [read] uint32 Milliseconds;
};
```

Figure 2-41. *MOF contents for Win32_CurrentTime*

Although this is not directly related to CIM cmdlets or PowerShell, it is important to have a basic idea about MOF, as the Desired State Configuration heavily leverages the MOF format to define the configurations. Let us take a look at some basics of MOF and how to create and compile a simple MOF file.

MOF Language Elements

MOF files are represented as text saved in UTF-8 format. These files contain class and instance definitions. Before we start to write a simple WMI class using an MOF file, let us take a look at some of the language elements used in MOF files.

Compiler Directives

Compiler directives direct the processing of MOF files. If you are familiar with programming languages, you can relate the compiler directives to #include in C and the Using keyword in C#. For example, a #pragma Include ("C:\ MOF\MyMOF.mof") directive specifies that the referenced MOF file should be included as a part of the resulting MOF compilation unit.

Qualifiers

Qualifiers in MOF files provide information about how to describe a class, instance, property, methods, and their parameters. These qualifiers are enclosed in square brackets. The **standard qualifiers** are defined by WMI. For example, the Dynamic qualifier indicates that the instances of a class are dynamically created. The Key qualifier indicates that the specified property is a key property in the class and can be used as a unique reference. There are many standard WMI qualifiers that can be used in MOF file definitions. The following example provides a sample definition of a class using standard qualifiers.

```
[Dynamic]
class SampleClassName : ParentClass
{
    [key] string KeyName;
};
```

Type Declarations

The CIM model defines a hierarchy of types to be used in an MOF file. At the root of the hierarchy is a namespace, and this is usually termed a **root namespace**. We can create a namespace under the root namespace as a container for the classes we would define. The following example illustrates how to define a namespace.

```
#pragma namespace("\\\\.\\Root")

instance of __Namespace
{
    Name = "MyCustomNamespace";
};
```

In the preceding example, the `instance of` keyword is used to create an instance of a `__Namespace` system class. The next element in the type hierarchy is a class. We can create a class under the new namespace we just defined.

```
#pragma namespace("\\\\.\\Root\\MyCustomNamespace")

class MyCN_MyClass
{
};
```

The `class` keyword indicates that the type of the element we are defining is a class. We have to add properties to this custom class. We can associate data types to these properties, and qualifiers also can be associated to the properties.

```
#pragma namespace("\\\\.\\Root\\MyCustomNamespace")
class MyCN_MyClass
{
    [Key] String KeyName;
    string MyValue;
    boolean UseValidation = false;
};
```

The CIM model is based on object-oriented programming specification and allows the creation of a hierarchy of classes. This means that we can derive child classes from a parent class. The child classes inherit the properties and methods defined in the parent class, while having their own set of properties and methods.

```
#pragma namespace("\\\\.\\Root\\MyCustomNamespace")
class MyCN_MyChildClass : MyCN_MyClass
{
    String ChildProperty;
    String ChildValueArray [];
};
```

Instances

An instance of a class describes a specific object of the managed element. For example, we can create an instance of the `MyCN_MyClass` class that we just defined. There can be multiple instances of this class. As we have seen earlier, we use the `instance of` keyword to create the instance of a class.

```
instance of MyCN_MyClass
{
    KeyName = "PowerShell";
    MyValue = "4.0";
    UseValidation = True;
};
```

Comments

We can add comments to an MOF file, to document certain areas. MOF language allows two styles of comments in an MOF file. // can be used for a single line comment, and /* and */ can be used to define multiline comments.

```
/*
This is the first instance of MyCN_MyClass class
*/
instance of MyCN_MyClass
{
    KeyName = "PowerShell";
    MyValue = "4.0";
    UseValidation = True; //The default value of this property is false.
};
```

Compiling MOF

We have seen the basics of class and instance creation using MOF language elements. Let us now look at a complete example of an MOF file and see how it can be compiled and then accessed, using the PowerShell CIM cmdlets. We will use the same namespace, class, and instance definitions as previously. As I mentioned earlier, we can use mofcomp.exe to compile this MOF file and add it to the WMI repository.

To start with, place the following example in the ISE script editor and run the code. This creates the MOF file and then compiles it. You'll see a warning that the #pragma Autorecover directive is missing. This is fine with our example, as we don't want to reconstruct this test MOF every time the WMI repository is rebuilt. Once the MOF compilation is complete, we can use the CIM cmdlets to verify if the namespace, class, and instance have been added to WMI repository.

```
$mof = @'
#pragma namespace("\\\\.\\Root")

Instance of __Namespace
{
  Name = "MyCustomNamespace";
};

#pragma namespace("\\\\.\\Root\\MyCustomNamespace")
class MyCN_MyClass
{
  [Key] string KeyName;
  String MyValue;
  Boolean UseValidation = false;
};
```

```
instance of MyCN_MyClass
{
    KeyName="PowerShell";
    MyValue="4.0";
    UseValidation=True;
};
'@
$mof | Out-file -Encoding ascii $env:TMP\myMOF.mof

mofcomp.exe $env:TMP\myMOF.mof
```

We can now use the CIM cmdlets to verify this new namespace and class. First, let us see if we can find this namespace. We already know how to get all namespaces under the root namespace. An example of this is shown in Figure 2-42.

```
Get-CimInstance -Namespace root -ClassName __NAMESPACE | Where-Object { $_.Name -eq
"MyCustomNamespace" }
```

```
PS C:\> Get-CimInstance -Namespace root -ClassName __NAMESPACE | Where-Object { $_.Name -eq "MyCustomNamespace" }

Name                                                    PSComputerName
----                                                    --------------
MyCustomNamespace
```

Figure 2-42. *Custom namespace existence in WMI repository*

We can now use the Get-CimClass cmdlet to see if the MyCN_MyClass exists under this new namespace.

```
Get-CimClass -Namespace root\myCustomNamespace -ClassName MyCN_MyClass
```

Because the new class exists, as shown in Figure 2-43, we can now look at the instances of this class.

```
   NameSpace: ROOT/MyCustomNamespace

CimClassName                    CimClassMethods        CimClassProperties
------------                    ---------------        ------------------
MyCN_MyClass                    {}                     {KeyName, MyValue, UseValidation}
```

Figure 2-43. *Existence of CIM class under the new namespace*

We have defined a static instance in the MOF file, so we should be able to see the values of that instance when we use the Get-CimInstance cmdlet. The output in Figure 2-44 demonstrates this.

```
Get-CimInstance -Namespace root\MyCustomNamespace -ClassName MyCN_MyClass
```

```
KeyName                         MyValue                                UseValidation PSComputerName
-------                         -------                                ------------- --------------
PowerShell                      4.0                                    True
```

Figure 2-44. *Instance of the custom class*

So far, we have seen the basics of MOF files and understand how to create custom namespaces, classes, and instances. This is only a foundation, and there is much more to learn, if you want to delve more deeply into this subject. If you would like to obtain more information on this topic, I suggest that you look at the MOF specification published by DMTF.

Summary

The DSC feature is built on CIM standards and uses WinRM for pushing the configuration to remote systems. There is a common misconception that DSC requires the PowerShell remoting feature. This is mostly because enabling the PowerShell remoting feature creates WinRM listeners, and some find it the easiest way to configure WinRM. However, PowerShell remoting is not a requirement. WinRM listeners are only required so that the CIM can be used to push the configuration to remote systems. This chapter provided a basic overview of the Windows Remote Management and Common Information Model for describing management data and how CIM cmdlets can be used to work with the management data provided by various CIM providers in the Windows OS. It is important to understand how the CIM cmdlets are used. This knowledge helps in troubleshooting and debugging DSC deployment issues. The Managed Object Format (MOF) is used by the WMI providers to define classes and instances. The MOF files, when complied, become a part of the WMI repository. Using CIM cmdlets, we can access these newly created classes and instances.

In the later chapters, when we discuss DSC in detail, the knowledge we gained so far about MOF files and language semantics will be useful in understanding the DSC concepts more easily. Remember that this chapter is not a deep dive into CIM, CIM cmdlets, and MOF language. However, the knowledge gained from it should be sufficient to understand and work with DSC concepts. If you are interested in gaining in-depth knowledge of any of the topics covered in this chapter, I strongly recommend that you read the help topics for WQL, CIM cmdlets, and MOF specification available on the DMTF web site.

PART II

Desired State Configuration Essentials

This part of the book introduces the basic concepts related to Desired State Configuration (DSC). Understanding these concepts is essential for building custom DSC resources and a scalable DSC infrastructure.

Chapter 3 provides an overview of continuous delivery and configuration management processes in IT organizations. You will learn why it is necessary to automate these processes and get an overview of DSC and how you can configure your IT environment for using DSC.

Chapter 4 is where we get started with the architecture of DSC and start exploring various phases in configuration management by DSC. You will learn the semantics of a DSC configuration script and two modes of configuration delivery in DSC.

You will receive in-depth information on the built-in DSC resources, in Chapter 5. You will write your first configuration script. There are a variety of built-in resources, and we will see how they are used and some of the gotchas you must be aware of.

Building reusable configuration scripts is essential to ease the configuration authoring process in a large IT organization. Chapter 6 takes you through this and demonstrates, using several examples, how to build nested and reusable configurations. You will also learn how to use configuration data in DSC, to secure DSC credentials.

CHAPTER 3

Introducing Desired State Configuration

The only thing that is constant is change!

—Heraclitus

Heraclitus was a pre-Socratic Greek philosopher. He was famous for his insistence on ever-present change in the universe. The epigraph from Heraclitus resonates not only in human philosophy but in enterprise data centers too. A Gartner publication on the top-seven considerations for configuration management predicted that through 2015, 80% of outages impacting mission-critical services will be caused by people and process issues, and more than 50% of those outages will be caused by change or configuration or release integration and hand-off issues. In this era of cloud computing, the two most prevalent issues in IT service management are configuration management and continuous delivery. This chapter provides a brief overview of these challenges faced by every IT organization and describes the processes involved in handling them. The Desired State Configuration (DSC) feature helps address a large part of these challenges. Toward the end of the chapter, you will see what DSC is and how you can configure the IT environment to start using it.

The Configuration Management Challenge

Most IT organizations, small or big, have processes to manage configuration changes in a data center environment. A typical configuration change management process has different phases. This includes change submission, review, approval, deployment, and monitoring and reporting. All these combined form the configuration management cycle. Parts of this process are manual, and others can be automated or scripted. Overall, configuration change management is a process that involves both people and systems. Therefore, collaboration between teams and people is an important aspect.

A typical configuration management life cycle is shown in Figure 3-1. This is a high-level representation of different phases involved in configuration management and does not represent a granular configuration process.

Figure 3-1. *A typical configuration management cycle*

Each configuration change in the data center may include more than one configuration item and involve disparate systems. For example, deploying a new web application might require changes to the web servers and database servers. Depending on how the application is architected, there might be a middleware tier, too, that gets changed. The initial deployments are always easy and usually adhere to the standards defined in IT service management. However, the subsequent changes are not. Some of these changes may involve only updates at one of the tiers of the application architecture. This is where the stringent process or phases of the configuration life cycle play a critical part in IT service management. Each of the configuration items going through this life cycle finally gets stored in a configuration store usually referred to as a configuration management database (CMDB). In an ideal world, the CMDB must be up-to-date, with all changes performed on an entity within the data center. We should be able to use the information stored in the CMDB to trace faults in the data center management to their exact cause and location and, thus, help data center administrators avoid configuration drift. However, we are not always in an ideal world, especially when talking about enterprise data centers.

Configuration drift refers to the unmanaged changes made to an entity in the scope of IT service management. Going back to the example of a web application, the changes performed at any tier of the architecture must be properly documented and implemented. Any failure to do so while performing changes to the application or the infrastructure hosting the applications will result in a configuration drift. Simply put, this drift represents a deviation from the desired configuration state, and such a drift can have bad consequences for service management and make fault isolation difficult. It is essential for IT managers to address these challenges in configuration management and eliminate configuration drift. To this extent, we can extend the monitoring and reporting phase shown in Figure 3-1 to include the detection and remediation of configuration drift. This is shown in Figure 3-2.

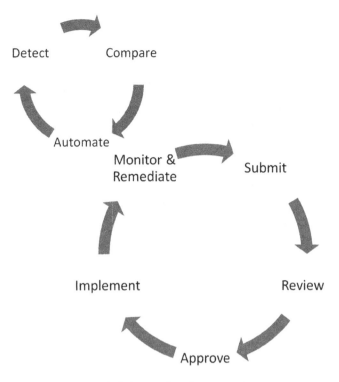

Figure 3-2. *Extended phases of configuration management*

The extended phases in the configuration management life cycle, shown in Figure 3-2, are used to enforce the configuration changes. Notice that I have changed the high-level configuration phase from *Monitor & Report* to *Monitor & Remediate*. This means we not only have the ability to report but also to take action based on how the remediation policies are created.

These extended phases provide a mechanism to *detect* the state of configuration items. This includes the ability to list what configuration items are being monitored and the means to retrieve the state of each configuration item. The *Compare* phase should provide the ability to the state of the configuration items retrieved in the *Detect* phase to a predefined baseline or a baseline that has been updated through a managed configuration change process. This phase also builds a report of the deviations, if there are any. *Detect* and *Compare* are the most important steps in the *Monitor & Remediate* phase of configuration management. These two phases provide insights into what has changed or not changed in the system being monitored. Without these insights, there is no meaning in monitoring and remediating a configuration drift. Through the final phase, *Automate*, we should be able to automate the actions, based on how we configure the remediation policies. You may choose to verify the configuration drift manually and then take action to remediate. This is perfectly fine, and that is what makes automation optional: it is not always mandatory to fix the configuration differences automatically.

The first three phases of the configuration management life cycle are related to IT service processes. There are various tools that help users to submit change requests and appropriate people to approve or reject the same. The next phases in the life cycle can be automated, using scripts and existing frameworks.

The Continuous Delivery Challenge

In order to enhance the time-to-market (TTM) and overall competitiveness of the products, companies have been following a *release small and release often* methodology. Using this methodology, products are built with one or more features at a time and in an incremental fashion. To enable this, the products have to be built, tested, and deployed often. The challenge here is the process to enable continuous delivery. This has to be well-thought and should be automated to eliminate any human errors in carrying it out. The complexity of such a process increases with the size of the release. The continuous delivery or continuous integration process must be capable of managing the complexities in product releases.

The workflow in Figure 3-3 shows only a high-level overview of the continuous delivery process. The different phases in this process involve different teams and infrastructure built for the purpose of software delivery. The *Build* phase involves different tools, such as development environments and version control systems. The *Test* phase is where the code that is built in an incremental manner gets tested through various small phases, such as a capacity or performance test, system test, user acceptance test, and so on. The final phase, *Release*, is when the tested and proven code is deployed into the production environment and maintained further.

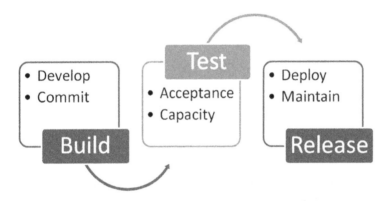

Figure 3-3. *High-level process in continuous delivery*

There are various challenges in this process. Some of them are addressed by the existing software development and build frameworks. The tests processes include both automated and manual test methods. For accurate test results, and to ensure that the product is functioning as designed, the releases must be tested on configuration exactly the same as for production. This leads to the requirements of building development and test environments that are similar to production. This, in turn, requires that the production build process and configuration management aspects are well documented and automated for ease of replication.

The final phase, *Release*, requires a solid process to deploy and then manage all configuration changes to the production environment. The changes implemented after the deployment of a new release must also be documented for creating the updated development and test environments.

Overall, configuration management plays a central role in continuous delivery and integration. We have already looked at what is involved in configuration management and how different tasks in the configuration management life cycle should be addressed. These processes, when automated, enable efficient continuous integration and/or configuration change management and help eliminate human errors. This is where the Desired State Configuration feature plays a role.

Understanding Desired State Configuration

Desired State Configuration (DSC) is the configuration management feature built into the Windows OS. DSC is a relatively new entrant in the configuration management space. This is significant, because it is a feature native to the OS, and the built-in tools can be used to perform configuration changes. We will look into the architecture of DSC in later chapters. To give a quick overview, DSC is based on standards-based management offered by the Windows OS. This includes the CIM and WS-Management remote management. DSC should be seen as a configuration management platform rather than a complete configuration management solution. Unlike the other configuration management tools or solutions, DSC does not provide an end-to-end tool set to manage and monitor configuration. Instead, DSC offers an application programming interface (API) and a platform that even other tools and frameworks can leverage. We will see more about this in Chapter 11. In the previous chapters, we built the foundational knowledge—CIM and WSMan concepts—required for understanding DSC.

DSC contains a set of CIM classes, PowerShell language extensions, cmdlets, and resources. Microsoft introduced declarative syntax for writing DSC configuration documents. In the next chapter, we will dive deep into the DSC architecture and components. But, before that, let us understand what declarative syntax is.

Imperative vs. Declarative Syntax

Windows PowerShell is imperative in nature. What that means is that when we write a script in PowerShell, we tell PowerShell how to perform a specific task, using either the built-in cmdlets or the functions or modules we write. Let us look at an example that describes this in detail.

```
Import-Module ServerManager

#Check and install ASP.NET 4.5 feature
If (-not (Get-WindowsFeature "Web-Asp-Net45").Installed) {
    try {
        Add-WindowsFeature Web-Asp-Net45 -ErrorAction Stop
    }
    catch {
        Write-Error $_
    }
}

#Check and install Web Server Feature
If (-not (Get-WindowsFeature "Web-Server").Installed) {
    try {
        Add-WindowsFeature Web-Server -ErrorAction Stop
    }
    catch {
        Write-Error $_
    }
}
#Create a new website
Import-Module WebAdministration
New-WebSite -Name MyWebSite -Port 80 -HostHeader MyWebSite -PhysicalPath "$env:systemdrive\inetpub\
WWWROOT\MyWebSite"

#Start the website
Start-WebSite -Name MyWebSite
```

The preceding example demonstrates how we can create and start a new web site. Before creating a web site, there are prerequisites, such as verifying if the web server feature is installed or not. If the role is not installed, the script installs that. Also, we have to take care of error handling explicitly. Without that, the script might result in failures. For example, toward the end of the preceding example, we are not checking if the web site is created successfully or not. Instead, we are assuming that it is created and using the `Start-WebSite` cmdlet to start the site. So, if the web site does not exist, we will see errors at this stage of the execution. So, essentially, the emphasis is on how to perform a given task and how to handle errors when they occur. This is the imperative style of programming.

In the declarative style of programming, we tell PowerShell what needs to be done and not how it needs to be done. In this programming style, we are not concerned about how things are done. We depend on the underlying automation or programming framework to know how to perform a given set of tasks. Of course, there has to be explicit support within the underlying framework to perform these tasks. Why not see an example of this style of programming?

```
Configuration WebSiteConfig
{
    Node MyWebServer
    {
        WindowsFeature IIS
        {
            Ensure = "Present"
            Name = "Web-Server"
        }

        WindowsFeature ASP
        {
            Ensure = "Present"
            Name = "Web-Asp-Net45"
        }

        Website MyWebSite
        {
            Ensure = "Present"
            Name = "MyWebSite"
            PhysicalPath = "C:\Inetpub\MyWebSite"
            State = "Started"
            Protocol = @("http")
            BindingInfo = @("*:80:")
        }
    }
}
```

The declarative programming style is more readable and easy to understand. To summarize, the *imperative syntax* defines *how a task should be performed* while *declarative syntax* describes *what needs to be done*. This is what DSC resources enable. A resource is a basic building block in managing system configuration using the Desired State Configuration feature. DSC provides a set of built-in resources to manage configuration of various components in the OS. Using the language extensions that DSC provides, we can even write our own resources. We will explore more DSC resources in later chapters.

The example showing the declarative syntax in PowerShell is indeed a DSC configuration document. Using the DSC configuration documents, we can specify what configuration items have to be managed and how. The configuration documents can be nested and use advanced configuration data by means of custom hash tables. We will look at these concepts in later chapters.

DSC provides methods to monitor the configuration items. Because DSC provides the PowerShell language extensions and cmdlets, it is easy to write reporting methods to identify any configuration drifts. We will see in later chapters how DSC configuration can be monitored and reported.

To summarize what we discussed so far, using PowerShell and DSC, we can achieve most of what needs to be done to streamline configuration or change management in a data center. Because DSC integrates with PowerShell and other technologies, such as CIM and WinRM, it is convenient to write custom DSC resource modules and extend what DSC can achieve out of the box.

Enabling Desired State Configuration

We have discussed in Chapter 1 that Windows Management Framework (WMF) 4.0 includes the Desired State Configuration (DSC) feature. Windows Server 2012 R2 and Windows 8.1 operating systems come with WMF 4.0 preinstalled; therefore, there is no WMF 4.0 download for these operating systems. The WMF 4.0 package is available for down-level operating systems, such as Windows Server 2012, Windows Server 2008 R2 SP1, and Windows 7 SP1. The procedure and the requirements for installing the WMF 4.0 package have already been described in Chapter 1. There is no WMF 4.0 package for the Windows 8 operating system. To get the DSC feature on Windows 8, the OS has to be upgraded to Windows 8.1.

On systems running Windows Server 2012 R2 and Windows 8.1 operating systems, make sure you install the update KB2883200. As described in the Microsoft support article for KB2883200, it also updates KB2894029 and KB2894179. This update package can either be installed using the Windows Update process or can be downloaded from the locations shown in Table 3-1.

Table 3-1. *KB2883200 Download Locations*

Operating System	Download Location
Windows 8.1 x64-based systems	www.microsoft.com/en-us/download/details.aspx?id=40749
Windows 8.1 x86-based systems	www.microsoft.com/en-us/download/details.aspx?id=40755
Windows Server 2012 R2	www.microsoft.com/en-us/download/details.aspx?id=40774

You can the `Get-HotFix` cmdlet to verify whether a system has this update installed. The result of this on my demo system is shown in Figure 3-4.

```
PS C:\> Get-HotFix -Id KB2883200

Source      Description     HotFixID      InstalledBy         InstalledOn
------      -----------     --------      -----------         -----------
WSR2-1      Update          KB2883200     WSR2-1\Ravikanth    9/30/2013 12:00:00 AM
```

Figure 3-4. *Using the* `Get-HotFix` *cmdlet to verify if KB2883200 is installed*

There are a couple of changes that this update package introduces in the DSC configuration. We will look at them in a later chapter, in which we discuss DSC resources and creating custom DSC resources.

■ **Note**   The DSC feature can be obtained by installing WMF 5.0 too. At the time of writing, WMF 5.0 is still in preview. Therefore, throughout this book, we will see references to changes or updates to DSC in WMF 5.0. The appendix at the end of this book has a section detailing changes in and fixes to DSC in WMF 5.0.

Configuring Your Environment for Desired State Configuration

Desired State Configuration (DSC) is built on standards-based management. It uses the Common Information Model (CIM), to describe the configuration that needs to be applied, and WinRM, as a communication vehicle. We looked at these two technologies in Chapter 2, so, I'll not go over them in detail here, but I will discuss some requirements needed for DSC to work in an Active Directory domain environment.

First and foremost, you will have to enable the WinRM service and create WinRM listeners on the systems that you want to manage using DSC. As we saw in Chapter 2, this can be done using the Set-WSManQuickConfig cmdlet. This cmdlet requires administrative privileges; therefore, ensure that you elevate the PowerShell console or ISE host to run as administrator, before using this cmdlet. In a larger domain environment, you can also enable the WinRM service and create WinRM listeners, using Group Policy.

Create WinRM Listeners Using Group Policy

We can configure Group Policy objects to enable the WinRM service and create WinRM listeners on domain-joined computers. For this, we will use the Group Policy Management MMC. This management console is available on Domain Controller systems or on systems in which the Group Policy Management feature is installed. You can use Server Manager PowerShell cmdlets to install this feature.

```
Add-WindowsFeature -Name GPMC -Verbose
```

Once the feature is installed, you can locate Group Policy Management in the Tools menu of Server Manager (or just type gpmc.msc in your Run dialog). In the Group Policy MMC, right-click the domain name and select the Create a GPO in this domain, and Link it here. . . menu option. In the New GPO dialog, enter "WinRM Listeners" in the text box next to New and click OK. This is shown in Figure 3-5.

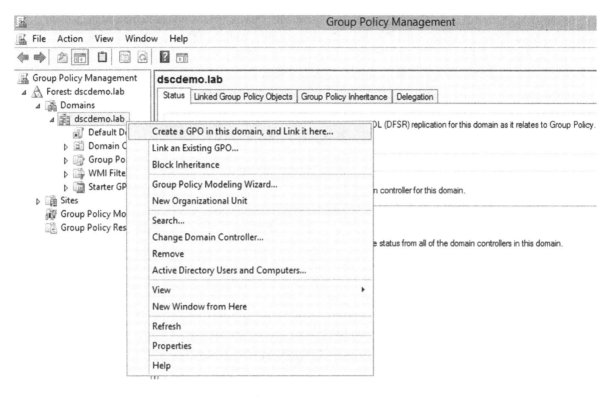

Figure 3-5. *Creating a new GPO in the Group Policy Management MMC*

Once you create the new GPO, right-click the GPO and select the Edit menu option. As shown in Figure 3-6, the Group Policy Management Editor opens.

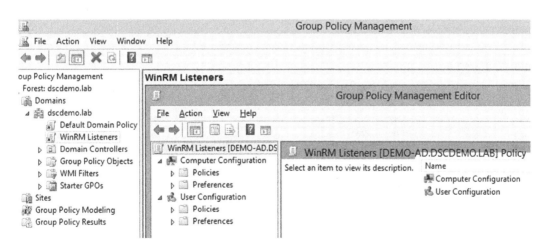

Figure 3-6. *Group Policy Management Editor*

As shown in Figure 3-7, in the Group Policy Management Editor, navigate to Windows Remote Management (WinRM) under Computer Configuration ➤ Policies ➤ Administrative Templates ➤ Windows Components.

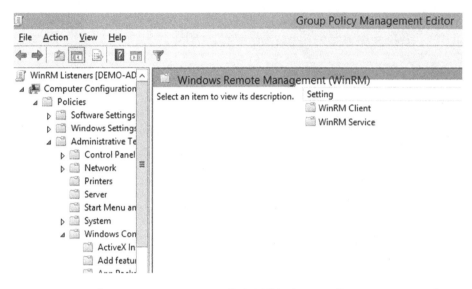

Figure 3-7. *Windows Remote Management (WinRM) in Group Policy Management Editor*

Under WinRM Service, double-click Allow remote server management through WinRM and select Enabled in the resulting configuration window. Enter "*" in the IPv4 filter option, to allow WinRM-based management from any system in the network, and click Apply to save the changes. The selected options are shown in Figure 3-8.

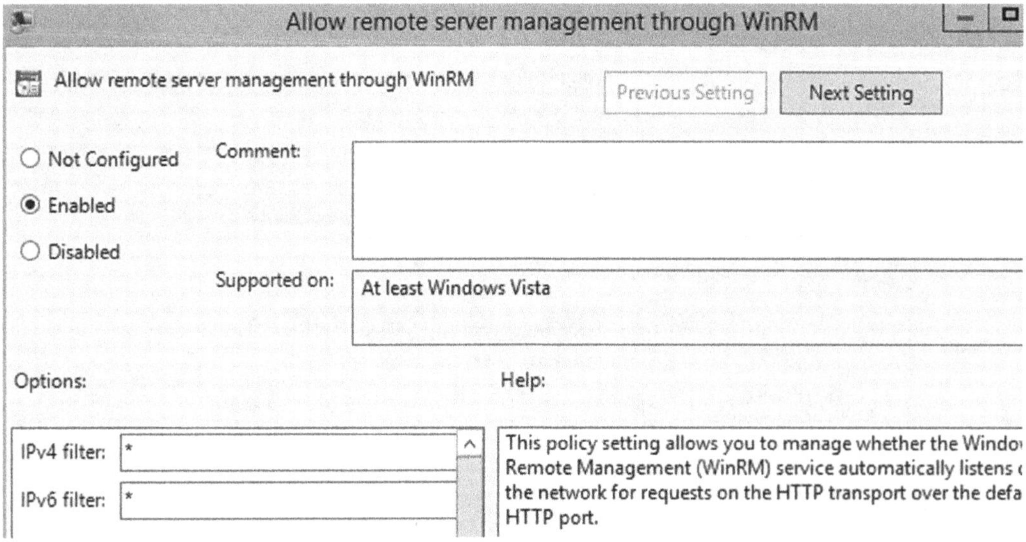

Figure 3-8. *Enabling remote management via WinRM*

We now have to ensure that the WinRM service starts by default on the remote computers. As shown in Figure 3-9, this can be done by setting Windows Remote Management (WS-Management) service to *"Automatic"* state by navigating to Computer Configuration ➤ Windows Settings ➤ Security Settings ➤ System Services in Group Policy Management Editor.

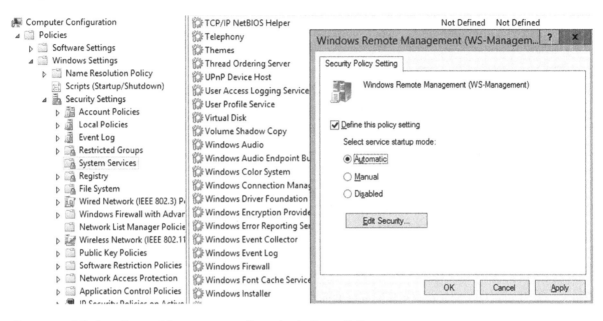

Figure 3-9. *Windows Remote Management configuration in Group Policy*

Finally, to complete the WinRM listener configuration through Group Policy, we have to configure the firewall inbound rules. Once again, this can be done using the Group Policy Editor. To do this, we have to create a new rule under Computer Configuration ➤ Windows Settings ➤ Windows Firewall with Advanced Security ➤ Windows Firewall with Advanced Security ➤ Inbound Rules. This is shown in Figure 3-10.

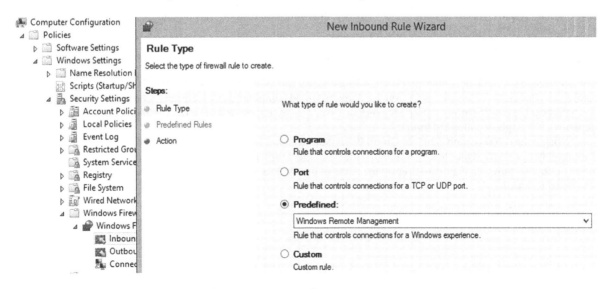

Figure 3-10. *Inbound rules in Group Policy Management Editor*

As shown in Figure 3-10, select Windows Remote Management under the Predefined option of New Inbound Rule Wizard. Click Next on the subsequent screens, by leaving the default values, and click Finish to complete creation of the new rule. Once the new GPO is created, you can see the report, shown in Figure 3-11, by selecting the Settings tab of the new GPO.

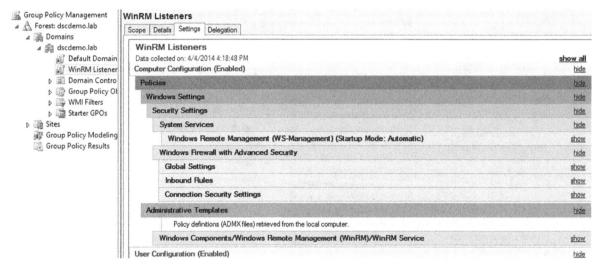

Figure 3-11. *WinRM Listener settings in GPO Management*

This completes the Group Policy configuration of WinRM listeners. You can either enforce this GPO or add a specific set of computers to which this GPO should be applied.

The second requirement for DSC is to set the PowerShell execution policy to allow script execution. We have seen this, as well, in Chapter 2. As with the WinRM listeners configuration, we can use Group Policy to change the execution policy settings in an Active Directory environment. Remember that the execution policy on systems running Windows Server 2012 R2 is Remote Signed. Therefore, if you have an all Windows Server 2012 R2 environment, you need not worry about changing it, unless you want to allow only digitally signed script execution.

Configure Execution Policy Using Group Policy

Just as we created a GPO for configuring WinRM listeners, we will follow a similar set of steps to create the GPO for configuring PowerShell execution policy on the domain-joined computers. The recommended execution policy setting is RemoteSigned. Through this policy setting, we enable execution of local scripts, while requiring digital signatures for scripts downloaded from the Internet.

To begin the GPO creation, start the Group Policy Management MMC from the Tools menu of Server Manager. In the Group Policy MMC, right-click the domain name and select the Create a GPO in this domain, and Link it here. . . menu option. As shown in Figure 3-12, enter the name of the GPO as "ExecutionPolicy," or whatever text of your choice, and click OK.

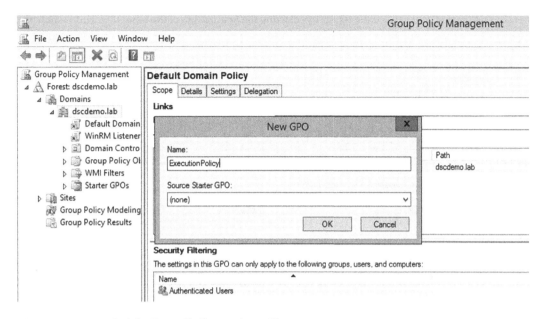

Figure 3-12. *New GPO for PowerShell execution policy*

Once the new GPO is created, right-click the GPO and select Edit. In the resulting Group Policy Management Editor, navigate to Computer Configuration ➤ Policies ➤ Administrative Templates ➤ Windows Components ➤ Windows PowerShell. Under the Windows PowerShell container, double-click Turn on Script Execution.

In the resulting dialog, shown in Figure 3-13, select the option labeled Enabled. In the Options area, select Allow local script and remote signed scripts from the drop-down menu. Click Apply to close the configuration window and exit to Group Policy Management Editor.

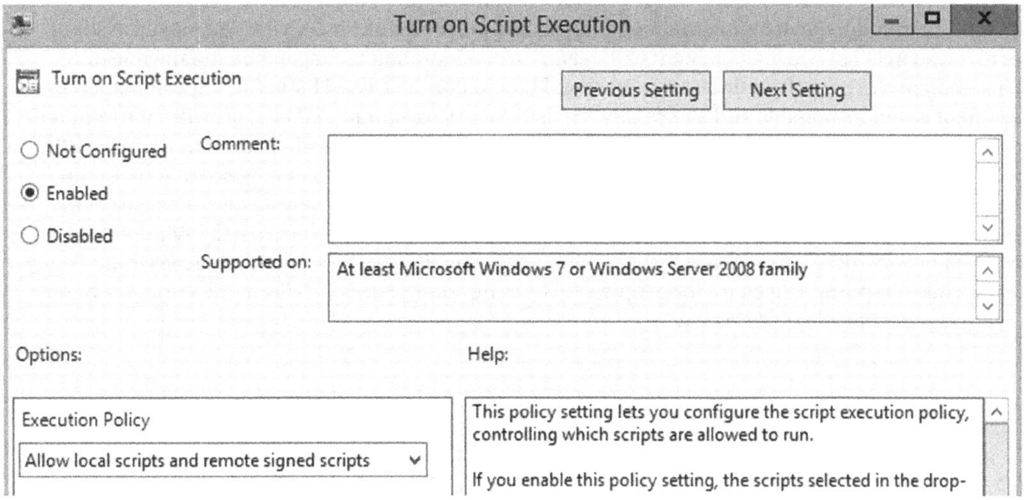

Figure 3-13. *Enabling RemoteSigned execution policy*

Once the new GPO is created, you can see the report by selecting the Settings tab of the new GPO. This is shown in Figure 3-14.

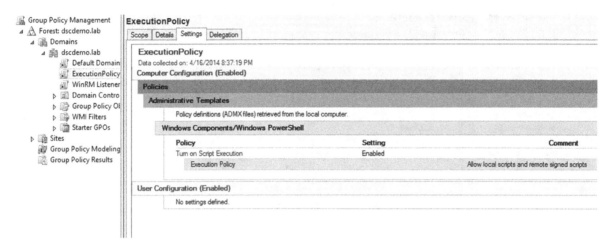

Figure 3-14. *Verifying settings of the GPO created for PowerShell execution policy*

This concludes this section on enabling or configuring the environment for implementing or using DSC in Windows PowerShell. We have looked at the environmental configuration for Active Directory domain-joined computers. There might be a need, however, to do the configuration for a hybrid environment where there is a combination of AD domain-joined and workgroup computers, or just a bunch of computers in a workgroup environment. I will cover, in a later chapter, the requirements for making DSC work in such an environment.

Summary

This chapter provided an introduction to configuration management and continuous delivery. We looked at some of the challenges involved in IT service management with regard to configuration management and the role of configuration management as a part of continuous delivery and integration. The need for enforcing automation in IT service management is unquestionable and a necessity. Desired State Configuration (DSC) provides the required feature set to enable the automation required for configuration change management and continuous delivery. DSC is designed to be a configuration management platform, and any existing configuration management tools in the enterprise can use the interfaces provided by DSC. The prerequisites for enabling this new feature are a part of the Windows operating system and are configurable using well-known administration interfaces in the Windows OS. For example, we have seen how WinRM listeners and PowerShell execution policy can be configured using Group Policy objects in Windows. This is important, because for people with existing administration skills in the Windows-based data center, the learning curve to adapt DSC is low.

CHAPTER 4

Getting Started with DSC

When I begin to learn a new technology, I usually start with the architecture. Understanding the architecture and the components within it helps to make better use of the technology. Also, when I am faced with issues, it helps me to go deeper into the problems at hand and determine their cause. Desired State Configuration (DSC) is no exception. DSC depends on such technologies as WinRM and CIM and has different components that make up the stack. Understanding the overall DSC component architecture helps users to gain deeper knowledge of DSC.

This chapter investigates DSC architecture and its components. Configuration management with DSC includes two different phases: configuration authoring and staging and configuration enacting. We will examine the DSC components that constitute each of these phases. By the end of this chapter, apart from an understanding of these DSC phases and components, you will be able to describe what the DSC Local Configuration Manager (LCM) is and how it works, explore and use DSC PowerShell cmdlets, and, finally, write your first DSC configuration script and apply the configuration on a target node.

DSC Configuration Management Architecture

The Desired State Configuration (DSC) configuration management architecture is fairly straightforward. Rather than using a typical architectural diagram, I prefer to represent the DSC and its components spread across various phases of configuration management. This representation not only helps us understand DSC architecture and its components but also provides a clear picture on what role these components play in the configuration life cycle.

In the overall architecture, shown in Figure 4-1, there are two distinct phases. Each of these phases involves DSC components having a specific purpose. As shown in Figure 4-1, these two phases include

1. Configuration authoring and staging
2. Configuration enacting

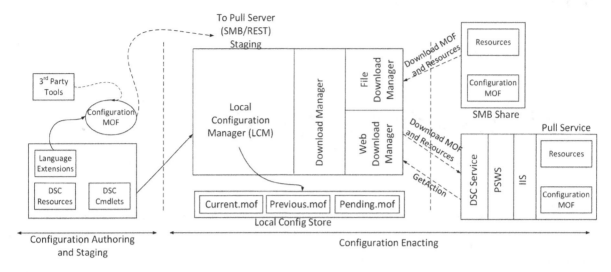

Figure 4-1. *High-level overview of DSC architecture and components*

The **configuration authoring and staging** phase is where we write configuration scripts that define what and how the resources on target systems must be configured and how this configuration gets staged for enacting. Although the authoring and staging refer to two different aspects of configuration management, it is prudent to discuss these together, as the configuration authoring phase leads to staging as a natural next step. We discussed the declarative style of writing configuration scripts and reviewed a related example in Chapter 3. While we understand the declarative scripts, we have not delved deep into the syntax and different parts of the configuration script. We will do so in this chapter. We will also look at different configuration staging modes available when using DSC.

The **configuration enacting** phase is when the configuration gets applied on a target system. There are two different modes, Push and Pull, through which we can deliver the configuration for enacting. While *configuration staging* refers to a place where the configuration Managed Object Format (MOF) gets stored, *enacting* refers to receiving this configuration MOF on a target system and performing the required configuration changes. In this chapter, we will look briefly at the different configuration delivery modes and learn how each of these methods can be used to enact configuration.

Each of these phases plays a specific role in the overall DSC architecture. In the sections that follow, we will take a detailed look at the components involved at each of these phases. As we move forward in our comprehension, the content of this chapter will play a major role in building the foundation on which to understand DSC.

Configuration Authoring and Staging

The first phase in the DSC configuration management architecture, called the *configuration authoring and staging phase*, provides the necessary components to author configuration scripts and stage them for configuration enacting. Let us begin our discussion with configuration authoring. Note that it is possible to generate a configuration MOF without using Windows PowerShell or the infrastructure provided by PowerShell.

■ **Note**   As we discussed in Chapter 3, DSC provides a platform for configuration management, and WMF 4.0 includes PowerShell language extensions to author and manage configurations, using PowerShell. You can certainly use any other programming or scripting language to work with DSC; however, any such discussion is outside the scope of this book.

Authoring

The configuration authoring includes Windows PowerShell declarative scripting. We looked at the declarative style of writing configuration scripts in Chapter 3. The language extensions that enable the declarative style of configuration authoring are a part of the DSC PowerShell module in WMF 4.0 and later. In this section, we will look at these language extensions and learn the role they play in configuration script authoring.

To understand the language extensions, let us first look at the configuration script that we already saw in Chapter 3. We will use this example to walk through different DSC keywords and components in the configuration authoring phase.

```
Configuration WebSiteConfig
{
    Node WSR2-1
    {
        WindowsFeature WebServer1
        {
            Name = "Web-Server"
        }

        WindowsFeature ASP
        {
            Name = "Web-Asp-Net45"
        }

        Website MyWebSite
        {
            Ensure = "Present"
            Name = "MyWebSite"
            PhysicalPath = "C:\Inetpub\MyWebSite"
            State = "Started"
            Protocol = @("http")
            BindingInfo = @("*:80:")
        }
    }
}
```

As I walk you through different language extensions enabled by DSC and the components involved in configuration authoring, we will reconstruct the preceding example, so that you can understand exactly how a configuration script is written and the details of each component within the configuration script.

DSC PowerShell Module

The first component that we must discuss when looking at writing configuration scripts is the DSC PowerShell module. The language extensions that are used in a configuration script, shown in the preceding example, are implemented within the DSC PowerShell module. This module is a script module, and it is stored as a .psm1 file at $PSHOME\Modules\PSDesiredStateConfiguration. We can use the Get-Command cmdlet to explore this module.

■ **Note**   You can open this module file, PSDesiredStateConfiguration.psm1, in your favorite PowerShell script editor and review how it implements the DSC language extensions. In fact, I recommend reading this module, to understand how some of the DSC-related keywords are created. However, do not make any modifications to this module file or any files within the folder path mentioned above.

As shown in Figure 4-2, the Configuration keyword appears as the function exported from the DSC PowerShell module.

```
PS C:\> Get-Command -Module PSDesiredStateConfiguration

CommandType     Name                                        ModuleName
-----------     ----                                        ----------
Function        Configuration                               PSDesiredStateConfiguration
Function        Get-DscConfiguration                        PSDesiredStateConfiguration
Function        Get-DscLocalConfigurationManager            PSDesiredStateConfiguration
Function        Get-DscResource                             PSDesiredStateConfiguration
Function        New-DSCCheckSum                             PSDesiredStateConfiguration
Function        Restore-DscConfiguration                    PSDesiredStateConfiguration
Function        Test-DscConfiguration                       PSDesiredStateConfiguration
Cmdlet          Set-DscLocalConfigurationManager            PSDesiredStateConfiguration
Cmdlet          Start-DscConfiguration                      PSDesiredStateConfiguration
```

Figure 4-2. *DSC PowerShell module commands*

If you read through the PowerShell module file for DSC, you will find the function definitions for only some of the exported commands or keywords, such as Configuration, New-DSCCheckSum, and Get-DscResource. This is because the PSDesiredStateConfiguration module loads a binary module as the root module. This can be seen from the module properties.

```
Import-Module -Name PSDesiredStateConfiguration
Get-Module -Name PSDesiredStateConfiguration
Get-Module -Name PSDesiredStateConfiguration | Select RootModule
```

The root module information for the PSDesiredStateConfiguration PowerShell module is shown in Figure 4-3. The Microsoft.Windows.DSC.CoreConfProviders.dll is located at C:\Windows\Microsoft.Net\assembly\GAC_MSIL\ Microsoft.Windows.DSC.CoreConfProviders. This binary module implements the Start-DscConfiguration and Set-DscLocalConfigurationManager cmdlets. However, this binary module does not export any of these cmdlets. Therefore, the PSDesiredStateConfiguration script module is used to export these cmdlets.

```
ModuleType Version    Name                              ExportedCommands
---------- -------    ----                              ----------------
Binary     1.0        PSDesiredStateConfiguration       {Set-DscLocalConfigurationManager, Start

RootModule : Microsoft.Windows.DSC.CoreConfProviders.dll
```

Figure 4-3. *Root module for the PSDesiredStateConfiguration module*

There are other cmdlets in this module, such as the Get-DscConfiguration, Get-DscLocalConfigurationManager, Restore-DscConfiguration, and Test-DscConfiguration. They are implemented as CDXML cmdlets to invoke the respective CIM methods of the MSFT_DSCLocalConfigurationManager CIM class implemented in the Desired State Configuration WMI Provider. This WMI provider implements more than just these CIM methods; it implements the root\Microsoft\Windows\DesiredStateConfiguration namespace. In the configuration authoring phase, there is no explicit need to call the WMI provider or any of its CIM class methods. Therefore, we will skip a detailed explanation for the WMI provider until the configuration enact phase. You will also encounter a detailed explanation of other DSC PowerShell cmdlets, in this chapter and throughout this book.

Configuration Keyword

The first keyword that you notice in the preceding example is Configuration. We can consider the Configuration keyword as the core component of DSC, as this keyword defines the desired configuration of a target system. What follows the Configuration keyword is a name or an identifier assigned to the configuration. The configuration of a target system is then defined using a PowerShell script block, identified using the code block wrapped in braces ({}). So, the general syntax for starting a configuration script using this keyword will be the following:

```
Configuration IdentifierString {

}
```

You can copy and paste the preceding code into PowerShell ISE and press F5 to run it. This loads the configuration command into the memory of the PowerShell ISE session.

■ **Note** The empty configuration script block is not useful or valid. This is used only to demonstrate what is discussed here.

Once you have done that, you can use the Get-Command cmdlet to explore the commands that are of Configuration type. In Chapter 1, when we looked at command types, we did not talk about the Configuration command type. This command type is added to WMF 4.0 to enable DSC configurations. In PowerShell 4.0 or above, whenever we create a configuration script and load it into memory, you will notice that the identifier used with the Configuration keyword appears as a command to the Get-Command cmdlet.

An example of this behavior is shown in Figure 4-4.

```
PS C:\> Get-Command  -CommandType Configuration

CommandType     Name                                                    ModuleName
-----------     ----                                                    ----------
Configuration   WebSiteConfig
```

Figure 4-4. Configuration command loaded, using a DSC configuration script

One thing to make a note of here is that the configuration we just created gets a few parameters automatically added to it. This is what the Configuration keyword adds. Once again, we can explore this using the Get-Command cmdlet. This is shown in Figure 4-5.

```
PS C:\> Get-Command -CommandType Configuration | Select -ExpandProperty Parameters

Key                                                 Value
---                                                 -----
InstanceName                                        System.Management.Automation.ParameterMetadata
OutputPath                                          System.Management.Automation.ParameterMetadata
ConfigurationData                                   System.Management.Automation.ParameterMetadata
```

Figure 4-5. *Parameters added to the configuration*

As a part of the discussion in this chapter, we will look at the OutputPath parameter and defer any discussion on the InstanceName and ConfigurationData parameters to a later chapter. These latter two keywords require a detailed understanding of resources and of writing advanced configuration scripts.

Although I stated that the Configuration keyword is the core aspect of DSC configuration management, this keyword alone does not define the configuration to be managed. To define the configuration that has to be managed, and the target system on which the configuration must be managed, we can use other DSC keywords and components.

Node Keyword

We use the Node keyword inside a Configuration script block to specify the target system(s) on which we want to apply configuration. As with the Configuration keyword, we have to specify an identifier along with the Node keyword, followed by a PowerShell script block. The general syntax for this keyword inside a Configuration keyword script block will be as follows:

```
Configuration IdentifierString {
    Node TargetSystemName {
    }
}
```

As shown in the preceding example, the Node script block is enclosed within a Configuration script block. The identifier is the target system hostname in which the configuration must be applied. Now that we have specified the Node script block, we can take a look at how we can specify the configuration that has to be managed on the target system specified by the Node identifier.

DSC Resources

In Desired State Configuration (DSC), the configuration that needs to be managed should be specified as resource script blocks. In DSC, a resource identifies an entity that can be managed by using a configuration script. These managed entities or resources can be anything from a simple file or folder to an operating system role or feature. Each resource that can be managed must have an associated DSC resource module. The DSC resource module is what takes care of the *how* part of the configuration management. Remember our discussion in Chapter 3? We talked about the differences between the imperative and declarative script styles. The DSC resource module is similar to a PowerShell module with special requirements. The DSC resource modules are implemented or written in imperative style, which means the resource module implements all the necessary details to manage the configuration settings of an entity. However, the DSC configuration makes it possible to abstract those imperative details from the end user, using a declarative configuration script.

To add a resource to the configuration script, there is no resource keyword, but each resource module that is available on the system, where the configuration script is being authored, is available within the Node script block. So, the keyword that we have to use here will be the name of the resource. But how do we know what resources are available, and what are the resource names? This is where the DSC PowerShell module helps. The module that implements the Configuration and Node keywords and enables the declarative scripting style of the configuration scripts is the PSDesiredStateConfiguration module.

Before we dive into a discussion on resources, let us take a small detour to explore the DSC PowerShell module. This will help us build a better understanding of the DSC resources and how we can explore DSC resources.

Now that we understand the cmdlets available within the DSC PowerShell module, let us go back to the discussion on the DSC resources. We can look at all DSC resources available on a system, using the Get-DscResource cmdlet (see Figure 4-6). In the WMF 4.0 release, this cmdlet is resource-intensive and takes longer, depending on the number of DSC resources that it has to enumerate. At the time of this writing, with the advent of WMF 5.0, the improvement in the performance of this cmdlet is manifold, and the output is retrieved much faster.

```
PS C:\> Get-DscResource

ImplementedAs   Name              Module                         Properties
-------------   ----              ------                         ----------
Binary          File                                             {DestinationPath, Attributes, Checksum, Content...
PowerShell      Archive           PSDesiredStateConfiguration    {Destination, Path, Checksum, DependsOn...}
PowerShell      Environment       PSDesiredStateConfiguration    {Name, DependsOn, Ensure, Path...}
PowerShell      Group             PSDesiredStateConfiguration    {GroupName, Credential, DependsOn, Description...}
Binary          Log               PSDesiredStateConfiguration    {Message, DependsOn}
PowerShell      Package           PSDesiredStateConfiguration    {Name, Path, ProductId, Arguments...}
PowerShell      Registry          PSDesiredStateConfiguration    {Key, ValueName, DependsOn, Ensure...}
PowerShell      Script            PSDesiredStateConfiguration    {GetScript, SetScript, TestScript, Credential...}
PowerShell      Service           PSDesiredStateConfiguration    {Name, BuiltInAccount, Credential, DependsOn...}
PowerShell      User              PSDesiredStateConfiguration    {UserName, DependsOn, Description, Disabled...}
PowerShell      WindowsFeature    PSDesiredStateConfiguration    {Name, Credential, DependsOn, Ensure...}
PowerShell      WindowsProcess    PSDesiredStateConfiguration    {Arguments, Path, Credential, DependsOn...}
```

Figure 4-6. *DSC resources list using the* Get-DscResource *cmdlet*

Using the -Verbose parameter of this cmdlet tells us exactly how this cmdlet works. It starts by enumerating all the PowerShell modules available at $env:PSModulePath, using the Get-Module cmdlet, and then checks for the DSC resource modules within that list. This is done by appending the DSCResources folder name to the module path for each module found. If the DSCResources folder is found, the Get-DscResource function iterates through the folder contents to find all DSC resources. What you see in Figure 4-6 is just the list of built-in resources.

DSC provides a method to create your own DSC resources and extend what you can configure using DSC. Such resources are written as PowerShell modules and are referred to as custom DSC resources. The method used to discover custom DSC resources isn't different. The same method I described earlier works with custom resources too. For example, the configuration script shown at the beginning of this chapter includes a Website resource that is a custom resource. We will talk more about creating custom DSC resources in Chapter 9.

DOWNLOAD AND VERIFY CUSTOM RESOURCES

As an exercise, download the DSC resource kit from http://gallery.technet.microsoft.com/scriptcenter/DSC-Resource-Kit-All-c449312d and extract the resource modules to $env:ProgramFiles\WindowsPowerShell\Modules. Now, try executing the Get-DscResource. You should be able to see a complete list of DSC resources, including custom resources.

Our First Configuration Script

The Name property of the resource in the output shown in Figure 4-6 becomes the dynamic keyword. This is valid to any DSC resource. The PSDesiredStateConfiguration module takes care of loading all the dynamic keywords. In fact, in PowerShell ISE, inside the Node block, if you type the first few letters of a DSC resource name and press the Tab key, you should be able to auto-complete resource names present on the local system.

So, to reconstruct our example, let us add the WindowsFeature resource to the configuration script.

```
Configuration WebsiteConfig {
    Node localhost {
        WindowsFeature WebServer1 {

        }
    }
}
```

Adding a resource script block is the same as Configuration or Node script blocks. We use the resource dynamic keyword, WindowsFeature in the preceding example, followed by an identifier and a script block. If you refer back to Figure 4-6, there are sets of properties associated with each resource. Using these properties, we can define what needs to be configured for the resource being managed. In this case, using the WindowsFeature resource properties, we can specify what Windows role or feature needs to be configured. An easy way to see all the properties and the syntax for any DSC resource is to use the -Syntax switch parameter of the Get-DscResource cmdlet (see Figure 4-7).

```
Get-DscResource -Name WindowsFeature -Syntax
```

```
PS C:\> Get-DscResource -Name WindowsFeature -Syntax
WindowsFeature [string] #ResourceName
{
    Name = [string]
    [ Credential = [PSCredential] ]
    [ DependsOn = [string[]] ]
    [ Ensure = [string] { Absent | Present }  ]
    [ IncludeAllSubFeature = [bool] ]
    [ LogPath = [string] ]
    [ Source = [string] ]
}
```

Figure 4-7. *WindowsFeature resource syntax*

The syntax shown in Figure 4-7 should be familiar. The properties enclosed within the square brackets are optional properties, and the rest are the key or mandatory properties. In the case of the WindowsFeature resource, we must at least specify the name of the role or feature we want to configure. The Ensure property is set by default to Present, and therefore, the WindowsFeature resource tries to install the role or feature specified, using the Name property.

■ **Tip**　When using the PowerShell ISE, another way to see the syntax for any DSC resource is to right-click the resource keyword, WindowsFeature in this example, and select the Start Intellisense option in the context menu. Another way to see valid property names is to type an invalid property name inside the Resource script block. When you move your mouse over the red wigley in the ISE, it shows a pop-up message with valid property names.

To reconstruct the example, we have to add the required properties to the resource definition. In our example, we must install the web server role, which is indicated by Web-Server.

```
Configuration WebsiteConfig {
    Node WSR2-1 {
        WindowsFeature WebServer1 {
            Name = "Web-Server"
        }
    }
}
```

As I mentioned earlier, the Ensure property is set by default to Present, so we need not specify that explicitly in the resource definition. Within a Node script block, we can specify any number of resource definitions, whether similar resources or different, as long as the values specified for the key properties of the same resources are different. For example, the following example is invalid, as we are specifying the same value for both WindowsFeature resource definitions. In addition, remember that the resource identifiers are resource names and must be unique. This is indicated using the strings WebServer1 and WebServer2 in the following example.

```
Configuration WebsiteConfig {
    Node WSR2-1 {
        WindowsFeature WebServer1 {
            Name = "Web-Server"
        }

        WindowsFeature WebServer2 {
            Name = "Web-Server"
        }
    }
}
```

However, the following example, in which we specify different values for the Name property, is valid, and using this configuration script, we can configure both the Web-Server role and the Web-Asp-Net45 feature.

```
Configuration WebsiteConfig {
    Node WSR2-1 {
        WindowsFeature WebServer1 {
            Name = "Web-Server"
        }

        WindowsFeature ASP {
            Name = "Web-Asp-Net45"
        }
    }
}
```

When using multiple resources inside a Node block, DSC also lets us specify the dependencies among the resources. Each DSC resource has a DependsOn property added to its list of properties. Using this property, we can specify what DSC resources must be configured before configuring the resource in which the DependsOn property is specified. For example, if we want to first ensure that the Web-Asp-Net45 feature is installed before attempting to install the Web-Server property, we can use the DependsOn property as a part of the WebServer1 resource definition. The following example demonstrates this.

```
Configuration WebSiteConfig
{
    Node WSR2-1
    {
        WindowsFeature WebServer1
        {
            Name = "Web-Server"
            DependsOn = "[WindowsFeature]ASP"
        }

        WindowsFeature ASP
        {
            Name = "Web-Asp-Net45"
        }
    }
}
```

We will delve into the DependsOn property and its use in Chapter 5, when we talk about the built-in DSC resources. We will see several examples that leave you with a better understanding of this property and its use.

If you have followed the examples shown in this section and tried what we discussed, congratulations! You have authored your first DSC configuration script. But this is not sufficient to make changes to the target systems. The configuration script we have seen so far is just a method to declaratively specify the configuration changes we intend to make. It is also possible to add multiple Node blocks in a configuration script and use parameters such as a usual PowerShell script. We will see all this in Chapter 6. In the example at the beginning of this chapter, we had a resource block for the Website resource. This is not a built-in resource. It is a custom DSC resource. We will learn more about custom resources in Chapter 9.

We now have to translate that into a format that the DSC Local Configuration Manager or the DSC Engine can understand. This is the Managed Object Format (MOF) representation of the configuration script.

We can generate the MOF representation of the configuration script by simply loading the configuration into memory and then calling the configuration. Take a look at the following example:

```
Configuration WebSiteConfig
{
    Node WSR2-1
    {
        WindowsFeature WebServer1
        {
            Name = "Web-Server"
            DependsOn = "[WindowsFeature]ASP"
        }

        WindowsFeature ASP
        {
            Name = "Web-Asp-Net45"
        }
    }
}
WebSiteConfig
```

In the preceding example, we added the name of the configuration at the end of the configuration script and saved it as a .ps1 file. Now, when we execute this PowerShell script, it generates the MOF file and stores it in a folder that has the same name as the configuration (see Figure 4-8).

```
PS C:\Scripts> .\WebSiteConfig.ps1


    Directory: C:\Scripts\WebSiteConfig


Mode                LastWriteTime     Length Name
----                -------------     ------ ----
-a---          5/6/2014    2:11 PM       1812 WSR2-1.mof
```

Figure 4-8. *Generating the MOF file for the configuration script*

Note that it is not necessary to save the configuration script. You can simply author the configuration script in the ISE script editor and press the F5 key to run the script. It will have the same impact as saving and then executing the .ps1 file. As you can see in Figure 4-8, running the configuration creates a folder with the same name as the configuration and stores an MOF file with the node name as the file name, followed by a .mof extension. You can open this MOF file in your favorite text editor and verify its contents. This is how it looks on my system, with the preceding configuration script. If you have executed the same configuration as we saw in the example, your MOF file shouldn't be much different from what I have here, except for the first few lines, in which the GeneratedBy, GenerationDate, and GenerationHost properties are shown, and the last few lines, in which an instance of the OMI_ConfigurationDocument class is specified. These are auto-generated using system environment variables when the MOF is generated, and it is not currently possible to change them from PowerShell.

```
/*
@TargetNode='WSR2-1'
@GeneratedBy=Ravikanth
@GenerationDate=05/06/2014 14:11:12
@GenerationHost=Home-Desk
*/

instance of MSFT_RoleResource as $MSFT_RoleResource1ref
{
ResourceID = "[WindowsFeature]WebServer1";
 DependsOn = {
    "[WindowsFeature]ASP"
};
 SourceInfo = "C:\\Scripts\\WebSiteConfig.ps1::5::9::WindowsFeature";
 Name = "Web-Server";
 ModuleName = "PSDesiredStateConfiguration";
 ModuleVersion = "1.0";

};
```

```
instance of MSFT_RoleResource as $MSFT_RoleResource2ref
{
ResourceID = "[WindowsFeature]ASP";
 SourceInfo = "C:\\Scripts\\WebSiteConfig.ps1::11::9::WindowsFeature";
 Name = "Web-Asp-Net45";
 ModuleName = "PSDesiredStateConfiguration";
 ModuleVersion = "1.0";

};

instance of OMI_ConfigurationDocument
{
 Version="1.0.0";
 Author="Ravikanth";
 GenerationDate="05/06/2014 14:11:12";
 GenerationHost="Home-Desk";
};
```

As you see in the above MOF for the configuration script, for each WindowsFeature resource definition inside the Node block, we see an entry specified as the instance of the MSFT_RoleResource class. This is true for any other resource in DSC. For any of the resources in the configuration script, the MOF will contain the instance of the implementing class for the same resource. You will also notice that the ModuleVersion specifies the version of the module that implements the resource.

You can use the -OutputPath parameter of the configuration to specify an alternate location for storing the MOF file, instead of using the default location, which is the working directory in which the configuration was executed. To do this, add the -OutputPath parameter next to the configuration name at the end of the script. For example, replace the last line of our configuration script with the following:

```
WebSiteConfig -OutputPath C:\DSCMofs
```

Requirements for Configuration Authoring

If you are using the Windows PowerShell language extensions provided by the PSDesiredStateConfiguration module for configuration script authoring and Managed Object Format (MOF) generation, then you would require WMF 4.0 or later on the system on which you author configuration scripts. This sounds very obvious, and we also looked at some system requirements from a WMF 4.0 point of view, such as enabling script execution and WinRM listeners for applying configuration changes. Relating to this, if you intend to use a system just to author configuration scripts, you wouldn't need WinRM listeners configured on the system. However, you'd still require the script execution enabled, using an appropriate execution policy.

Also, when using the PowerShell 4.0 or later language extensions for authoring configuration scripts, you will require all the DSC resource modules, both built-in and custom resources, on the authoring system.

This brings us to the discussion on third-party languages and tools in the configuration authoring phase shown in Figure 4-1. If you have read this section clearly, you'll understand that the PowerShell configuration script is just a declarative way of describing the configuration that has to be managed. It, by itself, cannot perform any changes. In fact, once we create the MOF representation, we probably won't require the configuration script until we have to change the configuration and regenerate the MOF. So, if we had another mechanism that can generate configuration scripts or the MOF representation of the configuration directly, we wouldn't really require the insight into how to author these scripts. In fact, if you can handwrite (or type, maybe) the MOF files for the configuration, you will never have to use the Configuration keyword or any other language extensions we've discussed so far. This is where the third-party languages and tools play a role. At the time of writing, Chef and ScriptRock have interfaces to generate the configuration files for DSC-based configuration management, and, using the interfaces provided in their framework, they make it possible to transparently use DSC without even requiring any knowledge of the DSC feature set. A discussion on these third-party tools or languages is outside the scope of this book; however, I recommend that you take a look at some of these resources available online.

■ **Note**   You can read more about ScriptRock GuardRail and DSC integration at www.scriptrock.com/blog/powershell-dsc-with-guardrail, and Chef has an open source cookbook available for DSC on Github at https://github.com/opscode-cookbooks/dsc.

Once we have the configuration MOF file generated from a script, or using any other method we just discussed, it has to be stored in a place that is accessible to target systems. This is called configuration staging. The choice of location for staging depends on how we plan to deliver the configuration to target systems. Delivering the configuration refers to how the target system receives the configuration MOF from a staging location for enacting. In the following section, we will look at configuration staging and how different configuration delivery modes in DSC influence this choice.

Staging and Delivery

Configuration staging is a natural step after authoring. In configuration authoring, we used the Configuration keyword and resulting configuration command to generate a Managed Object Format (MOF) representation of the change required. In our example, we stored the generated MOF file at C:\DSCMofs. However, you can also store such files at a central location, such as a Server Message Block (SMB) share. For example, in Figure 4-9, I used the -OutputPath parameter to store the configuration at a network share located on another server. Note that you will have to write permissions on the network share to be able to copy the generated MOF.

```
PS C:\> WebSiteConfig -OutputPath \\WSR2-2\DSCMofs


    Directory: \\WSR2-2\DSCMofs


Mode                LastWriteTime     Length Name
----                -------------     ------ ----
-a---          5/6/2014   6:23 PM       1644 WSR2-1.mof
```

Figure 4-9. Staging configuration MOFs in an SMB share

This is useful when you have a central location that is version-controlled. Using version control at this level, you can always go back to an earlier version of the configuration, when required. We will discuss more about this in Chapter 11, which covers best practices and recommendations when using Desired State Configuration (DSC) for configuration management.

In the preceding example, we have stored the generated MOF file at a network location. This alone isn't sufficient for target systems to receive this and enact it. This MOF must be delivered to the target system, and once the MOF is received on the target system, it gets enacted. DSC, as I briefly mentioned earlier, supports two modes of configuration delivery, and these modes influence where the configuration gets staged. These are called Push and Pull modes in DSC. Chapter 7 is dedicated to diving deep into these configuration delivery modes. That said, I will give a quick overview of the methods, so that we don't have to focus on the fundamentals when we examine these delivery modes in Chapter 7.

Push Mode

The target systems with WMF 4.0 or later are configured by default to receive configuration using the Push mode. So, when using the Push mode, the target system does not really go looking for configuration changes. Instead, it expects a configuration push every time a change is required.

As with configuration authoring, the Push mode uses the PSDesiredStateConfiguration module. Once we have a configuration script created and an MOF file generated, we can push the configuration changes to a target system, using the Start-DscConfiguration cmdlet. When using this cmdlet, the configuration is immediately applied to the target system(s). Therefore, the Start-DscConfiguration cmdlet actually results in configuration delivery from a staging location and immediately enacts that configuration on the target systems. In the "Configuration Enactment" section, we will look at enacting in Push mode.

The Push mode, while providing an easy way to enact configuration, isn't very scalable, because there is a limit to how many simultaneous Common Information Model (CIM) sessions can be created from a single computer and because of the complexities involved in connecting to target systems that are either in a workgroup environment or in a mixed-domain configuration. Also, when the configuration involves DSC resources that are not available on the target systems, Push mode won't work. The DSC resources must be copied to the target systems, before enacting configuration in Push mode. This is where the Pull mode of configuration delivery helps.

Pull Mode

The Pull mode of configuration delivery resolves the scalability issues and limitations of the Push mode, while providing a central store for both configurations and DSC resource modules. To implement this, Pull mode can be built using a file server (Server Message Block [SMB]) share or an OData web service. A target system can be configured to use the Pull mode of configuration delivery, which means the system would periodically poll a central repository or service to get the configuration changes and DSC resource modules required for the change. In this section, we will look at the two Pull mode configurations available and the pros and cons of these methods. For Pull mode, whether over an SMB or OData endpoint, we need this special configuration on the target systems. These settings are defined as the meta-configuration of a DSC component called the Local Configuration Manager (LCM). In the next section, "Configuration Enactment," we will look at LCM and how some of its configuration settings can be changed to enable Pull mode for the target systems.

Pull Mode over SMB

The Pull mode over SMB is the simplest method to implement. All we need is to create an SMB file share and copy all configurations we generate and the resources required for the configurations. The advantage of this method, of course, is the simplicity in setting it up. The only configuration we need is to assign proper permissions to the SMB file share. We will see this in detail when we discuss configuration delivery methods, in Chapter 7.

Pull Mode over OData or HTTP

This method requires special configuration of an OData endpoint. On Windows Server 2008 R2, 2012 systems with WMF 4.0 or later, or on systems with Windows Server 2012 R2, this OData endpoint can be configured by installing the Windows PowerShell Desired State Configuration Service (DSC-Service) feature. The target systems can then be configured to pull the configuration and the DSC resource modules from this OData endpoint. The steps needed to set up a DSC Pull service and configure the clients for Pull mode are discussed in Chapter 7.

When using the Pull mode, either over SMB or REST, we must create a checksum for the configuration MOF files being sent to the target systems for configuration change. This checksum can be created using the New-DscChecksum function in the PSDesiredStateConfiguration. This function is used only in staging the configuration for delivery in Pull mode. It is possible to create a file checksum without using the New-DscChecksum function. This function uses the SHA-256 hashing algorithm and the New-FileHash cmdlet to generate the checksum for each configuration MOF. Therefore, the DSC components that get involved in the Pull mode configuration staging are the DSC Pull Service (if implemented) and the PowerShell DSC module.

Third-Party Pull Servers

Microsoft released the DSC Pull mode protocol specification, with which anyone having a knowledge of writing web services can create a DSC pull server for configuration delivery over HTTP. This is where the third-party Pull services or OData endpoints will come into the picture. At the time of this writing, there are no third-party DSC pull servers.

■ **Note** The Desired State Configuration Pull mode protocol specification can be downloaded at http://msdn.microsoft.com/en-us/library/dn393548.aspx. I recommend reading through this material to understand how Pull mode is implemented.

Configuration Enactment

The configuration enactment phase is when the configuration changes get deployed on the target systems. In the configuration authoring and staging phase, we looked at how Push and Pull modes are used. These involve either pushing the configuration or pulling both configurations and resources from a central location. However, this is only the configuration delivery method. The component that actually performs the configuration change is the DSC Local Configuration Manager (LCM). The DSC LCM is the heart of Desired State Configuration. Let us take a look at LCM and its capabilities.

Local Configuration Manager

Local Configuration Manager is the DSC engine. It runs on all systems that have WMF 4.0 or later installed. However, it plays a role only in the configuration enactment phase on the target systems, and it is responsible for calling the configuration resources that are included in a DSC configuration script. When we discussed the configuration delivery methods, I mentioned that the LCM settings on the target systems can be changed. This includes settings such as configuration refresh mode to Push or Pull, configuration mode to allow auto-correction of any configuration drift, and so on. In this section, we will take a look at how LCM implements these configuration settings and the internals of the LCM configuration.

The LCM is implemented as a Common Information Model (CIM) class, called MSFT_DscLocalConfigurationManager, in the DSC WMI provider. The configurable settings for the LCM are defined in the CIM class MSFT_DSCMetaConfiguration. These CIM classes are available in the DSC WMI namespace at root/Microsoft/Windows/DesiredStateConfiguration. This Windows Management Instrumentation (WMI) provider is implemented as two dynamic-link libraries, DscCore.dll and DscCoreConfProv.dll, located in the C:\Windows\System32 folder. The CIM class for LCM implements several methods that are used not only in the configuration enact phase but also in the later part of configuration management (as we saw in Chapter 3), where we have to monitor the configuration drift and perform configuration restore or enforcement. We can see a list of these CIM methods in the LCM class by using the Get-CimClass cmdlet.

```
Get-CimClass -ClassName MSFT_DscLocalConfigurationManager -Namespace root/microsoft/Windows/
DesiredStateConfiguration | Select -ExpandProperty CimClassMethods
```

Table 4-1 provides a quick overview of the CIM methods of the MSFT_DscLocalConfigurationManager class.

Table 4-1. *Local Configuration Manager CIM Methods*

Method Name	Description
SendConfiguration	Sends the configuration document to the target system and saves it as a pending configuration change. This method is not available as a PowerShell cmdlet in the PSDesiredStateConfiguration module.
SendConfigurationApply	Sends the configuration document to the target system and applies the configuration immediately. The Start-DscConfiguration cmdlet invokes this method for pushing the configuration.
GetConfiguration	Gets the current state of each resource specified in the configuration that was last applied. This is implemented as the Get-DscConfiguration CDXML cmdlet in the PSDesiredStateConfiguration module.
TestConfiguration	Verifies if a there is a configuration drift after the last configuration change or if the specified configuration is matching what was applied during the last configuration enactment. This is implemented as the Test-DscConfiguration CDXML cmdlet in the PSDesiredStateConfiguration module.
ApplyConfiguration	Applies the pending configuration. If there is no pending configuration, this method reapplies the current configuration. This is not implemented as a cmdlet in the PSDesiredStateConfiguration module.
SendMetaConfigurationApply	Sets the LCM settings. This is implemented as the Set-DscLocalConfiguration Manager CDXML cmdlet in the PSDesiredStateConfiguration module.
GetMetaConfiguration	Gets the LCM settings. This is implemented as the Get-DscLocalConfiguration Manager CDXML cmdlet in the PSDesiredStateConfiguration module.
RollBack	Restores target system configuration to a previous version. This is available as the Restore-DscConfiguration CDXML cmdlet in the PSDesiredStateConfiguration module.
PerformRequired ConfigurationChecks	Starts a consistency check for the configuration last applied. This is not available as a cmdlet in the PSDesiredStateConfiguration module. This method is used by the DSC scheduled task to perform the consistency check at regular configured intervals.
StopConfiguration	Stops the configuration change in progress. This is not available as a cmdlet in the PSDesiredStateConfiguration module.

As you see in Table 4-1, not all of the methods are implemented as PowerShell cmdlets in the DSC PowerShell module. There is also no need to use these CIM methods directly. The DSC engine, or agent, as some refer it, takes care of the tasks implemented by these methods internally. However, when we discuss some common DSC issues in DSC-based configuration management in Chapter 10, we will see examples of how these methods can be used.

When we looked at different configuration delivery methods in the previous section, I mentioned that you can configure LCM settings to switch between different configuration delivery methods and the required settings for each configuration delivery method. These settings are called the DSC meta-configuration, and the properties that we can configure are presented as CIM properties of the class MSFT_DscMetaConfiguration. Once again, we can use the Get-CimClass to look into the details of this.

```
Get-CimClass -ClassName MSFT_DscMetaConfiguration -Namespace root/microsoft/Windows/
DesiredStateConfiguration | Select -ExpandProperty CimClassProperties | Select Name
```

Table 4-2 provides overview of the LCM meta-configuration settings.

Table 4-2. *LCM Meta-configuration Settings*

Method Name	Description
AllowModuleOverwrite	Specifies whether the modules downloaded from a pull server overwrite the old ones. This property takes Boolean values. The default value is False.
CertificateID	Specifies the certificate thumbprint for decrypting the DSC communication or credential used in a configuration script
ConfigurationMode	Specifies how LCM should apply the configuration. Valid values are **ApplyOnly**: Configuration is applied once. **ApplyAndMonitor**: Configuration is applied, and LCM monitors whether any changes occur. If configuration drift is detected, it is reported in logs. This is the default value. **ApplyAndAutoCorrect**: Configuration is applied, and LCM monitors whether changes occur. If configuration drift is detected, LCM reapplies the configuration.
RefreshMode	Refresh mode, which can accept one of the following two values: **Push**: Configuration is sent (pushed) to the node, by running the Start-DscConfiguration cmdlet (from the same or remote node). This is the default value. **Pull**: Node periodically checks for configuration updates on the pull server and gets (pulls) it when available. The pull server from which to pull the configuration is specified by values in DownloadManagerName and DownloadManagerCustomData properties.
ConfigurationId	GUID, which is used to get the configuration from the server when the RefreshMode is set to Pull mode
Credential	Credentials to access remote resources
DownloadManagerName	Specifies which download manager to use. There are two download managers available: **WebDownloadManager** (used with Pull mode over HTTP) and **DscFileDownloadManager** (used for Pull mode over SMB).
DownloadManagerCustomData	Specifies additional data to send to the download manager
RebootNodeIfNeeded	Specifies whether the target node is automatically restarted when configuration requires it. (For example, the machine might have to be restarted when adding or removing server roles and features.)
ConfigurationModeFrequencyMins	Specifies how often (in minutes) LCM ensures that the configuration is in the desired state
RefreshModeFrequencyMins	Specifies how often (in minutes) LCM attempts to obtain the configuration from the pull server. If configuration on the pull server differs from the current one on the target node, it is copied to the pending store and applied.

We can use the Get-DscLocalConfigurationManager cmdlet to get the LCM meta-configuration (see Figure 4-10).

```
PS C:\> Get-DscLocalConfigurationManager


AllowModuleOverwrite            : False
CertificateID                   :
ConfigurationID                 :
ConfigurationMode               : ApplyAndMonitor
ConfigurationModeFrequencyMins  : 30
Credential                      :
DownloadManagerCustomData       :
DownloadManagerName             :
RebootNodeIfNeeded              : False
RefreshFrequencyMins            : 15
RefreshMode                     : PUSH
PSComputerName                  :
```

Figure 4-10. *LCM default settings*

Figure 4-10 shows the default LCM settings on a system with WMF 4.0 or later. As you see, the RefreshMode is by default set to Push. Also, the ConfigurationMode is set to ApplyAndMonitor, with ConfigurationModeFrequencyMins set to 30. This means that the DSC engine performs a consistency check every 30 minutes and reports any configuration drift as an event log message. We will look further into DSC monitoring and reporting in Chapter 7.

I mentioned changing the LCM settings. So, how exactly can we do that? DSC provides a LocalConfigurationManager keyword to create a PowerShell script that can be used to change the meta-configuration on a target system. The syntax is very similar to configuration scripts we have seen so far.

```
Configuration LCMConfig {
    Node "WSR2-1" {
        LocalConfigurationManager {
            ConfigurationMode = "ApplyAndAutoCorrect"
        }
    }
}

LCMConfig
```

If you look at the preceding code snippet, it is very similar to a configuration script we created, except that there is no identifier next to the LocalConfigurationManager keyword inside the Node block. Now, we can run this configuration like any other configuration script we have written so far. This is a simple example of changing LCM settings. We are only modifying the ConfigurationMode to ApplyAndAutoCorrect. Using this setting, we can automatically correct any configuration drift. We are not changing the ConfigurationModeFrequencyMins, so the consistency check still occurs every 30 minutes.

If you observe Figure 4-11, the name given to the MOF file is different from that of the usual resource configuration MOF file. Here, the name describes that it is a meta-configuration MOF. We cannot use the Start-DscConfiguration cmdlet to apply this. We must use the Set-DscLocalConfigurationManager cmdlet for this purpose.

```
Directory: C:\FileDemo\LCMConfig


Mode                LastWriteTime     Length Name
----                -------------     ------ ----
-a---          5/7/2014  10:45 PM        824 WSR2-1.meta.mof
```

Figure 4-11. *Running a meta-configuration script*

The CIM method, SendMetaConfigurationApply, we discussed in Table 4-1 is that used to change the LCM settings on the target node. This is evident in the output shown in Figure 4-12. We will look at the LCM settings that impact the configuration delivery modes used in Chapter 7. It is more appropriate to connect these settings to the examples in which we see both Push and Pull modes of configuration delivery in detail.

```
VERBOSE: [WSR2-1]: LCM:  [ Start   Set         ]
VERBOSE: [WSR2-1]: LCM:  [ Start   Resource ]   [MSFT_DSCMetaConfiguration]
VERBOSE: [WSR2-1]: LCM:  [ Start   Set         ]  [MSFT_DSCMetaConfiguration]
VERBOSE: [WSR2-1]: LCM:  [ End     Set         ]  [MSFT_DSCMetaConfiguration]   in 0.0470 seconds.
VERBOSE: [WSR2-1]: LCM:  [ End     Resource ]   [MSFT_DSCMetaConfiguration]
VERBOSE: [WSR2-1]: LCM:  [ End     Set         ]
VERBOSE: Operation 'Invoke CimMethod' complete.
VERBOSE: Set-DscLocalConfigurationManager finished in 0.445 seconds.
```

Figure 4-12. *Changing LCM meta-configuration*

Now that we have a fair understanding of what LCM is and how LCM settings can be changed, let us look at some DSC components that are used in both Push and Pull modes.

Configuration Enactment in Push Mode

As we've discussed and observed in LCM default settings, Push mode is used by default for configuration enactment. For this, as we learned in the "Staging and Delivery" section, we can use the Start-DscConfiguration cmdlet locally or target it to a remote system.

```
Start-DscConfiguration -Wait -Verbose -Path \\wsr2-2\DSCMofs
```

In the preceding command, we use the Start-DscConfiguration cmdlet's -Path parameter to specify the path to the MOF file we generated in an earlier step. The -Wait parameter specifies that we want to wait until the configuration change is complete, and the -Verbose parameter specifies that the verbose output stream should be shown to reveal what changes are being made. We don't have to explicitly specify the -ComputerName parameter to describe where the configuration needs to be applied. We have already included that as the name of the Node block, and the resulting MOF file includes this information as the name of the MOF file. However, this method (of not specifying -ComputerName) looks at all MOF files at the specified path and pushes the configuration to all target nodes listed. If we specify the -ComputerName parameter, and an MOF file with that name does not exist, it results in an error. This parameter takes a comma-separated list of computer names. Using this, you can specify if you want to push configuration to a subset of target systems for which the MOF files are available at the specified path.

Figure 4-13 shows an example of applying DSC configuration to a target system, using the Push mode. There are other parameters available for this cmdlet. We will take a closer look at the complete usage when we discuss configuration delivery methods in detail.

```
VERBOSE: [WSR2-1]: LCM:  [ Start  Set       ]
VERBOSE: [WSR2-1]: LCM:  [ Start  Resource  ]  [[WindowsFeature]ASP]
VERBOSE: [WSR2-1]: LCM:  [ Start  Test      ]  [[WindowsFeature]ASP]
VERBOSE: [WSR2-1]:                              [[WindowsFeature]ASP]  The operation 'Get-WindowsFeature' started: Web-Asp-Net45
VERBOSE: [WSR2-1]:                              [[WindowsFeature]ASP]  The operation 'Get-WindowsFeature' succeeded: Web-Asp-Net45
VERBOSE: [WSR2-1]: LCM:  [ End    Test      ]  [[WindowsFeature]ASP]  in 0.3590 seconds.
VERBOSE: [WSR2-1]: LCM:  [ Start  Set       ]  [[WindowsFeature]ASP]
VERBOSE: [WSR2-1]:                              [[WindowsFeature]ASP]  Installation started...
VERBOSE: [WSR2-1]:                              [[WindowsFeature]ASP]  Prerequisite processing started...
VERBOSE: [WSR2-1]:                              [[WindowsFeature]ASP]  Prerequisite processing succeeded.
WARNING: [WSR2-1]:                              [[WindowsFeature]ASP]  Windows automatic updating is not enabled. To ensure that your newly-i
nstalled role or feature is automatically updated, turn on Windows Update.
VERBOSE: [WSR2-1]:                              [[WindowsFeature]ASP]  Installation succeeded.
VERBOSE: [WSR2-1]:                              [[WindowsFeature]ASP]  successfully installed the feature Web-Asp-Net45
VERBOSE: [WSR2-1]: LCM:  [ End    Set       ]  [[WindowsFeature]ASP]  in 32.5540 seconds.
VERBOSE: [WSR2-1]: LCM:  [ End    Resource  ]  [[WindowsFeature]ASP]
VERBOSE: [WSR2-1]: LCM:  [ Start  Resource  ]  [[WindowsFeature]WebServer1]
VERBOSE: [WSR2-1]: LCM:  [ Start  Test      ]  [[WindowsFeature]WebServer1]
VERBOSE: [WSR2-1]:                              [[WindowsFeature]WebServer1] The operation 'Get-WindowsFeature' started: Web-Server
VERBOSE: [WSR2-1]:                              [[WindowsFeature]WebServer1] The operation 'Get-WindowsFeature' succeeded: Web-Server
VERBOSE: [WSR2-1]: LCM:  [ End    Test      ]  [[WindowsFeature]WebServer1] in 0.3750 seconds.
VERBOSE: [WSR2-1]: LCM:  [ Skip   Set       ]  [[WindowsFeature]WebServer1]
VERBOSE: [WSR2-1]: LCM:  [ End    Resource  ]  [[WindowsFeature]WebServer1]
```

Figure 4-13. *Pushing DSC configuration*

As shown in Figure 4-13, the Start-DscConfiguration cmdlet invokes the SendConfigurationApply method of the MSFT_DSCLocalConfigurationManager CIM class on the target system. This indicates that if you have an alternate script or tool that can invoke remote CIM methods with appropriate parameters to push the configuration, you don't even have to use the Start-DscConfiguration cmdlet in the DSC PowerShell module.

Whether it is a local or remote system, the Start-DscConfiguration cmdlet creates a temporary CIM session and invokes the SendConfigurationApply method of the LCM CIM class with MOF file contents as a byte array input to the method. The MOF contents get validated for any syntactical or other errors. Also, for Push configuration to work, as we discussed earlier, all resources defined in the configuration must exist on the target system. Once this validation is complete, the SendConfigurationApply method saves the configuration as pending.mof in the C:\Windows\System32\Configuration folder. The configuration enactment begins immediately, and if the change is complete, the current.mof (if exists) will be renamed to previous.mof, and the pending.mof gets copied to current. mof and backup.mof. The backup.mof file gets used when the current.mof file gets corrupted for any reason. Because the Start-DscConfiguration is only invoking a CIM method on the target system with the configuration MOF as a byte array, we can do that using a simple PowerShell script, using the Invoke-CimMethod cmdlet. Therefore, it is possible for third-party tools to push DSC configuration without using the DSC PowerShell module. This is illustrated in Figure 4-1.

I will conclude this section by briefly describing one of the limitations of the Push mode. When using Push mode, the DSC resource modules that are needed to perform the configuration change must exist on the target system. Therefore, it is not possible to store the modules in a central location such as a network share and then push the modules also as a part of the configuration delivery. There are other limitations, too, such as scalability. We will look at this in detail in a Chapter 7.

Configuration Enactment in Pull Mode

When using Pull mode for configuration and resource-module retrieval, the LCM uses the DownloadManagerName property to identify the method by which to download the configuration to the local system. If the DownloadManagerName is set to WebDownloadManager, LCM uses HTTP to retrieve the configuration from the pull server. The URL for the pull server service should be given as a hash table value to the DownloadManagerCustomData property of LCM. The interfaces required to perform the communication over HTTP are defined in the WebDownloadManager module, within the PSDesiredStateConfiguration module. Similarly, if the DownloadManagerName is set to FileDownloadManager, the LCM uses the SMB share name defined in the DownloadManagerCustomData property, to retrieve the configuration and any necessary resource modules. For communicating with the SMB file server, the FileDownloadManager module is used. To pull the right configuration from the pull server, the value of the `ConfigurationID` property is used. This value gets suffixed with `.mof`, and the pull server gets checked for an MOF with this name. As we have seen earlier, a checksum file for each MOF must also exist on the pull server and should have the `ConfigurationID` defined in the LCM as its file name, suffixed with `.mof.checksum`.

Both `WebDownloadManager` and `FileDownloadManager` modules export the `Get-DscAction`, `Get-DscDocument`, and `Get-DscModule` cmdlets. When the LCM is configured for Pull mode, these cmdlets are used to retrieve the configuration MOFs (`Get-DscDocument`) and missing DSC resource modules (`Get-DscModule`) from the pull server. The `Get-DscAction` cmdlet helps the LCM find what should be done at the interval defined using `RefreshModeFrequencyMins`. When this triggers, the `Get-DscAction` compares the checksum of the local MOF to the one available at the pull server location. If it matches, no action will be taken; otherwise, the MOF from the pull server gets copied as `pending.mof`, and the configuration is applied.

This brings us to the end of our discussion of the configuration enactment phase. In this section, we only touched upon the fundamentals of what occurs for various configuration delivery modes in this phase, and we examined the need and the role of LCM in DSC. We, however, have not seen any details about setting up a pull server or verifying how the configuration drift gets checked and corrected. We will see these concepts in detail in the upcoming chapters. Also, once we apply the configuration to a target system, there is a need to monitor and report any configuration drift. There are cmdlets in the `PSDesiredStateConfiguration` module for performing these activities. Apart from these cmdlets, we can create custom scripts to report the state of configuration on the target systems. This will be discussed in Chapter 8.

Summary

What we have seen in this chapter forms the basis of understanding Desired State Configuration (DSC) and how it works. The implementation of a configuration change typically occurs in two different phases. These include configuration authoring and staging and enacting. DSC architecture has multiple components and language extensions that facilitate each of these phases. Understanding DSC language extensions and components in relation to the two phases of implementing configuration change is more helpful than discussing each component in silos. This chapter provided an overview of the components at each phase and sufficient details for you to get started; however, there is more. The later parts of this book will delve into the details of each of these components and how they are used.

CHAPTER 5

■ ■ ■

Using Built-in DSC Resources

The configuration scripts in Windows PowerShell Desired State Configuration (DSC) are based on the building blocks called resources. We discussed the concept of DSC resources in the previous chapter, and you learned why DSC resources are needed. As discussed, the DSC resources are PowerShell modules with a specific set of functions. At the time of writing, there are 12 DSC resources that come built in as a part of Windows Management Framework (WMF) 4.0. The future releases of Windows Management Framework may add more such built-in resources. These resources enjoy Microsoft support, and you can create requests for bug fixes and feature changes.

In this chapter, we look at each of the built-in resources in depth and learn how to use it. Doing so not only improves our understanding of the DSC resources and how they work but also helps us understand the best practices in writing DSC resources. We will look at writing custom DSC resources in the next chapter, and knowledge gained from this chapter will certainly be valuable. For each of the built-in DSC resources, we will discuss multiple examples to understand the syntax and usage in detail. To try the examples in this chapter, you will require at least two systems. One system will be used to author the configuration scripts, and a second as the target for applying the configuration. In my lab setup for these examples, I have multiple virtual machines running a mix of operating systems that DSC supports. This helps me to understand what the exact requirements for each of these operating systems are and to uncover any gotchas in that process. If not the same number of systems, I suggest that you have a mix of operating systems that support the DSC feature.

Exploring Built-in Resources

As we saw in Chapter 4, the `Get-DSCResource` cmdlet lists all the DSC resources, built-in and custom, on the local system. This cmdlet looks at the value of the `$env:PSModulePath` variable to find the DSC resources. You can run the cmdlet without any parameters to see a list of DSC resources. This cmdlet returns a list of both built-in and custom resources. Run the following command on a Windows Server 2012 R2, Windows 8.1, or a system with WMF 4.0 and no custom resources.

```
Get-DSCResource
```

In the output shown in Figure 5-1, there are 12 built-in DSC resources in Windows Server 2012 R2 or on systems with WMF 4.0. We saw in Chapter 4 that the DSC resources can either be binary or PowerShell script modules. The `ImplementedAs` property tells us that the `File` and `Log` resources are the binary modules.

```
PS C:\> Get-DscResource

ImplementedAs    Name            Module                        Properties
-------------    ----            ------                        ----------
Binary           File                                          {DestinationPath, Attrib...
PowerShell       Archive         PSDesiredStateConfiguration   {Destination, Path, Chec...
PowerShell       Environment     PSDesiredStateConfiguration   {Name, DependsOn, Ensure...
PowerShell       Group           PSDesiredStateConfiguration   {GroupName, Credential, ...
Binary           Log             PSDesiredStateConfiguration   {Message, DependsOn}
PowerShell       Package         PSDesiredStateConfiguration   {Name, Path, ProductId, ...
PowerShell       Registry        PSDesiredStateConfiguration   {Key, ValueName, Depends...
PowerShell       Script          PSDesiredStateConfiguration   {GetScript, SetScript, T...
PowerShell       Service         PSDesiredStateConfiguration   {Name, BuiltInAccount, C...
PowerShell       User            PSDesiredStateConfiguration   {UserName, DependsOn, De...
PowerShell       WindowsFeature  PSDesiredStateConfiguration   {Name, Credential, Depen...
PowerShell       WindowsProcess  PSDesiredStateConfiguration   {Arguments, Path, Creden...
```

Figure 5-1. *List of built-in DSC resources*

Each of the resources shown in Figure 5-1 has a unique purpose. Table 5-1 provides an overview of the resources. In the subsequent sections, we will look at each of the resources in depth and learn their usage.

Table 5-1. *Overview of Built-in DSC Resources in WMF 4.0*

DSC Resource Name	Purpose
Archive	Provides a method to extract zip archives at a specified path
Environment	Provides a mechanism to manage system environment variables
File	Provides a mechanism to create/manage files and folders
Group	Provides a method to manage local groups
Log	Provides a mechanism to write event logs to the Microsoft-Windows-Desired State Configuration/Analytic event log
Package	Provides a mechanism to install or uninstall packages, such as Windows Installer and setup.exe packages
WindowsProcess	Provides a mechanism to configure Windows processes
Registry	Provides a mechanism to manage registry configurations
Script	Provides a mechanism to run Windows PowerShell script blocks
Service	Provides a mechanism to manage Windows Services
User	Provides a mechanism to manage local user accounts
WindowsFeature	Provides a mechanism to manage Windows Roles and Features

■ **Note** In the subsequent sections, we will look at each built-in DSC resource and learn how each property in the resource definition is used. However, we will defer any discussion of the Credential property to a later chapter 6 in this book. This is because we have to understand parameterizing the configuration scripts and using configuration data before we can discuss how to use the Credential property. Also, there are potential security pitfalls when using the Credential property. We will discuss this in Chapter 6.

Archive Resource

The Archive resource can be used to unpack zip archives on a target node at a specified path. We have seen, in Chapter 4, how to see a list of properties available and the syntax for a resource using the DSC cmdlets. We used the Get-DSCResource cmdlet with the -Syntax parameter. The properties of the Archive resource are described in Table 5-2.

Table 5-2. *Properties of the Archive DSC Resource*

Property Name	Description	Required?
Destination	Specifies the destination location or folder on the target node	Yes
Path	Specifies the path of the zip archive to unpack or extract. This zip must exist at a location reachable from the target computer.	Yes
Checksum	Specifies the type of checksum that should be used when determining whether two files are the same. If Checksum is not specified, only the file or directory name is used for comparison. Valid values include SHA-1, SHA-256, SHA-512, createdDate, modifiedDate, none (default).	No
Validate	Specifies whether the resource configuration must be validated or not	No. Required when Checksum property is specified
DependsOn	Specifies the resources that must be configured before this resource is configured	No
Ensure	Specifies if the archive should be Present or Absent at the destination. The default value is Present.	No
Force	Specifies if a configuration change must always be enforced	No. Required when the changes must be enforced based on validation

With this knowledge, let us proceed to some examples on how to use the Archive resource. The following code snippet shows the basic usage of the Archive resource in a configuration script.

```
Archive ArchiveDemo {
    Path = "C:\Scripts"
    Destination = "C:\downloads\scripts.zip"
}
```

The preceding code shows the bare minimum properties required to use the Archive resource. In this example, we should make sure that the zip archive specified as a value for the Destination property exists on the target node. The value of the Path argument may or may not exist. When this resource is configured, the Local Configuration Manager (LCM) checks if the destination already exists and, if it exists, compares the contents at the destination path to what is available in the zip archive. If the file and folder names in the zip archive match, LCM skips the resource configuration. Let's see an example, to understand this better.

■ **Note**   We have looked at the fundamentals of executing configuration scripts and pushing DSC configuration to remote systems using the Start-DscConfiguration cmdlet. For the examples in this chapter and those ahead, we will not revisit any of these basics. This is to keep the chapter content concise and useful.

```
Configuration ArchiveDemo {
    Node WSR2-1 {
        Archive ArchiveDemo {
            Destination = "C:\Scripts"
            Path = "C:\downloads\scripts.zip"
        }
    }
}
```

ArchiveDemo

To understand the behavior of this resource, I had created a zip archive with a few files placed on the target node at C:\Downloads. Also, I created a folder, C:\Scripts, on the target node. When we apply this configuration using the Start-DscConfiguration cmdlet, we can clearly see from the verbose output that the existence of the files at the target node is being verified.

■ **Note**   For all examples in this chapter, configuration must be enacted using the Start-DscConfiguration cmdlet. You have to use –Verbose and –Wait parameters, along with –Path parameter, to specify the path of the folder that contains the configuration Managed Object Format (MOF). For the sake of brevity, the output from the Start-DscConfiguration cmdlet has been cropped to show only the details that are necessary.

As shown Figure 5-2, LCM checks for the existence of files, and when it does not find the files, it unpacks the zip archive. What happens if only a subset of files, but not all, exists on the target node? Try it yourself.

```
[ Start  Set      ]
[ Start  Resource ]   [[Archive]ArchiveDemo]
[ Start  Test     ]   [[Archive]ArchiveDemo]
                      [[Archive]ArchiveDemo]  The destination file C:\Scripts\Common.dll was missing or was not a file
                      [[Archive]ArchiveDemo]  The destination file C:\Scripts\Common.pdb was missing or was not a file
                      [[Archive]ArchiveDemo]  The destination file C:\Scripts\Content.txt was missing or was not a file
[ End    Test     ]   [[Archive]ArchiveDemo]   in 0.5310 seconds.
[ Start  Set      ]   [[Archive]ArchiveDemo]
                      [[Archive]ArchiveDemo]  The configuration of MSFT_ArchiveResource is starting
                      [[Archive]ArchiveDemo]  The archive at C:\downloads\scripts.zip was unpacked to destination C:\Scripts
                      [[Archive]ArchiveDemo]  The configuration of MSFT_ArchiveResource has completed
[ End    Set      ]   [[Archive]ArchiveDemo]   in 0.2500 seconds.
[ End    Resource ]   [[Archive]ArchiveDemo]
[ End    Set      ]
```

Figure 5-2. *Applying the* Archive *resource configuration*

As we have seen in the properties description in Table 5-2, the checksum validation happens only at the file and folder name level when there is no explicit mention of the Checksum property in the configuration script. If the file and folder names in the zip archive match the destination, but one of the files' content is updated, the Archive resource won't replace the file at the destination. This is where the Checksum property plays a role.

```
Configuration ArchiveDemo {
    Node WSR2-1 {
        Archive ArchiveDemo {
            Destination = "C:\Scripts"
            Path = "C:\downloads\scripts.zip"
            Checksum = "SHA-256"
            Validate = $true
            Force = $true
        }
    }
}
```

ArchiveDemo

In the updated configuration script (see Figure 5-3), we are specifying that the contents at the destination and zip archive must be validated using SHA-256 checksum. In addition, based on the result of the checksum, we want to enforce the configuration change. This is what the Force property specifies.

```
VERBOSE: [WSR2-1]: LCM:  [ Start  Set     ]
VERBOSE: [WSR2-1]: LCM:  [ Start  Resource ]  [[Archive]ArchiveDemo]
VERBOSE: [WSR2-1]: LCM:  [ Start  Test    ]  [[Archive]ArchiveDemo]
VERBOSE: [WSR2-1]:                             [[Archive]ArchiveDemo] The destination file C:\Scripts\Content.txt exists but i
ts checksum did not match the origin file
VERBOSE: [WSR2-1]: LCM:  [ End    Test    ]  [[Archive]ArchiveDemo]  in 0.0470 seconds.
VERBOSE: [WSR2-1]: LCM:  [ Start  Set     ]  [[Archive]ArchiveDemo]
VERBOSE: [WSR2-1]:                             [[Archive]ArchiveDemo] The configuration of MSFT_ArchiveResource is starting
VERBOSE: [WSR2-1]:                             [[Archive]ArchiveDemo] The archive at C:\downloads\scripts.zip was unpacked to
destination C:\Scripts
VERBOSE: [WSR2-1]:                             [[Archive]ArchiveDemo] The configuration of MSFT_ArchiveResource has completed
VERBOSE: [WSR2-1]: LCM:  [ End    Set     ]  [[Archive]ArchiveDemo]  in 0.0310 seconds.
VERBOSE: [WSR2-1]: LCM:  [ End    Resource ]  [[Archive]ArchiveDemo]
VERBOSE: [WSR2-1]: LCM:  [ End    Set     ]
VERBOSE: [WSR2-1]: LCM:  [ End    Set     ]   in  0.1090 seconds.
VERBOSE: Operation 'Invoke CimMethod' complete.
VERBOSE: Time taken for configuration job to complete is 0.157 seconds
```

Figure 5-3. *Enforcing an archive content change*

As you see in the output shown in Figure 5-3, the LCM validates the checksum and finds that the content.txt at the destination is different from the source. The LCM, then, unpacks the contents of the zip archive at the destination specified in the configuration script. If the Force property is not set to True, the LCM halts the configuration change after finding the mismatch in the checksum.

What happens if we specify Ensure = "Absent" in the above configuration script? Try it yourself!

The example that we discussed earlier made an assumption that the zip archive is locally available on the target node. What if we want to use a network share to store the zip archive and then unpack it over the network to a target system? This sounds reasonable. Let us try it with an example.

```
Configuration ArchiveDemo {
    Node WSR2-1 {
        Archive ArchiveDemo {
            Destination = "C:\Scripts"
            Path = "\\Demo-Ad\Share\Scripts.zip"
        }
    }
}
```

ArchiveDemo

So, as we see in the example, I used a Universal Naming Convention (UNC) path to the zip archive. When I apply this configuration, see what happens! (See Figure 5-4.)

```
VERBOSE: [WSR2-1]: LCM:  [ Start  Set     ]
VERBOSE: [WSR2-1]: LCM:  [ Start  Resource ]  [[Archive]ArchiveDemo]
VERBOSE: [WSR2-1]: LCM:  [ Start  Test    ]  [[Archive]ArchiveDemo]
VERBOSE: [WSR2-1]: LCM:  [ End    Test    ]  [[Archive]ArchiveDemo]  in 0.2810 seconds.
PowerShell provider MSFT_ArchiveResource  failed to execute Test-TargetResource functionality with error message:
The running command stopped because the preference variable "ErrorActionPreference" or common parameter is set to
Stop: Access is denied
    + CategoryInfo          : InvalidOperation: (:) [], CimException
    + FullyQualifiedErrorId : ProviderOperationExecutionFailure
    + PSComputerName        : WSR2-1

VERBOSE: [WSR2-1]: LCM:  [ End    Set     ]
The SendConfigurationApply function did not succeed.
    + CategoryInfo          : NotSpecified: (root/Microsoft/...gurationManager:String) [], CimException
    + FullyQualifiedErrorId : MI RESULT 1
    + PSComputerName        : WSR2-1

VERBOSE: Operation 'Invoke CimMethod' complete.
VERBOSE: Time taken for configuration job to complete is 0.852 seconds
```

Figure 5-4. *Failure in unpacking a zip archive from network share*

The verbose output shown in Figure 5-4 clearly tells us that the LCM was unable to access the UNC path. The logged-in domain credentials do not matter here, as the LCM service itself runs as the SYSTEM account. The workaround here is to give the computer account permissions to access the UNC path. This can be done by navigating to folder security and selecting the target node computer account. To do this, follow the steps listed below.

1. Right-click the folder that is shared and select **Properties**.

2. Navigate to the **Security** tab and click **Edit** (see Figure 5-5).

3. In the Permissions for <foldername> dialog, click **Add**.

4. In the Select Users, Computers, Service Account, or Groups dialog, click **Object Types...**

5. Select **Computers** and click OK.

6. In the text box named **Enter the object names to select:** dialog, type the name of the target node(s) to which you want to push the configuration and select **Check Names**.

7. Click OK to close all the open dialogs.

The share permissions should look like what is shown in Figure 5-5. Before we can apply the configuration script shown in the preceding example, we have to ensure that the share permissions also reflect the computer name we just added to the folder security. Once the previously listed steps are complete, we can apply the configuration script from the preceding example. The result is shown in Figure 5-6.

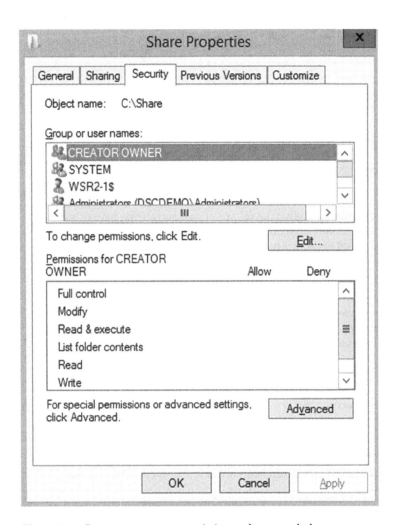

Figure 5-5. *Computer account permission to the network share*

```
VERBOSE: [WSR2-1]: LCM:  [ Start  Set       ]
VERBOSE: [WSR2-1]: LCM:  [ Start  Resource ]  [[Archive]ArchiveDemo]
VERBOSE: [WSR2-1]: LCM:  [ Start  Test      ]  [[Archive]ArchiveDemo]
VERBOSE: [WSR2-1]:                             [[Archive]ArchiveDemo] The destination file C:\Scripts\Common.dll was m
issing or was not a file
VERBOSE: [WSR2-1]:                             [[Archive]ArchiveDemo] The destination file C:\Scripts\Common.pdb was m
issing or was not a file
VERBOSE: [WSR2-1]:                             [[Archive]ArchiveDemo] The destination file C:\Scripts\Content.txt was
missing or was not a file
VERBOSE: [WSR2-1]: LCM:  [ End    Test      ]  [[Archive]ArchiveDemo]  in 0.0630 seconds.
VERBOSE: [WSR2-1]: LCM:  [ Start  Set       ]  [[Archive]ArchiveDemo]
VERBOSE: [WSR2-1]:                             [[Archive]ArchiveDemo] The configuration of MSFT_ArchiveResource is sta
rting
VERBOSE: [WSR2-1]:                             [[Archive]ArchiveDemo] The archive at \\Demo-Ad\Share\Scripts.zip was u
npacked to destination C:\Scripts
VERBOSE: [WSR2-1]:                             [[Archive]ArchiveDemo] The configuration of MSFT_ArchiveResource has co
mpleted
VERBOSE: [WSR2-1]: LCM:  [ End    Set       ]  [[Archive]ArchiveDemo]  in 0.2340 seconds.
VERBOSE: [WSR2-1]: LCM:  [ End    Resource ]  [[Archive]ArchiveDemo]
VERBOSE: [WSR2-1]: LCM:  [ End    Set       ]
VERBOSE: [WSR2-1]: LCM:  [ End    Set       ]    in  0.3280 seconds.
VERBOSE: Operation 'Invoke CimMethod' complete.
VERBOSE: Time taken for configuration job to complete is 0.36 seconds
```

***Figure 5-6.** Unpacking archive from a UNC path*

The process just described may not be the right method, given the volume of systems you may have to manage. Also, it is not appropriate security practice to give computer account permissions to access folders on remote systems. In addition, unpacking large archives over a low-speed network is not a good idea.

Environment Resource

The Environment resource is used to manage the system environment variables on the target nodes. For example, you can use this resource to set the PATH variable on target nodes to include a path to a specific line-of-business (LOB) application that you have recently installed on systems in your organization. The properties of the Environment resource are described in Table 5-3.

***Table 5-3.** Properties of the Environment DSC Resource*

Property Name	Description	Required?
Name	Specifies the name of the Environment variable to create, delete, or modify	Yes
Path	Specifies if the Environment variable is a Path variable. Set this to True for variables such as Path and PSModulePath.	No
Value	Specifies the value for the Environment variable	No
DependsOn	Specifies the resources that must be configured before this resource is configured	No
Ensure	Specifies if the Environment variable should be present or absent on the target node	No

When this resource is used with only the Name property, a system Environment variable will be created with no value.

```
Configuration EnvironmentDemo {
    Node WSR2-1 {
        Environment EnvironmentDemo {
            Name = "DemoVariable"
        }
    }
}
```

EnvironmentDemo

In the preceding example, we did not specify any value for the variable named DemoVariable. When this configuration is applied, the Environment resource module checks whether there is an existing system Environment variable with the given name and creates a variable, if required (see Figure 5-7).

```
VERBOSE: [WSR2-1]: LCM:  [ Start  Set       ]
VERBOSE: [WSR2-1]: LCM:  [ Start  Resource  ]  [[Environment]EnvironmentDemo]
VERBOSE: [WSR2-1]: LCM:  [ Start  Test      ]  [[Environment]EnvironmentDemo]
VERBOSE: [WSR2-1]:                              [[Environment]EnvironmentDemo] (NOT FOUND) Environment variable
 'DemoVariable'
VERBOSE: [WSR2-1]: LCM:  [ End    Test      ]  [[Environment]EnvironmentDemo]  in 7.9740 seconds.
VERBOSE: [WSR2-1]: LCM:  [ Start  Set       ]  [[Environment]EnvironmentDemo]
VERBOSE: [WSR2-1]: LCM:  [ End    Set       ]  [[Environment]EnvironmentDemo]  in 0.0940 seconds.
VERBOSE: [WSR2-1]: LCM:  [ End    Resource  ]  [[Environment]EnvironmentDemo]
VERBOSE: [WSR2-1]: LCM:  [ End    Set       ]
VERBOSE: [WSR2-1]: LCM:  [ End    Set       ]    in  8.7700 seconds.
```

Figure 5-7. *Creating an Environment variable with no value*

It can be seen clearly from Figure 5-7 that the variable did not exist on the target node, and the LCM completes the configuration, by adding the variable with the specified name. However, as shown in the configuration script, there is no value assigned to that variable. To assign a value to this variable, you can simply add the Value property and specify a value to that. For example, add Value = "Demo" to the configuration script shown in this example and apply the configuration. You will see that LCM finds a mismatch in the variable values and enforces the configuration change. Figure 5-8 shows what happens when I added the Value property to the configuration script in the preceding example.

```
VERBOSE: [WSR2-1]: LCM:  [ Start  Set       ]
VERBOSE: [WSR2-1]: LCM:  [ Start  Resource  ]  [[Environment]EnvironmentDemo]
VERBOSE: [WSR2-1]: LCM:  [ Start  Test      ]  [[Environment]EnvironmentDemo]
VERBOSE: [WSR2-1]:                              [[Environment]EnvironmentDemo] (FOUND MISMATCH) Environment var
iable 'DemoVariable' with value '' mismatched the specified value 'Demo'
VERBOSE: [WSR2-1]: LCM:  [ End    Test      ]  [[Environment]EnvironmentDemo]  in 0.0000 seconds.
VERBOSE: [WSR2-1]: LCM:  [ Start  Set       ]  [[Environment]EnvironmentDemo]
VERBOSE: [WSR2-1]: LCM:  [ End    Set       ]  [[Environment]EnvironmentDemo]  in 0.0160 seconds.
VERBOSE: [WSR2-1]: LCM:  [ End    Resource  ]  [[Environment]EnvironmentDemo]
VERBOSE: [WSR2-1]: LCM:  [ End    Set       ]
VERBOSE: [WSR2-1]: LCM:  [ End    Set       ]    in  0.0470 seconds.
```

Figure 5-8. *Adding a value to the system Environment variable*

When using the `Environment` resource to set the variables that are path variables, we must be extra careful. For example, variables such as `Path` and `PSModulePath` have multiple path values separated by a semicolon (`;`). So, setting values of these variables using the `Environment` resource will overwrite the earlier value, instead of appending to it. To resolve this, the `Environment` resource includes an additional property called `Path`.

```
Configuration EnvironmentDemo {
    Node WSR2-1 {
        Environment EnvironmentDemo {
            Name = "Path"
            Value = "C:\Scripts\MyModules"
            Path = $true
        }
    }
}

EnvironmentDemo
```

The `Path` property takes a `Boolean` value. So, if the system variable we are configuring is a `Path` variable, we have to set the `Path` property of the `Environment` resource to `True`.

The result of the preceding configuration script is shown in Figure 5-9. The `Environment` resource finds a mismatch with the current value and appends the variable value specified to the variable.

```
VERBOSE: [WSR2-1]: LCM:  [ Start  Set      ]
VERBOSE: [WSR2-1]: LCM:  [ Start  Resource ]  [[Environment]EnvironmentDemo]
VERBOSE: [WSR2-1]: LCM:  [ Start  Test     ]  [[Environment]EnvironmentDemo]
VERBOSE: [WSR2-1]:                            [[Environment]EnvironmentDemo] (FOUND MISMATCH) Environment var
iable 'Path' with value 'C:\Windows\system32;C:\Windows;C:\Windows\System32\Wbem;C:\Windows\System32\WindowsP
owerShell\v1.0\' mismatched the specified value 'C:\Scripts\MyModules'
VERBOSE: [WSR2-1]: LCM:  [ End    Test     ]  [[Environment]EnvironmentDemo]  in 0.0470 seconds.
VERBOSE: [WSR2-1]: LCM:  [ Start  Set      ]  [[Environment]EnvironmentDemo]
VERBOSE: [WSR2-1]: LCM:  [ End    Set      ]  [[Environment]EnvironmentDemo]  in 0.0670 seconds.
VERBOSE: [WSR2-1]: LCM:  [ End    Resource ]  [[Environment]EnvironmentDemo]
VERBOSE: [WSR2-1]: LCM:  [ End    Set      ]
VERBOSE: [WSR2-1]: LCM:  [ End    Set      ]     in  0.1450 seconds.
```

Figure 5-9. *Configuring a Path variable*

File Resource

The `File` DSC resource is used to manage files and folders on target nodes. We can use this resource to copy files or folder contents to remote systems using a configuration script. The functionality of this resource is often misunderstood and requires some explanation. First of all, this resource, unlike most of the other built-in resources, is not implemented as a PowerShell script module. Instead, it is a Management Infrastructure (MI) provider. We will discuss different types of DSC resource modules further in Chapter 9.

Table 5-4 shows a list of properties of the `File` resource.

Table 5-4. *Properties of the File DSC Resource*

Property Name	Description	Required?
DestinationPath	Specifies the destination path of file or folder that has to be configured	Yes
Attributes	Specifies the state of the attributes for the file or folder that has to be configured	No
Checksum	Specifies the type of checksum that has to be validated for the resource. Valid values include SHA-1, SHA-256, SHA-512, createdDate, modifiedDate.	No
Contents	Specifies the contents of the file	No
Credential	Specifies the credentials to access the file or folder at a network location	No
Ensure	Specifies if a file or folder resource must be present or absent	No
Force	Specifies if certain file operations, such as overwriting file, must be enforced	No
Recurse	Specifies if the subdirectories should be included as a part of configuration	No
SourcePath	Specifies the path of the File or Folder resource to be copied to destination	No
DependsOn	Specifies the resources that must be configured before this resource is configured	No
Type	Specifies if the resource to be configured is a File or Folder. Default value is File	No
MatchSource	Specifies if the File or Folder contents at the destination should always match that at the source	No

If you examine the list of properties in Table 5-4, the only mandatory property is DestinationPath, and the default value of Type property is File. This means that when we specify only the DestinationPath property and apply the configuration, the File resource tries to create a file at the destination path. However, when creating a file, we must specify the contents of the file. This makes the Contents property mandatory, to create an empty file.

```
Configuration FileDemo {
    Node WSR2-1 {
        File FileDemo {
            DestinationPath = "C:\Scripts\Test.txt"
            Contents = ""
        }
    }
}

FileDemo
```

If you note the code above, I have set the Contents property to an empty string. As shown in Figure 5-10, when we apply this configuration, an empty file named test.txt is created on the target node at C:\Scripts.

```
VERBOSE: [WSR2-1]: LCM:  [ Start  Set      ]
VERBOSE: [WSR2-1]: LCM:  [ Start  Resource ]  [[File]FileDemo]
VERBOSE: [WSR2-1]: LCM:  [ Start  Test     ]  [[File]FileDemo]
VERBOSE: [WSR2-1]:                            [[File]FileDemo] The system cannot find the file specified.
VERBOSE: [WSR2-1]:                            [[File]FileDemo] The related file/directory is: C:\Scripts\Test.txt.
VERBOSE: [WSR2-1]: LCM:  [ End    Test     ]  [[File]FileDemo]  in 0.0160 seconds.
VERBOSE: [WSR2-1]: LCM:  [ Start  Set      ]  [[File]FileDemo]
VERBOSE: [WSR2-1]:                            [[File]FileDemo] The system cannot find the file specified.
VERBOSE: [WSR2-1]:                            [[File]FileDemo] The related file/directory is: C:\Scripts\Test.txt.
VERBOSE: [WSR2-1]:                            [[File]FileDemo] C:\Scripts\Test.txt was successfully created.
VERBOSE: [WSR2-1]: LCM:  [ End    Set      ]  [[File]FileDemo]  in 0.0160 seconds.
VERBOSE: [WSR2-1]: LCM:  [ End    Resource ]  [[File]FileDemo]
VERBOSE: [WSR2-1]: LCM:  [ End    Set      ]
VERBOSE: [WSR2-1]: LCM:  [ End    Set      ]     in  0.0470 seconds.
```

Figure 5-10. *Creating an empty file*

What if we want to create an empty folder? Simple: We set the Type property to Directory and remove the Contents property from the configuration script. This is shown in Figure 5-11.

```
Configuration FileDemo {
    Node WSR2-1 {
        File FileDemo {
            DestinationPath = "C:\DSCScripts"
            Type = "Directory"
        }
    }
}

FileDemo
```

```
VERBOSE: [WSR2-1]: LCM:  [ Start  Set      ]
VERBOSE: [WSR2-1]: LCM:  [ Start  Resource ]  [[File]FileDemo]
VERBOSE: [WSR2-1]: LCM:  [ Start  Test     ]  [[File]FileDemo]
VERBOSE: [WSR2-1]:                            [[File]FileDemo] The system cannot find the file specified.
VERBOSE: [WSR2-1]:                            [[File]FileDemo] The related file/directory is: C:\DSCScripts.
VERBOSE: [WSR2-1]: LCM:  [ End    Test     ]  [[File]FileDemo]  in 0.0160 seconds.
VERBOSE: [WSR2-1]: LCM:  [ Start  Set      ]  [[File]FileDemo]
VERBOSE: [WSR2-1]:                            [[File]FileDemo] The system cannot find the file specified.
VERBOSE: [WSR2-1]:                            [[File]FileDemo] The related file/directory is: C:\DSCScripts.
VERBOSE: [WSR2-1]: LCM:  [ End    Set      ]  [[File]FileDemo]  in 0.0000 seconds.
VERBOSE: [WSR2-1]: LCM:  [ End    Resource ]  [[File]FileDemo]
VERBOSE: [WSR2-1]: LCM:  [ End    Set      ]
VERBOSE: [WSR2-1]: LCM:  [ End    Set      ]     in  0.0470 seconds.
```

Figure 5-11. *Creating an empty folder with the* File *resource*

We can use the Recurse property to copy the contents of a source folder to the destination. Using the Recurse property ensures that the files and subdirectories at the source are copied to the destination. Try this yourself!

Yet another property that we have to discuss is the Attributes property. Using this property, we can set the attributes on a file or folder. The following configuration script demonstrates how to use this.

```
Configuration FileDemo {
    Node WSR2-1 {
        File FileDemo {
            DestinationPath = "C:\MyScripts1\Test.txt"
            Attributes = "Hidden"
        }
    }
}
```

FileDemo

The configuration script is simple to follow. It doesn't require a lot of explanation, except for the fact that the Attributes property in WMF 4.0 cannot be used to specify multiples of attributes. For example, Attributes = "Hidden","System" is not valid. Because the DestinationPath property is a key property, it is not possible to have two different File resource configurations for the same file. Therefore, configuring multiple file/folder attributes in the current implementation is not possible.

```
Configuration FileDemo {
    Node WSR2-1 {
        File FileDemo {
            DestinationPath = "C:\MyScripts1\Test.txt"
            Attributes = "Hidden","System"
        }
    }
}
```

FileDemo

One limitation with File resource is that there is no method to remove attributes on a file or folder using the Attributes property.

There are a few other properties in the File resource that we have not seen yet. One of these is the Force property. When we set the Force property to True in a configuration script, if a file or folder that we want to create using DSC already exists at the destination, it will be overwritten. We can use this property, set to True, for deleting nonempty folders from the target systems.

Now that we covered some basic usage of the File resource, let us examine the File resource functionality. There are a few scenarios we must consider when using the File resource. For example, suppose you have copied source folder contents to a destination path on the target system. What will happen if you add, delete, or modify files at the source or at the destination? The answer largely depends on the properties used and the DSC LCM settings on the target system.

DSC LCM on the target systems can be configured to auto-correct any configuration drift. This is done as a part of regular consistency checks performed by DSC. So, when a consistency check gets triggered, the File resource looks at a local cache of the source contents and compares the contents of destination with this cache. When there is a mismatch, and depending on LCM settings and the attributes used in the File resource configuration, the contents at the destination path get overwritten from the cache. After enaction of the initial configuration, and during normal operation, the File resource never uses the source path again. This is done to avoid going over the network to fetch files again and again during a consistency check. However, this can be worked around by setting the MatchSource property to True in the File resource configuration. During a consistency check, when MatchSource is set to True, the local cache is always ignored.

Also, sending the configuration to a target system again ignores the local cache and rebuilds it. This results in the source contents getting copied over to the destination path.

■ **Note** To understand the behavior I just described, it is important that you understand different configuration delivery models and how the configuration mode settings of LCM are used. When there is a configuration drift, if LCM is configured only to monitor and report the drift, the resource configuration will never be fixed automatically. These details are discussed in Chapters 7 and 8. Once you have familiarity with the concepts described there, I recommend that you revisit the File resource configuration and experiment with the different scenarios we discussed.

We have not seen an explanation of how the Credential property can be used; however, you can follow the procedure described in the "Archive Resource" section for working around using a network path for the SourcePath property. This is not a recommended practice. In Chapter 6, we will discuss the right method for using the Credential property for any DSC resource and securing DSC credentials.

Group Resource

The Group resource helps us to manage the local groups. Remember: I'd mentioned local groups and not Active Directory groups. Using this resource, we can create, delete, and modify properties of local group(s). Table 5-5 lists the properties of this DSC resource.

Table 5-5. *Properties of the Group DSC Resource*

Property Name	Description	Required?
GroupName	Specifies the name of the local group to be configured	Yes
Credential	Specifies the credentials required to access the target node	No
Description	Specifies a description for the local group	No
Ensure	Specifies whether the local group has to be present or absent	No
Members	Specifies the usernames to be included in the local group. This property cannot be used with MembersToExclude and MembersToInclude properties.	No
MembersToExclude	Specifies the users to be excluded or removed from group membership	No
MembersToInclude	Specifies the users to be included or added to group membership	No
DependsOn	Specifies the resource(s) that must be configured before configuring the group resource	No

The basic usage of the Group resource is very simple. We just specify the GroupName property with a value to be assigned as the group name, and the local group gets created, if it does not exist already. We can specify Ensure = "Absent" to remove an existing group.

```
Configuration GroupDemo {
    Node Home-Desk {
        Group GroupDemo {
            GroupName = "Group1"
        }
    }
}
```

GroupDemo

As shown in Figure 5-12, the LCM finds that there is no group that exists with the name Group1 and then creates it.

```
VERBOSE: [HOME-DESK]: LCM:  [ Start  Set       ]
VERBOSE: [HOME-DESK]: LCM:  [ Start  Resource ]  [[Group]GroupDemo]
VERBOSE: [HOME-DESK]: LCM:  [ Start  Test      ]  [[Group]GroupDemo]
VERBOSE: [HOME-DESK]:                              [[Group]GroupDemo] A group with the name Group1 does not exist.
VERBOSE: [HOME-DESK]: LCM:  [ End    Test      ]  [[Group]GroupDemo]  in 3.2633 seconds.
VERBOSE: [HOME-DESK]: LCM:  [ Start  Set       ]  [[Group]GroupDemo]
VERBOSE: [HOME-DESK]:                              [[Group]GroupDemo] Performing the operation "Add" on target "Group: Group1".
VERBOSE: [HOME-DESK]:                              [[Group]GroupDemo] Group Group1 exists on this node with the desired propert
ies. No action required.
VERBOSE: [HOME-DESK]: LCM:  [ End    Set       ]  [[Group]GroupDemo]  in 2.9341 seconds.
VERBOSE: [HOME-DESK]: LCM:  [ End    Resource ]  [[Group]GroupDemo]
VERBOSE: [HOME-DESK]: LCM:  [ End    Set       ]     in  6.9684 seconds.
```

Figure 5-12. *Group creation with DSC*

Using the other properties, such as Members, MembersToInclude, and MembersToExclude, we can manage the group membership as well. Let us a see a few examples.

```
Configuration GroupDemo {
    Node Home-Desk {
        Group GroupDemo {
            GroupName = "Group1"
            Members = "User1","User2"
        }
    }
}
```

GroupDemo

To add users to a group as members, we can simply specify a list of users as a value of the Members property. The group membership changes are shown in Figure 5-13. Note, however, that when using the Members property, the group membership gets overwritten as a result of configuration change. For example, if User1 and User2 are already members of Group1, specifying Members = "User3" in a subsequent configuration change will remove User1 and User2, while adding User3. This can have unintended results. This is where the MembersToInclude and MembersToExclude properties are useful.

```
VERBOSE: [HOME-DESK]: LCM:  [ Start  Set       ]
VERBOSE: [HOME-DESK]: LCM:  [ Start  Resource ]   [[Group]GroupDemo]
VERBOSE: [HOME-DESK]: LCM:  [ Start  Test     ]   [[Group]GroupDemo]
VERBOSE: [HOME-DESK]:                              [[Group]GroupDemo] A group with the name Group1 exists.
VERBOSE: [HOME-DESK]:                              [[Group]GroupDemo] Property Members. The number of provided unique group mem
bers 2 is different from the number of actual group members 0.
VERBOSE: [HOME-DESK]: LCM:  [ End    Test     ]   [[Group]GroupDemo]  in 8.9845 seconds.
VERBOSE: [HOME-DESK]: LCM:  [ Start  Set      ]   [[Group]GroupDemo]
VERBOSE: [HOME-DESK]:                              [[Group]GroupDemo] Performing the operation "Set" on target "Group: Group1".
VERBOSE: [HOME-DESK]:                              [[Group]GroupDemo] Group Group1 properties updated successfully.
VERBOSE: [HOME-DESK]: LCM:  [ End    Set      ]   [[Group]GroupDemo]  in 8.3249 seconds.
VERBOSE: [HOME-DESK]: LCM:  [ End    Resource ]   [[Group]GroupDemo]
VERBOSE: [HOME-DESK]: LCM:  [ End    Set      ]    in  18.2262 seconds.
```

Figure 5-13. *Adding group members using DSC*

Let us look at an example to understand this. In the following example, we will remove User1 from Group1 membership and add User3 as a member.

```
Configuration GroupDemo {
    Node Home-Desk {
        Group GroupDemo {
            GroupName = "Group1"
            MembersToInclude = "User3"
            MembersToExclude = "User1"
        }
    }
}

GroupDemo
```

In the preceding example, we are not using the Members property. In fact, the Members property is mutually exclusive to the MembersToInclude and MembersToExclude properties. The configuration script in the example specifies that we want to add User3 to the group while removing User1. If you do not want to overwrite the existing group membership configuration, ensure that you use the MembersToInclude and MembersToExclude properties, instead of the Members property.

Log Resource

The Log DSC resource is used to write event logs to the DSC analytic event channel. Remember that this resource is not for any event logs but specific to DSC events. There are only two properties that are available with the Log resource. These are shown in Table 5-6.

Table 5-6. *Properties of the Log DSC Resource*

Property Name	Description	Required?
Message	Specifies the message that should appear in the DSC analytic log	Yes
DependsOn	Specifies the resource(s) that must be configured before configuring the group resource	No

The Log resource is not something we use like other resources. It does not perform any configuration change, per se. It simply logs the message specified as a value to the Message property to the DSC Analytic event log.

■ **Note**   The DSC Analytic log, located at "Microsoft-Windows-Desired State Configuration/Analytic" under "Application and Services Logs," is not enabled by default. To enable it, follow the procedure outlined at
http://technet.microsoft.com/en-us/library/cc749492.aspx.

Once you have the Analytic event log enabled, you can use the following code snippet to write an event message to the DSC logs.

```
Configuration LogDemo {
    Node WSR2-1 {
        Log LogDemo {
            Message = "This is a test message from DSC Demo"
        }
    }
}
```

LogDemo

After you apply this configuration by using the Start-DscConfiguration cmdlet, to verify if an event log message is written or not, you can use the Get-WinEvent cmdlet or the Event Viewer.

```
Get-WinEvent -FilterHashtable @{LogName='Microsoft-Windows-Dsc/Analytic'; Id=4098} -Oldest
```

The same messages can be seen in the Event Viewer by navigating to Application and Services Logs ➤ Microsoft ➤ Desired State Configuration ➤ Analytic logs container. This is shown in Figure 5-14.

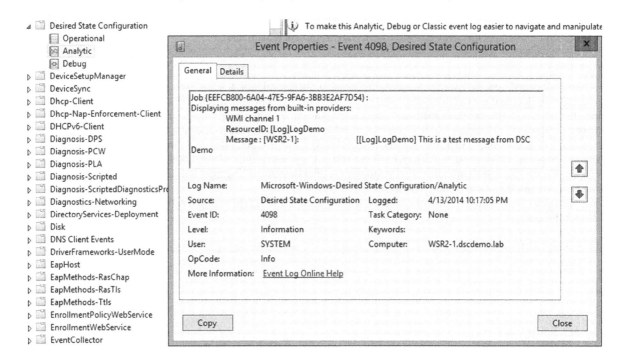

Figure 5-14. *DSC Log resource messages in the event log*

The Log resource is certainly not something we would use often. We will revisit the DSC logging methods when we discuss monitoring and reporting the DSC state.

Package Resource

The Package resource is used to install and uninstall setup.exe and Windows Installer packages on target nodes. We cannot use it for installing Windows Update packages. Table 5-7 provides a list of properties associated with this resource and a brief description of each property.

Table 5-7. *Properties Associated with the Package DSC Resource*

Property Name	Description	Required?
Name	Specifies the name of the package that has to configured	Yes
ProductId	Specifies a product ID that uniquely identifies the product being configured	Yes
Arguments	Specifies a list of arguments required to configure the product	No
Credential	Specifies the credentials required to access the network share containing package installer	No
DependsOn	Specifies the resource(s) that must be configured before configuring the group resource	No
Ensure	Specifies whether the package needs to be present or absent	No
LogPath	Specifies the full path of a log file to which install or uninstall information must be written to	No
Path	Specifies the full path to the package installer	Yes
ReturnCode	Specifies the expected return code from a successful install	No

To understand how the Package resource can be used, we should look at a few examples. To start with, let us try to install a product that uses Windows Installer or MSI technology. I chose to install the 7-Zip package on my target node for this demo. You can download the 7-Zip MSI package from 7-zip.org. Once you have the package, copy it to the remote node at C:\Package folder. If you look at Table 5-7, the ProductId property is a required property. This is, in reality, a Globally Unique Identifier (GUID) associated with the product. Using any random GUID will result in a failure. The product code must be derived from the MSI package and requires Win32 API access. So, to make things easy, I will use a PowerShell module called Windows Installer PowerShell module. This has been developed by Heath Stewart at Microsoft and can be downloaded at psmsi.codeplex.com.

Once you have the module downloaded and installed, the Get-MSITable cmdlet can be used to retrieve the ProductID value.

```
Get-MSITable -Path .\7z920-x64.msi -Table Property | Where-Object { $_.Property -eq " ProductCode" }
```

We now have the product code for the 7-Zip MSI package. So, the configuration script for deploying this package on a target node can be written.

```
Configuration PackageDemo {
    Node WSR2-1 {
        Package PackageDemo {
            Name = "7-Zip"
            Path = "C:\Package\7z920-x64.msi"
            ProductId = "23170F69-40C1-2702-0920-000001000000"
        }
    }
}

PackageDemo
```

The value of the Name property can be anything and does not have to match the package name while installing a package. The Path property is required and points to the full path of the MSI package. We have already discussed the ProductId property and understand its significance. When we apply this configuration, the MSI package gets installed on the target node, and the result of that configuration change is shown in Figure 5-15.

```
VERBOSE: [WSR2-1]: LCM:   [ Start   Set       ]
VERBOSE: [WSR2-1]: LCM:   [ Start   Resource ]   [[Package]PackageDemo]
VERBOSE: [WSR2-1]: LCM:   [ Start   Test     ]   [[Package]PackageDemo]
VERBOSE: [WSR2-1]:                                [[Package]PackageDemo] The package Anything is not installed
VERBOSE: [WSR2-1]: LCM:   [ End     Test     ]   [[Package]PackageDemo]  in 0.0320 seconds.
VERBOSE: [WSR2-1]: LCM:   [ Start   Set       ]  [[Package]PackageDemo]
VERBOSE: [WSR2-1]:                                [[Package]PackageDemo] The package Anything is not installed
VERBOSE: [WSR2-1]:                                [[Package]PackageDemo] Package configuration starting
VERBOSE: [WSR2-1]:                                [[Package]PackageDemo] Package has been installed
VERBOSE: [WSR2-1]:                                [[Package]PackageDemo] Package configuration finished
VERBOSE: [WSR2-1]: LCM:   [ End     Set       ]  [[Package]PackageDemo]  in 0.8280 seconds.
VERBOSE: [WSR2-1]: LCM:   [ End     Resource ]   [[Package]PackageDemo]
VERBOSE: [WSR2-1]: LCM:   [ End     Set       ]
VERBOSE: [WSR2-1]: LCM:   [ End     Set       ]     in  0.8910 seconds.
VERBOSE: Operation 'Invoke CimMethod' complete.
VERBOSE: Time taken for configuration job to complete is 0.946 seconds
```

Figure 5-15. *Package installation using DSC*

What happens when we try to install an MSI package is simple. The Package resource verifies whether the package is locally available on the target node. If not, and the package is at a UNC path, a PS drive is mapped, using the credentials provided by the Credential property. Once this process is complete, the Package resource sets up the command line for installing the MSI package. This includes the full path to MSIEXEC.exe and the MSI package name with /i and /quiet command-line arguments.

You can also use an HTTP-based URL as the path to the MSI package. For example, it is completely valid to specify http://downloads.sourceforge.net/sevenzip/7z920-x64.msi as the value of Path property. In this case, the package resource will attempt to download a package to the target node, before starting the installation. If you have a target node connected to the Internet, try the preceding example with the URL just mentioned.

The next example in our discussion is about uninstalling the package (see Figure 5-16). The configuration script will be similar to that we have seen in the earlier example, except that the Ensure property will be used to specify that the package must be uninstalled.

```
Configuration PackageDemo {
    Node WSR2-1 {
        Package PackageDemo {
            Name = "Test"
            ProductId = "23170F69-40C1-2702-0920-000001000000"
            Path = "C:\Package\7z920-x64.msi"
            Ensure = "Absent"
        }
    }
}

PackageDemo
```

```
VERBOSE: [WSR2-1]: LCM:    [ Start  Set      ]
VERBOSE: [WSR2-1]: LCM:    [ Start  Resource ]  [[Package]PackageDemo]
VERBOSE: [WSR2-1]: LCM:    [ Start  Test  |  ]  [[Package]PackageDemo]
VERBOSE: [WSR2-1]:                             [[Package]PackageDemo] The package 7-Zip 9.20 (x64 edition) is already installed
VERBOSE: [WSR2-1]: LCM:    [ End    Test     ]  [[Package]PackageDemo]  in 0.0630 seconds.
VERBOSE: [WSR2-1]: LCM:    [ Start  Set      ]  [[Package]PackageDemo]
VERBOSE: [WSR2-1]:                             [[Package]PackageDemo] The package 7-Zip 9.20 (x64 edition) is already installed
VERBOSE: [WSR2-1]:                             [[Package]PackageDemo] Package configuration starting
VERBOSE: [WSR2-1]:                             [[Package]PackageDemo] Package has been uninstalled
VERBOSE: [WSR2-1]:                             [[Package]PackageDemo] Package configuration finished
VERBOSE: [WSR2-1]: LCM:    [ End    Set      ]  [[Package]PackageDemo]  in 0.8210 seconds.
VERBOSE: [WSR2-1]: LCM:    [ End    Resource ]  [[Package]PackageDemo]
VERBOSE: [WSR2-1]: LCM:    [ End    Set      ]
VERBOSE: [WSR2-1]: LCM:    [ End    Set      ]     in  0.8990 seconds.
```

Figure 5-16. *Uninstalling a package using DSC*

There is a gotcha here. When uninstalling a package, the ProductId need not be specified. The property should still be present in the configuration script, but it can be an empty string value. In this case, you have to specify the value of the Name property as it appears in Programs and Features in the control panel. For example, the following configuration, when applied, will result in a message that there is no package with the name "Test" installed on the target node (see Figure 5-17).

```
Configuration PackageDemo {
    Node WSR2-1 {
        Package PackageDemo {
            Name = "Test"
            ProductId = ""
            Path = "C:\Package\7z920-x64.msi"
            Ensure = "Absent"
        }
    }
}
PackageDemo
```

```
VERBOSE: [WSR2-1]: LCM:  [ Start   Set      ]
VERBOSE: [WSR2-1]: LCM:  [ Start   Resource ] [[Package]PackageDemo]
VERBOSE: [WSR2-1]: LCM:  [ Start   Test     ] [[Package]PackageDemo]
VERBOSE: [WSR2-1]:                            [[Package]PackageDemo] The package Test is not installed
VERBOSE: [WSR2-1]:                            [[Package]PackageDemo]  in 0.2500 seconds.
VERBOSE: [WSR2-1]: LCM:  [ End     Test     ] [[Package]PackageDemo]
VERBOSE: [WSR2-1]: LCM:  [ Skip    Set      ] [[Package]PackageDemo]
VERBOSE: [WSR2-1]: LCM:  [ End     Resource ] [[Package]PackageDemo]
VERBOSE: [WSR2-1]: LCM:  [ End     Set      ]
VERBOSE: [WSR2-1]: LCM:  [ End     Set      ]       in  0.7030 seconds.
```

Figure 5-17. *Configuration failure with an invalid package name*

To fix this, we have to use the same name for the package as in Programs and Feature under Control Panel. For the 7-Zip package we installed, the name of the package is 7-Zip 9.20 (x64 Edition).

■ **Note**   Be aware that the full name of this package might differ, depending on the version you are downloading.

In the preceding configuration script, we can replace the value of the Name property with the correct name for the package and apply the configuration. Try this yourself.

We have only talked about installing MSI packages using the Package resource. However, as per the resource documentation and the way it is implemented, it is possible to install .exe-based setup packages too. However, the Package resource expects a registry key with the specified Product ID to be available under the Uninstall key at HKEY_LOCAL_MACHINE\SOFTWARE\MICROSOFT\WINDOWS\Current Version. Many of the setup.exe-based installers do not create this key with the GUID. Therefore, the Package DSC resource may complete such package installs but will complete the configuration change with an error stating that the product ID specified did not match. In this context, it makes more sense to use the Process resource to install such setup.exe packages, rather than the Package resource. Given this instruction from Microsoft, we won't be discussing the install or uninstall of setup.exe packages using the Package resource.

WindowsProcess Resource

The WindowsProcess resource in DSC is used to manage running processes on a target node. This includes starting and stopping processes. Table 5-8 lists the properties available as a part of this resource.

Table 5-8. *Properties of the WindowsProcess DSC Resource*

Property Name	Description	Required?
Path	Specifies the path to the process that needs to be configured	Yes
Arguments	Specifies any optional arguments to the process	Yes
Credential	Specifies the credentials required to manage the process on the target node	No
Ensure	Specifies whether you want to the process to be present or absent	No
StandardErrorPath	Specifies the file location to which the standard error stream must be redirected to	No
StandardInputPath	Specifies the file location from which the standard input should be gathered	No
StandardOutputPath	Specifies the file location to which the standard output stream must be redirected	No
DependsOn	Specifies the resource(s) that must be configured before configuring this resource	No

Let us consider a few examples, to understand this DSC resource. To begin, let us see how we can start a process.

```
Configuration ProcessDemo {
    Node WSR2-1 {
        WindowsProcess ProcessDemo {
            Path = "Notepad.exe"
            Arguments = ""
        }
    }
}
```

ProcessDemo

In the preceding example, we have not specified the complete path to the process we want to start. This is acceptable, because notepad.exe is available at the system path and can be found easily. However, if the process you have to start is not available at the system path or not a part of the location specified in $env:Path, you must specify the full path to the executable. The preceding example is very trivial. Let us see something more useful. We observed, in an earlier section, that the Process resource can be used to perform installs of setup.exe-based packages. For most setup.exe types of installer packages, command-line arguments are provided for the silent installs of products. We can use the Process resource to automate such installs, by providing the package path as the value to Path property and command-line arguments as values to the Arguments property. Here is an example of that in action:

```
Configuration ProcessDemo {
    Node WSR2-1 {
        WindowsProcess ProcessDemo {
            Path = "C:\Package\winrar-x64-51b2.exe"
            Arguments = "/S"
        }
    }
}
```

ProcessDemo

In the preceding example, we are installing a WinRAR package that is available on the target node at the C:\Packages folder. The WinRAR installer supports the /S command-line parameter to install the package in a silent and automated manner. So, the preceding configuration script, when applied, helps us install the WinRAR package on the target node.

Let us move on to discuss how other properties can be used. As described in Table 5-8, the StandardOutputPath property can be used to redirect all the standard output from a process to a file we specify. To explain this, I will use ping.exe and a network computer name as an argument. We will use the StandardOutputPath to redirect the output from this command to a text file on the remote node.

```
Configuration ProcessDemo {
    Node WSR2-1 {
        WindowsProcess ProcessDemo {
            Path = "Ping.exe"
            Arguments = "Demo-Ad"
            StandardOutputPath = "C:\Scripts\ping.txt"
        }
    }
}
```

ProcessDemo

The parent path specified as a part of the value to the StandardOutputPath property must exist. For example, in our example, a C:\Scripts folder must exist. The WindowsProcess DSC resource will create the text file with the name we specify; however, we won't see any errors during the configuration change, even when the path specified for the StandardOutputPath, or any such similar property, is not valid. This is shown in Figure 5-18. On my target system, the file specified as StandardOutputPath does not exist and, as discussed, it won't result in an error.

```
VERBOSE: [WSR2-1]: LCM:  [ Start  Set       ]
VERBOSE: [WSR2-1]: LCM:  [ Start  Resource ]  [[WindowsProcess]ProcessDemo]
VERBOSE: [WSR2-1]: LCM:  [ Start  Test     ]  [[WindowsProcess]ProcessDemo]
VERBOSE: [WSR2-1]: LCM:  [ End    Test     ]  [[WindowsProcess]ProcessDemo]  in 0.1560 seconds.
VERBOSE: [WSR2-1]: LCM:  [ Start  Set      ]  [[WindowsProcess]ProcessDemo]
VERBOSE: [WSR2-1]:                             [[WindowsProcess]ProcessDemo] Process matching path 'C:\Windows
\system32\Ping.exe' started
VERBOSE: [WSR2-1]: LCM:  [ End    Set      ]  [[WindowsProcess]ProcessDemo]  in 0.4850 seconds.
VERBOSE: [WSR2-1]: LCM:  [ End    Resource ]  [[WindowsProcess]ProcessDemo]
VERBOSE: [WSR2-1]: LCM:  [ End    Set      ]
VERBOSE: [WSR2-1]: LCM:  [ End    Set      ]      in  0.7190 seconds.
```

Figure 5-18. *Starting a process with DSC WindowsProcess resource*

To stop or terminate a process, we simply have to set Ensure="Absent". If there are multiple processes with the same path, the arguments that are used to start the process identify the right process to terminate.

```
Configuration ProcessDemo {
    Node WSR2-1 {
        WindowsProcess ProcessDemo {
            Path = "Notepad.exe"
            Arguments = "C:\Scripts\Archive.ps1"
            Ensure = "Absent"
        }
    }
}
```

ProcessDemo

In the preceding example, I am trying to terminate the Notepad process that has one of the scripts open. When I apply this configuration, the WindowsProcess resource tries to find the process that matches both the path and arguments values. If a match is found, the matching process will be terminated.

The result of the preceding configuration script is shown in Figure 5-19. If the value to the Arguments property is an empty string, a process that is started with no arguments and matching process path will be terminated. In this example, LCM finds no matching process, and you can see that any resource configuration on the target system gets skipped.

```
VERBOSE: [WSR2-1]: LCM:  [ Start  Set      ]
VERBOSE: [WSR2-1]: LCM:  [ Start  Resource ]  [[WindowsProcess]ProcessDemo]
VERBOSE: [WSR2-1]: LCM:  [ Start  Test     ]  [[WindowsProcess]ProcessDemo]
VERBOSE: [WSR2-1]: LCM:  [ End    Test     ]  [[WindowsProcess]ProcessDemo]  in 0.0000 seconds.
VERBOSE: [WSR2-1]: LCM:  [ Skip   Set      ]  [[WindowsProcess]ProcessDemo]
VERBOSE: [WSR2-1]: LCM:  [ End    Resource ]  [[WindowsProcess]ProcessDemo]
VERBOSE: [WSR2-1]: LCM:  [ End    Set      ]
VERBOSE: [WSR2-1]: LCM:  [ End    Set      ]      in  0.0460 seconds.
```

Figure 5-19. *Terminating the process started with specific arguments*

Registry Resource

Using the `Registry` resource, we can manage the registry keys and values on the target node. The properties of the resource are shown in Table 5-9.

Table 5-9. *Properties of the Registry DSC Resource*

Property Name	Description	Required?
Key	Specifies the path of the registry key that needs to be configured	Yes
ValueName	Specifies the name of the registry value that is being configured	Yes
DependsOn	Specifies the resource(s) that must be configured before configuring this resource	No
Ensure	Specifies whether you want the specified registry configuration to be present or absent	No
Force	Specifies whether you want to force the configuration change to overwrite the existing configuration	No
Hex	Specifies if the ValueData is expressed in hexadecimal format. If specified, the DWORD/QWORD value data will be in hex format.	No
ValueData	Specifies the data for the registry value specified using the ValueName property	No
ValueType	Specifies the type of the registry value. The valid values are String, Multistring, ExpandString, Binary, Dword, and Qword.	No

Most of the properties listed in Table 5-9 are self-explanatory. Let us examine a few examples, to learn how to use the ValueType and Hex properties.

```
Configuration RegistryDemo {
    Node WSR2-1 {
        Registry RegistryDemo {
            Key = "HKEY_LOCAL_MACHINE\SOFTWARE\Demo"
            ValueName = "DemoValue"
            ValueData = "This is a demo value"
            ValueType = "String"
        }
    }
}
```

RegistryDemo

The preceding example is a simple one. We just want to create a new registry key called Demo under HKEY_LOCAL_MACHINE\SOFTWARE and a new string value called DemoValue with data "This is a demo value" assigned to it. The result is straightforward and shown in Figure 5-20.

```
VERBOSE: [WSR2-1]: LCM:  [ Start  Set      ]
VERBOSE: [WSR2-1]: LCM:  [ Start  Resource ]  [[Registry]RegistryDemo]
VERBOSE: [WSR2-1]: LCM:  [ Start  Test     ]  [[Registry]RegistryDemo]
VERBOSE: [WSR2-1]:                            [[Registry]RegistryDemo] Registry key 'HKLM:\software\demo' does not exist
VERBOSE: [WSR2-1]: LCM:  [ End    Test     ]  [[Registry]RegistryDemo]  in 0.4840 seconds.
VERBOSE: [WSR2-1]: LCM:  [ Start  Set      ]  [[Registry]RegistryDemo]
VERBOSE: [WSR2-1]: LCM:  [ End    Set      ]  [[Registry]RegistryDemo]  in 0.3280 seconds.
VERBOSE: [WSR2-1]: LCM:  [ End    Resource ]  [[Registry]RegistryDemo]
VERBOSE: [WSR2-1]: LCM:  [ End    Set      ]
VERBOSE: [WSR2-1]: LCM:  [ End    Set      ]     in  1.3120 seconds.
```

Figure 5-20. *Registry key and value creation using DSC* `Registry` *resource*

In the preceding example, we looked at how we can create a registry value of type `REG_SZ` or `String`. In the next example, we will see how we can create a `DWORD` value type and assign a hexadecimal value to it. When creating `DWORD` or `QWORD` type values, it is a requirement to specify the `Hex` property and assign a value `$true` to it. This is what we will observe in the following example.

```
Configuration RegistryDemo {
    Node WSR2-1 {
        Registry RegistryDemo {
            Key = "HKEY_LOCAL_MACHINE\SOFTWARE\Demo"
            ValueName = "IsDemo"
            ValueData = "0x01"
            ValueType = "Dword"
            Hex = $true
        }
    }
}

RegistryDemo
```

This concludes our discussion on the `Registry` resource. Using the knowledge you've gained so far in using the DSC resources, try to determine the need for setting the `Force` property to `$true` and create a configuration script that demonstrates this behavior.

Script Resource

The `Script` resource is a special DSC resource. It does not represent any specific resource that can be configured, but this resource provides a way to execute script blocks on the target node(s). This is equivalent to executing any random or ad hoc code on a target node. While this may not sound very interesting to some of you, the `Script` resource actually has a couple of very good use cases. First of all, the way the `Script` resource works is how the DSC resources work internally. The properties of the `Script` resource, shown in Table 5-10, can be used to visualize the working internals of a DSC resource. So, it is important that we look at a few examples of this, so that it becomes familiar by the time we start discussing how to create custom DSC resources. The second advantage of the `Script` resource is that it provides a quick method to validate the code you want to create for a custom resource.

Table 5-10. *Properties of the Script DSC Resource*

Property Name	Description	Required?
GetScript	Specifies the script block that returns a hash table of the configuration	Yes
TestScript	Specifies the script block that verifies the state of configuration on the target system. This function should return only a Boolean value based on the tests.	Yes
SetScript	Specifies the script block that can be used to configure a resource	Yes
Credential	Specifies the credentials to use for executing the script resource	No
DependsOn	Specifies the resource(s) that must be configured before configuring this resource	No

As shown in Table 5-10, the three properties, GetScript, TestScript, and SetScript are mandatory. The Script resource works by first executing the script block supplied as an argument to the TestScript property. This script block must return a Boolean value. Let us see an example of this and understand what happens when we the script block doesn't result in or return a Boolean value.

```
Configuration ScriptDemo {
    Node WSR2-1 {
        Script ScriptDemo {
            GetScript = {
                #Ignore this for now
            }

            SetScript = {
                #Ignore this for now
            }

            TestScript = {
                "This is what we return"
            }
        }
    }
}

ScriptDemo
```

In the preceding example, we are not returning any Boolean value as a part of the TestScript execution. Instead, we are simply returning a string. When we apply this configuration, we see an error message indicating what is expected from the TestScript execution. This is shown in Figure 5-21.

```
VERBOSE: [WSR2-1]: LCM:  [ Start  Set      ]
VERBOSE: [WSR2-1]: LCM:  [ Start  Resource ]  [[Script]ScriptDemo]
VERBOSE: [WSR2-1]: LCM:  [ Start  Test     ]  [[Script]ScriptDemo]
VERBOSE: [WSR2-1]: LCM:  [ End    Test     ]  [[Script]ScriptDemo]  in 0.2810 seconds.
PowerShell provider MSFT_ScriptResource  failed to execute Test-TargetResource functionality with error
message: Failure to get a valid result from the execution of TestScript. The Test script should return True
or False.
    + CategoryInfo          : InvalidOperation: (:) [], CimException
    + FullyQualifiedErrorId : ProviderOperationExecutionFailure
    + PSComputerName        : WSR2-1

VERBOSE: [WSR2-1]: LCM:  [ End    Set      ]
The SendConfigurationApply function did not succeed.
    + CategoryInfo          : NotSpecified: (root/Microsoft/...gurationManager:String) [], CimException
    + FullyQualifiedErrorId : MI RESULT 1
    + PSComputerName        : WSR2-1
```

Figure 5-21. *Error when the* TestScript *does not return a Boolean value*

So, the script block associated with the TestScript property must return a Boolean value. If the TestScript returns $false, the script block assigned to the SetScript property will be executed. So, to understand this, think of TestScript as a method of verifying whether or not an entity on the target node is configured the way we want. If it is not, the TestScript should return $false, and the SetScript should execute to configure the entity as desired. With this knowledge, let us look at another example that explains this behavior.

```
Configuration ScriptDemo {
    Node WSR2-1 {
        Script ScriptDemo {
            GetScript = {
                #Ignore this for now
            }

            SetScript = {
                Set-service -Name AudioSrv -Status Running
            }

            TestScript = {
                (Get-Service -Name Audiosrv).Status -eq 'Running'                }
        }
    }
}

ScriptDemo
```

As you see in the example here, we are using the TestScript property to verify whether or not AudioSrv service is running. If it is not running, we are returning $false. The SetScript then gets executed and starts the AudioSrv service. If the service is already in the running status, you can see that the resource skips the SetScript script block (see Figure 5-22).

```
VERBOSE: [WSR2-1]: LCM:  [ Start  Set       ]
VERBOSE: [WSR2-1]: LCM:  [ Start  Resource  ]  [[Script]ScriptDemo]
VERBOSE: [WSR2-1]: LCM:  [ Start  Test      ]  [[Script]ScriptDemo]
VERBOSE: [WSR2-1]: LCM:  [ End    Test      ]  [[Script]ScriptDemo]  in 0.2500 seconds.
VERBOSE: [WSR2-1]: LCM:  [ Skip   Set       ]  [[Script]ScriptDemo]
VERBOSE: [WSR2-1]: LCM:  [ End    Resource  ]  [[Script]ScriptDemo]
VERBOSE: [WSR2-1]: LCM:  [ End    Set       ]
VERBOSE: [WSR2-1]: LCM:  [ End    Set       ]     in  0.7030 seconds.
```

Figure 5-22. *TestScript and SetScript usage in the Script resource*

Now, the other mandatory property we did not yet see is the GetScript property. As you can infer from the preceding examples, the script block associated with this property has no direct impact on the configuration change. It is used only when we run the Get-DscConfiguration cmdlet. The script block for this property must always return a hash table. Let's suppose we don't return a hash table from GetScript. After we reenact this configuration using the Start-DscConfiguration cmdlet, what will the Get-DscConfiguration cmdlet result in? An error, of course! See Figure 5-23.

```
Configuration ScriptDemo {
    Node WSR2-1 {
        Script ScriptDemo {
            GetScript = {
                "Return a string for now"
            }

            SetScript = {
                Set-service -Name AudioSrv -Status Running
            }

            TestScript = {
(Get-Service -Name Audiosrv).Status -eq 'Running'            }
        }
    }
}

ScriptDemo

$CimSession = New-CimSession -ComputerName WSR2-1
Get-DscConfiguration -CimSession $CimSession


Get-DscConfiguration : PowerShell provider MSFT_ScriptResource  failed to execute Get-TargetResource
functionality with error message: Failure to get the results from the script in a hash table format.
At line:2 char:1
+ Get-DscConfiguration -CimSession $CimSession
+ ~~~~~~~~~~~~~~~~~~~~~~~~~~~~~~~~~~~~~~~~~~~~~~
    + CategoryInfo          : InvalidOperation: (MSFT_DSCLocalConfigurationManager:root/Microsoft/...gurati
   onManager) [Get-DscConfiguration], CimException
    + FullyQualifiedErrorId : ProviderOperationExecutionFailure,Get-DscConfiguration
    + PSComputerName        : WSR2-1
```

Figure 5-23. *Error from Get-DscConfiguration when the GetScript property does not return a hash table*

The hash table that the GetScript script block returns should have the same properties defined in the Script resource schema definition. We can get this information by looking at the Script resource schema file MSFT_ScriptResource.schema.mof located at $pshome\Modules\PSDesiredStateConfiguration\DSCResources\MSFT_ScriptResource\. This is shown in Figure 5-24.

```
[ClassVersion("1.0.0"),FriendlyName("Script")]
class MSFT_ScriptResource : OMI_BaseResource
{
  [Key] string GetScript;
  [Key] string SetScript;
  [Key] string TestScript;
  [write,EmbeddedInstance("MSFT_Credential")] string Credential;
  [Read] string Result;
};
```

Figure 5-24. *The MOF schema contents for the Script resource*

As we see in the Script resource MOF schema, there are five properties, but the Credential property cannot be returned as a part of the hash table. So, the hash table that we construct as a part of GetScript should include the properties GetScript, SetScript, TestScript, and Result. The Result property should contain the result from the configuration change done by SetScript. Going back to our example, Result should contain the status of the AudioSrv service on the target node. For the rest of the properties, such as GetScript, SetScript, and TestScript, we simply assign the same script block that was in the configuration script. So, the final code for our Script resource example would look like the following:

```
Configuration ScriptDemo {
    Node WSR2-1 {
        Script ScriptDemo {
            GetScript = {
                @{
                    GetScript = $GetScript
                    SetScript = $SetScript
                    TestScript = $TestScript
                    Result = (Get-Service -Name Audiosrv).Status
                }
            }

            SetScript = {
                Set-service -Name AudioSrv -Status Running
            }

            TestScript = {
                (Get-Service -Name Audiosrv).Status -eq 'Running'            }
        }
    }
}

ScriptDemo
```

In this example, we assign $GetScript, $SetScript, and $TestScript variables to the hash table values GetScript, SetScript, and TestScript. For the Result property, we determine the status of the AudioSrv service. So, after we reapply this configuration, we use the Start-DscConfiguration cmdlet and then the Get-DscConfiguration to verify what the result of the configuration change or the current state of the configuration we pushed was. The result from the Get-DscConfiguration is shown in Figure 5-25.

```
PS C:\> $CimSession = New-CimSession -ComputerName WSR2-1
Get-DscConfiguration -CimSession $CimSession


Credential     :
GetScript      :
                         @{
                             GetScript = $GetScript
                             SetScript = $SetScript
                             TestScript = $TestScript
                             Result = (Get-Service -Name Audiosrv).Status
                         }

Result         : Running
SetScript      :
                         Set-service -Name AudioSrv -Status Running

TestScript     :
                         if ((Get-Service -Name Audiosrv).Status -eq "Running") {
                             $true
                         } else {
                             $false
                         }

PSComputerName : WSR2-1
```

Figure 5-25. *Output from the Get-DscConfiguration*

While this does not make a lot of sense in a real-world scenario, I like the fact that the Script resource helps us understand how the DSC resources actually work. We will see more about writing custom DSC resources in Chapter 9. I am sure that the knowledge you gained here will be helpful in understanding custom resource development.

Before we conclude this discussion of the Script resource, it is important to note that the values provided as arguments to the GetScript, SetScript, and TestScript properties get converted to a string representation when the configuration MOF is generated. Variable expansion is not done in these script blocks. So, if you use any variable names inside the script blocks used as the arguments to any of the Script resource properties, they won't be replaced by the variable values. You can observe this by editing the resulting configuration MOF file. If you need to expand variable values in these script blocks, you can use Using scope modifier. Try this yourself.

Service Resource

In the previous section, we looked at a script resource in which we retrieved the status of the AudioSrv service. We can, of course, add more properties and make the script resource complete enough to manage services on the remote nodes. However, we need not subject ourselves to that hardship. Microsoft shipped a DSC resource to manage services on the remote node. It is called—no surprises—the Service resource. Table 5-11 shows a complete list of this resource's properties.

Table 5-11. *Properties of the Service DSC Resource*

Property Name	Description	Required?
Name	Specifies the name of the service you need to configure	Yes
BuiltInAccount	Specifies the sign-in account to use for the service. The valid values are LocalService, LocalSystem, and NetworkService.	No
Credential	Specifies the credentials for running the service. This cannot be used with the BuiltInAccount property.	No
StartupType	Specifies the startup type for the service being configured	No
State	Specifies the state in which the service being configured should be set	No
DependsOn	Specifies the resource(s) that should be configured before configuring this service	No

The Service resource is a simple one. If you note the contents in Table 5-11, you will see that there is no Ensure property. This means we can't create or delete services using the DSC resource. We can only manage the existing services and configure their StartupType, State, and service sign-in account or credentials. Let us see some examples.

```
Configuration ServiceDemo {
    Node WSR2-1 {
        Service ServiceDemo {
            Name = "AudioSrv"
            State = "Running"
        }
    }
}

ServiceDemo
```

What we are trying to achieve in the preceding example is similar to what we did with the Script resource. We are setting the state of the service to running (see Figure 5-26).

```
VERBOSE: [WSR2-1]: LCM:  [ Start  Set      ]
VERBOSE: [WSR2-1]: LCM:  [ Start  Resource ]  [[Service]ServiceDemo]
VERBOSE: [WSR2-1]: LCM:  [ Start  Test     ]  [[Service]ServiceDemo]
VERBOSE: [WSR2-1]: LCM:  [ End    Test     ]  [[Service]ServiceDemo]  in 0.0000 seconds.
VERBOSE: [WSR2-1]: LCM:  [ Start  Set      ]  [[Service]ServiceDemo]
VERBOSE: [WSR2-1]:                             [[Service]ServiceDemo] Service 'AudioSrv' started
VERBOSE: [WSR2-1]: LCM:  [ End    Set      ]  [[Service]ServiceDemo]  in 0.0930 seconds.
VERBOSE: [WSR2-1]: LCM:  [ End    Resource ]  [[Service]ServiceDemo]
VERBOSE: [WSR2-1]: LCM:  [ End    Set      ]
VERBOSE: [WSR2-1]: LCM:  [ End    Set      ]  in  0.1410 seconds.
```

Figure 5-26. *Starting AudioSrv using the Service DSC resource*

As seen in Figure 5-26 and in the configuration script, setting the State property to Running changes the state of the service on the target node. Similarly, we can set the other properties, such as StartupType and BuiltInAccount, too.

```
Configuration ServiceDemo {
    Node WSR2-1 {
        Service ServiceDemo {
            Name = "AudioSrv"
            State = "Running"
            BuiltInAccount = "LocalService"
            StartupType = "Automatic"
        }
    }
}
```

```
ServiceDemo
```

The configuration script in the preceding example is not very different from what we have seen earlier. We are just setting more than one property here. Let us move on to the other DSC resources we have not yet covered.

User Resource

As a part of our discussion on built-in DSC resources, we have seen examples of using the Group resource that is used to create local groups on target nodes. We have seen examples where we added multiple users as members of those groups. Now, what if those users did not exist? Is there a way to create the users before adding them to the local groups? Yes; this is where we can use the User resource. The User resource is used to create local users on target nodes. Remember that this is about local users and not Active Directory users. Table 5-12 shows the properties of this DSC resource.

Table 5-12. *Properties of the User DSC Resource*

Property Name	Description	Required?
UserName	Specifies the name of the user account that has to be configured	Yes
Description	Specifies description text for the user account being configured	No
Disabled	Specifies whether the user account is disabled or enabled. This is a Boolean value.	No
Ensure	Specifies whether the user account has to be present or absent	No
FullName	Specifies a full name for the user account being configured	No
Password	Specifies the credentials for the user account. This is a PSCredential type.	No
PasswordChangeNotAllowed	Specifies whether or not the user account can change the password	No
PasswordChangeRequired	Specifies if the user account must change the password on first logon	No
PasswordNeverExpires	Specifies whether the user account password expires as per the password policies on the system or never expires	No
DependsOn	Specifies the resource(s) that should be configured before configuring this service	No

As shown in the list of properties, it is simple to create a new user. We just have to specify the UserName property, and as the default value for Ensure is Present, the user account gets created if it doesn't already exist.

```
Configuration UserDemo {
    Node Home-Desk {
        User UserDemo {
            UserName = "User1"
        }
    }
}
```

UserDemo

The preceding example is way too simple. Let us add some more properties to it and then apply the configuration to create the user account. For the next example, we will add such properties as FullName, PasswordNeverExpires, and PasswordChangeRequired.

```
Configuration UserDemo {
    Node Home-Desk {
        User UserDemo {
            UserName = "User1"
            FullName = "User One"
            PasswordChangeRequired = $false
            PasswordNeverExpires = $false
        }
    }
}
```

UserDemo

In this example, we are creating a user account and setting the full name to a string that is specified in the configuration script (see Figure 5-27). The other properties take Boolean values to specify that the new user account does not need to change the password at first logon, and the user account password never expires.

```
VERBOSE: [HOME-DESK]: LCM:  [ Start  Set      ]
VERBOSE: [HOME-DESK]: LCM:  [ Start  Resource ] [[User]UserDemo]
VERBOSE: [HOME-DESK]: LCM:  [ Start  Test     ] [[User]UserDemo]
VERBOSE: [HOME-DESK]:                            [[User]UserDemo] A user with the name User1 does not exist.
VERBOSE: [HOME-DESK]: LCM:  [ End    Test     ] [[User]UserDemo]  in 3.3901 seconds.
VERBOSE: [HOME-DESK]: LCM:  [ Start  Set      ] [[User]UserDemo]
VERBOSE: [HOME-DESK]:                            [[User]UserDemo] Configuration of user User1 started.
VERBOSE: [HOME-DESK]:                            [[User]UserDemo] Performing the operation "Add" on target "Us
er: User1".
VERBOSE: [HOME-DESK]:                            [[User]UserDemo] User User1 created successfully.
VERBOSE: [HOME-DESK]:                            [[User]UserDemo] Configuration of user User1 completed succes
sfully.
VERBOSE: [HOME-DESK]: LCM:  [ End    Set      ] [[User]UserDemo]  in 2.9017 seconds.
VERBOSE: [HOME-DESK]: LCM:  [ End    Resource ] [[User]UserDemo]
VERBOSE: [HOME-DESK]: LCM:  [ End    Set      ]    in  7.0150 seconds.
```

Figure 5-27. *Creating a new user account using the* User *DSC resource*

We left out a few more properties, such as Description, Disabled, and so on. It isn't difficult to figure out what they are meant to do. So, give it a try yourself and write a configuration script that uses most or all of the properties of this resource. Also, if you have noticed, we have not given the user account any password using the Password property. This requires an understanding of handling passwords in a configuration script. We shall encounter this in Chapter 6.

WindowsFeature Resource

The final resource in the list of built-in resources is the WindowsFeature resource. This one tops my list of most useful built-in DSC resources. This resource can be used to manage roles and features in Windows Server operating systems. As the resource modules use the Server Manager cmdlets to manage roles and features, we cannot use this resource to do the same on the client OS. So, the target nodes are limited to systems running Server OS only. Table 5-13 provides a description of the properties of this DSC resource.

Table 5-13. *Properties of the WindowsFeature DSC Resource*

Property Name	Description	Required?
Name	Specifies the name of the role or feature that has to be configured	Yes
Credential	Specifies the credentials required to configure the roles or features on the target node	No
DependsOn	Specifies the resource(s) that must be configured before configuring this resource	No
Ensure	Specifies whether the user account has to be present or absent	No
IncludeAllSubFeature	Specifies if the sub-features of the role or feature must be enabled or not	No
LogPath	Specifies the log file path for the feature installation	No
Source	Specifies an alternate source path for the feature or roles that have to installed	No

Like many other built-in DSC resources, there is only one mandatory property, and that is the Name property. We can create a configuration script with the property alone and configure the role or feature. The IncludeAllSubFeature property is useful when the role we are configuring has sub-features, such as management tools and so on. Within a single configuration script, it allows us to configure the role, as well as all the management tools and required sub-features.

```
Configuration WindowsFeatureDemo {
    Node WSR2-1 {
        WindowsFeature WindowsFeatureDemo {
            Name = "AD-Domain-Services"
            IncludeAllSubFeature = $true
            Ensure = "Present"
        }
    }
}

WindowsFeatureDemo
```

In the preceding example, we are installing the Active Directory Domain Service role, if it is not already installed. We are also specifying that all sub-features be installed, as required. The WindowsFeature resource uses the Server Manager cmdlets to check for the roles and features on the target node and installs or uninstalls them, as required. As you can see in Figure 5-28, the output clearly indicates the usage of Server Manager cmdlets, such as the Get-WindowsFeature and so on.

```
VERBOSE: [WSR2-1]: LCM:  [ Start  Set      ]
VERBOSE: [WSR2-1]: LCM:  [ Start  Resource ]  [[WindowsFeature]WindowsFeatureDemo]
VERBOSE: [WSR2-1]: LCM:  [ Start  Test     ]  [[WindowsFeature]WindowsFeatureDemo]
VERBOSE: [WSR2-1]:                            [[WindowsFeature]WindowsFeatureDemo] The operation 'Get-WindowsFeatur
e' started: AD-Domain-Services
VERBOSE: [WSR2-1]:                            [[WindowsFeature]WindowsFeatureDemo] The operation 'Get-WindowsFeatur
e' succeeded: AD-Domain-Services
VERBOSE: [WSR2-1]: LCM:  [ End    Test     ]  [[WindowsFeature]WindowsFeatureDemo]  in 1.1100 seconds.
VERBOSE: [WSR2-1]: LCM:  [ Start  Set      ]  [[WindowsFeature]WindowsFeatureDemo]
VERBOSE: [WSR2-1]:                            [[WindowsFeature]WindowsFeatureDemo] Installation started...
VERBOSE: [WSR2-1]:                            [[WindowsFeature]WindowsFeatureDemo] Prerequisite processing started.
..
VERBOSE: [WSR2-1]:                            [[WindowsFeature]WindowsFeatureDemo] Prerequisite processing succeede
d.
WARNING: [WSR2-1]:                            [[WindowsFeature]WindowsFeatureDemo] Windows automatic updating is no
t enabled. To ensure that your newly-installed role or feature is automatically updated, turn on Windows Update.
VERBOSE: [WSR2-1]:                            [[WindowsFeature]WindowsFeatureDemo] Installation succeeded.
VERBOSE: [WSR2-1]:                            [[WindowsFeature]WindowsFeatureDemo] successfully installed the featu
re AD-Domain-Services
VERBOSE: [WSR2-1]: LCM:  [ End    Set      ]  [[WindowsFeature]WindowsFeatureDemo]  in 28.5930 seconds.
VERBOSE: [WSR2-1]: LCM:  [ End    Resource ]  [[WindowsFeature]WindowsFeatureDemo]
```

***Figure 5-28.** AD Domain Services installation using DSC*

Some of the role's installation or uninstallation may require a reboot. For example, in the earlier configuration script, we installed AD Domain Services role. Now, if we try to uninstall the same role by setting the Ensure property to Absent, the WindowsFeature resource will indicate the requirement for any reboots in the verbose output from the resource. An example of this is shown in Figure 5-29.

```
VERBOSE: [WSR2-1]: LCM:  [ Start  Set      ]
VERBOSE: [WSR2-1]: LCM:  [ Start  Resource ]  [[WindowsFeature]WindowsFeatureDemo]
VERBOSE: [WSR2-1]: LCM:  [ Start  Test     ]  [[WindowsFeature]WindowsFeatureDemo]
VERBOSE: [WSR2-1]:                            [[WindowsFeature]WindowsFeatureDemo] The operation 'Get-WindowsFeatur
e' started: AD-Domain-Services
VERBOSE: [WSR2-1]:                            [[WindowsFeature]WindowsFeatureDemo] The operation 'Get-WindowsFeatur
e' succeeded: AD-Domain-Services
VERBOSE: [WSR2-1]: LCM:  [ End    Test     ]  [[WindowsFeature]WindowsFeatureDemo]  in 0.5480 seconds.
VERBOSE: [WSR2-1]: LCM:  [ Start  Set      ]  [[WindowsFeature]WindowsFeatureDemo]
VERBOSE: [WSR2-1]:                            [[WindowsFeature]WindowsFeatureDemo] Uninstallation started...
VERBOSE: [WSR2-1]:                            [[WindowsFeature]WindowsFeatureDemo] Prerequisite processing started.
..
VERBOSE: [WSR2-1]:                            [[WindowsFeature]WindowsFeatureDemo] Prerequisite processing succeede
d.
WARNING: [WSR2-1]:                            [[WindowsFeature]WindowsFeatureDemo] You must restart this server to
finish the removal process.
VERBOSE: [WSR2-1]:                            [[WindowsFeature]WindowsFeatureDemo] Uninstallation succeeded.
VERBOSE: [WSR2-1]:                            [[WindowsFeature]WindowsFeatureDemo] successfully unInstalled the fea
ture AD-Domain-Services.
VERBOSE: [WSR2-1]:                            [[WindowsFeature]WindowsFeatureDemo] The Target machine needs to be r
estarted.
VERBOSE: [WSR2-1]: LCM:  [ End    Set      ]  [[WindowsFeature]WindowsFeatureDemo]  in 22.6350 seconds.
```

***Figure 5-29.** DSC messages from the WindowsFeature resource indicating a reboot*

When a DSC resource requires a reboot to complete the configuration change, we can instruct the LCM to perform the reboot automatically. This behavior is disabled by default. We will discuss this in depth in Chapter 9 in which we talk about creating custom DSC resources and how LCM can be configured to handle the reboots automatically.

Coming back to our discussion on the WindowsFeature resource, there is one more property that deserves some discussion in this section. It's the Source property. If you have ever installed .NET Framework 3.5 core on a Windows Server 2012 or 2012 R2 system, you will know that you have to provide an external source path. This can be done with DSC too. Let us see how. Before we proceed, you have to attach, based on the Windows Server 2012 version OS you are using, the OS ISO or DVD to the target node and note down the drive letter assigned to it. Once you have this, push the following configuration to install the .NET Framework 3.5 from an external source.

```
Configuration WindowsFeatureDemo {
    Node WSR2-1 {
        WindowsFeature WindowsFeatureDemo {
            Name = "NET-Framework-Core"
            Source = "D:\Sources\SxS"
        }
    }
}
```

WindowsFeatureDemo

The preceding code sample shows how to use the Source property. This is just one example of a Windows OS feature that requires an external source. Some of the administrators remove the Windows OS source files from the OS install folder, to save on the hard drive space on server systems. In such a scenario, the Source property can be quite useful.

Using the DependsOn Property

Every resource in DSC receives the DependsOn property. For both built-in and custom DSC resources, the PSDesiredStateConfiguration module automatically adds this property. As I had mentioned in the description of properties of each DSC resource, the DependsOn property is used to specify what other DSC resource or resources must be configured prior to configuring the resource in which the dependency is defined. I have intentionally skipped any discussion of the DependsOn property when providing the built-in resource examples. The way we use this property is independent of the DSC resource. To understand this, let us look at a few examples.

To start with, we will revisit the Group resource example we used earlier. We used this DSC resource to create a local group and then to add members to that group. However, we did not verify whether those user accounts really existed. This is where DependsOn is used. Using the DependsOn property with the Group resource, we can specify that we want to verify whether or not the user accounts exist, before creating a group.

```
Configuration DependsOnDemo {
    Node Home-Desk {
        Group GroupDemo {
            GroupName = "Group1"
            MembersToInclude = "User1"
            DependsOn = "[user]UserDemo1"
        }

        User UserDemo1 {
            UserName = "User1"
        }
    }
}
```

DependsOnDemo

In the preceding configuration script, I have defined both Group and User resources within the same node block. Within the Group resource definition, I have added the DependsOn property and assigned it a value, to indicate that it depends on the User resource within the configuration. If you look at the value of the DependsOn property, it has a specific syntax. The general syntax is "[Resource Type] ResourceName". So, following that, "[User] UserDemo1" defines that the Group resource is dependent on the User resource defined by UserDemo1.

When this configuration is applied, LCM first tries to run the User resource, as the Group resource has a dependency on the User resource. This is best illustrated in an example, as shown in Figure 5-30.

```
VERBOSE: [HOME-DESK]: LCM:  [ Start  Set      ]
VERBOSE: [HOME-DESK]: LCM:  [ Start  Resource ]  [[User]UserDemo1]
VERBOSE: [HOME-DESK]: LCM:  [ Start  Test     ]  [[User]UserDemo1]
VERBOSE: [HOME-DESK]:                             [[User]UserDemo1] A user with the name User1 does not exist.
VERBOSE: [HOME-DESK]: LCM:  [ End    Test     ]  [[User]UserDemo1]  in 4.1496 seconds.
VERBOSE: [HOME-DESK]: LCM:  [ Start  Set      ]  [[User]UserDemo1]
VERBOSE: [HOME-DESK]:                             [[User]UserDemo1] Configuration of user User1 started.
VERBOSE: [HOME-DESK]:                             [[User]UserDemo1] Performing the operation "Add" on target "User: User1".
VERBOSE: [HOME-DESK]:                             [[User]UserDemo1] User User1 created successfully.
VERBOSE: [HOME-DESK]:                             [[User]UserDemo1] Configuration of user User1 completed successfully.
VERBOSE: [HOME-DESK]: LCM:  [ End    Set      ]  [[User]UserDemo1]  in 3.4614 seconds.
VERBOSE: [HOME-DESK]: LCM:  [ End    Resource ]  [[User]UserDemo1]
VERBOSE: [HOME-DESK]: LCM:  [ Start  Resource ]  [[Group]GroupDemo]
VERBOSE: [HOME-DESK]: LCM:  [ Start  Test     ]  [[Group]GroupDemo]
VERBOSE: [HOME-DESK]:                             [[Group]GroupDemo] A group with the name Group1 does not exist.
VERBOSE: [HOME-DESK]: LCM:  [ End    Test     ]  [[Group]GroupDemo]  in 2.9209 seconds.
VERBOSE: [HOME-DESK]: LCM:  [ Start  Set      ]  [[Group]GroupDemo]
VERBOSE: [HOME-DESK]:                             [[Group]GroupDemo] Performing the operation "Add" on target "Group: Group1".
VERBOSE: [HOME-DESK]:                             [[Group]GroupDemo] Group Group1 created successfully.
VERBOSE: [HOME-DESK]: LCM:  [ End    Set      ]  [[Group]GroupDemo]  in 7.1054 seconds.
VERBOSE: [HOME-DESK]: LCM:  [ End    Resource ]  [[Group]GroupDemo]
VERBOSE: [HOME-DESK]: LCM:  [ End    Set      ]   in  22.1258 seconds.
```

Figure 5-30. *Demonstration of DependsOn property in DSC*

As shown in Figure 5-30, LCM finds a dependency on the User resource and begins configuring the User resource first. If a user account with specified configuration is not found, the user account gets created, and then the Group resource gets configured. Now, how do we add multiple such dependencies? For example, what if we want to add multiple user accounts to the group membership and use the DependsOn property, to ensure all those user accounts exist? The DependsOn property is a string array, and therefore, we can add multiple resource definitions to the DependsOn value as a comma-separated list. This is shown in the following example.

```
Configuration DependsOnDemo {
    Node Home-Desk {
        Group GroupDemo {
            GroupName = "Group1"
            MembersToInclude = "User1"
            DependsOn = "[user]UserDemo1","[user]UserDemo2"
        }

        User UserDemo1 {
            UserName = "User1"
        }

        User UserDemo2 {
            UserName = "User2"
        }
    }
}

DependsOnDemo
```

The use of the DependsOn property must be clear now. When we apply this configuration, you can see that the LCM walks through all resources defined as the value of the DependsOn property and configures each resource, as required. This is shown in Figure 5-31.

```
VERBOSE: [HOME-DESK]: LCM:  [ Start  Set       ]
VERBOSE: [HOME-DESK]: LCM:  [ Start  Resource  ] [[User]UserDemo1]
VERBOSE: [HOME-DESK]: LCM:  [ Start  Test      ] [[User]UserDemo1]
VERBOSE: [HOME-DESK]:                             [[User]UserDemo1] A user with the name User1 exists.
VERBOSE: [HOME-DESK]:                             [[User]UserDemo1] All User User1 properties match.
VERBOSE: [HOME-DESK]: LCM:  [ End    Test      ] [[User]UserDemo1]  in 2.8911 seconds.
VERBOSE: [HOME-DESK]: LCM:  [ Skip   Set       ] [[User]UserDemo1]
VERBOSE: [HOME-DESK]: LCM:  [ End    Resource  ] [[User]UserDemo1]
VERBOSE: [HOME-DESK]: LCM:  [ Start  Resource  ] [[User]UserDemo2]
VERBOSE: [HOME-DESK]: LCM:  [ Start  Test      ] [[User]UserDemo2]
VERBOSE: [HOME-DESK]:                             [[User]UserDemo2] A user with the name User2 does not exist.
VERBOSE: [HOME-DESK]: LCM:  [ End    Test      ] [[User]UserDemo2]  in 2.7476 seconds.
VERBOSE: [HOME-DESK]: LCM:  [ Start  Set       ] [[User]UserDemo2]
VERBOSE: [HOME-DESK]:                             [[User]UserDemo2] Configuration of user User2 started.
VERBOSE: [HOME-DESK]:                             [[User]UserDemo2] Performing the operation "Add" on target "User: User2".
VERBOSE: [HOME-DESK]:                             [[User]UserDemo2] User User2 created successfully.
VERBOSE: [HOME-DESK]:                             [[User]UserDemo2] Configuration of user User2 completed successfully.
VERBOSE: [HOME-DESK]: LCM:  [ End    Set       ] [[User]UserDemo2]  in 3.1660 seconds.
VERBOSE: [HOME-DESK]: LCM:  [ End    Resource  ] [[User]UserDemo2]
VERBOSE: [HOME-DESK]: LCM:  [ Start  Resource  ] [[Group]GroupDemo]
VERBOSE: [HOME-DESK]: LCM:  [ Start  Test      ] [[Group]GroupDemo]
VERBOSE: [HOME-DESK]:                             [[Group]GroupDemo] A group with the name Group1 exists.
VERBOSE: [HOME-DESK]: LCM:  [ End    Test      ] [[Group]GroupDemo]  in 5.5631 seconds.
VERBOSE: [HOME-DESK]: LCM:  [ Skip   Set       ] [[Group]GroupDemo]
VERBOSE: [HOME-DESK]: LCM:  [ End    Resource  ] [[Group]GroupDemo]
```

Figure 5-31. *Multiple dependent resources in a configuration script*

Make a note that the list of resources you specify as a value to the DependsOn property need not be of the same resource type. You can certainly mix different resource types as a part of another resource's dependency list. With the knowledge you've gained so far, is it possible to write a configuration script that a zip archive is available on the target node before you attempt to unpack it at a destination path on the target node? See for yourself.

Summary

Phew! This chapter is a long one. DSC resources are the heart of the configuration management capability offered by Desired State Configuration (DSC). Along with WMF 4.0, there are 12 built-in resources with which to perform some of the usual tasks performed by an administrator on a day-to-day basis. DSC also provides a way to create custom resources. Each resource, whether built-in or custom, has multiple properties that are used to define the attributes of an entity that is being configured. Understanding what each resource does and how each of the properties is used is the first step to mastering DSC. The DependsOn property is a common property across all DSC resources in a system. Using this property, you can define what other DSC resources must be configured before the resource that defines the DependsOn relation.

We may not have looked at each and every property and seen examples for each built-in DSC resource. I highly recommend that you try a few examples with each DSC resource and understand how the properties are used. To understand how DSC resources work internally, it is good to try a few examples with the Script DSC resource. As I've mentioned, this resource models closely how the custom DSC resources are written. So, any knowledge gained from your practice can be leveraged later when we look at creating custom DSC resources.

CHAPTER 6

■ ■ ■

Building Advanced DSC Configurations

Desired State Configuration (DSC) configuration scripts define what configuration has to be managed and where. The DSC resources enable this configuration change in an imperative way. As we learned from the previous chapter, there are several built-in DSC resources that enable us to perform basic system administration tasks using DSC declarative style. While discussing the built-in resources, we looked at several examples for each resource and how some of their properties are used. We, however, skipped discussion of properties such as `Credential`. Before we get to that, you have to understand a few more aspects of authoring configuration scripts, by parameterizing the scripts and using a technique called configuration data, to supply values to configuration scripts' properties. This chapter builds on the knowledge you've gained so far and shows how we can build advanced DSC configurations that are parameterized and reusable. We will see how we can use configuration data in DSC and how nested and composite configurations are used. With these techniques, and by the end of this chapter, you will have a complete understanding of how to use the built-in resources, building better, complex, and large configuration scripts that are reusable and composable.

Reusable Configurations

In all our examples in Chapters 4 and 5, we used a fixed Node block or two such Node blocks, with the target system name as the Node block identifier. Here is one such example:

```
Configuration ArchiveDemo {
    Node WSR2-1 {
        Archive ArchiveDemo {
            Path = "C:\Temp\Scripts.zip"
            Destination = "C:\Deployment\Scripts"
            Force = $true
        }
    }
}

ArchiveDemo
```

The preceding example has only one node identifier and generates a single MOF file, the specified target system. If we want to specify multiple systems, we can do so as a comma-separated list, as shown in the following example:

```
Configuration ArchiveDemo {
    Node ("WSR2-1","WSR2-2") {
        Archive ArchiveDemo {
            Path = "C:\Temp\Scripts.zip"
            Destination = "C:\Deployment\Scripts"
            Force = $true
        }
    }
}
```

Note well that when you want to specify multiple target system names within the Node block, they must be enclosed in parentheses. So, in these two examples, we have hard-coded the target system names. It does not, however, make these configuration scripts reusable. We will discuss the concepts that do make our configurations reusable and composable.

I'd mentioned in Chapter 4 that the Configuration keyword and the script block associated with it are not much different from how we write a PowerShell function, which means that we can add parameters to supply the configuration properties. This is done by adding a parameter block, as we saw in some of the PowerShell function examples. And, inside the parameter block, we define the parameter names as required. To start with, we will just add $ComputerName as the only parameter to this configuration.

```
Configuration ArchiveDemo {
    param (
        [String[]]$ComputerName
    )

    Node $ComputerName {
        Archive ArchiveDemo {
            Path = "C:\Temp\Scripts.zip"
            Destination = "C:\Deployment\Scripts"
            Force = $true
        }
    }
}
```

So, now we have a configuration script that is parameterized. Now, as we discussed in Chapter 4 and saw in Chapter 5, we load this configuration into memory by selecting the complete code and pressing F5 in PowerShell ISE. As you might have guessed, we can use the Get-Command cmdlet to look at the parameters available on this configuraton. This is shown in Figure 6-1.

```
PS C:\> Get-Command -Name ArchiveDemo | Select -ExpandProperty Parameters

Key                                          Value
---                                          -----
InstanceName                                 System.Management.Automation.ParameterMetadata
OutputPath                                   System.Management.Automation.ParameterMetadata
ConfigurationData                            System.Management.Automation.ParameterMetadata
ComputerName                                 System.Management.Automation.ParameterMetadata
```

Figure 6-1. *Parameters on the new configuration*

We see the new parameter, ComputerName, added to the configuration, and it can be used to specify the target system name.

```
ArchiveDemo -ComputerName WSR2-1
```

■ **Note** In this example, it is mandatory to use the -ComputerName parameter, along with the configuration command. A configuration command has other parameters, such as InstanceName, OutputPath, and ConfigurationData. Without the ComputerName parameter name in the command line, the value specified after the configuration command will be used as a value for the InstanceName parameter.

The preceding command generates the MOF file for the ArchiveDemo configuration (see Figure 6-2).

```
PS C:\> ArchiveDemo -ComputerName WSR2-1


    Directory: C:\ArchiveDemo


Mode                LastWriteTime     Length Name
----                -------------     ------ ----
-a---        5/9/2014     7:55 PM       1236 WSR2-1.mof
```

Figure 6-2. *Using parameters with configuration*

Because ArchiveDemo, the name given to our configuration, is like any other PowerShell command, we use the parameter name specified in the configuration to supply a value. This is shown in Figure 6-2. And, as you see in the output, this creates an MOF with the target system name specified as an argument to the -ComputerName parameter. Because the ComputerName parameter is a string array, we can provide multiple computer names to create MOF files for those target systems.

```
ArchiveDemo -ComputerName WSR2-1, WSR2-2, WC81-1
```

When you execute this configuration script, you will see that it creates different MOF files—one for every computer name provided in the collection. This is shown in Figure 6-3.

```
PS C:\> ArchiveDemo -ComputerName WSR2-1, WSR2-2, WC81-1


    Directory: C:\ArchiveDemo


Mode                LastWriteTime     Length Name
----                -------------     ------ ----
-a---        5/9/2014     7:59 PM       1236 WSR2-1.mof
-a---        5/9/2014     7:59 PM       1236 WSR2-2.mof
-a---        5/9/2014     7:59 PM       1236 WC81-1.mof
```

Figure 6-3. *ComputerName as a string array to build multiple configurations*

As shown in Figure 6-3, adding the $ComputerName parameter as a string array is enough to generate the configuration for multiple target systems. We have essentially built a reusable configuration already by parameterizing the node identifiers.

In the preceding example, we only have the Node block identifier or the target system name. We have hard-coded the values of Archive resource properties in the resource script block. However, it is possible to use parameters for these values too and, in a similar way, add the ComputerName parameter. The following example demonstrates this:

```
Configuration ArchiveDemo {
    param (
        [String[]]
        $ComputerName,

        [String]
        $SourcePath,

        [String]
        $DestinationPath,

        [switch]
        $Force
    )

    Node $ComputerName {
        Archive ArchiveDemo {
            Path = $SourcePath
            Destination = $DestinationPath
            Force = $Force
        }
    }
}

ArchiveDemo -ComputerName WSR2-1, WSR2-2, WC81-1 -SourcePath "C:\Temp\Scripts.zip" -DestinationPath
"C:\Deployment\Scripts" -Force
```

This is useful only if you want all nodes to be configured in terms of the source path for the archive and where we want to unpack the archive. Also, you might not want to force overwriting on certain nodes. But, in our preceding example, we did not have a way to specify differently that property per target system. So, what if we want to have a different set of values for each target system in the configuration, based on the role or some other attribute that identifies the node? This is where the concept of configuration data comes in handy. Let us dive into this before we consider an example.

Understanding Configuration Data

The configuration data in DSC helps us to separate the environmental configuration from the structural configuration. What we defined in the preceding examples is the structural configuration. We want a zip archive unpacked on all the nodes that we specified using the ComputerName parameter. However, what if we want to set the Source property of the Archive resource to a different value, based on where we want the configuration applied? For example, for the target system named WSR2-1, I want the source of the archive to be C:\Temp\Development-Scripts.zip instead of C:\Temp\Scripts.zip. This is what we call *environmental configuration*, and as I've mentioned, this is where the configuration data plays a role.

To understand this in the context of DevOps and continuous delivery, let us consider, as an example, moving code from a development environment to production. In any of these environments, we want the software being developed or deployed to have a similar configuration. For example, whether it is a development server or a production server, we want a web server to host our web application. However, depending on the type of environment, the path where the web application source files are stored might be different. In this context, the structural configuration defines the need for always having a web server installed, and the environmental configuration defines the configuration of the web server specific to an environment.

Introduction

In these scenarios, using configuration data in DSC makes the configuration script independent of hard-coded values and makes it reusable. When there is a need to change the property values required for the configuration, we simply change the configuration data, and not the configuration script.

The configuration data in DSC is the structure for specifying the environmental configuration. This is a hash table with at least one key called AllNodes. The AllNodes key must be an array of hash tables. The following example demonstrates this syntax.

```
$ConfigData = @{
    AllNodes = @(
        @{
            NodeName="WSR2-1 "
            Source = 'C:\Temp\Development-Scripts.zip'
            Destination = 'C:\Deployment\Scripts'
            Force = 'False'
        }

        @{
            NodeName="WSR2-2"
            Source = 'C:\Temp\Production-Scripts.zip'
            Destination = 'C:\Deployment\Scripts'
            Force = 'True'

        }

        @{
            NodeName="WC81-1"
            Source = 'C:\Temp\Development-Scripts.zip'
            Destination = 'C:\Deployment\Scripts'
            Force = 'False'
        }
    )
}
```

Let us spend some time to understand how the configuration data is structured. First of all, the variable name, $ConfigData in the example, can be anything. You can name it as you like. I've mentioned that the configuration data is a hash table, and that is the reason it is enclosed in @{}. The configuration data hash table must have at least one key named AllNodes. This key's value must be an array of hash tables, which is what we have in the preceding example. Inside this array of hash tables, each hash table must contain at least one key named NodeName. This is mandatory. All other key names inside the hash table can be anything you choose to assign. If you look at the above configuration data structure, I have used the AllNodes array to specify multiple hash tables, each containing the Archive resource properties specific to each target system I want to configure. The NodeName key identifies the name of the target system. And, based on whether a target system is in production or development, we set the Source property to a different value.

So, how do we use all this? First of all, we have to modify the configuration logic or script, to use the configuration data. The following example illustrates this.

```
Configuration ArchiveDemo {
    Node $AllNodes.NodeName {
        Archive ArchiveDemo {
            Path = $Node.Source
            Destination = $Node.Destination
            Force = $Node.Force
        }
    }
}
```

If you compare the preceding example with an earlier one in which we parameterized a whole lot of things, we removed all the explicit parameter definition. We introduced two new variables, called $AllNodes and $Node. This deserves a bit of discussion. $AllNodes and $Node are the automatic variables in a configuration script block. The $AllNodes variable represents the AllNodes hash table array in the configuration data. The $AllNodes.NodeName gives us the values assigned all NodeName properties from each hash table in the AllNodes array. This is similar to using a string array with all the target system names. We have seen an example of this already. The $Node automatic variable represents a hash table in the AllNodes array. We can use the $Node variable to reference to the keys in each hash table. For example, $Node.Source gives the path assigned to it in the configuration data. But, how do we pass the configuration data to a configuration?

We discussed in Chapter 4 that additional parameters get added to each configuration we define. In Figure 6-1, we see that there is a parameter called ConfigurationData. The -ConfigurationData parameter of the configuration command can be used to provide the $ConfigData structure we created in our example (see Figure 6-4).

```
ArchiveDemo -ConfigurationData $ConfigData
```

```
    Directory: C:\ArchiveDemo


Mode                LastWriteTime     Length Name
----                -------------     ------ ----
-a---        5/10/2014   12:34 PM       1260 WSR2-1.mof
-a---        5/10/2014   12:34 PM       1258 WSR2-2.mof
-a---        5/10/2014   12:34 PM       1260 WC81-1.mof
```

Figure 6-4. *Using -ConfigurationData parameter*

Take a moment to open the MOF files generated and understand how the values provided in the configuration data are translated into the properties of instances in the MOF.

If we put all this code together, here is what our configuration script or logic will look like:

```
$ConfigData = @{
    AllNodes = @(
        @{
            NodeName="WSR2-1 "
            Source = 'C:\Temp\Development-Scripts.zip'
```

```
            Destination = 'C:\Deployment\Scripts'
             Force = 'False'
        }

        @{
            NodeName="WSR2-2"
            Source = 'C:\Temp\Production-Scripts.zip'
            Destination = 'C:\Deployment\Scripts'
             Force = 'True'

        }

        @{
            NodeName="WC81-1"
            Source = 'C:\Temp\Development-Scripts.zip'
            Destination = 'C:\Deployment\Scripts'
             Force = 'False'
        }
    )
}

Configuration ArchiveDemo {
    Node $AllNodes.NodeName {
        Archive ArchiveDemo {
            Path = $Node.Source
            Destination = $Node.Destination
            Force = $Node.Force
        }
    }
}
```

Separating Configuration Data

So far, so good. We can put the code from the preceding example into a single .PS1 file and then execute it to create the MOF files for each node. And, when we need to change any values in the configuration data, we simply open the PS1 file and edit the $ConfigData hash table. Sounds simple, but this is not a best practice. Remember what I mentioned in the beginning of this chapter. We want to create reusable configurations that separate what from where. That is, we want to separate the configuration logic and data, so that we don't have to edit the configuration script every time we need to change the configuration data. This can be achieved by storing the configuration data separately in the same hash table format in a .PSD1 file. So, all that we need to do is copy the $ConfigData variable definition into another file and name it something like ConfigurationData.PSD1. To reiterate what I just said, this is what I have in my ConfigurationData.PSD1. Note that I am not assigning the hash table to the $ConfigData variable. We don't need that when we are saving the configuration data in a PowerShell Script Data (PSD1) file.

```
@{
    AllNodes = @(
        @{
            NodeName="WSR2-1 "
            Source = 'C:\Temp\Development-Scripts.zip'
            Destination = 'C:\Deployment\Scripts'
            Force = 'False'
        }
```

```
    @{
        NodeName="WSR2-2"
        Source = 'C:\Temp\Production-Scripts.zip'
        Destination = 'C:\Deployment\Scripts'
        Force = 'True'

    }

    @{
        NodeName="WC81-1"
        Source = 'C:\Temp\Development-Scripts.zip'
        Destination = 'C:\Deployment\Scripts'
        Force = 'False'
    }
  )
}
```

Figure 6-5 shows the structure of the folder containing the configuration logic (Configuration.ps1) and the configuration data (ConfigurationData.psd1).

```
PS C:\Scripts> dir .\ConfigurationDemo


    Directory: C:\Scripts\ConfigurationDemo


Mode                LastWriteTime     Length Name
----                -------------     ------ ----
-a---         5/10/2014    6:47 PM        218 Configuration.ps1
-a---         5/10/2014    6:47 PM        537 ConfigurationData.psd1
```

Figure 6-5. *Configuration script and data files*

Once we load the configuration command using the dot-sourcing method, we can execute the configuration command with the -ConfigurationData parameter, by providing the path to the ConfigurationData.psd1 as the argument. Figure 6-6 shows this in action.

```
PS C:\Scripts\ConfigurationDemo> . .\Configuration.ps1

PS C:\Scripts\ConfigurationDemo> ArchiveDemo -ConfigurationData .\ConfigurationData.psd1


    Directory: C:\Scripts\ConfigurationDemo\ArchiveDemo


Mode                LastWriteTime     Length Name
----                -------------     ------ ----
-a---         5/10/2014    6:56 PM       1358 WSR2-1.mof
-a---         5/10/2014    6:56 PM       1356 WSR2-2.mof
-a---         5/10/2014    6:56 PM       1358 WC81-1.mof
```

Figure 6-6. *Using -Configuration Data in a file*

When we separate the logic from data, we achieve true reusability. In the preceding example, we still have some redundant data. For example, the `Destination` property value is the same across all target system hash tables. The configuration data provides a method to unify such redundant settings that apply to all nodes. Here is an example:

```
@{
    AllNodes = @(
        @{
            NodeName="*"
            Destination = "C:\Deployment\Scripts"
        }

        @{
            NodeName="WSR2-1"
            Source = 'C:\Temp\Development-Scripts.zip'
            Force = 'False'
        }

        @{
            NodeName="WSR2-2"
            Source = 'C:\Temp\Production-Scripts.zip'
            Force = 'True'
        }

        @{
            NodeName="WC81-1"
            Source = 'C:\Temp\Development-Scripts.zip'
            Force = 'False'
        }
    )
}
```

In the preceding example, we have introduced a new hash table in the `AllNodes` array, which has the `NodeName` key set to "*". Any settings that are specified here can be used with any target system. So, using this method, we can specify the settings that are common across multiple target systems. If there is a duplicate setting in the other hash tables in the array, the common configuration value takes precedence. For example, if we specify `Force = 'True'` in the hash table where `NodeName` is set to "*", all target system configuration will get this value for the `Force` property, irrespective of what is configured within individual node configuration.

You can load the configuration we previously defined that provides this new structure as the configuration data (as a PSD1, of course) and see if the MOF files are generated the way you require and are the same as the earlier MOF files.

Extended Configuration Data

The configuration data has many other uses. I've mentioned a scenario in which we wanted to move code from development to production. Now, based on the environment, we may have to configure certain other settings, rather than just copying files. Let us move beyond the simple `Archive` resource example and write some complex configuration logic. In the following example, we check for a different set of configuration parameters, based on the role of the target system in a deployment. Let us look at the example, and then we will walk through it, to understand it better. Let us start with the configuration data first.

```
$ConfigData = @{
    AllNodes = @(
        @{
            NodeName="*"
            SourcePath = "C:\Temp\Generic-Scripts.zip"
            Destination = "C:\Deployment\Scripts"
        }

        @{
            NodeName="WSR2-1"
            Role = "Web"
                Force = 'False'
        }

        @{
            NodeName="WSR2-2"
            Role = "Database"
                Force = 'True'
        }

        @{
            NodeName="WC81-1"
            Force = 'False'
        }
    )

    DBConfig = @{
        SourcePath = "C:\Temp\Database-Scripts.zip"
        ServiceToCheck = "MSSQLSERVER"
    }

    WebConfig = @{
        SourcePath = "C:\Temp\WebServer-Scripts.zip"
        ServiceToCheck = "inetsrv"
    }
}
```

In the preceding configuration data example, we have additional hash tables apart from the mandatory AllNodes hash table array. Inside each node-specific hash table, I added a new key, called Role, to help me identify a target system's role. Apart from that, I have also added two more hash tables, called DBConfig and WebConfig. These two hash tables define the environmental configuration for the nodes. For example, the DBConfig hash table specifies what service must be checked for the running state and the source archive path that must be extracted on the target node. Similarly, I have the WebConfig hash table that defines these settings for a target system with a web role. Also, observe that I have added SourcePath and Destination properties to the hash table where NodeName is set to "*". This is done to ensure that a Node with no Role property can use those settings for gathering and unpacking a zip archive. Now, how do we use this new structure for the configuration data? We need to modify the logic a little bit to ensure that we adopt these changes.

```
Configuration ComplexConfiguration {
    Node $AllNodes.NodeName {
        Switch ($Node.Role) {
            'Web' {
                WindowsFeature IIS {
                    Name = "Web-Server"
                    IncludeAllSubFeature = $true
                    Ensure = "Present"
                }

                Service ServiceCheck {
                    Name = $ConfigurationData.WebConfig.ServiceToCheck
                    State = "Running"
                }

                Archive ScriptArchive {
                    Path = $ConfigurationData.WebConfig.SourcePath
                    Destination = $Node.Destination
                    Force = $Node.Force
                }
            }

            'Database' {
                WindowsProcess SQL {
                    Path = "C:\Program Files\Microsoft SQL Server\MSSQL\Binn\sqlservr.exe"
                    Arguments = ""
                    Ensure = "Present"
                }

                Service ServiceCheck {
                    Name = $ConfigurationData.DBConfig.ServiceToCheck
                    State = "Running"
                }

                Archive ScriptArchive {
                    Path = $ConfigurationData.DBConfig.SourcePath
                    Destination = $Node.Destination
                    Force = $Node.Force
                }
            }

            Default {
                Archive ScriptArchive {
                    Path = $Node.SourcePath
                    Destination = $Node.Destination
                    Force = $Node.Force
                }
            }
        }
    }
}
```

As I've described in the example, this configuration logic checks for the role of the target node in the configuration data and changes the configuration definition for the node accordingly. In this example, we use the PowerShell Switch statement to check the role of the target system. $Node.Role provides the value of the Role property from each node's hash table. So, based on the role, we change the configuration definition for the node. For example, for the web role, we are using WindowsFeature, Service, and Archive resources and configuring them accordingly. To access the environmental configuration from the configuration data, we use the $ConfigurationData variable. Remember: -ConfigurationData is a configuration parameter, and any value assigned to it during command invocation can be accessed using $ConfigurationData. We can use the reference operator, a "." in this example, to access the properties in both WebConfig and DBConfig hash tables. For example, the $ConfigurationData. WebConfig.SourcePath gives us the source archive path for the web servers. The advantage of using a Switch statement to verify the role of the target system is very clear from the preceding configuration logic. We can use the Default condition to add only the Archive resource configuration for the nodes that do not have a Role property.

Once again, take your time to understand the configuration logic in the preceding example and run the configuration script to verify if the MOF files are generated without any errors and as you expected.

As with anything else in PowerShell, we can rewrite the above configuration logic to use different conditional constructs. The following example demonstrates the Where operator to check the Role of a target system. The following configuration script demonstrates this:

```
Configuration ComplexConfiguration {
    Node $AllNodes.Where({$_.Role -eq "Web"}).NodeName {
        WindowsFeature IIS {
            Name = "Web-Server"
            IncludeAllSubFeature = $true
            Ensure = "Present"
        }

        Service ServiceCheck {
            Name = $ConfigurationData.WebConfig.ServiceToCheck
            State = "Running"
        }

        Archive ScriptArchive {
            Path = $ConfigurationData.WebConfig.SourcePath
            Destination = $Node.Destination
            Force = $Node.Force
        }
    }

    Node $AllNodes.Where({$_.Role -eq "Database"}).NodeName {
        WindowsProcess SQL {
            Path = "C:\Program Files\Microsoft SQL Server\MSSQL\Binn\sqlservr.exe"
            Arguments = ""
            Ensure = "Present"
        }

        Service ServiceCheck {
            Name = $ConfigurationData.DBConfig.ServiceToCheck
            State = "Running"
        }
```

```
            Archive ScriptArchive {
                Path = $ConfigurationData.DBConfig.SourcePath
                Destination = $Node.Destination
                Force = $Node.Force
            }
    }

    Node $AllNodes.Where({-not ($_.Role) }).NodeName {
            Archive ScriptArchive {
                Path = $Node.SourcePath
                Destination = $Node.Destination
                Force = $Node.Force
            }
    }
}
```

The biggest change in the preceding example is how we are checking the role of a target system specified in the configuration data. We are using the $AllNodes.Where() operator to filter the nodes. The simplified Where syntax lets us filter an object collection, $AllNodes in this example, for any given condition within the Where() operator. Within this method, we need to specify the condition that matches each role. This is done using, for example, {$_.Role -eq "Web"}. To get a collection of nodes with no Role property, we use negation as the condition within the Where operator. This configuration logic results in the same MOF file content as the one using a Switch statement.

Now that you understand the need for and uses of configuration data, let us revisit our discussion on built-in resources and look at how configuration data can help use the resources in a better way.

Using Credentials in Configuration

In Chapter 5, when discussing the use of File, Package, User, Group, Service, WindowsProcess, and WindowsFeature resources, we had a very limited, or no, discussion related to the Credential property of these resources. When we looked at copying folder contents from a network share using the File resource, we had given the target system access to the share instead of using the Credential property. This is not a recommended way of handling permissions when using DSC.

Using Plain-Text Credentials

In this section, we look at how we can make use of configuration data to supply credentials within a resource configuration.

Before we see an example of using configuration data for credentials, let us look at how we can specify credentials in a resource and what happens when we use the Credential property.

```
Configuration FileDemo {
    Param (
        [pscredential]$Credential
    )
    Node WSR2-1 {
        File FileDemo1 {
            DestinationPath = "C:\Scripts2"
            SourcePath = "\\Demo-Ad\Share"
```

```
            Type = "Directory"
            Ensure = "Present"
            Credential = $Credential
            Recurse = $true
        }
    }
}
```

In the preceding example, we are using a Universal Naming Convention (UNC) path as the SourcePath and added a Credential parameter to the configuration, so that we can supply the username and password required to access the UNC path when applying the configuration. So, to enact this on the target system, we can load the configuration into the memory and use the -Credential parameter of the configuration command to provide the credentials. Here is how we do that:

```
$Cred = Get-Credential
FileDemo -Credential $Cred
```

As shown in Figure 6-7, the MOF file generation fails with an error, as the plain-text password provided through the Credential parameter is not allowed. The password has to be encrypted.

```
ConvertTo-MOFInstance : System.InvalidOperationException error processing property 'Credential' OF TYPE 'File': Converting and
storing an encrypted password as plaintext is allowed only if PSDscAllowPlainTextPassword is set to true.
At line:6 char:9
+    File
At line:164 char:16
+       $aliasId = ConvertTo-MOFInstance $keywordName $canonicalizedValue
+                  ~~~~~~~~~~~~~~~~~~~~~~~~~~~~~~~~~~~~~~~~~~~~~
    + CategoryInfo          : InvalidOperation: (:) [Write-Error], InvalidOperationException
    + FullyQualifiedErrorId : FailToProcessProperty,ConvertTo-MOFInstance
Errors occurred while processing configuration 'FileDemo'.
At C:\windows\system32\windowspowershell\v1.0\Modules\PSDesiredStateConfiguration\PSDesiredStateConfiguration.psm1:2088 char:5
+       throw $errorRecord
+       ~~~~~~~~~~~~~~~~~~
    + CategoryInfo          : InvalidOperation: (FileDemo:String) [], InvalidOperationException
    + FullyQualifiedErrorId : FailToProcessConfiguration
```

Figure 6-7. *Using the Credential property in the File resource*

The error message suggests a workaround, using a property called PSDscAllowPlainTextPassword. This property has to be set through the configuration data. See how we are connecting the dots from different resources and their properties to the configuration data? Here is how the configuration data for this looks:

```
@{
    AllNodes = @(
        @{
            NodeName="WSR2-1"
            PSDscAllowPlainTextPassword=$true
        }
    )
}
```

We can store this configuration structure in a PSD1 file and run the configuration command to generate the MOF files. As shown in Figure 6-8, the MOF file gets generated without any errors.

```
PS C:\Scripts> FileDemo -Credential $cred -ConfigurationData .\ConfigurationData.psD1

    Directory: C:\Scripts\FileDemo


Mode                LastWriteTime     Length Name
----                -------------     ------ ----
-a---          5/12/2014   3:34 PM       1628 WSR2-1.mof
```

Figure 6-8. *MOF generation after using configuration data*

The PSDscAllowPlainTextPassword property is a special property allowed within the configuration data. When DSC comes across this property in the configuration data, instead of encrypting the credentials, it simply puts the plain-text credentials in the MOF file for this configuration. Following is how the MOF file looks:

```
/*
@TargetNode='WSR2-1'
@GeneratedBy=Administrator
@GenerationDate=05/12/2014 15:34:28
@GenerationHost=DEMO-AD
*/

instance of MSFT_Credential as $MSFT_Credential1ref
{
Password = "Pass@W0rd";
 UserName = "dsc-demo\\administrator";

};

instance of MSFT_FileDirectoryConfiguration as $MSFT_FileDirectoryConfiguration1ref
{
ResourceID = "[File]FileDemo1";
 Type = "Directory";
 Credential = $MSFT_Credential1ref;
 Ensure = "Present";
 SourceInfo = "::6::9::File";
 DestinationPath = "C:\\Scripts2";
 ModuleName = "PSDesiredStateConfiguration";
 Recurse = True;
 ModuleVersion = "1.0";
 SourcePath = "\\\\Demo-Ad\\Share";

};

instance of OMI_ConfigurationDocument
{
 Version="1.0.0";
 Author="Administrator";
 GenerationDate="05/12/2014 15:34:28";
 GenerationHost="DEMO-AD";
};
```

In addition, you can enact this configuration, using the `Start-DscConfiguration` cmdlet. But once again, this is not a best practice. You should never leave passwords such as this in plain-text format. This might be allowed for development and testing purposes, but should never be in production. The best practice and recommendations are always to encrypt the password and have some means to decrypt it on the target system, for the purpose of enacting the configuration. This is achieved using server authentication certificates.

Encrypting Credentials

For encrypting the credentials, we need an encryption-capable certificate on the target node. To learn how this configuration works, we either need an Active Directory Certificate Server or any certificate authority that is capable of issuing certificates, or we can deploy a self-signed certificate on the target system. For the purpose of this demonstration, I will show you how to create a self-signed certificate and deploy it on the target system. The following steps must be run on the target system where the configuration has to be applied.

To create a self-signed certificate, we will use the `makecert.exe` and `pvk2pfx.exe` tools, which are available in the Visual Studio Tools or Windows SDK. We need to copy these tools to a folder on the target system.

If you have a certificate authority through which you can enroll a certificate, you can skip the following steps of creating a self-signed certificate and importing it in to the local machine certificate store on the target system.

```
makecert -r -pe -n "CN=WSR2-1.DSCDemo.Lab" -b 01/01/2014 -e 01/01/2036 -eku 1.3.6.1.5.5.7.3.2
-sky exchange -sp "Microsoft RSA SChannel Cryptographic Provider" -sy 12 -sv WSR2-1-DSCDEMO.pvk
WSR2-1-DSCDEMO.cer
```

In the preceding example, we are creating a Client Authentication certificate. This command will prompt you to create the private key. You can enter the password of your choice here, and it will be used as the private key. Once this command completes, we will find two files (`WSR2-1-DSCDemo.pvk` and `WSR2-1-DSCDemo.cer`) in the current working directory where you copied the tools. The `.pvk` file contains the private key information, and `.cer` contains the certificate and the public key.

Now, we need to use the `pvk2pfx.exe` tool to copy the public and private key information in to a Personal Information Exchange or `pfx` file.

```
pvk2pfx.exe -pvk WSR2-1-DSCDEMO.pvk -spc WSR2-1-DSCDEMO.cer -pfx WSR2-1-DSCDEMO.pfx -po PassW0rd1
```

This command will prompt for the private key password, and you have to provide the same password with which we created a private key in the previous step. The `-po` switch is used to provide a password for the `pfx` file itself. Once the `pfx` file is generated, we can use the `certutil.exe` to import the certificate into target system's local machine certificate store.

```
Certutil.exe -importpfx WSR2-1-DSCDemo.pfx
```

The preceding command prompts for the `pfx` file password, and upon completion, it imports the certificate into a personal store in the local machine scope. We can now obtain the thumbprint for this certificate, by using the certificate provider.

```
Get-ChildItem Cert:\LocalMachine\My | Where-Object { $_.Subject -eq "CN=WSR2-1.DSCDemo.lab" }
```

The certificate thumbprint for this new certificate is shown in Figure 6-9. Make a note of this certificate thumbprint. At this point, we have to make the Local Configuration Manager on the target system aware of the certificate, so that it is used for decrypting the credentials. This can be done by a change of meta-configuration settings, as we saw in Chapter 4. We will see an example illustrating this, later in this section.

```
PS C:\Scripts> Get-ChildItem Cert:\LocalMachine\My | Where-Object { $_.Subject -eq "CN=WSR2-1.DSCDemo.lab" }

    Directory: Microsoft.PowerShell.Security\Certificate::LocalMachine\My

Thumbprint                               Subject
----------                               -------
B261936C63B9966765A8752EB9B41431D9677D94  CN=WSR2-1.DSCDemo.Lab
```

Figure 6-9. *Thumbprint of the new self-signed certificate*

We now have the necessary infrastructure to encrypt the DSC configurations. We need the configuration data structure to provide the public key file and the thumbprint to the DSC configuration, along with the nodename. Here is how the configuration data should look:

```
$ConfigData = @{
    AllNodes = @(
        @{
            NodeName = "WSR2-1.dscdemo.lab"
            CertificateFile = "C:\Scripts\WSR2-1-DSCDEMO.cer"
        };
    );
}
```

Similar to the `PSDscAllowPlainTextPassword` property in the DSC configuration data, the `CertificateFile` is a special property allowed within the configuration data to specify the path to a public key to encrypt the DSC configuration. In our example, we are pointing this property to a certificate file we created in an earlier step. Our configuration logic should include the `Credential` property for the `File` resource, and it is always recommended that you specify the credential as a parameter to the configuration, to preserve the reusability factor.

```
Configuration FileDemo {
    Param (
        [pscredential]$Credential
    )
    Node $AllNodes.NodeName {
        File FileDemo1 {
            DestinationPath = "C:\Scripts2"
            SourcePath = "\\Demo-Ad\Share"
            Type = "Directory"
            Ensure = "Present"
            Credential = $Credential
            Recurse = $true
            Force = $true
        }
    }
}
```

As you see in the preceding configuration logic, I have specified `Credential` as a parameter to the configuration and used that as a value for the `File` resource's `Credential` property. We can generate an MOF file for this configuration by providing the credentials.

```
$Cred = Get-Credential
FileDemo -Credential $Cred -ConfigurationData $ConfigData
```

The Get-Credential cmdlet prompts for the username and password to be used to access the file share specified as the SourcePath. Because we are using a certificate to encrypt the credentials, we should be able to create the MOF file without any errors. The generated MOF, shown in Figure 6-10, should have the credentials encrypted.

```
$Cred = Get-Credential
FileDemo -Credential $Cred -ConfigurationData $ConfigData

cmdlet Get-Credential at command pipeline position 1
Supply values for the following parameters:


    Directory: C:\Scripts\FileDemo


Mode                LastWriteTime     Length Name
----                -------------     ------ ----
-a---        5/14/2014  12:28 AM        2080 WSR2-1.dscdemo.lab.mof
```

Figure 6-10. *Generating a configuration MOF with encrypted credentials*

We can open this file in a text editor and verify it. The sample MOF from my system is shown below.

```
/*
@TargetNode='WSR2-1.dscdemo.lab'
@GeneratedBy=Administrator
@GenerationDate=05/14/2014 00:28:59
@GenerationHost=WSR2-1
*/

instance of MSFT_Credential as $MSFT_Credential1ref
{
Password = "yDptAvGyCXWfs6h996FqwOyKjiVvjIJ1yN6DVA/mJxbOmw9nOrm9zM5ak6snBC1hzen6rNZ3kO/
F9fiAbTkaUeXbEXYRfHOXqpmwKesGZ1BNpc5A4wchwFwPrRdHmVqvCkP5rfO7yU1ImhC7hryMhRYiO1sfAyw4UBAnM+eq96A=";
 UserName = "dscdemo\\administrator";

};

instance of MSFT_FileDirectoryConfiguration as $MSFT_FileDirectoryConfiguration1ref
{
ResourceID = "[File]FileDemo1";
 Type = "Directory";
 Credential = $MSFT_Credential1ref;
 Ensure = "Present";
 SourceInfo = "::15::9::File";
 DestinationPath = "C:\\Scripts2";
 Force = True;
 ModuleName = "PSDesiredStateConfiguration";
 Recurse = True;
 ModuleVersion = "1.0";
 SourcePath = "\\\\Demo-Ad\\Share";

};
```

```
instance of OMI_ConfigurationDocument
{
 Version="1.0.0";
 Author="Administrator";
 GenerationDate="05/14/2014 00:28:59";
 GenerationHost="WSR2-1";
 ContentType="PasswordEncrypted";
};
```

From the preceding code listing, it should be clear. This is the difference between using PSDscAllowPlainTextPassword and certificates to encrypt the DSC configurations. So, we have the credentials encrypted in the MOF file, but is this good enough to enact the configuration? No. The Local Configuration Manager on the target system must be configured to use the right certificate that contains the private key to decrypt the credentials.

To configure the LCM to use the certificate we created, we have to provide the value of the Thumbprint property, shown in Figure 6-9, as the value of LCM's CertificateID property. In Chapter 4, we saw how we can use a configuration script to manage the meta-configuration of the LCM. So, we shall use the same method here too.

```
Configuration LCMCertConfig {
    param (
        $thumbprint
    )
    Node Localhost {
        LocalConfigurationManager {
            CertificateID = $Thumbprint
        }
    }
}

$Thumbprint = (Get-ChildItem Cert:\LocalMachine\My | Where-Object { $_.Subject -eq "CN=WSR2-1.
DSCDemo.Lab" }).Thumbprint

LCMCertConfig -thumbprint $Thumbprint
```

The above code sample is used to generate the LCM meta-configuration MOF to update the LCM settings to include the CertificateID for decryption purposes. This is shown in Figure 6-11.

```
PS C:\Scripts> LCMCertConfig -thumbprint $Thumbprint

    Directory: C:\Scripts\LCMCertConfig


Mode                LastWriteTime     Length Name
----                -------------     ------ ----
-a---         5/12/2014     5:11 PM       860 Localhost.meta.mof
```

Figure 6-11. *Creating a meta-configuration MOF*

We can use the Set-DscLocalConfigurationManager with the -Path parameter to perform the LCM meta-configuration changes. The Get-DscLocalConfigurationManager cmdlet should show us the updated settings.

```
Set-DscLocalConfigurationManager -Path .\LCMCertConfig
```

```
Get-DscLocalConfigurationManager
```

Figure 6-12 shows the certificate thumbprint value as the value for the CertificateID property of the LCM. We can now try and push the File resource configuration that was using the UNC path for the SourcePath property.

```
AllowModuleOverwrite            : False
CertificateID                   : B261936C63B9966765A8752EB9B41431D9677D94
ConfigurationID                 :
ConfigurationMode               : ApplyAndMonitor
ConfigurationModeFrequencyMins  : 30
Credential                      :
DownloadManagerCustomData       :
DownloadManagerName             :
RebootNodeIfNeeded              : False
RefreshFrequencyMins            : 15
RefreshMode                     : PUSH
PSComputerName                  :
```

Figure 6-12. *Updated LCM settings*

We will enact the configuration, using the Start-DscConfiguration cmdlet.

```
Start-DscCofiguration -Wait -Verbose -Path .\FileDemo
```

As I mentioned earlier, and as I hope you have followed, we ran all the steps on the target system on which we needed to enact the configuration. However, this may not always be the case. As discussed in Chapter 4, we may, at times, author a configuration on a different system altogether. In such a scenario, the system from which we are authoring the configuration must have the target system's certificate. This is a simple task. We just copy the .cer file created at the beginning of our process of deploying certificates to the system that will be used for authoring the configuration. It is not necessary to import the certificate into a local certificate store. The configuration logic shown in the preceding example can be run to generate the MOF file with encrypted credentials. Once we have the MOF with encrypted credentials, it can be pushed from any machine, without really needing the public key or the certificate from the target system.

Creating Nested Configurations

We have seen several examples of making our configurations reusable by using parameters and configuration data. The configuration parameters help us supply the values for the configuration, instead of hard-coding them in a configuration script. The configuration data structure helps us separate the configuration logic from the data. This enables reusability as well. There are other methods to make configurations reusable. In all our examples so far, we have a single configuration script that defines the configuration that has to be managed on target system(s). So, depending on the number of resources we add to this script, it can become quite big and cumbersome to manage. This is where nested configurations help us simplify authoring complex configuration scripts. In this section, we will look at how we create nested configurations and see how this can help take the configuration reusability to a next level.

To understand this, we will start with an example. We will begin with the configuration data first. We have seen the following example earlier, so let us build a nested configuration that uses this configuration data.

```
@{
    AllNodes = @(
        @{
            NodeName="*"
            SourcePath = "C:\Temp\Generic-Scripts.zip"
            Destination = "C:\Deployment\Scripts"
        }

        @{
            NodeName="WSR2-1"
            Role = "Web"
            Force = 'False'
        }

        @{
            NodeName="WSR2-2"
            Role = "Database"
            Force = 'True'
        }

        @{
            NodeName="WSR2-3"
            Force = 'False'
        }
    )

    DBConfig = @{
        SourcePath = "C:\Temp\Database-Scripts.zip"
        ServiceToCheck = "MSSQLSERVER"
    }

    WebConfig = @{
        SourcePath = "C:\Temp\WebServer-Scripts.zip"
        ServiceToCheck = "inetsrv"
    }
}
```

We will now build several small configurations to compose a larger nested configuration at the end. The first one we need is a web server configuration. This is simple, and we just want to ensure that the Web-Server role is installed.

```
Configuration IIS {
    WindowsFeature WebServer {
        Name = 'Web-Server'
        IncludeAllSubFeature = $true
        Ensure = 'Present'
    }
}
```

If you review the preceding configuration, you'll note that it doesn't have the Node block. If you refer back to the discussion in Chapter 4, I stated that the general syntax is to include a Node block inside a configuration script. However, that is not completely mandatory, and we see an example here. So, let us move on. The next configuration we need is a service check configuration. Based on the role of the target system, database, or web, we want to check if a specific service is running or not. This is how we can accomplish that.

```
Configuration ServiceCheck {
    param (
        $Name
    )

    WindowsService SQLCheck {
        Name = $Name
        State = 'Running'
    }
}
```

We have parameterized this configuration so that it can be reused, based on the role to provide a different set of input values. The third configuration we require is an Archive resource configuration that takes only the different input parameters and unpacks an archive. Once again, we have the parameters defined on this to make it reusable.

```
Configuration ArchiveUnpack {
    param (
        $Source,
        $Destination,
        $Force
    )
    Archive ScriptArchive {
        Path = $Source
        Destination = $Destination
        Force = $Force
    }
}
```

We can copy all these configuration definitions into a PS1 file and load them into the memory. Once the configuration is loaded into the memory, we can use the Get-DscResource cmdlet to see a list of configurations that are defined in the PS1 file (see Figure 6-13).

```
PS C:\> Get-DscResource

ImplementedAs   Name              Module                        Properties
-------------   ----              ------                        ----------
Composite       ArchiveUnpack                                   {Source, Destination}
Binary          File                                            {DestinationPath, Attributes, Checksum, Content...
Composite       IIS                                             {}
Composite       ServiceCheck                                    {Name}
PowerShell      Archive           PSDesiredStateConfiguration   {Destination, Path, Checksum, DependsOn...}
PowerShell      Environment       PSDesiredStateConfiguration   {Name, DependsOn, Ensure, Path...}
PowerShell      Group             PSDesiredStateConfiguration   {GroupName, Credential, DependsOn, Description...}
Binary          Log               PSDesiredStateConfiguration   {Message, DependsOn}
PowerShell      Package           PSDesiredStateConfiguration   {Name, Path, ProductId, Arguments...}
PowerShell      Registry          PSDesiredStateConfiguration   {Key, ValueName, DependsOn, Ensure...}
PowerShell      Script            PSDesiredStateConfiguration   {GetScript, SetScript, TestScript, Credential...}
PowerShell      Service           PSDesiredStateConfiguration   {Name, BuiltInAccount, Credential, DependsOn...}
PowerShell      User              PSDesiredStateConfiguration   {UserName, DependsOn, Description, Disabled...}
PowerShell      WindowsFeature    PSDesiredStateConfiguration   {Name, Credential, DependsOn, Ensure...}
PowerShell      WindowsProcess    PSDesiredStateConfiguration   {Arguments, Path, Credential, DependsOn...}
```

Figure 6-13. *Configurations in the Get-DscResource output*

Oh, wait! Did I just say Get-DscResource instead of Get-Command? In all our earlier discussions, I've mentioned that the loaded configuration will be appearing as a command, and that you can verify that by using the Get-Command cmdlet. Well, that is still true. However, the configurations we just defined are special. If we execute the configuration command, it creates an MOF targeted at the localhost, and this configuration cannot be directly targeted at a remote system. The idea of using these configurations is to make them reusable. So, let us move on with that discussion, by assessing an example of how these configurations are used in a nested manner.

```
Configuration NestedConfiguration {
    Node $AllNodes.NodeName {
        Switch ($Node.Role) {
            'Web' {
                IIS IISInstall { }

                ServiceCheck SvcCheck {
                    Name = $ConfigurationData.WebConfig.ServiceToCheck
                }

                ArchiveUnpack ExtractZip {
                    Source = $ConfigurationData.WebConfig.SourcePath
                    Destination = $Node.Destination
                    Force = 'False'
                }
            }

            'Database' {
                ServiceCheck SvcCheck {
                    Name = $ConfigurationData.DBConfig.ServiceToCheck
                }

                ArchiveUnpack ExtractZip {
                    Source = $ConfigurationData.DBConfig.SourcePath
                    Destination = $Node.Destination
                    Force = 'True'
                }
            }

            Default {
                ArchiveUnpack ExtractZip {
                    Source = $Node.SourcePath
                    Destination = $Node.Destination
                    Force = 'True'
                }
            }
        }
    }
}
```

This example should be familiar. We have used a similar one when talking about using the Switch statement and Where() operator to filter the resource definitions, based on the target system role. However, as you can see in the preceding example, we are using the configurations defined earlier as the nested configurations. The IIS configuration takes no parameters, and, therefore, we need not specify any resource properties in the configuration definition. However, the ServiceCheck and ArchiveUnpack configurations take parameters, and we define those values using the configuration data supplied to the nested configuration. As with the standard resource definitions, we have to assign an identifier for the nested configurations too. Once we have a nested configuration created, we can use it, like any other configuration, to generate the MOF. So, to complete this example, we will use the -ConfigurationData parameter to provide the path to the PSD1 file containing the configuration data and generate MOF files for all the nodes.

```
NestedConfiguration -ConfigurationData .\ConfigurationData.psd1
```

As you see in Figure 6-14, the MOF files are generated without any errors. The configuration data supplied to the NestedConfiguration command, in turn, gets passed to each configuration defined within that and, therefore, makes it possible to use a single configuration data structure.

```
    Directory: C:\Scripts\NestedConfiguration


Mode                LastWriteTime     Length Name
----                -------------     ------ ----
-a---        5/14/2014   2:35 AM        2424 WSR2-1.mof
-a---        5/14/2014   2:35 AM        1800 WSR2-2.mof
-a---        5/14/2014   2:35 AM        1228 WSR2-3.mof
```

Figure 6-14. *MOFs generated from a nested configuration*

There are multiple benefits to this approach. First, you can create a configuration with all default property values and resource definitions, without ever specifying all of them every time you create or update a configuration script. This is what we are doing with the WindowsFeature resource in the first configuration. There are only two properties specified there, and when we make it a part of the nested configuration, we simply add an empty configuration block. The second benefit is the obvious reusable nature of this method. It is possible to reuse these configurations, as shown in the NestedConfiguration example, across multiple nodes and completely different configuration scripts. For example, imagine a scenario in which you have hundreds, if not thousands, of servers that require identical base configuration. If not for the nested configurations, you would end up duplicating the same configuration across multiple configuration scripts, which is a nightmare when it comes to maintaining consistent base configuration across multiple target systems.

While the benefits are good, there is one limitation to using nested configurations. It is not possible to use the DependsOn property of the resources when the resources are used in a nested configuration. At the time of writing, this is a bug that is being actively looked at.

At the beginning of this section, in Figure 6-13, when we saw the configurations listed in the Get-DscResource output, did you notice the type of the resource? If not, take a quick look at the figure again. You will notice that the configurations IIS, ArchiveUnpack, and ServiceCheck are listed as *composite* resources. So, what is a composite resource? Composite resources are an extension of nested configuration—at least, in theory. Unlike nested configurations, the composite resources are more discoverable and behave like DSC resources. Before we dig into the concept of composite resources, it is better that you understand custom resources, as well as how the custom DSC resources are written, deployed, and used in the DSC environment. In Chapter 9, we will discuss custom resources and then relate them to the discussion of composite resources.

Summary

The Desired State Configuration (DSC) resources become the heart of configuration scripts. These resources have a certain set of properties. When creating configuration scripts, it is both ideal and recommended to parameterize them, so that the configuration can be reused across multiple target nodes. The configuration data is an important structure within the DSC framework and is a key enabler for creating reusable and composable configurations. This chapter provided a complete overview of configuration data and several examples on how to use configuration data for creating complex configurations. Other methods of creating composable configurations include nested configurations and composite resources. Using these methods to create configuration scripts should be looked upon as a standard, when working with DSC.

PART III

Advanced DSC Concepts and Tips

Once you have understood the fundamentals of DSC, you can advance to much more complex topics, such as how to use the two configuration delivery modes in DSC, monitoring and correcting configuration delivered using DSC, building custom DSC resources, and so on. This part of the book navigates you through these subjects.

Chapter 7 discusses configuration delivery modes in depth. You will learn how to configure DSC pull servers and target systems as pull clients. You will also look at how to enact configuration in both delivery modes.

Chapter 8 builds on the knowledge you acquired in Chapter 7, to demonstrate how to monitor the DSC configuration and report when there is a configuration drift. The Local Configuration Manager (LCM) can be configured to auto-correct the configuration drift. This is done using scheduled tasks in Windows. You will learn, in depth, how the LCM is configured to create these tasks and how these tasks work. You will learn to deploy and use DSC conformance endpoint.

Chapter 9 shows you how to build custom DSC resources. This is the most essential aspect of making DSC work for you. This chapter explains the semantics of writing a DSC resource module. You will write your first DSC resource and learn how to package it, along with help topics and localized data.

Chapter 10 provides information on how to troubleshoot some common DSC problems. This chapter can be used as a reference when working with DSC. It provides a list of the most common problems that you may come across and how to resolve them.

Using DSC in the real world is different from using it in a test lab. You have to consider the security restrictions and other environmental configuration that affects the functionality of DSC. Chapter 11 offers you a set of tips from the field.

CHAPTER 7

■ ■ ■

DSC Configuration Delivery Modes

In the configuration management life cycle, configuration delivery plays a major role. Once a configuration is authored, a delivery mode helps to enact the configuration on the target systems. These modes dictate how the configuration is enforced and corrected, as required. DSC supports two types of delivery modes: Push and Pull. We have briefly touched upon these modes in Chapter 4. This chapter helps to build on that knowledge and provides additional details on how exactly these modes work.

Push Mode

The first DSC configuration delivery mode we discussed was the Push mode. By this mode, the configuration to be enacted gets *pushed* to the node, whether it is local or remote. This is unidirectional and immediate. By *unidirectional*, we mean that the configuration is pushed from a management system to a target node. The configuration pushed to the node is enacted immediately. This is done using the Start-DscConfiguration cmdlet. Whether the target node is local or remote, you are required to run the WinRM service and configure the WinRM listeners. In the preceding chapters, we saw how to configure WinRM and looked at several examples using the Start-DscConfiguration cmdlet. In this section, we will expand on that knowldedge and explore some of the parameters that we did not discuss as well as an alternate method to push the configuration to target systems.

In our earlier examples, we saw the Wait, Verbose, and Path parameters of the Start-DscConfiguration cmdlet. In this chapter, we will first conduct a quick overview of all the parameters on this cmdlet and then look at some examples that demonstrate the use of the cmdlet's remaining parameters. Table 7-1 provides an overview of the parameters of the Start-DscConfiguration cmdlet, excluding its common parameters.

Table 7-1. Overview of the Start-DscConfiguration Cmdlet Parameters

Parameter Name	Description
CimSession	Specifies a Common Information Model (CIM) session that should be used to run the cmdlet. This can either be a computer name or a CIM session created using the New-CimSession cmdlet.
ComputerName	Specifies the target system computer name for matching with an MOF file at the path specified using the Path parameter
Credential	Specifies the credentials required to perform configuration change on the target system
Force	Specifies if the configuration should be pushed, even when the target system is configured to use the Pull mode

(continued)

179

Table 7-1. (*continued*)

Parameter Name	Description
JobName	Specifies the name of the job. The configuration change runs in a background job when this parameter is specified.
Path	Specifies the path of a folder containing the configuration MOF files
ThrottleLimit	Specifies the maximum number of concurrent operations that can be used to run the cmdlet
Verbose	Specifies whether the configuration enactment verbose messages from the target system should be displayed or not
Wait	Specifies whether the console will be blocked until the configuration change is complete

In the next section, we will look at some of these parameters in detail and examine their need and proper use. We have already seen several examples of the Wait, Verbose, and Path parameters. After reviewing the parameters, we will consider some of the Push mode's limitations.

Using Start-DscConfiguration Parameters

When using the Start-DscConfiguration cmdlet, I recommend that you always use these parameters when you are dealing with a fewer number of target systems. When dealing with a larger number of target systems, it does not make a lot of sense either to wait at the console for the configuration change to complete or to look at the verbose stream of messages from the configuration resources. So, this is where the -JobName parameter plays a role.

■ **Tip** You can simply remove the -Wait parameter to run the configuration as a background job. It is not mandatory to use the -JobName parameter to start the configuration enactment process as a background job. However, the -JobName parameter makes it easy to identify the configuration job and access the state of the configuration job(s).

When using the -JobName parameter, the Start-DscConfiguration cmdlet starts the configuration enactment process as a background job and returns a job object. This job object can be used to monitor the job progress and receive the output from the configuration change process. This job object is a PowerShell configuration job object, and we can examine it by accessing its members.

Let us start with a configuration script that helps us understand this.

```
Configuration ScriptDemo {
    Node ("WC7-1", "WC81-1") {
        Script ScriptDemo {
            GetScript = {
                @{
                    GetScript = $GetScript
                    SetScript = $SetScript
                    TestScript = $TestScript
                    Result = "TestScript"
                }
            }
```

```
        SetScript = {
            Write-Verbose "Sleeping for 50 seconds"
            Start-Sleep 50
            Write-Verbose "Completed Script task"
        }

        TestScript = {
            $false
        }
    }
  }
}
```

ScriptDemo

The preceding configuration script uses the Script resource that just waits for some time. Apart from that, what we do in the SetScript script block is to write some verbose messages. The following code snippet shows how to use the -JobName parameter:

```
$ConfigJob = Start-DscConfiguration -JobName scriptjob -Path .\ScriptDemo -Verbose
```

It's simple. This starts the configuration enactment process for all the MOF files that exist in the ScriptDemo folder. The $ConfigJob variable becomes a container job for all the configuration jobs started for every target system MOF in the ScriptDemo folder. This is shown in Figure 7-1.

```
PS C:\Scripts> ScriptDemo

    Directory: C:\Scripts\ScriptDemo

Mode            LastWriteTime     Length Name
----            -------------     ------ ----
-a---      5/26/2014   8:04 PM      2008 WC7-1.mof
-a---      5/26/2014   8:04 PM      2010 WC81-1.mof


PS C:\Scripts> $ConfigJob = Start-DscConfiguration -JobName scriptjob -Path .\ScriptDemo -ComputerName WC7-1 -Verbose
VERBOSE: Time taken for configuration job to complete is 0.015 seconds
```

Figure 7-1. *Using the -JobName parameter*

The ChildJobs property of the $ConfigJob object gives a list of jobs started for each MOF at the ScriptDemo directory (see Figure 7-2).

```
PS C:\Scripts> $ConfigJob.ChildJobs

Id    Name      PSJobTypeName    State       HasMoreData    Location     Command
--    ----      -------------    -----       -----------    --------     -------
9     Job9      Configuratio...  Completed   True           WC7-1        $ConfigJob = Start-Dsc...
10    Job10     Configuratio...  Completed   True           WC81-1       $ConfigJob = Start-Dsc...
11    Job11     Configuratio...  Failed      True           WC811        $ConfigJob = Start-Dsc...
```

Figure 7-2. *Child jobs started for configuration enactment*

As we see in Figure 7-2, one of the child jobs failed for some reason. In fact, there is no computer named WC811. I had copied an MOF with that name to the ScriptDemo folder. To understand why that job failed, we have to look at the job object properties.

We can use the Get-Member cmdlet to see all the properties of the job object.

```
Get-Job -Name Job11 | Get-Member -MemberType Properties
```

As shown in Figure 7-3, there are five properties that give us the output from the configuration change. These are the Debug, Error, Output, Verbose, and Warning properties.

```
   TypeName: Microsoft.PowerShell.DesiredStateConfiguration.Commands.PSConfigurationJob

Name            MemberType      Definition
----            ----------      ----------
ChildJobs       Property        System.Collections.Generic.IList[System.Management.Automation.Job]
Command         Property        string Command {get;}
Debug           Property        System.Management.Automation.PSDataCollection[System.Management.Au
Error           Property        System.Management.Automation.PSDataCollection[System.Management.Au
Finished        Property        System.Threading.WaitHandle Finished {get;}
HasMoreData     Property        bool HasMoreData {get;}
Id              Property        int Id {get;}
InstanceId      Property        guid InstanceId {get;}
JobStateInfo    Property        System.Management.Automation.JobStateInfo JobStateInfo {get;}
Location        Property        string Location {get;}
Name            Property        string Name {get;set;}
Output          Property        System.Management.Automation.PSDataCollection[psobject] Output {ge
Progress        Property        System.Management.Automation.PSDataCollection[System.Management.Au
PSBeginTime     Property        System.Nullable[datetime] PSBeginTime {get;}
PSEndTime       Property        System.Nullable[datetime] PSEndTime {get;}
PSJobTypeName   Property        string PSJobTypeName {get;}
StartParameters Property        System.Collections.Generic.List[System.Management.Automation.Runsp
StatusMessage   Property        string StatusMessage {get;}
Verbose         Property        System.Management.Automation.PSDataCollection[System.Management.Au
Warning         Property        System.Management.Automation.PSDataCollection[System.Management.Au
State           ScriptProperty  System.Object State {get=$this.JobStateInfo.State.ToString();}
```

Figure 7-3. *Properties of the configuration job object*

Each of these five properties corresponds to an output stream from the configuration. The following code snippet shows how to access the values from these output streams:

```
Get-Job -Name job11 | Select Debug, Error, Output, Verbose, Warning
```

The result of this is shown in Figure 7-4.

```
Debug   : {}
Error   : {HRESULT 0x80070035}
Output  : {}
Verbose : {Perform operation 'Invoke CimMethod' with following parameters, ''methodName' = SendConfig
          root/Microsoft/Windows/DesiredStateConfiguration'., Operation 'Invoke CimMethod' complete.}
Warning : {}
```

Figure 7-4. *Output streams from the configuration change*

The error that we have seen in Figure 7-4 is a WinRM error, and it can be translated to a helpful message, using the winrm command. The helpmsg sub-command of the winrm.exe native command takes the hexdecimal error number and provides a meaningful message related to that.

```
Winrm helpmsg 0x80070035
```

So, what information do we have in the output streams of jobs that succeeded? Try this yourself. If you have used the -Verbose parameter with the Start-DscConfiguration cmdlet, you should be able to see that as the value of the Verbose property.

If all you are interested in is the verbose output stream, you can simply use the Receive-Job cmdlet with -Verbose parameter. For example, as shown in Figure 7-2, Job9 and Job10 have succeeded. These two job objects should have the verbose output, and that can be retrieved using the Receive-job cmdlet.

```
Get-Job -Name Job9, Job10 | Receive-Job -Verbose
```

By default, the Receive-Job cmdlet clears the values of output streams associated with each job object. If you want to retain those values in the job object for later use, you need to use the -Keep switch parameter with the Receive-Job cmdlet.

There are many other properties associated with the job object. We shall look at some of these when we discuss monitoring and reporting of DSC configurations, in Chapter 8.

The -ThrottleLimit parameter of the Start-DscConfiguration cmdlet governs how many concurrent operations are performed within the CIM session established by the cmdlet. For example, in the preceding example, I had three target systems on which the configuration was being enacted. All three configuration jobs we saw in Figure 7-2 executed concurrently. This is a much smaller set, and we need not worry about the resource consumption or limitations on the system from where the configuration is being pushed. However, in a scenario in which you are pushing configuration to hundreds, if not thousands, of target systems, you must ensure that these configuration jobs are throttled, so that none of them fails for lack of resources on the system used for pushing the configuration.

The default value for the -ThrottleLimit parameter is 32. However, if zero is provided as an argument to this parameter, an optimum throttle limit is calculated based on the number of CIM cmdlets running on the local computer. Following is an example of this parameter in action. I have only three target systems, so I will try to limit the concurrent actions to two. You can see the result in Figure 7-5.

```
PS C:\> Start-DscConfiguration -Verbose -Path .\ScriptDemo -JobName ScriptConfig -ThrottleLimit 2

Id   Name          PSJobTypeName    State     HasMoreData   Location            Command
--   ----          -------------    -----     -----------   --------            -------
28   ScriptConfig  Configuratio...  Running   True          WC7-1,WC81-1,WC811  Start-DscConfiguration...
VERBOSE: Time taken for configuration job to complete is 52.667 seconds
```

Figure 7-5. *Using the ThrottleLimit parameter*

As shown in Figure 7-5, the time it takes with a throttle limit of two is longer than starting all three jobs concurrently. This difference can be clearly seen from the output shown in Figure 7-1. When using the ThrottleLimit parameter, the Start-DscConfiguration cmdlet starts some jobs (based on the value specified as an argument to the ThrottleLimit parameter) and then waits for them to complete. In the Script resource example, we used the Start-Sleep command in the SetScript block to create the wait time. The result of the wait is shown in Figure 7-5.

We have already discussed the -ComputerName parameter, in Chapter 5. To summarize, the -ComputerName parameter can be used to push configuration to a specific target system on which there are many other configuration MOF files at the path specified using the -Path parameter. So, for example, if I specify WC7-1 as the argument for the -ComputerName parameter, the Start-DscConfiguration cmdlet looks for a file named WC7-1.mof at the path specified and push configuration only to this target system. This also brings up another point, which is that the MOF files present at the path value should have the target system names with .mof as an extension. When the -ComputerName parameter is not specified, the Start-DscConfiguration cmdlet uses the base name of the file as the target system name.

The -CimSession parameter has multiple-use cases. As we discussed in Chapter 4, when the Start-DscConfiguration cmdlet is used, a temporary CIM session is created to the target system, and the configuration is pushed. Instead of setting up a CIM session and tearing it down, one can use an existing CIM session to a target computer. While this is the primary-use case, there are a couple of other use cases for the -CimSession parameter. When we looked at creating WinRM listeners in Chapter 2, I had mentioned that we can create both HTTP and HTTPS listeners. By default, these listeners use port number 5895 and 5896, respectively. We also looked at changing the default port numbers for these listeners.

The first-use case for the -CimSession parameter is the non-default WinRM endpoint ports. To demonstrate this, I changed the WinRM HTTP listener port number of one of the systems, named WC7-1, to 5900. Now, with this change, pushing configuration using the Start-DscConfiguration cmdlet will fail.

Here are commands I used to change the default endpoint port number for the HTTP listener:

```
Set-Location wsman:
Set-Item -Path .\localhost\Listener\Listener_1084132640\Port -Value 5900 -Force
```

■ **Note** If you have configured the WinRM listeners using the Active Directory Group Policy, you won't be able to update the WinRM port numbers using the preceding code. You have to revoke the Group Policy and then change the port numbers, as required.

Now, with the port number reset to 5900, pushing the configuration, either using the -ComputerName parameter or simply the -Path parameter, will result in an error (see Figure 7-6).

```
PS C:\> Start-DscConfiguration -ComputerName WC7-1 -Path C:\ScriptDemo -Verbose -Wait
VERBOSE: Perform operation 'Invoke CimMethod' with following parameters, ''methodName' = SendConfigurationApp
ly,'className' = MSFT_DSCLocalConfigurationManager,'namespaceName' = root/Microsoft/Windows/DesiredStateConfi
guration'.
The client cannot connect to the destination specified in the request. Verify that the service on the
destination is running and is accepting requests. Consult the logs and documentation for the WS-Management
service running on the destination, most commonly IIS or WinRM. If the destination is the WinRM service,
run the following command on the destination to analyze and configure the WinRM service: "winrm
quickconfig".
    + CategoryInfo          : ConnectionError: (root/Microsoft/...gurationManager:String) [], CimException
    + FullyQualifiedErrorId : HRESULT 0x80338012
    + PSComputerName        : WC7-1

VERBOSE: Operation 'Invoke CimMethod' complete.
VERBOSE: Time taken for configuration job to complete is 3.075 seconds
```

Figure 7-6. *Failure in pushing configuration to a system with non-default WinRM configuration*

As shown in Figure 7-6, the Start-DscConfiguration cmdlet fails to reach the target system, as the WinRM HTTP listener is configured for port number 5900. This is our first-use case for the -CimSession parameter.

```
$CimSession = New-CimSession -ComputerName WC7-1 -Port 5900
Start-DscConfiguration -CimSession $CimSession -Path .\ScriptDemo -Verbose -Wait
```

In the preceding example, we are using the -CimSession cmdlet to create a new session and specifying the non-default WinRM listener port that we configured on the remote system. When a configuration is pushed using the Start-DscConfiguration cmdlet and the -CimSession parameter, the Start-DscConfiguration cmdlet takes the target system computer name from the CIM session properties. To be precise, the ComputerName property of the CIM session is used to identify the MOF file that contains the configuration for the target system (see Figure 7-7).

```
VERBOSE: Perform operation 'Invoke CimMethod' with following parameters, ''methodName' = SendConfigurationApp
ly,'className' = MSFT_DSCLocalConfigurationManager,'namespaceName' = root/Microsoft/Windows/DesiredStateConfi
guration'.
VERBOSE: An LCM method call arrived from computer WC7-1 with user sid S-1-5-21-3906674661-2793090968-24913020
47-500.
VERBOSE: [WC7-1]: LCM:  [ Start  Set      ]
VERBOSE: [WC7-1]: LCM:  [ Start  Resource ]  [[Script]ScriptDemo]
VERBOSE: [WC7-1]: LCM:  [ Start  Test     ]  [[Script]ScriptDemo]
VERBOSE: [WC7-1]: LCM:  [ End    Test     ]  [[Script]ScriptDemo]  in 0.0150 seconds.
VERBOSE: [WC7-1]: LCM:  [ Start  Set      ]  [[Script]ScriptDemo]
VERBOSE: [WC7-1]:                            [[Script]ScriptDemo] Sleeping for 50 seconds
VERBOSE: [WC7-1]:                            [[Script]ScriptDemo] Completed Script task
VERBOSE: [WC7-1]: LCM:  [ End    Set      ]  [[Script]ScriptDemo]  in 50.0000 seconds.
VERBOSE: [WC7-1]: LCM:  [ End    Resource ]  [[Script]ScriptDemo]
VERBOSE: [WC7-1]: LCM:  [ End    Set      ]
VERBOSE: [WC7-1]: LCM:  [ End    Set      ]  in  50.0460 seconds.
VERBOSE: Operation 'Invoke CimMethod' complete.
VERBOSE: Time taken for configuration job to complete is 50.073 seconds
```

Figure 7-7. *Using CIM session for pushing configuration*

The second-use case for the -CimSession parameter is when the target systems are configured to use HTTPS WinRM listeners. With the knowledge you have gained so far about using this parameter, try it yourself, to push configuration to a target system with HTTPS listeners. Here is a hint. You need to use the CIM session option to specify that the target system has to be accessed over SSL. If you don't have a system that is configured to use HTTPS WinRM endpoints, take a look at Chapter 2 again, to create an HTTPS endpoint. The final parameter that we have to look at is the -Force parameter. This is used to push configuration to a target system that is configured as a client for the Pull mode of configuration delivery (see Figure 7-8). We will talk more about the Pull mode in a bit, but this is what happens if we don't use the -Force parameter and try push configuration to a system configured as a pull client.

```
PS C:\> Start-DscConfiguration -ComputerName WSR2-2 -Path .\ScriptDemo -Verbose -Wait
VERBOSE: Perform operation 'Invoke CimMethod' with following parameters, ''methodName' = SendConfigurationApp
ly,'className' = MSFT_DSCLocalConfigurationManager,'namespaceName' = root/Microsoft/Windows/DesiredStateConfi
guration'.
VERBOSE: An LCM method call arrived from computer DEMO-AD with user sid S-1-5-21-3906674661-2793090968-249130
2047-500.
VERBOSE: [WSR2-2]: LCM:  [ Start  Set      ]
VERBOSE: [WSR2-2]: LCM:  [ End    Set      ]
A PUSH operation was requested without -Force while configured for PULL processing.
    + CategoryInfo          : InvalidArgument: (root/Microsoft/...gurationManager:String) [], CimException
    + FullyQualifiedErrorId : MI RESULT 4
    + PSComputerName        : WSR2-2

VERBOSE: Operation 'Invoke CimMethod' complete.
VERBOSE: Time taken for configuration job to complete is 0.138 seconds
```

Figure 7-8. *Pushing configuration to a system configured as a pull client*

What we see in Figure 7-8 is self-explanatory. To be able to push configuration to a pull client, we have to use the -Force parameter. Let us now look at the Pull mode configuration delivery, and then you can try using the -Force parameter to push the configuration to a target system you've configured as pull client.

Limitations of the Push Mode

Let us conclude our discussion on the Push mode of configuration delivery by pointing out the limitations of this mode. Push mode is simple and easy. It does not require any infrastructure services, such as a central shared location to host the configurations, and so on. However, the Push mode is not scalable. Pushing configuration to hundreds, if not thousands, of systems would take quite long and can be limited, based on the resources available on the system on which the Start-DscConfiguration cmdlet is being run. Of course, this is where I said the ThrottleLimit parameter will help, but it increases the overall time it takes to complete configuration enactment.

To enact configuration, we need all resource modules to be present on the target system. This represents another limitation of the Push mode. For example, if you have custom DSC resources used in a configuration script, the modules for these resources must be copied to target systems prior to pushing the configuration. You can, of course, do this using another configuration script, but there are better ways to solve this problem. Also, when using Push mode, once the configuration is pushed to the target systems, there is no simple and easy method to get an overview of the configuration state from all the target systems.

This is where the Pull mode of configuration delivery helps. Using the Pull mode, we can solve both the scalability and configuration and resource module distribution problems. In the following sections, we will look at the Pull mode of configuration delivery, different methods of configuring Pull mode, and configuring target systems as pull clients.

Pull Mode

Unlike the Push mode for configuration delivery, the Pull mode is bidirectional. This means that the pull server and the client both communicate with each other to manage the client configuration. Figure 7-9 depicts an overview of this process. It also depicts the components involved in the Pull mode of configuration delivery.

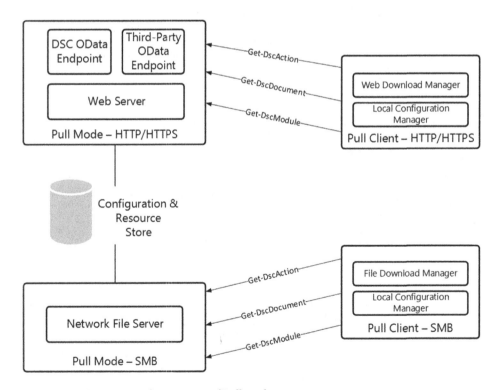

Figure 7-9. *Overview and component of Pull mode*

Before we go into details about the flow of configuration in Pull mode, let us look into those of setting up a pull service and configuring a pull client. DSC supports two types of pull servers:

- OData-based pull service

- SMB-based pull service

Each of the methods we are going to see has its pros and cons. We will look at each of these in depth and consider the configuration steps involved.

OData-Based (HTTP/HTTPS) Pull Service

The Windows Management Framework 4.0 release includes a feature called Windows PowerShell Desired State Configuration Service. This is the official name, but you will find that many in the community simply refer to this as DSC pull service. So, we, too, shall stick to the short form. Using this feature, we can configure either an HTTP or HTTPS endpoint for the pull service. This feature implements the required support for setting up an OData-based pull service. Installing this feature alone does not ensure a functional pull service but does require that a bunch of additional steps be performed. We will look at these steps to manually configure the pull service provided as a part of WMF 4.0. In simple terms, we will learn it the hard way first! This is necessary in order to understand the intricate details of how this pull service is configured. It will help us to troubleshoot any problems that arise after we set up the service.

■ **Note** The Windows PowerShell Desired State Configuration Service feature is available only on systems running Windows 8.1, Windows Server 2012, and Windows Server 2012 R2. This chapter assumes that you are setting up the DSC pull service on either Windows Server 2012 or Windows Server 2012 R2.

There is an easy method to configure the DSC pull service, using a custom DSC resource written by the Windows PowerShell team at Microsoft. There is an explanation on how to use this custom resource in Appendix A. And, by the way, the steps I am going to describe in this section are derived from this custom resource. If you prefer the quick way of getting the pull service running, skip to Appendix A, to complete the pull service configuration. Continue reading, if you want to understand the steps involved.

Configuring OData Endpoints

As I've mentioned, there are multiple steps in installing and configuring the DSC pull service. We start by installing the Windows PowerShell Desired State Configuration Service also known as the DSC-Service. We can use the Add-WindowsFeature cmdlet for this.

```
Add-WindowsFeature -Name DSC-Service
```

■ **Note** This chapter focuses only on deploying and configuring the pull service on Windows Server 2012 and Windows Server 2012 R2. With regard to the down-level server OS, such as Windows Server 2008 R2, while the DSC-Service feature is not available in Server Manager, it is possible to deploy and configure the pull service using the DISM command line. Dave Wyatt, a PowerShell MVP, describes this in his blog post at http://davewyatt.wordpress.com/2014/06/07/how-to-install-a-dsc-pull-server-on-windows-2008-r2/.

This service depends on other roles and/or features, such as Web-Server (Internet Information Server) and so on. The dependent features get installed as a part of the DSC pull service installation. Once the feature is installed, you can see that there is a folder named DSCService at the path $env:ProgramFiles\WindowsPowerShell and another folder named PullServer at the path $pshome\modules\PSDesiredStateConfiguration.

The next step in configuring the DSC pull service is setting up an IIS web site. The following code snippet helps us do that. First, we set up some default values that we will use later.

```
#Path to the PullServer service and configuration files
$pathPullServer = "$pshome\modules\PSDesiredStateConfiguration\PullServer"

#Path where the DscService data is stored
$rootDataPath ="$env:PROGRAMFILES\WindowsPowerShell\DscService"

#Database Provider settings for target system inventory
$jet4provider = "System.Data.OleDb"
$jet4database = "Provider=Microsoft.Jet.OLEDB.4.0;Data Source=$env:PROGRAMFILES\WindowsPowerShell\
DscService\Devices.mdb;"

#Language settings for retrieving right MUI files
$culture = Get-Culture
$language = $culture.TwoLetterISOLanguageName

#Dependent service binaries
$dependentBinaries = "$pathPullServer\Microsoft.Powershell.DesiredStateConfiguration.Service.dll"

#Dependent service MUI files based on $Language value
$dependentMUIFiles = "$pathPullServer\$language\Microsoft.Powershell.DesiredStateConfiguration.
Service.Resources.dll"

#Path to the ASAX file used for the endpoint
$asax = "$pathPullServer\Global.asax"

#Application Pool name
$appPool = "PSWS"

#Path to the web.config file for the Pull Service endpoint
$cfgfile = "$pathPullServer\PSDSCPullServer.config"

#Path to the pull service definition file
$svc = "$pathPullServer\PSDSCPullServer.svc"

#Path to the Pull service MOF file
$mof = "$pathPullServer\PSDSCPullServer.mof"

#Path to the Pull service dispatch XML configuration file
$dispatch = "$pathPullServer\PSDSCPullServer.xml"

#Name of the IIS site for pull service
$Site = "PullSvc"
```

```
#Name of the IIS web application for the pull service
$App = "PullSvc"

#Port number to be used for the Pull Service endpoint
$Port = "8080"

#Path to the site root directory
$Path = "$env:SystemDrive\inetpub\wwwroot\$Site"

#Path where the custom resource modules for distribution be stored
$ModulePath = "$env:PROGRAMFILES\WindowsPowerShell\DscService\Modules"

#Path where the configuration for distribution be stored
$ConfigurationPath = "$env:PROGRAMFILES\WindowsPowerShell\DscService\Configuration"
```

That is one long list of default values! I have added the comments for each variable defined here, so that you get an idea of why that variable is defined and how the value will be used. Once we have these values set, we can start copying the files necessary to enable the pull service endpoint.

```
$null = New-Item -ItemType container -Path $path
$binFolderPath = Join-Path $path "bin"
$null = New-Item -path $binFolderPath  -itemType "directory" -Force
Copy-Item $dependentBinaries $binFolderPath -Force

$muiPath = Join-Path $binFolderPath $language

if (!(Test-Path $muiPath))
{
    $null = New-Item -ItemType container $muiPath
}
Copy-Item $dependentMUIFiles $muiPath -Force

Copy-Item $cfgfile (Join-Path $path "web.config") -Force
Copy-Item $svc $path -Force
Copy-Item $mof $path -Force
Copy-Item $dispatch $path -Force
Copy-Item $asax $path -Force
```

In the preceding code snippet, we are taking the necessary files to the root directory of the IIS site created for the pull service endpoint. This list includes files, such as the service definition file, the MOF, and the dispatch XML files, along with the web.config file.

```
Restart-WebAppPool - Name "DefaultAppPool"
```

We stop any existing sites and restart the Default Web Application pool in IIS. We are now all set to create the new IIS site and pull server endpoint. As I mentioned, we can either create an HTTP or HTTPS endpoint. The HTTPS endpoint is what is recommended but requires that we have a web server certificate on the system hosting the pull service endpoint. The HTTP endpoint is not secure and does not need any certificates. So, it is easy to create an HTTP endpoint. However, to use an HTTP endpoint for the pull clients, we need additional configuration on the pull client. We will see that toward the end of this chapter.

Whether we are creating an HTTP or HTTPS endpoint, we need an application pool for that. Let us create that first.

```
$null = New-WebAppPool -Name $appPool
$appPoolItem = Get-Item IIS:\AppPools\$appPool
$appPoolItem.managedRuntimeVersion = "v4.0"
$appPoolItem.enable32BitAppOnWin64 = $true
$appPoolItem.processModel.identityType = 0
$appPoolItem | Set-Item
```

We have set $appPool to "PSWS." The preceding code snippet creates an application pool and sets the application pool identity to 0, which indicates a local system.

Creating an HTTP Endpoint

Creating an HTTP endpoint is simple. We just have to create an IIS site and assign the port number we had already provided as $Port in the default values.

```
$siteID = (Get-Website | Sort-Object ID | Select-Object -Last 1 ID).ID+1 $webSite = New-WebSite
-Name $site -Id $siteID -Port $port -IPAddress "*" -PhysicalPath $path -ApplicationPool $appPool
```

The $SiteID variable is used to generate a unique ID for the new endpoint, and we use the values of the $Site and $Port variables and the New-Website cmdlet to create the HTTP endpoint for the pull service. We point this site to the folder specified, as a value to the $Path variable.

Creating an HTTPS Endpoint

Creating an HTTPS endpoint requires a certificate bound to the IIS endpoint. If you already have an Active Directory Certificate authority and other means for generating a certificate, go ahead to the next steps for creating an IIS site and binding the certificate to it. If not, you can create a self-signed certificate and install it on the system on which the pull service is being configured. You can use the Get-ChildItem cmdlet to see the thumbprint associated with the certificate on the web server. Note that you will require a web server certificate that is capable of server authentication, and not the client authentication certificate, as we saw in Chapter 6. So, if you are using the instructions given in Chapter 6 to create a self-signed certificate using makecert.exe, make sure that you change the Enhanced Key Usage (EKU) value to 1.3.6.1.5.5.7.3.1, which represents server authentication.

```
#Use a Web Server certificate and not a client authentication cert
$ServerCert = (Get-ChildItem Cert:\LocalMachine\my).Where({$_.EnhancedKeyUsageList.FriendlyName -eq
'Server Authentication'})
if ($ServerCert) {
    $certificate = $ServerCert.Thumbprint
} else {
    throw "there is no server authentication certificate"
}
```

Once we have the certificate thumbprint, we can create an IIS site and bind the certificate to it.

```
$webSite = New-WebSite -Name $site -Id $siteID -Port $port -IPAddress "*" -PhysicalPath $path
-ApplicationPool $appPool -Ssl
Remove-Item IIS:\SSLBindings\0.0.0.0!$port -ErrorAction Ignore
$null = Get-Item CERT:\LocalMachine\MY\$certificate | New-Item IIS:\SSLBindings\0.0.0.0!$port
```

We now have to create a web application for the IIS site we created. The steps from here onward are same for both HTTP and HTTPS endpoints.

```
$null = New-WebApplication -Name $app -Site $site -PhysicalPath $path -ApplicationPool $appPool
```

Once we have the web application created, we can start configuring the other aspects of the IIS endpoint. We start by allowing different authentication methods.

```
$Auths = "anonymous","basic","windows"
[System.Reflection.Assembly]::LoadWithPartialName("Microsoft.Web.Administration") | Out-Null
foreach ($auth in $Auths) {
    $webAdminSrvMgr = new-object Microsoft.Web.Administration.ServerManager
    $appHostConfig = $webAdminSrvMgr.GetApplicationHostConfiguration()
    $authenticationType = "$($auth)Authentication"
    $appHostConfigSection = $appHostConfig.GetSection("system.webServer/security/authentication/$aut
    henticationType", $Site)
    $appHostConfigSection.OverrideMode="Allow"
    $webAdminSrvMgr.CommitChanges()
    Start-Sleep 4
}
```

The final few steps in configuring the pull service endpoint are to set up the device inventory database for the pull clients, set up the directories for configuration and module distribution, and update the IIS web.config file to ensure we have the right database provider settings. The devices.mdb file available at the $PathPullServer is used for the device inventory.

```
Copy-Item "$pathPullServer\Devices.mdb" $rootDataPath -Force
```

We have to create the folders in which we intend to store the configuration MOF and resource modules files for distribution to the pull clients.

```
$null = New-Item -path "$ConfigurationPath" -itemType "directory" -Force
$null = New-Item -path "$ModulePath" -itemType "directory" -Force
```

To conclude the configuration, we have to update the web.config of the IIS endpoint. We will use a hash table that contains the keys and values that we have to add to the web.config file.

```
[hashtable] $PullSettingHash = [Ordered] @{
    dbprovider = $jet4provider
    dbconnectionstr = $jet4database
    ConfigurationPath = $ConfigurationPath
    ModulePath = $ModulePath
}
```

We must use the Jet DB provider for the pull service endpoint. Also, the configuration and module paths have to be added to the web.config file, so that the endpoint can use that for distribution to the pull clients. We will use a function (derived from the xPSDesiredStateConfiguration resource) to update the web.config file. Here is the function definition:

```
function Set-AppSettingsInWebconfig
{
    param (

        # Physical path for the IIS Endpoint on the machine (possibly under inetpub/wwwroot)
        [parameter(Mandatory)]
        [ValidateNotNullOrEmpty()]
        [String] $path,

        # Key to add/update
        [parameter(Mandatory)]
        [ValidateNotNullOrEmpty()]
        [String] $key,

        # Value
        [parameter(Mandatory)]
        [ValidateNotNullOrEmpty()]
        [String] $value

    )

    $webconfig = Join-Path $path "web.config"
    [bool] $Found = $false

    if (Test-Path $webconfig)
    {
        $xml = [xml](get-content $webconfig)
        $root = $xml.get_DocumentElement()

        foreach( $item in $root.appSettings.add)
        {
            if( $item.key -eq $key )
            {
                $item.value = $value;
                $Found = $true;
            }
        }

        if( -not $Found)
        {
            $newElement = $xml.CreateElement("add")
            $nameAtt1 = $xml.CreateAttribute("key")
            $nameAtt1.psbase.value = $key;
            $null = $newElement.SetAttributeNode($nameAtt1)
```

```
        $nameAtt2 = $xml.CreateAttribute("value")
        $nameAtt2.psbase.value = $value;
        $null = $newElement.SetAttributeNode($nameAtt2)

        $null = $xml.configuration["appSettings"].AppendChild($newElement)
    }
}

$xml.Save($webconfig)
}
```

We will now iterate over the hash table and update the web.config file, using the Set-AppSettingsInWebConfig function. Here is how we do it:

```
foreach ($key in $PullSettingHash.Keys) {
    Set-AppSettingsInWebconfig -path $Path -key $key -value $PullSettingHash[$key]
}
```

That's it. We should have a functional pull server endpoint at this stage, and we can verify it by accessing the URL represented by some of the default variable values we defined earlier. For example, based on the values I showed in this section, the URL to the pull service will be either

```
http://wsr2-1.dscdemo.lab:8080/PullSvc/PSDSCPullServer.svc/
```

or

```
https://wsr2-1.dscdemo.lab:8080/PullSvc/PSDSCPullServer.svc/
```

based on the type of endpoint you created. When we access this endpoint in a browser, we should see XML output with the available methods Action and Module.

The XML output you see must be similar to what is shown in Figure 7-10. The Action and Module methods shown in the output represent the service methods available to the pull clients. We will discuss more about this when we look at configuring a pull client and enacting configuration in Pull mode.

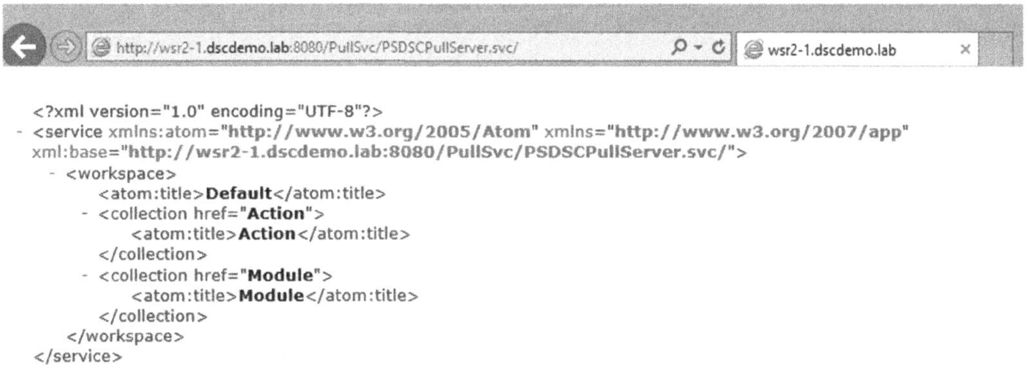

Figure 7-10. *Successful configuration of the DSC pull service*

So far, we have looked at creating representational state transfer (REST)-based pull service endpoints that either use HTTP or HTTPS. As you have seen in this section, the configuration of these endpoints is complex and requires separate services deployed for each protocol. The pull service can also be deployed to support an SMB (Server Message Block) file share too. The next section shows you how to configure this.

SMB-Based Pull Server

The process of configuring a Server Message Block (SMB)–based pull server is much simpler. In fact, we just create an SMB share for storing the configuration Managed Object Format (MOF) files and resource modules. All you have to do is identify a system that will host the SMB file share, create the file share, and assign appropriate permissions. Once you have a system identified for hosting the file share, you can use the New-SmbShare cmdlet to create a file share for storing configuration and modules.

```
New-SmbShare -Name SMBpull -Path C:\SMBPull -ReadAccess Everyone -Description "SMB Share
for Pull Mode"
```

This is really it! You have just configured the pull service over SMB! Okay, there is more. What we created is really a staging area for the configuration and resource modules. But, when using the SMB mode, you need not do anything on the server that is hosting the file share but configure the target system to look at the SMB file share for any configuration and required modules. Also, notice that in the preceding command, I have given read access to everyone. This gives all systems configured as pull clients access to the SMB file share in which the configuration and modules are stored. Is this really a best practice? Not necessarily, but there are limitations in DSC packaged with WMF 4.0. We will have that discussion in the following sections, when we look at how we can configure the target systems as pull clients for using either an OData-based or SMB-based pull service.

Configuring Pull Clients

As we have seen so far, it is possible to create either an OData-based or a SMB-based pull service for configuration and module distribution. The pull client configuration on the target systems depends on your choice of pull service. As shown in Figure 7-9, each service in the Pull mode, whether SMB or REST, has an associated download manager that helps the Local Configuration Manager (LCM) on the target systems download configurations and modules that are required. Therefore, the pull client configuration settings needed for the LCM are specific to the type of pull service being used. Before looking at the different configuration options for each type of pull service, let us revisit the LCM and examine its settings related to pull client configuration. To recap, Table 7-2 shows a subset of LCM properties that are used for pull client configuration.

Table 7-2. *LCM Properties Used in Pull Client Configuration*

Method Name	Description
AllowModuleOverwrite	Specifies if the modules downloaded from a pull server overwrite the old ones. This property takes Boolean values. The default value is False.
ConfigurationMode	Specifies how the LCM should apply the configuration. Valid values are as follows:
	ApplyOnly: Configuration is applied once.
	ApplyAndMonitor: Configuration is applied, and the LCM monitors whether any changes occur. If configuration drift is detected, it is reported in logs.
	ApplyAndAutoCorrect: Configuration is applied, and the LCM monitors whether changes occur. If configuration drift is detected, the LCM reapplies the configuration.
RefreshMode	Refresh mode, which can accept one of two values:
	Push: Configuration is sent (pushed) to the node by running the Start-DscConfiguration cmdlet (from the same or remote node). This is the default value.
	Pull: Node periodically checks for configuration updates on the pull server and gets (pulls) it when available. The pull server from which to pull the configuration is specified by values in DownloadManagerName and DownloadManagerCustomData properties.
ConfigurationId	GUID, which is used to get the configuration from the server when the RefreshMode is set to Pull mode
Credential	Credentials to access remote resources when using Pull mode over SMB
DownloadManagerName	Specifies which download manager to use. There are two download managers available:
	WebDownloadManager (used with Pull mode over HTTP)
	DscFileDownloadManager (used for Pull mode over SMB)
DownloadManagerCustomData	Specifies additional data to send to the download manager
ConfigurationModeFrequencyMins	Specifies how often (in minutes) the LCM ensures that the configuration is in the desired state
RefreshModeFrequencyMins	Specifies how often (in minutes) the LCM attempts to obtain the configuration from the pull server. If configuration on the pull server differs from the current one on the target node, it is copied to the pending store and applied.

The first step that we need perform to make the target system a pull client is to update the RefreshMode property to PULL. However, changing this property to Pull mode does not help retrieve the configuration and resource modules from pull servers. We need to assign a unique GUID to the pull client on target system. This unique GUID must be assigned as the value of the ConfigurationID property of the LCM meta-configuration. The pull client uses this unique ID to identify the configuration documents on the pull server whether it is SMB-based or OData-based. For now, you can use the NewGuid() method of the System.GUID class in .NET. This method generates a random GUID that can be used as the value of ConfigurationID. For example, [System.Guid]::NewGuid() generates the random GUID.

Download Manager for Pull Clients

We need to choose the right download manager, based on the pull server implementation, and then add the custom data for the download manager we choose to configure. Therefore, the properties we need to update for this are the DownloadManagerName and the DownloadManagerCustomData.

As we have seen in Table 7-2, the DownloadManagerName property can take two values: DscFileDownloadManager or WebDownloadManager. Each of these download managers is a binary PowerShell module that is written to access the pull server (SMB or REST) and download the configuration and modules required. Each of these PowerShell modules has three cmdlets, as shown in Table 7-3. These cmdlets help retrieve the configuration and modules from the pull servers Note that these modules are not exposed as PowerShell modules in the Get-Module cmdlet (with -ListAvailable switch parameter) output, as they are not in the path represented by the $env:PSModulePath variable. However, you can import these modules, using the Import-Module cmdlet, into the current session, by using the full path.

Table 7-3. *Overview of File and Web Download Managers in Pull Mode*

Download Manager	Description
DscFileDownloadManager	**Location:** $PSHOME\Modules\PSDesiredStateConfiguration\DownloadManager\ DSCFileDownloadManager
	Module Name: DSCFileDownloadManager
WebDownloadManager	**Location:** $PSHOME\Modules\PSDesiredStateConfiguration\WebDownloadManager
	Module Name: WebDownloadManager
Cmdlets in Download Manager Modules	Get-DscAction This cmdlet is used by the pull client to determine if configuration on the pull server is different from that on the target system.
	Get-DscDocument This cmdlet is used by the pull client to retrieve the configuration document from the pull server.
	Get-DscModule This cmdlet is used by the pull client to retrieve the dependent modules and unpack them on the target system, to enact the configuration specified in the configuration document.

■ **Note**   It is not necessary to use the cmdlets in the download manager modules manually at any time. They are meant to enable the pull client to function. In addition, it is useful to understand their purpose, so that in the event of debugging or troubleshooting issues with pull client configurations, you know where to start from.

Once we understand and chose the right pull server for our environment, we can get started with configuring the pull clients. Apart from the download managers, we also discussed that the DownloadManagerCustomData property must be set to point the pull client to the right pull server. The value to this property is a hash table containing key-value pairs that describe how the download managers (web or file) can reach the pull server (REST or SMB). Table 7-4 provides an overview of the valid key-value pairs used for each download manager.

Table 7-4. *Download Manager Custom Data for Each Module*

Download Manager Name	Custom Data
DscFileDownloadManager	**SourcePath:** Represents the SMB file share UNC path
	SkipChecksum: Specifies that the checksum at the source path on the pull server is to be ignored
WebDownload Manager	**SourceUrl:** Represents the HTTP or HTTPS endpoint URL of the pull server
	AllowUnSecureConnection: Used when the pull server REST endpoint is HTTP and not HTTPS

Pull Client Configuration for an OData-Based Service

When using a REST or OData-based pull server, there are two types of endpoints we can use. We have already seen that we can create HTTP- or HTTPS-based endpoints. In this section, we will see how to configure each of these endpoints. There is not much difference in using either of these endpoints, except for the use of the AllowUnSecureConnection property in the DownloadManagerCustomData.

HTTP Endpoints

The HTTP endpoints provide an unsecure connection between the pull clients and the pull server for transferring configuration and modules. The following configuration documents show an example of this meta-configuration.

```
Configuration PullClientConfig {
    Node Localhost {
        LocalConfigurationManager {
            ConfigurationID = 'e86549dc-7a5f-45b6-9d66-560d980587a8'
            RefreshMode = "Pull"
            DownloadManagerName = "WebDownloadManager"
            DownloadManagerCustomData = @{
                ServerUrl = "http://wsr2-1.dscdemo.lab:8080/PullSvc/PSDSCPullServer.svc/";
                AllowUnSecureConnection="True"}
        }
    }
}
 =PullClientConfig

Set-DscLocalConfigurationManager -Path .\PullClientConfig
```

What is shown in the preceding code snippet is sufficient to configure LCM on the target system as a pull client for an HTTP-based pull server. As you can see, we have specified the AllowUnsecureConnection property and set it to True. Similar to what is shown in Chapter 6 for creating advanced configurations, it is possible to use configuration data or parameterize the above configuration script to enact this LCM meta-configuration across multiple servers in the domain.

The HTTP endpoints are easy to set up and configure, but they are not secure. It is recommended that you use HTTPS endpoints instead of HTTP endpoints for Pull mode configuration delivery using OData.

HTTPS Endpoints

Using an HTTPS-based pull service endpoint provides a secure way to distribute configurations. As we saw in the pull service configuration section, we need a trusted server authentication certificate on the pull server hosting the IIS endpoint. For the pull client configuration, we need nothing special. We can take the same meta-configuration script as in the preceding example, sans the AllowUnsecureConnection property in the DownloadManagerCustomData.

```
Configuration PullClientConfig {
    Node Localhost {
        LocalConfigurationManager {
            ConfigurationID = 'e86549dc-7a5f-45b6-9d66-560d980587a8'
            RefreshMode = "Pull"
            DownloadManagerName = "WebDownloadManager"
            DownloadManagerCustomData = @{
                ServerUrl = "https://wsr2-1.dscdemo.lab:8080/PullSvc/PSDSCPullServer.svc/"}
        }
    }
}

PullClientConfig

Set-DscLocalConfigurationManager -Path .\PullClientConfig
```

The preceding meta-configuration document enables us to change the pull client, to get the configuration and modules using an HTTPS-based endpoint. This concludes the basic configuration of pull client that uses HTTP- or HTTPS-based pull service endpoints. Once again, it is recommended that you use HTTPS-based endpoints, configured with certificates to ensure that the communication between the pull clients and the server is encrypted and secure.

Pull Client Configuration for an SMB-Based Pull Server

When using an SMB file-share-based pull server, the pull clients use the File Download Manager module to retrieve the configuration modules. When configuring the pull client for the SMB Pull mode, we have to provide the SourcePath in the DownloadManagerCustomData. Let us see how.

```
Configuration PullClientConfig {
    Node Localhost {
        LocalConfigurationManager {
            ConfigurationID = 'e86549dc-7a5f-45b6-9d66-560d980587a8'
            RefreshMode = "Pull"
            DownloadManagerName = "DscFileDownloadManager"
            DownloadManagerCustomData = @{SourcePath = "\\WSR2-1\SMBPull"}
        }
    }
}

PullClientConfig

Set-DscLocalConfigurationManager -Path .\PullClientConfig
```

Using the preceding meta-configuration script, the target system can be configured to pull configuration and modules from the SMB file share specified as the SourcePath in the DownloadManagerCustomData property. As we saw in Table 7-4, with the SMB Pull mode, SkipChecksum can be used in the DownloadManagerCustomData. We will see more about this in a later section.

If you go back and look at the way we configured the SMB file share, you will note that we gave Everyone read access to the share, so that all pull clients can connect and read the configuration MOF files from the share. However, this is not a best practice. Alternatively, you can give each computer account, or the Domain Computers group in AD, permissions to read the SMB file share. This is what we did when we looked at Archive and File resources in Chapter 5. This method is not scalable and is a management nightmare. The right method is to provide a domain user account (specifically created to allow access by the SMB pull client) read permissions to the SMB file share. We can then use this user account's credentials as a value to the Credential property of the LCM meta-configuration. Similar to how we encrypted credentials for the built-in resources, we can use the same certificate-based method to encrypt the user credentials required for SMB file share access. The following code snippet shows an example of using the encrypted credentials. As with a DSC resource, we would require client authentication certificates installed on the target system for using the encrypted credentials. However, at the time of writing (in WMF 4.0 release), LCM is not capable of decrypting the credentials provided for SMB file share access. Therefore, the following method, although it gets configured with no errors, won't work in pulling the configuration and modules from the SMB-based pull server.

```
mkdir C:\cert -force
$cert = Get-ChildItem Cert:\LocalMachine\my | Where-Object { $_.Subject -eq 'CN=WSR2-2.dscdemo.lab' }
$thumbprint = $cert.Thumbprint

#Export-Certificate available only on Windows 8.1 & above and Windows Server 2012 R2 & above
#For other down-level OS look at ther alternate method shown below
Export-Certificate -Type CERT -Cert $cert -FilePath 'C:\Cert\WSR2-2.cer'

#Un comment and use the following method to export a certificate on down-level OS
#$cert | Foreach-Object {
#    [system.IO.file]::WriteAllBytes("$home\$($_.thumbprint).cer", ($_.Export('CER')))
#}

$ConfigData = @{
    AllNodes = @(
        @{
            NodeName = "WSR2-2.dscdemo.lab"
            CertificateFile = "C:\cert\WSR2-2.cer"
        }
    )
}


Configuration LCMMetaDemo {
    Param (
        [pscredential]$Credential,
        $thumbprint
    )

    Node $AllNodes.NodeName {
        LocalConfigurationManager {
            CertificateID = $thumbprint
            ConfigurationID = 'e86549dc-7a5f-45b6-9d66-560d980587a8'
            RefreshMode = "PULL"
```

```
                DownloadManagerName = "DSCFileDownloadManager"
                Credential = $Credential
                DownloadManagerCustomData = @{SourcePath = '\\WSR2-1\SMBPull\'}
        }
    }
}

LCMMetaDemo -Credential (Get-Credential) -ConfigurationData $ConfigData -thumbprint $thumbprint

Set-DscLocalConfigurationManager -Path .\LCMMetaDemo
```

Because the preceding method cannot be used with the current implementation, what is the alternative to supplying credentials? You can use the configuration data to specify that you want to use a plain text password. This is done by setting the PsDscAllowPlainTextPassword property to True in the configuration data for all nodes. We have seen examples of this in Chapter 6. You can refer back to those examples and build one for the LCM meta-configuration. I am sure that you are aware of the risks involved in transferring passwords as plain text in a data center network. Therefore, I do not suggest or recommend using this method for LCM configuration.

In this section, so far, we have seen how to configure the pull services (OData/SMB) and how to configure the target systems as pull clients by changing the RefreshMode property to PULL, choosing a download manager for the environment, and finally, using DownloadManagerCustomData to provide the pull server coordinates for the chosen download manager.

So far, we have looked at how the pull client can be configured to access the pull server configuration store. But how does the pull client perform the configuration change that is available in the pull server store? This is where the RefreshFrequencyMins setting in LCM meta-configuration is used. Let us examine this.

Refresh Mode Frequency

By default, the LCM is configured to be in Push mode. This means the default value of the RefreshMode property of LCM is PUSH. When we change this setting to PULL, two scheduled tasks are created, if not present already, in the task library, under Microsoft\Windows\Desired State Configuration. You can see these tasks on a target system, using the task scheduler cmdlets.

■ **Note** By default, on a fresh WMF 4.0 installation, these scheduled tasks do not exist. We have to set the Local Configuration Manager (LCM) properties through a meta-configuration script, to ensure that these tasks are created. We can simply reapply the same LCM default settings to create these tasks. It is not mandatory to configure LCM to be in Pull client mode for the tasks to be created. These tasks are used in Push mode too.

```
Get-ScheduledTask -TaskPath '\Microsoft\Windows\Desired State Configuration\'
```

As shown in Figure 7-11, two scheduled tasks, named Consistency and DSCRestartBootTask, are created.

```
PS C:\> Get-ScheduledTask -TaskPath '\Microsoft\Windows\Desired State Configuration\'

TaskPath                                      TaskName                State
--------                                      --------                -----
\Microsoft\Windows\Desired State Configurat... Consistency            Ready
\Microsoft\Windows\Desired State Configurat... DSCRestartBootTask     Ready
```

Figure 7-11. *Scheduled tasks on a target system configured as a pull client*

This configuration will be the same for both REST- and SMB-based pull servers. The `Consistency` task is configured to run every 15 minutes by default. This task starts what is called a consistency check, using the consistency engine that is a part of the LCM. When using the pull client for configuration changes, if there is a new or updated configuration in the pull server configuration store, the consistency task downloads the new configuration and applies it immediately. Can we change how often this task runs? Yes, we can update the `RefreshFrequencyMins` property of the LCM meta-configuration. Before we go there, let us understand one more property in LCM meta-configuration, called `ConfigurationModeFrequencyMins`.

■ **Note**   The `RefreshFrequencyMins` property is used only when the `RefreshMode` setting is set to `PULL`.

Configuration Mode Frequency

As shown in Table 7-2, there is a `ConfigurationModeFrequencyMins` property in the LCM that is set by default to 30 minutes. It is important that we understand the difference between this and the `RefreshFrequencyMins` property.

The `RefreshFrequencyMins` property is used to define *how often the pull client checks for new or changed configuration on the pull server*. Whereas, the `ConfigurationModeFrequencyMins` defines *how often the target system configuration is checked for the desired state*.

For example, let us say we have a configuration applied on a target system using the pull client. Also, assume that this configuration ensures that there is a specific text file in the `C:\Windows` folder with some predefined text content. In this scenario, with the default values for both these intervals, the pull client checks the pull server configuration store every 15 minutes, to see if there is an updated configuration that is different from the existing one stored in the local configuration store. If the pull client finds a different configuration, the new configuration will be downloaded and applied. Now, when the `ConfigurationModeFrequencyMins` triggers, the target system will be checked for the configuration that is already applied—a text file with specific contents, in this example. If the target system has drifted from what is available in the local configuration store, LCM uses the settings defined for the `ConfigurationMode` property to take an action. The behavior of the configuration mode is the same for both the Push and Pull modes of configuration. Table 7-5 summarizes this.

Table 7-5. Summary of ConfigurationMode Behavior

ConfigurationMode Setting	LCM behavior
ApplyOnly	Apply configuration once; omit monitoring or reenacting, even when the target system configuration is different
ApplyAndMonitor	Apply configuration once and monitor the target system for noncompliance; report any noncompliance in event logs
ApplyAndAutoCorrect	Apply configuration once and reenact the same, without checking the target system for any noncompliance

Note that when a new configuration becomes available, either through the Push mode or Pull mode, the configuration mode settings have no impact. The new configuration will be applied. In the case of Push, the configuration change occurs immediately. And, in the Pull mode, the configuration change occurs when the consistency task is triggered, based on the `RefreshFrequencyMins` setting.

Although the purpose of these two intervals, which we discussed, is different, it is important to note that these two values depend on each other. The value provided as `ConfigurationModeFrequencyMins` should be a multiple of the value provided as `RefreshFrequencyMins`, and when we don't specify it that way, LCM automatically rounds it off to a nearest multiple. If you look at the default values of these two properties, you will notice that they are set to 30 and 15 minutes, respectively. These are the minimum configurable values.

Let us look at an example to understand this behavior and see how to change these settings, using the LCM meta-configuration.

```
Configuration PullClientConfig {
    Node Localhost {
        LocalConfigurationManager {
            ConfigurationID = 'e86549dc-7a5f-45b6-9d66-560d980587a8'
            RefreshMode = "Pull"
            DownloadManagerName = "DscFileDownloadManager"
            DownloadManagerCustomData = @{SourcePath = "\\WSR2-1\SMBPull"}
            ConfigurationModeFrequencyMins = 50
            RefreshFrequencyMins = 20
        }
    }
}

PullClientConfig

Set-DscLocalConfigurationManager -Path .\PullClientConfig
```

In the preceding meta-configuration script, we are intentionally setting ConfigurationModeFrequencyMins to 50, which is not a multiple of RefreshFrequencyMins, which is set to 20. When we apply this configuration, LCM finds this discrepancy and automatically chooses an optimal value for the ConfigurationModeFrequencyMins property (see Figure 7-12).

```
PS C:\> Get-DscLocalConfigurationManager

AllowModuleOverwrite            : False
CertificateID                   :
ConfigurationID                 : e86549dc-7a5f-45b6-9d66-560d980587a8
ConfigurationMode               : ApplyAndMonitor
ConfigurationModeFrequencyMins  : 60
Credential                      :
DownloadManagerCustomData       : {MSFT_KeyValuePair (key = "SourcePath")}
DownloadManagerName             : DscFileDownloadManager
RebootNodeIfNeeded              : False
RefreshFrequencyMins            : 20
RefreshMode                     : Pull
PSComputerName                  :
```

Figure 7-12. *LCM chooses the optimal value of ConfigurationModeFrequencyMins*

We can see in Figure 7-12 the result of LCM choosing the optimal value. Here the configuration mode frequency gets set to 60 minutes instead of the value provided in the meta-configuration script. This change in RefreshFrequencyMins value changes how often the consistency scheduled task is run. This is shown in Figure 7-13, which shows this interval in seconds (1200 seconds).

```
PS C:\> (Get-ScheduledTask -TaskName Consistency).Triggers.Repetition
```

Duration	Interval	StopAtDurationEnd	PSComputerName
--------	--------	-----------------	--------------
	PT1200S	False	

Figure 7-13. *Consistency task interval*

When the client is configured in Push mode, the RefreshFrequencyMins property is not used. However, ConfigurationModeFrequencyMins is used to perform a consistency check. So, when the LCM is in Push mode, the consistency schedule task gets set to a trigger interval that is the same as the ConfigurationModeFrequencyMins. So, when the task gets triggered, all it really does is check the target system for a compliance act based on the configuration mode settings.

With the LCM settings and the discussion of those settings out of the way, let us see how the configuration gets enacted in Pull mode.

Enacting Configuration in Pull Mode

We have already discussed that when the Local Configuration Manager (LCM) is in Pull mode, the consistency scheduled task is used to poll the pull server configuration store for a configuration. In this section, let us look at how we prepare the pull server configuration store, so that pull clients can retrieve the configuration. When looking at the pull client configuration, I had mentioned that each target system must have a unique GUID. This is specified in the LCM meta-configuration as ConfigurationID. For any target system that is a pull client to be able to retrieve the appropriate configuration associated with it, a Managed Object Format (MOF) file should exist in the pull server store. The base name of the MOF file should be same as the GUID assigned within the LCM meta-configuration.

In the case of the Push mode, we used the configuration command to generate an MOF file, and that MOF had the same base name as the target system computer name. So, in the case of a pull store, we just modify that to contain the GUID. Here is an example:

```
Configuration DemoConfig {
    Node 'e86549dc-7a5f-45b6-9d66-560d980587a8' {
        WindowsProcess ProcessDemo {
            Path = 'Notepad.exe'
            Arguments = ''
            Ensure = 'Absent'
        }
    }
}

DemoConfig -OutputPath C:\SMBPull
```

In the preceding example, I am using the SMB-based pull configuration store, so when I generate the MOF file for a configuration script, I am using the GUID assigned to the target system LCM and storing that file in the SMB file share. Now, this alone is not enough. We have to generate a file hash for the MOF file, so that the pull client can identify when the configuration changes. This is done using the New-DscChecksum cmdlet in the PSDesiredStateConfiguration PowerShell module.

```
New-DscCheckSum -ConfigurationPath C:\SMBPull -OutPath C:\SMBPull -Force
```

The New-DscCheckSum cmdlet uses the Get-FileHash cmdlet with the SHA-256 hashing algorithm, to generate the file hash and store it at the path specified using the -OutPath parameter. So, you can write your own wrapper around the Get-FileHash cmdlet to do this job. Note that this cmdlet stores the generated hash as <GUID>.checksum.mof. So, if you plan to write your own function to do this, make sure you follow the same file-naming format.

Once both these files are generated and the LCM is configured with the same GUID as the value for the `ConfigurationID` property, the pull client can automatically pull this configuration when the consistency scheduled task runs. But what happens when we change the configuration available in the pull server store? In such a case, when the consistency task runs, the LCM first tries to find if the configuration on the pull server is different from that which is available in the local configuration store. This is done by computing the checksum of the MOF file in the local configuration store and comparing it to the one available on the pull server. If the checksum is different, the LCM downloads the new configuration MOF from the pull server and applies it on the target system. Do you understand now why we need a checksum for the MOF?

When using an SMB-based pull server, we copy both the configuration MOF and the checksum into the same folder that is shared. However, when using a REST- or OData-based pull service, we have to copy the configuration MOF and checksum files to the folder created for storing configuration. For example, in the pull service configuration script in this chapter, we used `$env:PROGRAMFILES\WindowsPowerShell\DscService\Configuration` for the configuration store. So, this is where all configuration MOF and checksum files should be stored. Instead of using a randomly generated GUID for each target system, it is recommended that you use the GUID from the computer

In this overall process, the pull client also looks for any missing resource modules required to enact the configuration on the target system. We already discussed that this is one of the advantages of using the Pull mode. So, how do we package these resource modules for distribution using a pull server?

Simple, we need to pack them as a zip archive and create a checksum file for the zip archive as well. To demonstrate this, I will use a custom DSC resource that I built for managing hosts file. We will be going through the details of creating a custom DSC resource in detail, in Chapter 9. For now, just try to understand the process of distributing custom DSC resources using a pull service endpoint. This resource is available in the source code for this chapter, located in the Source Code/Download area of the Apress web site (`www.apress.com`). So, if you want to follow the instructions in this section, grab the zip file named `HostsFile_1.0.zip` from this chapter's source code. As you can see from the file name, I have named it `<ResourceModuleName>_<Version>.zip`.

■ **Note**   In the LCM meta-configuration properties, `AllowModuleOverwrite` can be set to `True` on the target systems, so that updated versions of modules can be downloaded to the same module folder, as required. Without this, the automatic module download from the pull server will fail, if a resource module with the same name already exists.

You have to generate the checksum for this zip archive, using the following command, and save it in a checksum file named `HostsFile_1.0.zip.checksum`.

```
New-DscCheckSum -ConfigurationPath C:\SMBPull\HostsFile_1.0.zip -OutPath C:\SMBPull
```

■ **Note**   When using an SMB file share for the pull server, you can use the `SkipChecksum` property, set to `True` in the `DownloadManagerCustomData`,to skip verifying the checksum of configuration and module files.

Once we have these files, we can copy them over to the pull server configuration store. In the case of the SMB pull server, this path will be the SMB file share and, in the case the of OData-based pull server, a configurable path. In the script sample that was shown in this chapter, we used `$env:PROGRAMFILES\WindowsPowerShell\DscService\Modules` for storing zip archives of DSC modules.

Once the configuration and any required modules are copied to the configuration store on the pull server, we can either wait for the consistency task to get triggered at the configured interval or manually invoke it by using the task scheduler cmdlets, as in the following:

```
$CimSession = New-CimSession -ComputerName WSR2-2
Start-ScheduledTask -CimSession $CimSession -TaskName Consistency
```

If you have enacted the configuration by using the preceding commands, you can check the target system configuration by using the Common Information Model (CIM) session with the Get-DscConfiguration cmdlet.

```
Get-DscConfiguration -CimSession $CimSession
```

This brings us to the end of this chapter. One thing we have not discussed is monitoring what exactly happens when you enact a configuration—either in Push or Pull mode. Also, the DSC Service in WMF 4.0 has another feature, called compliance endpoint. This can be used to monitor or query the compliance state of the target systems configured as pull clients. There is no centralized method in the Push mode of configuration delivery to report the compliance status of all target systems to which the configuration was pushed. We will explore some of these issues in detail in Chapter 8.

Summary

Configuration delivery methods play a major role in the overall configuration management process. Choosing the right method is important and depends on the number of target systems in the environment. In this chapter, we looked at both Push and Pull modes of configuration delivery. Each of these modes has pros and cons. Choosing between these modes depends on the flexibility required in delivering configuration to the target systems. If you need a scalable solution in which the custom DSC resources and updates to the target system configurations can be distributed without the need for any manual intervention, the Pull mode of configuration delivery should be your choice. Again, the Pull mode itself can be configured by using HTTP or HTTPS endpoints, or a simple SMB file share. Once again, the choice here should be based on the ease of configuration and management vs. security. The HTTPS pull service endpoints provide a secure way to transfer configuration and modules between the pull service and the pull clients, whereas the SMB-based pull service configuration is nothing but a simple SMB file share.

■ ■ ■

CHAPTER 8

Monitoring, Correcting, and Reporting Configuration

In the configuration management processes, after the configuration is enacted, the most important step is to monitor the target systems for configuration drift. Over time, in the life cycle of target systems and the applications running on those systems, there is a high probability of configuration drifting away from the original configuration. In an ideal world, all the changes on the target system would go through the designated configuration management system. This would help to prevent configuration drift. This, however, is certainly not the case in many IT organizations. IT and application administrators prefer quick fixes to the problems that arise in day-to-day operations. Eventually, this leads to a configuration drift. And, when a disaster strikes, with a target system that drifted away from the baseline configuration, it may take more than a few hours to restore services offered to the end users.

Desired State Configuration (DSC) provides interfaces to monitor and report configuration from the target systems, in addition to a method to auto-correct a configuration drift. In this chapter, we take a look at internals of configuration management using DSC, monitoring and correcting configuration on target systems, and finally, reporting configuration from target systems using built-in methods.

Configuration Enactment

As seen in Chapter 4, the configuration enactment phase is that in which the target systems apply the configuration Managed Object Format (MOF), received either through the push or pull configuration delivery models. We did not discuss what happens internally when the configuration is either pushed or pulled. Also, we looked at the scheduled tasks that get created on the target systems, talked about the ConfigurationModeFrequencyMins and RefreshModeFrequencyMins, but did not discuss what goes on behind the scenes when these scheduled tasks are triggered at the respective intervals. In the following section, we will look at these processes in depth. This knowledge will be helpful in understanding the monitoring and correction aspects of the configuration when using Desired State Configuration (DSC). Let us start.

Target System Configuration

We have seen in some earlier examples that when the configuration gets pushed, the Start-DscConfiguration cmdlet invokes the SendConfigurationApply method of the MSFT_DscLocalConfigurationManager CIM class in the DesiredStateConfiguration namespace. This method takes one parameter that is Configuration, which is a byte array representation of the MOF file. In the Pull mode, the download manager receives the configuration MOF from the pull server and then calls the Apply method of the MSFT_DscLocalConfigurationManager CIM class. This method, too, takes a byte array representation of the received configuration MOF as the argument.

If we set aside the configuration delivery methods, that is how the configuration MOF is transported to the target system. What goes on behind the scenes during the configuration enactment process is the same. Figure 8-1 provides an overview of this.

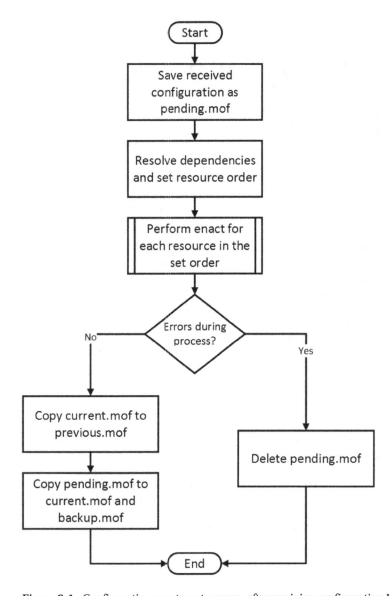

Figure 8-1. *Configuration enactment process, after receiving configuration MOF*

As shown in Figure 8-1, when a configuration MOF is either pushed or pulled, the Local Configuration Manager (LCM) copies the received configuration as pending.mof at the C:\Windows\System32\Configuration folder. LCM then tries to find all the dependencies in the configuration. We have seen in earlier chapters that we can use the DependsOn property to set these dependencies between resources. Once the dependencies are resolved and the resource execution order is determined, LCM starts configuring each resource in the set order. This execution involves checking if the resource is in the desired state or not. If the resource is already in the desired state, no action is needed. In Chapter 9, when we look at building custom DSC resources, you will see more about this and learn exactly how the DSC resources work.

■ **Caution**   As a domain or local administrator on a target system, you will be able to access the current.mof, backup.mof, and previous.mof files in the C:\Windows\System32\Configuration folder. However, under normal circumstances, you should not tamper or delete these files manually.

Once the execution for each resource in the set order is complete with no errors, the current.mof, if present, gets renamed to previous.mof, and pending.mof gets renamed and copied as current.mof and backup.mof, respectively. These changes mean that we can always go back to the previous configuration, provided previous.mof exists at C:\Windows\System32\Configuration. You can roll back to a previous configuration using the Restore-DscConfiguration cmdlet. If a previous configuration does not exist, this cmdlet results with an error, shown in Figure 8-2.

```
PS C:\> Restore-DscConfiguration
Restore-DscConfiguration : A previous configuration does not exist. DSC can rollback only when there is a previous configuration.
At line:1 char:1
+ Restore-DscConfiguration
+ ~~~~~~~~~~~~~~~~~~~~~~~~~
    + CategoryInfo          : NotSpecified: (MSFT_DSCLocalConfigurationManager:root/Microsoft/...gurationManager) [Restore-DscCon
    + FullyQualifiedErrorId : MI RESULT 1,Restore-DscConfiguration
```

Figure 8-2.   *Rollback to previous configuration without a previous.mof*

The current.mof and backup.mof contain the current configuration that represents the desired state. The contents of these files are the same. If, for some reason, current.mof is corrupt, the backup.mof is used as the current configuration MOF.

What happens if one of the resources in the configuration fails to complete the configuration change during the enactment process? Does it roll back the changes done to the point of failure in enactment? No. In fact, as you can see in Figure 8-1, upon a failure during the enactment process, LCM deletes the pending.mof and does not roll back any changes executed prior to failure. The changes executed until the failure are not updated in the current configuration, and therefore, the Get-DscConfiguration won't reflect the changes made to the target system. This gives an impression that the system is in an inconsistent state. You can, however, resolve the issues causing the resource failure and enact the configuration again. Because the DSC resources are idempotent, no changes will be made if a specific resource is already in the desired state. Deleting the pending.mof upon a failure is a bug in WMF 4.0 release and will be fixed in future releases of DSC.

When we run the Get-DscConfiguration cmdlet, the current.mof, if present, gets parsed for the resources, and the dependency order gets created. The GetConfiguration method of the MSFT_DscLocalConfigurationManager gets invoked with a byte array representation of the current.mof as input. During this process, the configuration does not get enacted; instead, the resource module is used to get the current configuration (which need not be in the desired state) of each resource in the configuration document. When we look at building custom DSC resources in Chapter 9, we will look at how the resource modules can be authored to enable the functionality required for the Get-DscConfiguration cmdlet to work.

Target System Meta-Configuration

In the previous section, we looked at the configuration enactment process on the target systems. We saw in Chapter 7 how to update the LCM meta-configuration using a configuration script. The LCM meta-configuration cannot be obtained from a pull server. In the current implementation of DSC, the LCM meta-configuration can only be pushed to the target systems using the Set-DscLocalConfigurationManager cmdlet. We have seen several examples of this already. So, what goes on behind the scenes is what we need to discuss now.

The LCM meta-configuration gets stored at the same location as current.mof or as other MOF files we looked at in the previous section. The current LCM meta-configuration gets stored as MetaConfig.mof in the C:\Windows\System32\Configuration folder. By default, on a target system with no earlier configuration managed by DSC, MetaConfig.mof does not exist. This file is created when the configuration gets enacted for the first time via Push or when the LCM meta-configuration is updated using a configuration script and the Set-DscLocalConfigurationManager cmdlet. LCM stores the previous meta-configuration as MetaConfig.Backup.mof. Make a note of the differences in nomenclature for meta-configuration. For a normal configuration, the previous configuration gets stored as previous.mof, whereas for a meta-configuration, it gets stored as MetaConfig.Backup.mof.

■ **Caution**   Deleting the MetaConfig.mof file resets the LCM configuration to defaults.

In the previous There is no CIM method or PowerShell cmdlet to restore to a previous meta-configuration. This process, in the current implementation, is manual. You can delete the MetaConfig.mof file and rename MetaConfig.Backup.mof to MetaConfig.mof. This restores the LCM configuration to an earlier state.

Configuration Monitoring and Correction

From what we have discussed so far, we understand what happens when a new configuration is received either via Push or Pull methods. We've also looked at what happens when LCM meta-configuration is pushed. Once the configuration is applied, there is a need to continuously monitor the target systems, to ensure that they are in the desired state. DSC has a component, the consistency engine, that does this job. Monitoring is performed using two scheduled tasks in the Windows operating system: Consistency and DSCRebootTask.

■ **Note**   These scheduled tasks do not appear until the LCM meta-configuration is updated at least once. You can create a meta-configuration script with default values and push the same, using the Set-dscLocalConfigurationManager cmdlet to create these scheduled tasks.

We briefly discussed these scheduled tasks in Chapter 7, where we looked at the configuration delivery methods. In the Pull configuration, a schedule task is used to check the pull server at regular intervals for any change in configuration. When there is no configuration change from the pull server, the scheduled task simply performs a consistency check to ensure that the target system is still in the desired state. When using Push mode, the same scheduled task is used to monitor and, optionally, correct the target system's configuration state. So, how is this controlled?

DSC Consistency Checks

We discussed, in Chapter 7, that the LCM configuration contains two properties defined as time intervals: the ConfigurationModeFrequencyMins and the RefreshFrequencyMins. We also observed that the values of these intervals are dependent on each other. For example, when the target system is configured as a pull client, the value of the ConfigurationModeFrequencyMins will be a multiple of the value provided as the RefreshFrequencyMins. And, in Pull mode, the scheduled task will be set to trigger at regular intervals indicated by the RefreshFrequencyMins, whereas in Push mode, the ConfigurationModeFrequencyMins is used as a trigger for the consistency scheduled task. Whether the target system is in Push or Pull mode, these scheduled tasks invoke a consistency check. Figure 8-3 shows an overview of what happens when the consistency scheduled task is invoked.

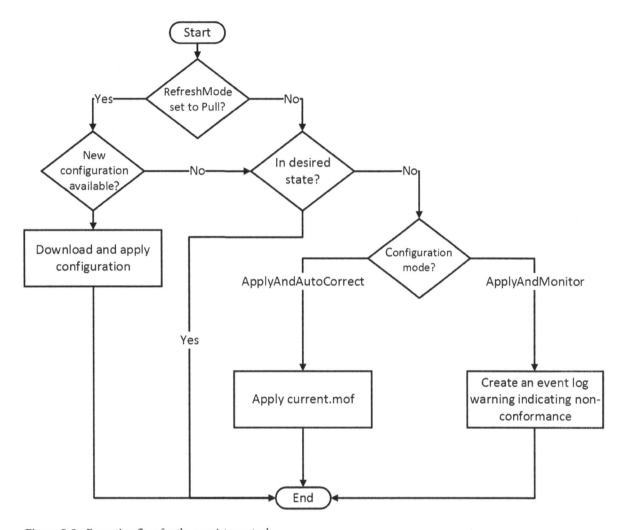

Figure 8-3. *Execution flow for the consistency task*

A picture is a worth a thousand words. Figure 8-3 explains what the consistency engine does. The execution flow depends on whether the target system is a pull client or not.

If the target system is a pull client, LCM uses the configured download manager to see if the checksum of the configuration on the local system is different from that on the pull server. This is done using the Get-DscAction cmdlet. If the configuration on the pull server is different, download manager interfaces (Get-DscDocument and Get-DscModule) are used to get the configuration MOF and resource modules, as required. The received configuration is then enacted. So, in this process of enacting a new configuration, the value of the ConfigurationMode property of the LCM meta-configuration is ignored or has no meaning.

The value of the ConfigurationMode property comes into play when there is no new configuration on the pull server or when the LCM is in Push mode. This property takes one of three values: ApplyOnly, ApplyAndMonitor, or ApplyAndAutoCorrect. At the time of the consistency check, the LCM verifies if the target system configuration is still in the desired state. This is done using the Test-TargetResource function within each resource module. If the target system is not in a desired state, the value of the ConfigurationMode property is used to take a necessary action. When the ConfigurationMode is set to ApplyOnly, the LCM takes no action, even if the target system is not in a desired state. This is precisely the reason why I did not include that in Figure 8-3. However, when the LCM is left in the default configuration for the ConfigurationMode property, which is ApplyAndMonitor, the LCM reports, as a warning message in the DSC event logs, nonconformance of the target system configuration. When the LCM meta-configuration is set to ApplyAndAutoCorrect, and when the target system is not in the desired state, the LCM simply reenacts the current.mof, bringing the system to a desired state.

As you see in Figure 8-3, if the LCM is configured for Push mode, there is no check for a new configuration. Because the configuration gets pushed, LCM has no place to go to verify whether there is a new configuration. However, if you place a configuration MOF as pending.mof at C:\Windows\System32\Configuration, it will be used as the new configuration during the consistency check. In such a scenario, the value of the ConfigurationMode property will be ignored, and the pending.mof will be applied on the target system.

All these details that we have looked at so far are not really hard to figure out, if you understand the event logs written by the DSC LCM. As with any other component of the Windows OS, DSC writes operational logs and can be configured to write both analytical and debug logs in Event Viewer, under Applications and Services Logs\ Microsoft\Windows\Desired State Configuration. In the following section, we will look at the DSC event logs and you will learn how to make sense of event log entries.

DSC Event Logs

Desired State Configuration event logs can be found in Event Viewer, under Application and Services Logs\ Microsoft\Windows\Desired State Configuration. By default, only operational logs are enabled. The operational logs do not provide much information about the resource execution. The analytic and debug logs, however, provide deeper insights into what happens when a configuration is enacted or when a consistency check is performed. These logs are not enabled by default. To enable these logs, you can execute the following commands:

```
wevtutil.exe set-log "Microsoft-Windows-Dsc/Analytic" /q:true /e:true
wevtutil.exe set-log "Microsoft-Windows-Dsc/Debug" /q:True /e:true
```

The preceding commands enable the Debug and Analytic channels for DSC logs. The event log messages from the three channels (Operational, Analytic, and Debug) can be accessed using the Get-WinEvent cmdlet. As you see in the following example, Microsoft-Windows-Dsc is the primary log provider, and we can retrieve the log messages by appending the Operational, Analytic, or Debug channel to the primary log (see Figure 8-4). The Analytic channel contains messages that identify errors that have occurred and verbose messages from the LCM. The Debug channel can be used for troubleshooting and debugging purposes.

```
Get-WinEvent -LogName "Microsoft-Windows-Dsc/Operational"
```

```
    ProviderName: Microsoft-Windows-DSC

TimeCreated                     Id LevelDisplayName Message
-----------                     -- ---------------- -------
6/26/2014 3:15:20 PM          4115 Information      Job {9F171F79-9473-47B6-8037-D896DD8A624...
6/26/2014 3:15:20 PM          4114 Information      Job {9F171F79-9473-47B6-8037-D896DD8A624...
6/26/2014 3:15:20 PM          4102 Information      Job {9F171F79-9473-47B6-8037-D896DD8A624...
6/26/2014 2:29:53 PM          4115 Information      Job {B9742B67-9D73-43FD-9414-7956887828A...
6/26/2014 2:29:53 PM          4114 Information      Job {B9742B67-9D73-43FD-9414-7956887828A...
6/26/2014 2:29:53 PM          4102 Information      Job {B9742B67-9D73-43FD-9414-7956887828A...
6/26/2014 1:28:55 PM          4115 Information      Job {A6ED4438-34EC-4EF4-896C-1ECED7E8B43...
6/26/2014 1:28:55 PM          4114 Information      Job {A6ED4438-34EC-4EF4-896C-1ECED7E8B43...
6/26/2014 1:28:55 PM          4102 Information      Job {A6ED4438-34EC-4EF4-896C-1ECED7E8B43...
6/26/2014 1:15:58 PM          4115 Information      Job {AEBEFD0E-0763-48B5-9771-545A55C7DD6...
6/26/2014 1:15:58 PM          4114 Information      Job {AEBEFD0E-0763-48B5-9771-545A55C7DD6...
6/26/2014 1:15:58 PM          4102 Information      Job {AEBEFD0E-0763-48B5-9771-545A55C7DD6...
6/26/2014 12:15:03 PM         4115 Information      Job {5FDA2E9C-BC34-43AE-9F1A-191194B6630...
6/26/2014 12:15:03 PM         4114 Information      Job {5FDA2E9C-BC34-43AE-9F1A-191194B6630...
6/26/2014 12:15:03 PM         4102 Information      Job {5FDA2E9C-BC34-43AE-9F1A-191194B6630...
6/26/2014 12:14:43 PM         4102 Information      Job {F933EF7D-B3DC-42F2-BDB9-096BC743972...
6/26/2014 12:14:10 PM         4115 Information      Job {D3E27995-6632-4986-8AF8-FE5E326A70D...
6/26/2014 12:14:10 PM         4114 Information      Job {D3E27995-6632-4986-8AF8-FE5E326A70D...
6/26/2014 12:14:10 PM         4102 Information      Job {D3E27995-6632-4986-8AF8-FE5E326A70D...
6/26/2014 12:13:21 PM         4102 Information      Job {8C2CD14F-5EDC-4499-8B02-B90A4636593...
6/26/2014 12:13:16 PM         4102 Information      Job {3890EA36-09BA-4F8C-9EF1-86CC26CF824...
6/26/2014 12:12:09 PM         4115 Information      Job {9A82CF0C-3A22-4D07-AF64-004FB561230...
6/26/2014 12:12:09 PM         4114 Information      Job {9A82CF0C-3A22-4D07-AF64-004FB561230...
6/26/2014 12:12:09 PM         4102 Information      Job {9A82CF0C-3A22-4D07-AF64-004FB561230...
```

Figure 8-4. *Operational logs from DSC*

Each time a consistency check runs or a configuration is either pulled or pushed, DSC generates these messages. Each of those activities can be grouped under a single operation. Within these DSC logs, the Message property contains the information relevant to identify or group messages pertaining to a specific operation. To be specific, the Job ID, which is a Globally Unique Identifier (GUID), as shown in Figure 8-4, uniquely identifies a DSC operation. We can use this information to group the log messages pertaining to a single operation.

Because we are interested in log messages from all three channels, we can use the Get-WinEvent cmdlet to construct an array containing all event log messages.

```
$AllDscLogs = Get-WinEvent -LogName Microsoft-Windows-DSC/* -Oldest
```

In the preceding command, we have used the -Oldest switch parameter. This is because the event logs store the newest messages at the top. By using the -Oldest parameter, we can receive the messages in oldest to newest order. The Properties attribute of an event log object contains the values of event properties published by the providers. In fact, the Properties attribute returns an object array of type System.Diagnostics.Eventing.Reader. EventProperty. In this array, the first element contains the GUID of the job. So, the following code gives us the JobID of all DSC activities.

```
$AllDscLogs | Foreach-Object { $_.Properties[0].Value }
```

We've already seen that the JobID can be used to group a set of DSC operations. We can use the Group-Object cmdlet for this purpose.

```
$AllDscLogs | Group-Object { $_.Properties[0].Value }
```

Each set of DSC operations shown in Figure 8-5 contains the log messages from all three DSC event log channels.

```
Count Name                          Group
----- ----                          -----
    3 {9A82CF0C-3A22-4D07-AF...     {System.Diagnostics.Eventing.Reader.EventLogRecord, System.Diagnostics.Ev...
    1 {3890EA36-09BA-4F8C-9E...     {System.Diagnostics.Eventing.Reader.EventLogRecord}
    1 {8C2CD14F-5EDC-4499-88...     {System.Diagnostics.Eventing.Reader.EventLogRecord}
    3 {D3E27995-6632-4986-8A...     {System.Diagnostics.Eventing.Reader.EventLogRecord, System.Diagnostics.Ev...
    1 {F933EF7D-B3DC-42F2-BD...     {System.Diagnostics.Eventing.Reader.EventLogRecord}
    3 {5FDA2E9C-BC34-43AE-9F...     {System.Diagnostics.Eventing.Reader.EventLogRecord, System.Diagnostics.Ev...
    3 {AEBEFD0E-0763-48B5-97...     {System.Diagnostics.Eventing.Reader.EventLogRecord, System.Diagnostics.Ev...
    3 {A6ED4438-34EC-4EF4-89...     {System.Diagnostics.Eventing.Reader.EventLogRecord, System.Diagnostics.Ev...
    3 {B9742B67-9D73-43FD-94...     {System.Diagnostics.Eventing.Reader.EventLogRecord, System.Diagnostics.Ev...
    3 {9F171F79-9473-47B6-80...     {System.Diagnostics.Eventing.Reader.EventLogRecord, System.Diagnostics.Ev...
  134 {75803515-BF92-466D-BA...     {System.Diagnostics.Eventing.Reader.EventLogRecord, System.Diagnostics.Ev...
  134 {FF2D0416-ACB3-4CD5-B3...     {System.Diagnostics.Eventing.Reader.EventLogRecord, System.Diagnostics.Ev...
  134 {D7030A10-A999-46B9-AC...     {System.Diagnostics.Eventing.Reader.EventLogRecord, System.Diagnostics.Ev...
  134 {87AAFDBE-1E02-4061-9F...     {System.Diagnostics.Eventing.Reader.EventLogRecord, System.Diagnostics.Ev...
```

Figure 8-5. *A partial set of DSC operations*

We can retrieve the messages in each group by selecting the Message property of the event log record (see Figure 8-6).

```
PS C:\> $DSCOperations = $AllDscLogs | Group-Object { $_.Properties[0].Value }

PS C:\> $DSCOperations[0].Group.message
Job {9A82CF0C-3A22-4D07-AF64-004FB5612301} :
Configuration is sent from computer NULL by user sid S-1-5-18.
Job {9A82CF0C-3A22-4D07-AF64-004FB5612301} :
Running consistency engine.
Job {9A82CF0C-3A22-4D07-AF64-004FB5612301} :
Consistency engine was run successfully.
```

Figure 8-6. *Event messages from a DSC operation*

■ **Note** The discussion so far is only to understand how the DSC event messages pertaining to a specific operation can be retrieved. The xDscDiagnostics module in the DSC resource kit provides a much easier way to work with DSC event logs. This module and its usage is discussed in Appendix A.

Once you have the events grouped by a specific DSC operation, similar to what is shown in Figure 8-6, it is easy to filter it for errors or any such criteria. This can be done using the Where-Object cmdlet.

```
$AllDscLogs | Group-Object { $_.Properties[0].Value } | Where-Object { $_.Group.LevelDisplayName -eq
"Warning" }
```

Configuration Reporting

In the preceding section, we looked at how we can monitor the configuration on the target system, using DSC consistency checks and the DSC event logs to determine when errors occur, either during the configuration change process and/or during consistency checks. These event logs provide a way to understand what happens during the enact process or during the subsequent consistency check processes, but the information or the number of messages we receive is simply overwhelming. When scripting the monitoring processes for reporting purposes, parsing event logs may not be a useful method. In the following section, we will see a few alternatives to event logs, for reporting DSC configuration status.

Using DSC PowerShell Cmdlets

The Test-DscConfiguration and the Get-DscConfiguration cmdlets in the PSDesiredStateConfiguration module provide a way to see whether the target system is in a desired state or not and determine what the current state of the configuration is. For the purpose of demonstration, I am using the following configuration script:

```
Configuration DemoConfig {
    Node Localhost {
        File DemoFile {
            DestinationPath = "C:\Scripts\Demo.txt"
            Contents = ""
            Ensure = "Present"
        }

        WindowsProcess DemoProcess {
            Path = "Notepad.exe"
            Arguments = "C:\Scripts\Demo.txt"
            DependsOn = "[File]DemoFile"
        }
    }
}

DemoConfig
```

When this configuration is applied, it creates Demo.txt, if it does not exist, and a notepad process with C:\Scripts\Demo.txt as an argument. So, the target system to which this configuration is applied will be in a desired state only if the Demo.txt file exists at C:\Scripts as an empty file and a notepad process exists with this Demo.txt file as an argument. Therefore, deleting either the Demo.txt or stopping the notepad process puts the target system's configuration in nonconformance. For this example, I deleted the Demo.txt file on the target system, and Figure 8-7 is what Test-DscConfiguration returns.

```
PS C:\Scripts> del *.*

PS C:\Scripts> dir

PS C:\Scripts> Test-DscConfiguration
False

PS C:\Scripts>
```

Figure 8-7. *Testing if a system is in a desired state*

As you see in Figure 8-7, deleting the file created by using the configuration script puts my target system in a nonconformance state.

The Test-DscConfiguration cmdlet returns a Boolean value. False indicates that the system is not in a desired state. But how exactly do we know which resource is not in a desired state? It is not easy. In our example, I know very well the resource that is not in a desired state, as I manually deleted the file from the C:\scripts folder. However, when you are using a configuration script with many resources, it won't be easy to determine which resource is not in a desired state. This is where the Get-DscConfiguration cmdlet helps a little bit.

As shown in Figure 8-8, the Get-DscConfiguration cmdlet returns the current state of the configuration. It is clear from the output that the file resource in my configuration is not in a desired state. I wanted the file to be present, but it is not, and that signals nonconformance. However, to identify the resource, from among many others, that is not in a desired state, you should know what the desired state for that particular resource is.

```
PS C:\Scripts> Get-DscConfiguration


Attributes      :
Checksum        :
Contents        :
CreatedDate     :
Credential      :
DestinationPath : C:\Scripts\Demo.txt
Ensure          : absent
Force           :
MatchSource     :
ModifiedDate    :
Recurse         :
Size            :
SourcePath      :
SubItems        :
Type            :
PSComputerName  :

Arguments            : C:\Scripts\Demo.txt
Credential           :
Ensure               : Present
HandleCount          : 86
NonPagedMemorySize   : 7920
PagedMemorySize      : 1097728
Path                 : C:\Windows\system32\Notepad.exe
ProcessId            : 1916
StandardErrorPath    :
StandardInputPath    :
StandardOutputPath   :
VirtualMemorySize    : 60710912
WorkingDirectory     :
PSComputerName       :
```

Figure 8-8. *Current state of the configuration*

In the current implementation of DSC, there is no easy way to pinpoint the specific resource that is not in a desired state. We can, of course, build some workarounds to read the configuration MOF and compare it to the output of the Get-DscConfiguration cmdlet. Some of this requires explanation of how the configuration MOF can be parsed, and so on. Let us save that discussion until Appendix B, where we will explore some expert tips. If you are looking for a way to generate reports for multiple target systems, skip to Appendix B.

We can use the -CimSession parameter of these cmdlets to retrieve the configuration current state and test remote systems for a desired state. We have looked at several examples of using CIM sessions in this book. So, try and create a script that generates a report for all target systems, using the cmdlets we have encountered so far.

When using the Get-DscConfiguration and Test-DscConfiguration cmdlets, it does not matter what configuration delivery method was used. However, when using a Pull mode with representative state transfer (REST) endpoints, the state of the configuration from the target systems gets sent to the pull server. This is stored in a database represented by devices.mdb. We discussed these details when looking at configuring REST-based Pull service endpoints. The DSC Pull service that comes with WMF 4.0 on Windows Server 2012 and 2012 R2 includes another service called conformance service or conformance endpoint. Using this service, we can query for the configuration run status from the target systems configured as clients of a REST-based Pull service. In this section, we will look at configuring the conformance endpoint and explore how to use that.

Conformance Endpoint for Pull Clients

In Chapter 7, we looked at how we can create a DSC Pull Service endpoint using the DSC-Service Windows Feature available on Windows Server 2012 R2. In this section, we extend that to add a conformance endpoint. The process is very similar, except for a few settings that we have to configure and the files that we must copy to the IIS endpoint directories. The conformance endpoint requires DSC Service and Windows Authentication features. Also, there is no point deploying only conformance service, if the same system is not hosting the REST-based endpoint feature offered by DSC-Service. Therefore, you should use the following guidance as a continuation of what we have seen in Chapter 7.

The following code example shows this process, and the comments in each line should help clarify what we are doing.

```
#For Conformance Server
Add-WindowsFeature -Name Web-Windows-Auth

#Default Values for non-Windows 8.1  endpoints
$pathPullServer = "$pshome\modules\PSDesiredStateConfiguration\PullServer"
$rootDataPath ="$env:PROGRAMFILES\WindowsPowerShell\DscService"

#Culture to identify the right binaries
$culture = Get-Culture
$language = $culture.TwoLetterISOLanguageName

#List of dependent binaries for the IIS endpoint
$dependentBinaries = "$pathPullServer\Microsoft.Powershell.DesiredStateConfiguration.Service.dll"
$dependentMUIFiles = "$pathPullServer\$language\Microsoft.Powershell.DesiredStateConfiguration.
  Service.Resources.dll"

#Path of the ASAX file
$asax = "$pathPullServer\Global.asax"

#Application pool identity. This has to be an existing one
#If you want to create a new app pool, refer to chapter 7
$appPool = "PSWS"

#Database Provider settings for target system inventory
$jet4provider = "System.Data.OleDb"
$jet4database = "Provider=Microsoft.Jet.OLEDB.4.0;Data Source=$env:PROGRAMFILES\WindowsPowerShell\
  DscService\Devices.mdb;"

#Compliance Server Files
#Template web.config file for the conformance endpoint
$cfgfile = "$pathPullServer\PSDSCComplianceServer.config"

# WCF service endpoint file
$svc = "$pathPullServer\PSDSCComplianceServer.svc"

#MOF file that defines the schema for the endpoint
$mof = "$pathPullServer\PSDSCComplianceServer.mof"

#Conformance endpoint XML
$dispatch = "$pathPullServer\PSDSCComplianceServer.xml"
```

```
#Name of the Conformance Endpoint
$Site = "DscConformance"

#Name of the web application for the conformance endpoint site
$App = "DscConformance"

#Port number for the conformance endpoint
$Port = "9090"

#Physical path for storing endpoint files
$Path = "$env:SystemDrive\inetpub\wwwroot\$Site"

#Service Name
$svcName = Split-Path $svc -Leaf

#Create physical path for the endpoint
$null = New-Item -ItemType container -Path $path
$binFolderPath = Join-Path $path "bin"
$null = New-Item -path $binFolderPath  -itemType "directory" -Force

#Copy files required for the endpoint to physical path
Copy-Item $dependentBinaries $binFolderPath -Force
$muiPath = Join-Path $binFolderPath $language

if (!(Test-Path $muiPath))
{
    $null = New-Item -ItemType container $muiPath
}
Copy-Item $dependentMUIFiles $muiPath -Force

Copy-Item $cfgfile (Join-Path $path "web.config") -Force
Copy-Item $svc $path -Force
Copy-Item $mof $path -Force
Copy-Item $dispatch $path -Force
Copy-Item $asax $path -Force

#Restart Default App Apool
Restart-WebAppPool -Name "DefaultAppPool"

#Create the endpoint site and web application
#For steps on HTTPS endpoint, refer to chapter 7
$siteID = (Get-Website | Sort-Object ID | Select-Object -Last 1 ID).ID+1
$webSite = New-WebSite -Name $site -Id $siteID -Port $port -IPAddress "*" -PhysicalPath $path
 -ApplicationPool $appPool
$null = New-WebApplication -Name $app -Site $site -PhysicalPath $path -ApplicationPool $appPool

#Start all web sites
Get-WebSite | Start-Website
```

```
#Set the authentication for the endpoint
$Auths = "anonymous","basic","windows"
[System.Reflection.Assembly]::LoadWithPartialName("Microsoft.Web.Administration") | Out-Null
foreach ($auth in $Auths) {
    $webAdminSrvMgr = new-object Microsoft.Web.Administration.ServerManager
    $appHostConfig = $webAdminSrvMgr.GetApplicationHostConfiguration()
    $authenticationType = "$($auth)Authentication"
    $appHostConfigSection = $appHostConfig.GetSection("system.webServer/security/authentication/$aut
        henticationType", $Site)
    $appHostConfigSection.OverrideMode="Allow"
    $webAdminSrvMgr.CommitChanges()
    Start-Sleep 4
}

#Set the web.config
[hashtable] $ConformanceSettingHash = [Ordered] @{
    dbprovider = $jet4provider
    dbconnectionstr = $jet4database
    AdminEndPoint = "True"
}

#For Set-AppSettingsInWebConfig function, refer to Chapter 7
foreach ($key in $ConformanceSettingHash.Keys) {
    Set-AppSettingsInWebconfig -path $Path -key $key -value $ConformanceSettingHash[$key]
}
```

Remember: As shown and explained in the preceding example, this code must run on the same system that is configured as the pull server, and the web application pool used in this script must exist. I recommend using the same pool as the Pull service endpoint.

Once the conformance endpoint is set up, you can access the service at http://localhost:9090/ DscConformance/PSDSCComplianceServer.svc. This provides a list of methods in the service. At the time of this writing, there is only one method, called Status, shown in Figure 8-9.

```
<?xml version="1.0" encoding="UTF-8"?>
- <service xmlns:atom="http://www.w3.org/2005/Atom" xmlns="http://www.w3.org/2007/app"
  xml:base="http://localhost:9090/DscConformance/PSDSCComplianceServer.svc/">
    - <workspace>
        <atom:title>Default</atom:title>
        - <collection href="Status">
            <atom:title>Status</atom:title>
        </collection>
    </workspace>
</service>
```

Figure 8-9. *Status method in the conformance endpoint service*

We can retrieve the metadata for the Status method by appending the $metadata query token to the service URI. The result from this URI is shown in Figure 8-10. As you can see from that XML output, there are multiple properties that identify the conformance status of the target system. Table 8-1 provides a brief overview of these properties.

Figure 8-10. *Metadata for the conformance endpoint service*

Table 8-1. *Overview of Status Method Output Properties*

Property Name	Description
TargetName	IP address of the target system configured as pull client. This is the key property too.
ConfigurationId	Value of the GUID configured as the ConfigurationId on the pull client
ServerCheckSum	Checksum value of the configuration MOF on the Pull service server
TargetCheckSum	Checksum value from the target system configured as pull client
NodeCompliant	Boolean value that specifies if configuration run on the target system was successful or not
LastComplianceTime	Last time the target system ran the configuration successfully
LastHeartBeatTime	Last time the target system connected to the pull server
Dirty	True, if the target system status was recorded in the database; if not, False
StatusCode	Status code indicating the target system's configuration run status

As shown in Figure 8-10, the Status endpoint provides details about an entity type called MSFT.PSDSCDevices. The XML output shown in Figure 8-10 gives the properties associated with the PSDSCDevices entity type. A short description of these properties is provided in Table 8-1.

With this information, we can access the Status method of the endpoint to retrieve the conformance status of the target systems. This can be done using the Invoke-RestMethod cmdlet. Here is an example:

```
$Url = 'http://localhost:9090/DscConformance/PSDSCComplianceServer.svc/Status'
$ContentType = "application/json"
$response = Invoke-WebRequest -Uri $Url -Method Get -ContentType $ContentType -UseDefaultCredentials
  -Headers @{Accept = $ContentType}
$jsonResponse = ConvertFrom-Json $response.Content
$jsonResponse.value
```

In the preceding example, we have set the content type of the response to application/json. It is possible to get an XML response by setting the content type to application/atom+xml. If you are retrieving an XML response, the subsequent steps must be changed accordingly. Also, it is necessary to use the -UseDefaultCredentials switch parameter, as the conformance server endpoint is set for Windows authentication.

The NodeCompliant property contains a Boolean value indicating whether or not the target system is in a desired state. If target system(s) pulled configuration from the Pull service only once and the subsequent consistency checks were not run yet, the NodeCompliant may still show as False, as illustrated in Figure 8-11. This is because when the pull client uses the Pull service for the first time, there is no compliance status available on the target system.

```
TargetName          : 192.168.100.107
ConfigurationId     : 437c669b-803b-4bc5-bb67-9c6d949b5a8c
ServerCheckSum      : E1814EC5F9A336363B77232B8D594E8A0F34C1EF7F55949337AABF3A4E2999D6
TargetCheckSum      :
NodeCompliant       : False
LastComplianceTime  : 0001-01-01T00:00:00|
LastHeatbeatTime    :
Dirty               : True
StatusCode          : 0

TargetName          : 192.168.100.103
ConfigurationId     : deb8c9e7-8462-4d33-957a-bf0fefa56830
ServerCheckSum      : 494D31CA94877157AADD96A7DC907BB04FF268A044D7B444C68AF56C665E2B30
TargetCheckSum      :
NodeCompliant       : False
LastComplianceTime  : 0001-01-01T00:00:00
LastHeatbeatTime    :
Dirty               : True
StatusCode          : 0
```

Figure 8-11. *NodeCompliant showing* False *when the pull configuration occurred only once*

In such a scenario, triggering the consistency scheduled task manually or as per the configured interval will fix this. The result from a subsequent consistency check is shown in Figure 8-12.

```
TargetName          : 192.168.100.107
ConfigurationId     : 437c669b-803b-4bc5-bb67-9c6d949b5a8c
ServerCheckSum      : E1814EC5F9A336363B77232B8D594E8A0F34C1EF7F55949337AABF3A4E2999D6
TargetCheckSum      : E1814EC5F9A336363B77232B8D594E8A0F34C1EF7F55949337AABF3A4E2999D6
NodeCompliant       : True
LastComplianceTime  : 2014-06-30T06:32:44.1048313Z
LastHeatbeatTime    :
Dirty               : True
StatusCode          : 0

TargetName          : 192.168.100.103
ConfigurationId     : deb8c9e7-8462-4d33-957a-bf0fefa56830
ServerCheckSum      : 494D31CA94877157AADD96A7DC907BB04FF268A044D7B444C68AF56C665E2B30
TargetCheckSum      : 494D31CA94877157AADD96A7DC907BB04FF268A044D7B444C68AF56C665E2B30
NodeCompliant       : True
LastComplianceTime  : 2014-06-30T06:32:39.7776434Z
LastHeatbeatTime    :
Dirty               : True
StatusCode          : 0
```

Figure 8-12. *NodeCompliant status after a subsequent consistency check*

In a deployment that has hundreds, if not thousands, of pull clients, you may not really want to retrieve the complete data set. This is where the OData query tokens can be used to filter the data set at the server. The following example demonstrates one such query.

```
$Url = 'http://localhost:9090/DscConformance/PSDSCComplianceServer.svc/Status?$top=2'
$ContentType = "application/json"
$response = Invoke-WebRequest -Uri $Url -Method Get -ContentType $ContentType -UseDefaultCredentials
 -Headers @{Accept = $ContentType}
$jsonResponse = ConvertFrom-Json $response.Content
$jsonResponse.value
```

The preceding example uses the $top query token to retrieve only the top-two results from the conformance endpoint. You can use the HTML reporting techniques in PowerShell to convert the objects returned by the conformance endpoint into beautiful reports. Try this yourself.

The current implementation in WMF 4.0 is limited. The NodeCompliant property only describes whether the configuration on the target system is or is not the same as that on the pull server. If the checksum matches, the NodeCompliant will be set to True. This does not include checks to find configuration drift on the target systems. Also, one more thing you must have noticed in the output of conformance endpoint is the lack of detail about what resource is not in a desired state. This is the same limitation we saw earlier with the Test-DscConfiguration cmdlet. In the current implementation, the conformance endpoint does not have the capability to pinpoint to a specific resource that is not in a desired state. Future releases of DSC may include some new features to address this.

Summary

When working with any configuration management system, once the configuration enactment process is complete, it is necessary to monitor the configuration on the target system, to identify any configuration drift. Configuration drift from the baseline can be harmful in a production environment and can have negative effects on the disaster recovery. To prevent this, it is ideal to monitor the systems on a regular basis and take corrective action. Desired State Configuration provides features to enable configuration monitoring and reporting. At this time of writing, in the current WMF 4.0 implementation, there are certain limitations that prevent insights into what specific resource is not in desired state. However, using whatever skills you have gained so far, it is not hard to write custom scripts that provide these missing insights in the base product. When using the pull REST-based endpoints, we can configure the conformance endpoint to retrieve the node compliance report from a central repository. Even this can be extended, if you know how to program in ASP.NET or web services. This is outside the scope of this book, but if you have expertise in these areas, you may want to explore building your own custom dashboards and reports.

■ ■ ■

CHAPTER 9

Building Custom DSC Resources

The resource modules are the heart of configuration management using the management platform provided by Desired State Configuration (DSC). The initial release of DSC, as a part of WMF 4.0, included only 12 built-in resources. These resources enable basic management of a target system, which includes modules for unpacking zip archives, installing and uninstalling MSI and setup packages, managing services, processes, managing Windows roles and features, and so on. While these built-in resources are a good starting point, there are still quite a few gaps and scope for creating DSC resources. DSC as a management platform provides a framework for creating custom DSC resources. It is important for administrators and developers alike to understand how to create custom DSC resource modules. For administrators, this knowledge provides a way to go beyond what is offered by DSC in-box. Developers can leverage the knowledge of writing custom DSC resources to provide support for configuring the applications they are developing using DSC.

This chapter equips you with all the information required to develop PowerShell script modules to implement custom DSC resources. You will learn how the DSC resources work, what the requirements for writing a DSC resource module are, and, finally, what composite resources are and how they are used.

Introduction to DSC Resource Development

DSC custom resources can be written as PowerShell script modules, Binary PowerShell modules (written in C#), or as Management Infrastructure (MI) providers.

Of all three, the MI providers are the most complex, and at this time of writing, only providers written in C or C++ are supported. The built-in File resource in DSC is an MI provider. The decision to create an MI provider depends on the existing functionality that can be leveraged as a part of the DSC resource. If you already have the required functionality and an MI provider that is used to manage your application settings, extending that functionality to an MI provider for DSC makes sense. Also, if an application or software that you want to manage is written in the native code, it is easier to program such application configuration using an MI provider than creating a module written either in C# or PowerShell.

The choice between the PowerShell script-based resource modules and the binary modules written in C# depends mostly on your expertise. If you are already proficient in writing PowerShell script modules, you are already equipped to write DSC resources. However, if your area of expertise is C# and you believe that the resource configuration using .NET is more performant than PowerShell, a binary DSC resource would be a better choice.

In this chapter, we will look at implementing PowerShell script modules as DSC resources. The semantics for writing a DSC resource are the same for both script and binary modules. Before we go into the details of building custom DSC resources, it is important to understand the key elements in a DSC resource and the execution flow of a DSC resource. This section introduces these concepts, and the subsequent sections build upon this and demonstrate building DSC resources.

As we have seen in the preceding paragraphs, a DSC resource module can be written as a PowerShell script module. This means we write the necessary logic to perform the configuration and store it as a .psm1 file. Along with a .psm1 file, a DSC resource must have the following:

- A *Schema MOF file* containing the properties of a DSC resource

- A *Module Manifest file* that describes the module and specifies how it should be processed

Optionally, the DSC resource can contain any .ps1 files or other PowerShell script modules files required and the help content as text files. We will cover more about writing help content for DSC resources, later in this chapter. Let us dive into each of the mandatory elements.

■ **Note**   The Resource Designer module in the DSC resource kit provides an easier way to create the resource schema Managed Object File (MOF) and a skeleton for the resource script module. For understanding what this module creates, and for a better understanding of how custom DSC resources are created, it is better that we go through this process manually. In Appendix A, we will look at the DSC resource designer and some examples of using some of its functions.

DSC Resource Schema

The schema MOF of a DSC resource defines the properties of a resource. In Chapter 2, we defined what an MOF file is and how to write CIM classes as MOF files. If you need a quick refresher, I suggest that you go back to the "Understanding MOF" section toward the end of Chapter 2. Each MOF file written for a DSC resource must have, at a minimum, one or more properties. Each custom resource class must derive from the OMI_BaseResource class. Also, the ClassVersion and FriendlyName attributes of the class are mandatory. In Chapter 2, we looked at the basic syntax for writing MOF files and discussed some of the qualifiers used in an MOF schema. Table 9-1 describes valid qualifiers and their purpose and provides examples for each qualifier.

Table 9-1. *Qualifiers in a DSC Schema MOF*

Qualifier	Description	Example
Key	The key qualifier on a property indicates that the property uniquely identifies the resource instance.	[Key] string VMName;
Write	The write qualifier indicates that a value can be assigned to the property in a configuration script.	[write] string Description;
Read	The read qualifier indicates that the property value cannot be assigned or changed in a configuration script.	[read] string VMID;

(*continued*)

Table 9-1. *(continued)*

Qualifier	Description	Example
Description	This qualifier is used to provide a description for a property. This is used along with read or write or key qualifiers.	`[Key, description("Specifies the name of the VM to be created.")] string VMName;`
Required	This qualifier specifies that the property value is mandatory and cannot be null. Make a note that this is not the same as the key qualifier. The key qualifier uniquely identifies a resource instance.	`[required] string VHDPath;`
ValueMap and Values	This restricts the values that can be assigned to a property to that defined in ValueMap.	`[write,ValueMap{"Present", "Absent"},Values{"Present", "Absent"}] string Ensure;`

As shown in Table 9-1, these are the basic qualifiers required for creating a DSC resource schema MOF. There are many other standard WMI qualifiers. We usually don't need all that when writing DSC resource schema files. For a complete list of standard qualifiers, refer to `http://msdn.microsoft.com/en-us/library/aa393650(v=vs.85).aspx`. Make a note of the syntax shown in the "Example" column. The property qualifiers are enclosed in square brackets. The `ValueMap` and `Values` qualifiers are used along with the `write` qualifier to define a set of valid values for a resource property. The `read` property is used to define properties of a resource that cannot be changed or assigned in a configuration script. For example, the `VMID` is not something we can change or assign while creating a VM. The hypervisor assigns a `VMID` during the creation of the VM. With an understanding of these qualifiers, let us look at an example and discuss a few more details about authoring DSC resource schema files.

```
[ClassVersion("1.0.0.0"), FriendlyName("VirtualMachine")]
class MyDSC_VirtualMachine : OMI_BaseResource
{
    [key, Description("Specifies the name of the Virtual Machine.")] string VMName;
    [write, Description("Specifies description for the Virtual Machine")] string Description;
    [required, Description("Specifies the path of the VHD")] string VHDPath;
    [read, Description("Specifies the virtual machine identifer")] string VMID;
    [write,ValueMap{"Present", "Absent"},Values{"Present", "Absent"}] string Ensure;
};
```

In the preceding example, we have used all the qualifiers we saw in Table 9-1. In addition to that, we have also specified the `ClassVersion` and `FriendlyName` attributes that define the version of the DSC resource class we are creating and a friendly name that identifies the DSC resource. The value of the `FriendlyName` attribute is what we see in the output of the `Get-DscResource` cmdlet. The value of the `ClassVersion` attribute can be used to uniquely identify the version of a DSC resource. Finally, as you see in the example, it is recommended to have a property called `Ensure` in the DSC resource, with `"Present"` and `"Absent"` as the possible values.

Once we have the resource schema file authored, we must store it as `<ClassName>.Schema.mof`. For instance, in the MOF schema we authored in the preceding example, the file name will be `MyDSC_VirtualMachine.Schema.mof`. Also, make a note that this file has to be stored with Unicode or ANSI encoding. Using other encoding schemes will result in errors. So, how do we pre-validate an MOF file for errors? We can use `mofcomp.exe` for that.

```
mofcomp.exe -check <mofilename>
```

DSC Resource PowerShell Module

The PowerShell script module that we have to author as a DSC resource module has special requirements. These resource modules must contain the three functions described in Table 9-2. The name of the functions has to be the same as shown in the table, and these functions are used in the resource configuration flow. We will discuss the execution flow further, after we see a brief description of these functions in the resource module.

Table 9-2. *Mandatory Functions in a DSC Resource Module*

Function Name	Description	Input	Output
Get-TargetResource	This function is used to retrieve the current state of the configuration. For example, by taking the key resource properties as input, the function should check the state of the resource on the target system and return all its properties.	The resource properties identified as key properties in the schema MOF	A configuration hash table containing the values of all resource instance properties in the current state
Set-TargetResource	This function should contain the logic required to perform the configuration change. This function is used to ensure that the resource instance is in the requested state. Ideally, the Ensure property must be used to identify the requested state.	The resource properties identified as key properties and any other optional properties defined in the schema MOF	None
Test-TargetResource	This function is used to identify if the resource instance is in a desired state or not. The output from this function is used to decide if the Set-TargetResource function must be called or not. Again, the value of the Ensure parameter is used to test if the resource instance is in a desired state or not.	This function must have the same parameters as the Set-TargetResource function. The Test-DscConfiguration cmdlet calls this function to verify if the resource instance is in a desired state or not.	A Boolean value indicating if the resource instance is in a desired state (True) or not (False)

Before we delve into creating a custom resource module, let us take a look at how the functions shown in Table 9-2 are used in the resource module execution flow. Understanding this execution flow is important to enable the right logic in the resource module functions.

DSC Resource Execution Flow

The Test-TargetResource and Set-TargetResource functions are the important of those used in the configuration enactment process. As described in Table 9-2, the Set-TargetResource function gets called if, and only if, the Test-TargetResource function returns False. Figure 9-1 provides an overview of this in the form of a flow chart.

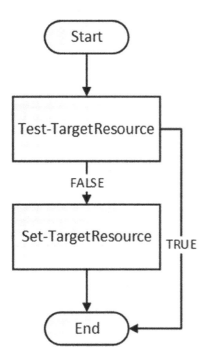

Figure 9-1. *DSC resource execution flow*

We saw in Table 9-2 that the Test-TargetResource function must return a Boolean value. This function has the same parameters as the Set-TargetResource function. When this function is called, it looks at the current state of the resource instance we are configuring and then returns either True or False. For example, when we create a virtual machine, we specify VMName as the key property. If we use a custom DSC resource to create the VM, the Test-TargetResource function in the resource module must check if a resource instance with the same name already exists. If it exists, this function must return True; it should return False otherwise. The Set-TargetResource function must be executed to create the virtual machine if and only if the Test-TargetResource function returned False. So, in essence, how we write the Test-TargetResource function decides whether our custom DSC resource works as expected or not.

The Set-TargetResource function performs the configuration change required. As this function gets executed only if the resource instance is not in a desired state, the error handling and prerequisite checks can be offloaded to the Test-TargetResource function.

The Get-TargetResource function, unlike the Set and Test functions, is not a part of the configuration enactment process. This is evident from the flow shown in Figure 9-1; however, the Get-TargetResource function is used to retrieve the current state of the resource instance. The Get-DscConfiguration cmdlet uses this function for all resources in a configuration script.

Once we have the logic for all the three functions, we can save it as a PowerShell script module with the name <ResourceClassName>.psm1. As a part of this module script, make sure you add the Export-ModuleMember cmdlet and export at least the three functions that we described so far. This is an important step, and we will see why when we author a custom DSC resource later in this chapter.

Resource Module Manifest

The DSC resource module manifest is nothing but a PowerShell module manifest. We can use the New-ModuleManifest cmdlet to generate this manifest for the DSC resource module. The module manifest should be stored as <ResourceName>.psd1.

The version specified in the module manifest is used as a reference in the MOF file generated for the configuration that uses this resource module. The target system uses the resource version in the configuration MOF to identify the version of the resource module to be used on the target system. We will see how to generate the module manifest data and how it is used in the configuration MOF files, later in this chapter.

The need for a module manifest file for a custom resource depends on how we package the custom resource module. We will see this in the next section.

Packaging DSC Resource Modules

We already understand that the custom DSC resource modules are nothing but PowerShell script modules. There are two methods of packaging DSC resources. We can put all the files for the resource module in a single folder. For example, in this configuration, the folder containing the module files must be stored at $PSHOME\Modules\ PSDesiredStateConfiguration\DSCResources. The folder structure should be as shown in Figure 9-2.

```
PS C:\Windows\System32\WindowsPowerShell\v1.0\Modules\PSDesiredStateConfiguration\DSCResources> tree /F /A
Folder PATH listing for volume Windows
Volume serial number is 627C-C198
C:.
+---HostsFile
|   |   HostsFile.psd1
|   |   HostsFile.psm1
|   |   HostsFile.schema.mof
|   |
```

***Figure 9-2.** Packaging of a DSC resource module placed in a system path*

The second method of packaging custom DSC resources is as a nested PowerShell module. Using this method, multiple DSC resources can be packaged as a single module. The folder containing the nested DSC resource modules can be placed at any path represented by $env:PSModulePath.

A typical folder structure for nested DSC resource modules is shown in Figure 9-3. When using this method for packaging DSC resources, remember that you need a module manifest for the nested module and not the DSC resource. This is different from what we discussed earlier in this section. You can author multiple DSC resources that can be categorized according to the functionality of the resource. For example, the modules in the DSC resource kit are organized based on the category and as nested PowerShell modules.

```
PS C:\Users\ravikanth_chaganti\Documents\WindowsPowerShell\Modules> tree /F /A
Folder PATH listing for volume Windows
Volume serial number is 627C-C198
C:.
\---DSCDeepDive
    |   DSCDeepDive.psd1
    |
    \---DSCResources
        \---HostsFile
            |   HostsFile.psm1
            |   HostsFile.schema.mof
```

***Figure 9-3.** DSC resource as a PowerShell nested module*

As shown in Figure 9-3, the module manifest is named-based on the nested module name. Also, notice the DSCResources folder under the nested module folder. We have to place all custom resource modules as folders in the DSCResources folder. The .psm1 file should have the same base name as the containing folder name. In our example, and as shown in Figure 9-3, the PowerShell script module is named HostsFile.psm1, and the parent folder is named HostsFile. Without this, the HostsFile resource won't get imported. Again, note that there is no module manifest file in the resource folder. So, as with this, we can store multiple such DSC resource module folders under the DSCResources folder.

■ **Tip**   You can look at the PSDesiredStateConfiguration module script to see how the Get-DscResource cmdlet retrieves a list of all DSC resources in the system. This gives a clear idea of how this cmdlet detects DSC resources from the nested modules and the reason for the folder structure required for DSC resources implemented as nested modules.

I recommend that you use the nested module option when packaging your custom DSC resources.

■ **Note**   When the custom DSC resource structured as nested modules is stored at a location other than the $PSHOME\Modules, we have to use the Import-DscResource cmdlet in the configuration script. We will see a few examples that demonstrate this, later in the chapter.

So far, in this section, we covered the concepts required to build custom DSC resources. In the following section, we will look at building a custom DSC resource. For the purposes of demonstration, I chose to write a DSC resource for managing hosts files in the Windows OS. I chose this simple resource because we don't want to spend time discussing how the logic for the resource module is implemented. Instead, we will discuss how the required functions are implemented, one at a time, and see the concepts we learned so far in action. Let's begin.

Writing Our First DSC Resource

The first step in writing a custom DSC resource is to write down the properties of a resource we want to configure. In our example, we will look to write a resource module for managing hosts files. A hosts file in the Windows OS is located at $env:SystemRoot\system32\drivers\etc. This file is a simple text file that takes the host entries as space-separated values. For example, the following string represents a host entry.

```
10.10.10.10 estserver10
```

The DSC resource must be capable of managing these entries. In our example, a hosts file entry is the resource instance we intend to configure. The mandatory input parameters are IPAddress and HostName. So, both these parameters become key properties in the resource schema. We also have to use the Ensure property, either to add or remove a host entry. The possible values for this property are Present and Absent. We can now create the schema MOF for the resource. Here is how it looks:

```
[ClassVersion("1.0"), FriendlyName("HostsFile")]
class DSC_HostsFile : OMI_BaseResource
{
  [Key] string HostName;
  [Key] string IPAddress;
  [write,ValueMap{"Present", "Absent"},Values{"Present", "Absent"}] string Ensure;
};
```

We have used HostsFile as the friendly name for the resource and DSC_HostsFile as the class name. We have added all relevant properties to the schema MOF. If you observe the MOF contents, we have set both IPAddress and HostName properties as key properties. This should be obvious, as we cannot construct a hosts file entry without both these values, and a combination of these values is what uniquely identifies the entry in the hosts file. We must save this file as DSC_HostsFile.schema.mof.

With the schema file handy, let us look at each of the three functions we have to create.

Test-TargetResource

We will start with the Test-TargetResource function. As we discussed earlier, this function gets called first to verify the state of the resource instance. In this example, we have to verify whether or not a hosts file exists for the given input parameters. Then, based on the value of the Ensure property, we return the necessary Boolean value.

At a high level, the execution flow for this function should be as shown in Figure 9-4.

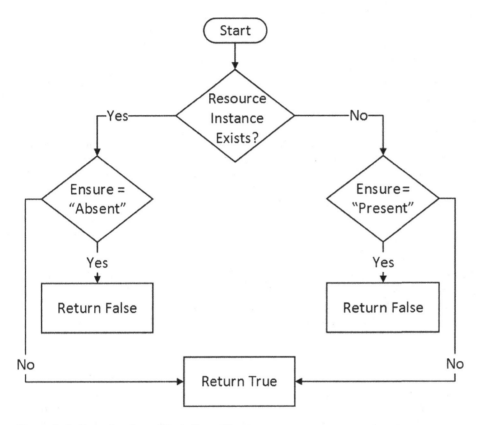

Figure 9-4. *Execution flow of* Test-TargetResource

Looking at the execution flow in Figure 9-4, it should be clear that we have to check if the resource instance already exists. The Test-TargetResource function enables idempotent nature in DSC resources. This means that we can apply the same configuration any number of times. If the current state is the same as the desired state, no action will be taken. When writing custom DSC resources, adhering to the idempotent principle is very important.

In our example, as discussed earlier, a resource instance is the hosts file entry constructed using the given input parameters HostName and IPAddress. Once we know if the resource instance exists or not, we have to look at the value of the Ensure property in the configuration script. Let us look at all the cases arising from this.

If the resource instance exists and the Ensure property is set to Present, we need not do anything. In this case, the Test-TargetResource function exits by returning True. This indicates that there is no need to execute the Set-TargetResource function.

If the resource instance exists and the Ensure property is set to Absent, we must remove the instance. In this case, the Test-TargetResource function exists by returning False, and the Set-TargetResource function will be used to remove the resource instance.

If the resource does not exist and Ensure is set to Absent, we need not do anything. In this case, the Test-TargetResource function exits by returning True. This indicates that there is no need to execute the Set-TargetResource function.

If the resource instance does not exist and the Ensure property is set to Present, we have to create the instance. In this case, the Test-TargetResource function exists by returning False, and the Set-TargetResource function will be used to create the resource instance.

Using what we have learned so far, let us put together the logic for the Test-TargetResource function in our DSC resource. Here is how it should look:

```
function Test-TargetResource
{
    [OutputType([boolean])]
    param (
        [parameter(Mandatory)]
        [string]
        $HostName,
        [parameter(Mandatory)]
        [string]
        $IPAddress,

        [ValidateSet('Present','Absent')]
        [string]
        $Ensure = 'Present'
    )

    try {
        Write-Verbose "Checking if the hosts file entry exists or not"
        $entryExist = ((Get-Content "${env:windir}\system32\drivers\etc\hosts" -ErrorAction Stop)
        -match "^[^#]*$ipAddress\s+$hostName")

        if ($Ensure -eq "Present") {
            if ($entryExist) {
                Write-Verbose "Hosts file entry exists for the given parameters; nothing to
                configure."
                return $true
            } else {
                Write-Verbose "Hosts file does not exist while it should; it will be added."
                return $false
            }
        } else {
            if ($entryExist) {
                Write-Verbose "Hosts file entry exists while it should not; it must be removed."
                return $false
            } else {
                Write-Verbose "Hosts file entry does not exist; nothing to configure."
                return $true
            }
        }
    }
}
```

```
catch {
    $exception = $_
    Write-Verbose "Error occurred while executing Test-TargetResource function"
    while ($exception.InnerException -ne $null)
    {
        $exception = $exception.InnerException
        Write-Verbose $exception.message
    }
}
}
```

Take a few minutes to understand the code we have here. First and foremost, note that the Test-TargetResource must return a Boolean value, and therefore, it is mandatory to mention the output type from this function. In the preceding code, this is done using [OutputType([boolean])] at the beginning of the function script block.

Writing a PowerShell function the way we declared the parameters and so on should not be new. It is worth noting that for all the resource properties marked with the key qualifier in the schema, we have created mandatory parameters in the PowerShell function. We are using regular expressions to check if the hosts file entry exists for the given input parameters. The $entryExist variable is used to hold a Boolean value from the regular expression matching. Once we have this value, we use that of the Ensure property to take the right execution path. This was explained earlier in this section, and I recommend that you compare what we discussed with the preceding code.

Set-TargetResource

As explained earlier, the Set-TargetResource function performs the configuration change. Because this function gets executed only when the resource instance is not in the desired state, we can safely assume that there is no error checking needed in this function. In our example, the Test-TargetResource function checks if a hosts file entry exists or not and relates it to the value of the Ensure property. So, all we have to write within the Set-TargetResource function is either remove or add the hosts file entry, based on the value of the Ensure property.

We can now look at the code required for implementing the Set-TargetResource function. Notice that the parameters of this function are the same as those of the Test-TargetResource function.

```
function Set-TargetResource
{
    param (
        [parameter(Mandatory)]
        [string]
        $HostName,
        [parameter(Mandatory)]
        [string]
        $IPAddress,
        [ValidateSet('Present','Absent')]
        [string]
        $Ensure = 'Present'
    )

    $hostEntry = "`n${ipAddress}`t${hostName}"
    $hostsFilePath = "${env:windir}\system32\drivers\etc\hosts" -
```

```
    try {

        if ($Ensure -eq 'Present')
        {
            Write-Verbose "Creating hosts file entry '$hostEntry'"
            Add-Content –Path $hostsFilePath Value $hostEntry -Force -Encoding ASCII –ErrorAction
            Stop
            Write-Verbose "Hosts file entry '$hostEntry' added"
        }
        else
        {
            Write-Verbose "Removing hosts file entry '$hostEntry'"
            ((Get-Content $hostsFilePath) -notmatch "^\s*$") -notmatch "^[^#]*$ipAddress\
s+$hostName" | Set-Content $hostsFilePath
            Write-Verbose "Hosts file entry '$hostEntry' removed"
        }
    }
    catch {
            $exception = $_
            Write-Verbose "An error occurred while running Set-TargetResource function"
            while ($exception.InnerException -ne $null)
            {
                $exception = $exception.InnerException
                Write-Verbose $exception.message
            }
    }
}
```

The logic here is simple. We check the value of the Ensure property and take the appropriate action. We use the try and catch block to report any errors in the process of updating the hosts file using this function.

The final function that we have to write is the Get-TargetResource.

Get-TargetResource

As we have seen in Table 9-2, the Get-TargetResource must have all resource properties marked with the key qualifier, in the schema MOF, as the input parameters. For our example, these are the HostName and IPAddress properties of the resource. Also, we discussed that the output from this function should be a hash table representing the current state of the resource instance. As you see in the following function script block, we are setting the output type of the function to a hash table.

Let us look at the function definition.

```
function Get-TargetResource
{
    [OutputType([Hashtable])]
    param (
        [parameter(Mandatory]
        [string]
        $HostName,
        [parameter(Mandatory)]
        [string]
        $IPAddress
    )
```

```
$Configuration = @{
    HostName = $hostName
    IPAddress = $IPAddress
}

Write-Verbose "Checking if hosts file entry exists or not"
try {
    if ((Get-Content "${env:windir}\system32\drivers\etc\hosts" -ErrorAction SilentlyContinue)
    -match "^[^#]*$ipAddress\s+$hostName") {
        Write-Verbose "Hosts file entry does exists"
        $Configuration.Add('Ensure','Present')
    } else {
        Write-Verbose "Hosts file entry does not exist"
        $Configuration.Add('Ensure','Absent')
    }
    return $Configuration
}

catch {
    $exception = $_
    Write-Verbose "Error occurred while running Get-TargetResource function"
    while ($exception.InnerException -ne $null)
    {
        $exception = $exception.InnerException
        Write-Verbose $exception.message
    }
}
}
```

The above function code is self-explanatory. Note that we do not have the Ensure property as a parameter of this function. The code in this function is almost the same as in the Test-TargetResource function. In this function, however, we set the Ensure property depending on whether the resource instance exists or not. So, the hash table returned from this function has the *current state* of the resource instance and not the desired state.

■ **Tip**   Using the Write-Verbose cmdlet in each of these functions helps to display messages from the resource execution on the console. If we use the Write-Debug cmdlet in the DSC resource module, the debug messages will be logged to the Debug channel of the DSC event logs. We have seen examples using these logs, in Chapter 8.

So, we have seen all the three functions and implemented the necessary logic to manage hosts file entries as a DSC resource. We can now package these functions as a PowerShell script module. Remember that we have to add the Export-ModuleMember command at the end of the script module file to export all the three functions. Because we have only three functions, we can use an asterisk (*) as an argument to the -Function parameter.

```
Export-ModuleMember -Function *-TargetResource
```

The script module with all three functions and the preceding command can be saved as DSC_HostsFile.psm1. For demonstration purposes, I saved in the C:\Scripts folder both the schema MOF and the script module.

We have to generate the module manifest for this script module. We can use the `New-ModuleManifest` cmdlet for this purpose. The following code snippet shows how this is done:

```
$param = @{
    guid = [Guid]::NewGuid()
    author = "Ravikanth"
    company = "DSC Demos LLC"
    moduleversion = "1.0"
    description = "DSC resource to manage hosts file entries"
    path= 'C:\Scripts\DSC_HostsFile.psd1'
}

New-ModuleManifest @param
```

This generates the module manifest file named `DSC_HostsFile.psd1` at `C:\Scripts`. With this, we have all the ingredients for a custom DSC resource. We can now store these files as a DSC resource module. Let us use the script module method to store this DSC resource at `$PSHOME\Modules\PSDesiredStateConfiguration\DSCResources`. If you recall, this is the first of the two methods we discussed for packaging DSC resources. Once we store the resource, we should be able to see the following (Figure 9-5) in the `Get-DscResource` cmdlet output:

```
PowerShell    Archive        PSDesiredStateConfiguration    {Destination, Path, Checksum, DependsOn...}
PowerShell    Environment    PSDesiredStateConfiguration    {Name, DependsOn, Ensure, Path...}
PowerShell    Group          PSDesiredStateConfiguration    {GroupName, Credential, DependsOn, Description...}
PowerShell    HostsFile      PSDesiredStateConfiguration    {HostName, IPAddress, DependsOn, Ensure}
Binary        Log            PSDesiredStateConfiguration    {Message, DependsOn}
```

Figure 9-5. *Partial output from* `Get-DscResource` *that shows* `HostsFile` *resource*

If you observe the partial output shown in Figure 9-5, the `HostsFile` DSC resource is shown as a part of the `PSDesiredStateConfiguration` module. This is because we have stored the DSC resource we created under the `DSCResources` folder in `PSDesiredStateConfiguration` module folder. When using a nested module structure, only the module manifest from the nested module is loaded. What if we want our own nested module for the DSC resource? Simple, we move to the nested module structure, as shown in the "Packaging DSC Resource Modules" section, earlier in this chapter. Remember that you have to rename the module manifest to that of the nested module.

For example, if we call our nested module DSCDeepDive, the module manifest name should be `DSCDeepDive.psd1` and not `DSC_HostsFile.psd1`. As shown in Figure 9-3, we have to ensure that we create a folder named `DSCResources` under the new nested module folder. Once this folder restructuring is complete, you can see that the name of the module in the `Get-DscResource` output changes to DSCDeepDive. Figure 9-6 shows the `HostsFile` resource as a part of the DSCDeepDive nested module.

```
PowerShell    HostsFile      DSCDeepDive                    {HostName, IPAddress, DependsOn, Ensure}
PowerShell    Archive        PSDesiredStateConfiguration    {Destination, Path, Checksum, DependsOn...}
PowerShell    Environment    PSDesiredStateConfiguration    {Name, DependsOn, Ensure, Path...}
PowerShell    Group          PSDesiredStateConfiguration    {GroupName, Credential, DependsOn, Description...}
Binary        Log            PSDesiredStateConfiguration    {Message, DependsOn}
PowerShell    Package        PSDesiredStateConfiguration    {Name, Path, ProductId, Arguments...}
```

Figure 9-6. `HostsFile` *resource under a nested module*

Let us write a configuration script to see how this DSC resource for managing a hosts file is used.

```
Configuration DemoConfig {
    Node localhost {
        HostsFile HostsDemo {
            IPAddress = "10.10.10.10"
            HostName = "TestHost10"
            Ensure = "Present"
        }
    }
}
```

DemoConfig

On my system, I copied the nested module I created for the HostsFile resource to the module path represented by $PSHOME\Modules. So, the preceding configuration script works without any errors. However, if you have copied the nested module to $env:ProgramFiles\WindowsPowerShell\Modules or $env:USERPROFILE\Documents\ WindowsPowerShell\Modules, you have to use the Import-DscResource cmdlet in the Configuration script block, to ensure that the DSC resource module is loaded. Without this, you will see an error that the resource module is not found. Following is a sample configuration script that uses the Import-DscResource:

```
Configuration DemoConfig {
    Import-DscResource -Name DSC_HostsFile
    Node Localhost {
        HostsFile DemoHosts {
            IPAddress = "10.10.10.10"
            HostName = "TestServer10"
            Ensure = "Present"
        }
    }
}
```

DemoConfig

As you see in the preceding code snippet, we have used the Import-DscResource cmdlet with the –Name parameter. When using this parameter, we must specify the class name of the DSC resource, as mentioned in the resource's schema MOF file. Using this method, we load the resource that is required for the configuration. Instead, if you want to import all DSC resources in a nested module, you can use the –ModuleName parameter to specify the nested module name. So, for our example, the modified configuration script will be as following:

```
Configuration DemoConfig {
    Import-DscResource -ModuleName DSCDeepDive
    Node Localhost {
        HostsFile DemoHosts {
            IPAddress = "10.10.10.10"
            HostName = "TestServer10"
            Ensure = "Present"
        }
    }
}
```

DemoConfig

■ **Note** If you are executing these examples on a Windows Server 2012 R2 or Windows 8.1 system and placed the DSC resource nested module under the `$env:ProgramFiles\WindowsPowerShell\Modules` folder, make sure you have KB2883200 installed. Without this, the program files location won't be searched for any PowerShell modules or DSC resources.

All the preceding configuration script examples generate the configuration MOF containing the `HostsFile` resource configuration. We have seen several examples of pushing or pulling resource configuration, so I'll leave it to you to verify whether the `HostsFile` resource we built is working as expected.

So far in this chapter, we have examined the concepts you must understand before creating a DSC resource, written a sample DSC resource that manages hosts file entries, and seen how and where the DSC resource module can be stored and some gotchas to be aware of. Now, there is more. In the next section, we will look at some of the patterns, best practices, and guidelines for writing and packaging DSC resources.

Custom DSC Resource Patterns

Writing a custom DSC resource is as simple as writing a PowerShell script module. However, as we have seen, there are best practices—covering how these modules are written to how they are packaged. In this section, we will explore more such patterns and see practical examples. In some cases, we will modify the `HostsFile` resource created earlier in this section, to demonstrate how to implement these patterns, best practices, and guidelines.

Inducing Reboot After a Configuration Change

When examining the DSC meta-configuration, we looked at an LCM property called `RebootIfNeeded`. This is set, by default, to `False`. In the default configuration, if the resource configuration requires a reboot, it displays a verbose message that the configuration requires a reboot. When this property is set to `True`, if a resource configuration requires a reboot, the DSC engine will automatically trigger the reboot. One such DSC resource example is the `WindowsFeature` resource discussed in Chapter 5. But how does a DSC resource signal a reboot?

A custom DSC resource can signal an LCM to reboot the system, by setting a global variable called `DSCMachineStatus` to 1. This, of course, has to be done in the `Set-TargetResource` function. Within this function, after the resource configuration is complete, if you determine that a reboot is needed to complete the configuration, you can signal the LCM on a target system, by adding the following line:

```
$global:DSCMachineStatus = 1
```

When LCM receives this signal, and the `RebootIfNeeded` property is set to `True`, the target system restarts to complete the configuration. If you are an administrator, I recommend that you exercise extreme caution before setting the `RebootIfNeeded` property to `True` in the LCM meta-configuration.

■ **Caution** Be sure that you have the `Test-TargetResource` doing the right checks and returning `False` only when needed. If the resource is inducing a reboot of the target system and the `Test-TargetResource` is not written according to the idempotent principles, the target system will end up in an infinite reboot loop.

Localizing Verbose and Debug Messages

In the three functions definitions we wrote for the HostsFile DSC resource, we used the Write-Verbose cmdlet to log messages from the resource execution to the console. This is a good and recommended way of writing custom DSC resources. If you have used the Start-DscConfiguration cmdlet, as we have in several examples so far, with the -Verbose switch parameter, you can see the verbose messages from the resource module. This gives to the user pushing the configuration an idea of what is happening on the target system. Similarly, we can use the Write-Debug cmdlet in the Set-TargetResource and other module functions to write log messages to the Debug channel of the DSC events. We have seen in Chapter 8 how useful the Debug and Analytic channels are when monitoring configuration changes.

If you plan on sharing your DSC resources, it is recommended that you localize the messages written, using either the verbose or debug streams, or, at least, enable the flexibility for someone to add localized messages to the resource module. This can be done by using the script internationalization techniques in PowerShell. This is not specific to DSC resources but can be used with any PowerShell modules or scripts.

■ **Tip**   I recommend that you read the about_Data_Sections and about_script_internationalization help topics to learn more about string localization in PowerShell.

To begin, we first must create a hash table that contains all the log message strings. This is what I have done for the HostsFile resource.

```
ConvertFrom-StringData @'
    CheckingHostsFileEntry=Checking if the hosts file entry exists.
    HostsFileEntryFound=Found a hosts file entry for {0} and {1}.
    HostsFileEntryNotFound=Did not find a hosts file entry for {0} and {1}.
    HostsFileShouldNotExist=Hosts file entry exists while it should not.
    HostsFileEntryShouldExist=Hosts file entry does not exist while it should.
    CreatingHostsFileEntry=Creating a hosts file entry with {0} and {1}.
    RemovingHostsFileEntry=Removing a hosts file entry with {0} and {1}.
    HostsFileEntryAdded=Created the hosts file entry for {0} and {1}.
    HostsFileEntryRemoved=Removed the hosts file entry for {0} and {1}.
    AnErrorOccurred=An error occurred while creating hosts file entry: {1}.
    InnerException=Nested error trying to create hosts file entry: {1}.
'@
```

The ConvertFrom-StringData takes the here-string content and converts it to a hash table. We now have to store this in a PowerShell data file. Let us call this file HostsFileProvider.psd1. The {0} and {1} in the here-string are used as placeholders for replacement with any values supplied, such as the IPAddress and HostName values in the configuration script. We will see how these are used later in this section. Because these messages are in English and the language culture on my system is set to en-US, we will create a folder named en-US, under the resource module folder.

For example, if you are using the nested module structure for the DSC custom resource, the folder structure should look similar to what is shown in Figure 9-7. The HostsFileProvider.psd1 file has to be stored in the en-US folder. If you have the localized data for any other cultures, create separate .psd1 files for each of the cultures and store them under folders representing each of those cultures.

```
PS C:\Program Files\WindowsPowerShell\Modules> tree DSCDeepDive /F /A
Folder PATH listing for volume Windows
Volume serial number is 627C-C198
C:\PROGRAM FILES\WINDOWSPOWERSHELL\MODULES\DSCDEEPDIVE
|   DSCDeepDive.psd1
|
\---DSCResources
    \---HostsFile
        |   HostsFile.psm1
        |   HostsFile.schema.mof
        |
        \---en-US
                HostsFileProvider.psd1
```

***Figure 9-7.** DSC resource with localization support*

We now have to make sure that the resource module file (.psm1) loads this localized data. But before that, we have to add the fallback localized strings. To achieve this, we must add a DATA section to the script module for the DSC resource. Add the following code snippet at the beginning of the resource module file (.psm1). The DATA section, in my example, simply contains the same here-string as in the HostsFileProvider.psd1 file.

```
DATA localizedData
{
    # same as culture = "en-US"
ConvertFrom-StringData @'
    CheckingHostsFileEntry=Checking if the hosts file entry exists.
    HostsFileEntryFound=Found a hosts file entry for {0} and {1}.
    HostsFileEntryNotFound=Did not find a hosts file entry for {0} and {1}.
    HostsFileShouldNotExist=Hosts file entry exists while it should not.
    HostsFileEntryShouldExist=Hosts file entry does not exist while it should.
    CreatingHostsFileEntry=Creating a hosts file entry with {0} and {1}.
    RemovingHostsFileEntry=Removing a hosts file entry with {0} and {1}.
    HostsFileEntryAdded=Created the hosts file entry for {0} and {1}.
    HostsFileEntryRemoved=Removed the hosts file entry for {0} and {1}.
    AnErrorOccurred=An error occurred while creating hosts file entry: {1}.
    InnerException=Nested error trying to create hosts file entry: {1}.
'@
}
```

The DATA section in the preceding code snippet is referred to using the identifier localizedData. Using this data section, we can access the message strings by using the key names of the hash table. One such example is shown here:

```
$localizedData.CheckingHostsFileEntry
```

The localized data can be loaded dynamically at the runtime of the resource module, using the Import-LocalizedData cmdlet. This, by default, takes the value of the $PSUICulture automatic variable to locate the right folder for importing the localized data. This is why when we create the folders, we name them the same as the culture names. Here is how this cmdlet is used in the module file:

```
if (Test-Path $PSScriptRoot\en-us)
{
    Import-LocalizedData LocalizedData -filename HostsFileProvider.psd1
}
```

This is it. We have created the necessary prerequisites to enable internationalization of the DSC resource. We have to use the localized data while displaying verbose or debug messages. The following example shows the Get-TargetResource function from the HostsFile DSC resource module using the localized data.

```
function Get-TargetResource
{
    [OutputType([Hashtable])]
    param (
        [parameter(Mandatory = $true)]
        [string]
        $hostName,
        [parameter(Mandatory = $true)]
        [string]
        $ipAddress,
        [parameter()]
        [ValidateSet('Present','Absent')]
        [string]
        $Ensure = 'Present'
    )

    $Configuration = @{
        HostName = $hostName
        IPAddress = $IPAddress
    }

    Write-Verbose $localizedData.CheckingHostsFileEntry
    try {
        if ((Get-Content "${env:windir}\system32\drivers\etc\hosts") -match "^[^#]*$ipAddress\
        s+$hostName") {
            Write-Verbose ($localizedData.HostsFileEntryFound -f $hostName, $ipAddress)
            $Configuration.Add('Ensure','Present')
        } else {
            Write-Verbose ($localizedData.HostsFileEntryNotFound -f $hostName, $ipAddress)
            $Configuration.Add('Ensure','Absent')
        }
        return $Configuration
    }

    catch {
        $exception = $_
        Write-Verbose ($LocalizedData.AnErrorOccurred -f $exception.message)
        while ($exception.InnerException -ne $null)
        {
            $exception = $exception.InnerException
            Write-Verbose ($LocalizedData.InnerException -f $exception.message)
        }
    }
}
```

In the preceding example, observe how the $LocalizedData variable is used along with the -f formatting operator. The {0} or {1} used in the here-string gets replaced with the values supplied after the -f operator. As with the Get-TargetResource function, you can update the Set-TargetResource and Test-TargetResource functions to use the localized data. Try this yourself.

Adding Help Content

When you author a PowerShell module, you can implement help for each of the cmdlets, as comment-based help. This ensures that end users can employ the Get-Help cmdlet to understand how each of your module's functions or cmdlets is used. However, if you look at the DSC resource modules, they all contain the same set of functions: Get, Set, and Test. So, even if you write comment-based help for these functions in your resource, it won't be of much use. So, how do we include help content for the DSC resources that we build?

For DSC resources, the help content should describe how the resource can be used, with examples describing each possible configuration scenario for the resource. The ideal place to put this help content is in an about topic. In Chapter 1, we have seen several examples of using about topics. We can author help content for the DSC resource and store it as a text file, with a relevant about topic name.

For instance, I have put a few examples describing how the HostsFile resource can be used in a text file and named it about_HostsFile.help.txt. Note that the file name must end in .help.txt and should be stored in UTF-8 encoding. Once we create this file, we can store it in a folder named identically as the language culture. If you are using the nested module structure, this folder must be created at the same level as the DSCResources folder. This will help to enable localization for the about topics for the DSC resource. Figure 9-8 shows an example of this.

```
PS C:\Program Files\WindowsPowerShell\Modules> tree .\DSCDeepDive /F /A
Folder PATH listing for volume Windows
Volume serial number is 627C-C198
C:\PROGRAM FILES\WINDOWSPOWERSHELL\MODULES\DSCDEEPDIVE
|    DSCDeepDive.psd1
|
+---DSCResources
|    \---HostsFile
|        |    HostsFile.psm1
|        |    HostsFile.schema.mof
|        |
|        \---en-US
|                HostsFileProvider.psd1
|
\---en-US
        about_HostsFile.help.txt
```

Figure 9-8. *Help content location for the nested modules*

■ **Note**   The localization of the resource message strings is different from the localization of the nested module. For each DSC resource in the nested module, you can create an about topic text file and store it in the language culture folder, as shown in Figure 9-8.

Once the help content is in place, we can use the Get-Help cmdlet to discover and access the about topic content. This is shown in Figure 9-9.

```
PS C:\> Get-Help About_HostsFile
Syntax

HostsFile [string] #ResourceName
{
    HostName = [string]

    IPAddress = [string]

    [ Ensure = [string] { Absent | Present }  ]
}
Properties

HostName - Name of the server or computer

IPAddress - IPv4 or IPv6 address of the server or computer

Ensure - Set this property to "Present" add the hosts file entry. Using "Absent" will remove the hosts entry, if it exists.
```

Figure 9-9. *Partial content from the about topic for the* HostsFile *resource*

Granularity in DSC Resources

DSC is fairly new, and it will be exciting to learn this technology and implement your own resource modules and so on. However, when developing or authoring custom DSC resources, make sure that you go to the most granular level of the resource. Let us consider this with an example.

A virtual machine as a resource will have many subcomponents, such as virtual hard disks, virtual network adapters, and so on. So, if you are writing a DSC custom resource module to manage virtual machines, it is recommended that you create multiple DSC resource modules for each manageable component. This simplifies the whole configuration and makes it easy to configure the VM-attached resources in an independent way.

This concludes our discussion on writing custom DSC resources and on patterns or guidelines for writing these resource modules. The next topic in this chapter is composite resources. Let us delve into that topic to understand what these resources are and how we can use them to simplify configurations.

Composite Resources

In Chapter 6, we looked at writing advanced DSC configurations. We learned how to parameterize and create nested configurations. These techniques made the configurations reusable. The concept of composite resources extends this further, by enabling composable configurations. Composite resources are technically not custom DSC resources. I saved this topic for this chapter because the composite configurations can be packaged like the custom resource modules. So, if you understand how to create custom resource modules and how to package them, it is much easier to understand composite resources. That's fine, but why do we need composite resources?

Creating Composite Resources

Composite resources enable reuse of existing configurations. This highly simplifies the configuration scripts that we must write for a target system. Reuse is what nested configurations also provide. So, why not settle for that?

Composite resources are discoverable like any other DSC resource. This is the reason composite resources have to be packaged. Let us first build a configuration that is reusable.

```
Configuration BaseServerConfiguration {
    param (
        [string]$HostName,
        [String]$IPAddress,
        [String]$ArchivePath,
        [String]$DestinationPath
    )
```

```
    Import-DscResource -ModuleName DSCDeepDive
    WindowsFeature WebServer {
        Name = "Web-Server"
        IncludeAllSubFeature = $true
        Ensure = "Present"
    }

    WindowsFeature NLB {
        Name = "NLB"
        Ensure = "Present"
    }

    Archive ScriptFolder {
        Path = $ArchivePath
        Destination = $DestinationPath
        Ensure = "Present"
        Force = $true
    }

    HostsFile HostsEntry {
        ipAddress = $IPAddress
        hostName = $HostName
        Ensure = "Present"
    }
}
```

In the preceding example, we added configuration for such resources as WindowsFeature, Archive, and the HostsFile resource we created earlier in this chapter. We have to save this as <resourcename>.schema.psm1. Yes, you read that right. There is no schema MOF required for a composite resource. Instead, the name for the composite resource should contain schema.psm1. So, for our example, I saved the configuration as BaseServerConfiguration. Schema.psm1. Also, notice that there is no Node script block in this. We don't need it, as we will be using this more like a DSC resource and not a configuration. The parameters specified in the configuration become properties of the composite resource. This is how we achieve another level of reusability with composite resources.

Once we have the schema.psm1 file created, we have to generate a module manifest for this. We can use the New-ModuleManifest cmdlet here.

```
New-ModuleManifest -Path .\BaseServerConfiguration.psd1 -ModuleVersion "1.0" -RootModule
"BaseServerConfiguration.Schema.psm1"
```

If you observe the command line, I have specified BaseServerConfiguration.Schema.psm1 as the root module. This is yet another difference from a custom DSC resource. The custom DSC resource modules need not have a manifest file, but for the composite resources, a manifest is mandatory. We have the composite resource generated, and it can be packaged in a folder structure similar to that we used for a nested DSC resource module. For example, the composite resource files (schema.psm1 and psd1) must exist in a folder named DSCResources. The nested module must have a manifest file. Once again, you can use the New-ModuleManifest cmdlet to create the manifest for the nested module. Without a manifest for the nested module, the composite resources cannot be discovered using the Get-DscResource cmdlet. Figure 9-10 shows the folder structure that I have on my system for this demonstration.

```
PS C:\Program Files\WindowsPowerShell\Modules> tree /F /A
Folder PATH listing
Volume serial number is 000000D7 6083:AF97
C:.
+---DSCComposite
|   |   DSCComposite.psd1
|   |
|   \---DSCResources
|       \---BaseServerConfiguration
|               BaseServerConfiguration.psd1
|               BaseServerConfiguration.Schema.psm1
```

Figure 9-10. *Folder structure for a DSC composite resource*

As shown in Figure 9-11, we can use the Get-DscResource cmdlet to discover the composite resources.

```
PS C:\> Get-DscResource -Name BaseServerConfiguration

ImplementedAs   Name                     Module          Properties
-------------   ----                     ------          ----------
Composite       BaseServerConfiguration  DSCComposite    {HostName, IPAddress, ArchivePat...
```

Figure 9-11. *Composite resource discovered using the Get-DscResource cmdlet*

We now have the composite resource ready. We can start using it in our configuration scripts like any other custom DSC resource. Because I have placed this in the program files path, I need to use the Import-DscResource cmdlet in the configuration script, to ensure that it can be compiled successfully to an MOF. The following example demonstrates this:

```
Configuration SharePointConfig {
    Import-DscResource -ModuleName DSCComposite
    Node SP-FE-1 {
        BaseServerConfiguration BaseConfig {
            HostName = "SQL-DB-1"
            IPAddress = "10.10.10.192"
            ArchivePath = "\\WDS-1\Staging\Server-FE.zip"
            DestinationPath = "C:\Scripts"
        }
    }
}
```

See how simple the configuration is? There are WindowsFeature resource configurations that are completely abstracted but will be included as a part of the MOF that gets generated from this configuration script. Unlike the custom DSC resource modules, the composite resources need not exist on the target system on which the configuration gets enacted. The composite resources are required on systems generating the configuration MOF files for the target systems.

■ **Note**   As in a nested configuration, a bug in WMF 4.0 prevents the use of the DependsOn property in a configuration script when using composite resources. This property does not get involved in the generated MOF, and, therefore, no dependency checks are performed. This leads to erroneous configuration changes on the target systems. This is fixed in WMF 5.0.

InstanceName Parameter of the Configuration Command

If you have noticed the parameters available for a configuration command, you have seen that there is a parameter named InstanceName along with the ConfigurationData, OutputPath, and any other parameters added to your configuration. We have had no discussion of what the InstanceName parameter is and how we use it. As an end-use, you will never have to use this parameter when executing a configuration command. DSC internally uses this when the configuration script contains composite resources. For example, we can extend our last example to contain two instances of the composite resource.

```
Configuration SharePointConfig {
    Import-DscResource -ModuleName DSCDeepDive
    Node SP-FE-1 {
        BaseServerConfiguration BaseConfig1 {
            HostName = "SQL-DB-1"
            IPAddress = "10.10.10.192"
            ArchivePath = "\\WDS-1\Staging\Server-FE.zip"
            DestinationPath = "C:\Scripts"
        }

        HostsFile HostEntry {
            IPaddress = "192.168.100.1"
            Hostname = "Gateway"
            Ensure = "Present"
        }
    }
}

SharePointConfig
```

If you look at the preceding example, it has an additional HostsFile resource configuration that has the same identifier, HostEntry, as the composite resource. In a normal configuration script, this would result in an error indicating that there is a duplicate resource identifier. However, when using composite resources, this is allowed, as DSC internally appends the composite resource identifier BaseConfig1 to the HostsEntry resource defined in the composite resource. This is done using the InstanceName parameter internally. This is why I mentioned that you will never have to use it yourself. The following code snippet shows partial contents of the MOF file generated from the preceding example.

```
instance of HostsFile as $HostsFile1ref
{
ResourceID = "[HostsFile]HostsEntry::[BaseServerConfiguration]BaseConfig1";
 Ensure = "Present";
 hostName = "SQL-DB-1";
 SourceInfo = "C:\\Program Files\\WindowsPowerShell\\Modules\\DSCDeepDive\\DSCResources\\
BaseConfig\\BaseConfig.Schema.psm1::28::5::HostsFile";
 ModuleName = "DSCDeepDive";
 ipAddress = "10.10.10.192";
 ModuleVersion = "1.0";

};
```

```
instance of HostsFile as $HostsFile2ref
{
ResourceID = "[HostsFile]HostEntry";
 Ensure = "Present";
 hostName = "Gateway";
 SourceInfo = "::11::9::HostsFile";
 ModuleName = "DSCDeepDive";
 ipAddress = "192.168.100.1";
 ModuleVersion = "1.0";

};
```

As you see in the MOF contents here, the first instance definition for the HostsFile resource has the composite resource identifier appended.

Summary

Desired State Configuration provides the patterns or framework to create custom resource modules. While the built-in modules are a great starting point, IT administrators require many more capabilities than that. For any administrator or developer with existing knowledge of PowerShell module authoring, it is very simple to translate that expertise into writing custom DSC resource modules. There are certain best practices and recommendations for writing DSC resources. These guidelines help improve the usability of custom DSC resources. Finally, the composite resources enable reusable and composable configurations that are as discoverable as any other DSC resources. Using the composite resources can simplify the management of target systems that share a baseline configuration.

CHAPTER 10

Troubleshooting Common DSC Issues

We've come a long way in our Desired State Configuration (DSC) journey. We started with what DSC is and moved all the way up to how to write custom DSC resources. By now, I assume that you have written some new custom DSC resources or at least attempted to write a few. Also, you might have started exploring where else you can deploy DSC and use it in your day-to-day job. Once you deploy and start to use any technology, it certainly requires a good amount of hands-on experience to troubleshoot issues that emerge in production or even during prototyping stages. It becomes complex when, to function, the technology in question depends on a set of other technologies or components. DSC is no exception. We've discussed how DSC uses WinRM and CIM as a foundation. Some of the DSC issues could arise because of the dependencies of these dependent technologies. In general, the DSC event logs and verbose messages from the resource execution provide details of what may be going wrong with the DSC configuration management. But that may not always be the case.

In this chapter, we will look at some of the most common problems you may come across when using DSC and the solutions to them. Let us start by identifying some common problems. I compiled a list based on my own experiences and from what I've learned helping others resolve issues in their own DSC deployment. By no means is this is a complete list of problems that you may have to tackle in your deployment. Let's work our way from the most basic to the most tricky situations one might encounter while deploying and using DSC.

All Systems Must Be at Least at WMF 4.0

All target systems involved in a DSC deployment must at least be at WMF 4.0 to receive configuration using either Push or Pull modes of configuration delivery. This is obvious, because DSC is a feature that is available only from PowerShell 4.0 onward. The configuration authoring process does not perform any checks to see if the target system mentioned as a node identifier has PowerShell 4.0 or later. So, any errors related to unavailability of WMF 4.0 on the remote systems will be seen when enacting the configuration. It is ideal to check whether or not the target system has Windows PowerShell 4.0 installed, before even generating the configuration MOF. There are different ways to do this. We can use the Get-HotFix cmdlet to check if the WMF 4.0 update is installed on the target systems. However, when we have different versions of the Windows operating system in the environment, we have first to check which OS the target system is running and then look at the appropriate update. This is a lengthy process, so here is a trick that I use for checking if the target systems have WMF 4.0 or later:

```
Function Test-DscNamespace {
    Param (
        $ComputerName = $env:COMPUTERNAME
    )
    if (Get-CimInstance -ComputerName $ComputerName `
                        -Namespace root\Microsoft\Windows `
                        -ClassName __NAMESPACE `
                        -Filter "name='DesiredStateConfiguration'" `
                        -ErrorAction SilentlyContinue)
```

```
    {
        $true
    }
    else
    {
        $false
    }
}
```

The preceding function checks for the DSC Window Management Instrumentation (WMI) namespace availability on the target systems. DSC as a feature is available only from WMF 4.0 onward, and checking for its WMI namespace confirms the availability of WMF 4.0. So, once we have this function, we can iterate through the MOF files and enact configuration only on those that have WMF 4.0 or later.

```
Configuration DemoConfig {
    param (
        [string[]]$ComputerName
    )
    Node ($ComputerName.Where{(Test-DscNameSpace -ComputerName $_)}) {
        WindowsProcess ProcessDemo {
            Path = "Notepad.exe"
            Arguments = ""
            Ensure = "Present"
        }
    }
}
```

```
DemoConfig –ComputerName WC7-1,WS8R2-1,WS8R2-2,WSR2-3-WMF50,WSR2-1
```

In my preceding example, the target system named WS8R2-2 did not have WMF 4.0 installed. The preceding code snippet should not generate an MOF file for that node. You can also use configuration data for providing the target system names. Following is how we modify the above code snippet to use configuration data:

```
$ConfigData = @{
    AllNodes = @(
                @{ NodeName = "*"},
                @{ NodeName = "WC7-1"},
                @{ NodeName = "WS8R2-1"},
                @{ NodeName = "WS8R2-2"},
                @{ NodeName = "WSR2-3-WMF50"},
                @{ NodeName = "WSR2-1"}
    );
}

Configuration DemoConfig {
    Node $AllNodes.Where{(Test-DscNameSpace -ComputerName $_.NodeName)}.NodeName {
        WindowsProcess ProcessDemo {
            Path = "Notepad.exe"
            Arguments = ""
            Ensure = "Present"
        }
    }
}

DemoConfig -ConfigurationData $ConfigData
```

Either of the methods shown in the preceding examples results in skipping MOF generation for the target systems that have no DSC WMI namespace. In my example, there should be no MOF generated for WS8R2-2. This is shown in Figure 10-1.

```
    Directory: C:\DemoConfig


Mode                LastWriteTime     Length Name
----                -------------     ------ ----
-a---        7/7/2014  11:16 AM         1156 WC7-1.mof
-a---        7/7/2014  11:16 AM         1160 WS8R2-1.mof
-a---        7/7/2014  11:16 AM         1170 WSR2-3-WMF50.mof
-a---        7/7/2014  11:16 AM         1158 WSR2-1.mof
```

Figure 10-1. Skipping MOF generation for systems with no DSC WMI namespace

Custom DSC Resources Not Available

Another common issue I've noted is the unavailability of custom DSC resources placed at $env:ProgramFiles\ WindowsPowerShell\Modules. Starting with Windows PowerShell 4.0, this new module location is used as one of the possible PowerShell module locations. However, on systems with Windows Server 2012 R2 and Windows 8.1 operating systems, DSC does not recognize this module path for DSC resources. This is fixed in an update rollup released as KB2883200. Without this update, although the path is available in $env:PSModulePath, DSC does not use it to find any DSC resources available at that location. On systems with Windows Server 2102 R2 and Windows 8.1, when you see this issue whereby the configuration MOF generation results in errors related to unavailability of DSC custom resources, use the Get-HotFix cmdlet to see if you have KB2883200 installed.

If KB2883200 is already installed but you still see this error, make sure that your configuration script has the Import-DscResource cmdlet added to the configuration script. This is a dynamic function available **only inside** the Configuration script block. We discussed this in depth in Chapter 9. Without explicitly importing the custom resources, we would not be able to use them in a configuration script.

Even after all this, if you still see errors related to custom DSC resource unavailability, check the folder structure used to package the custom DSC resource module. As I mentioned in Chapter 9, the custom DSC resources must follow the nested module structure, with all DSC resource modules placed under the DSCResources folder. Without this, DSC will not be able to recognize the custom DSC resources, therefore resulting in an error when a configuration MOF has to be generated for the resources in the configuration script.

WinRM Issues

DSC, as we've already discussed, depends on WinRM and CIM. Although CIM cmdlets in PowerShell 3.0 and later support DCOM-based remote connectivity, DSC neither provides a way to specify the usage of DCOM, unlike the CIM cmdlets, nor works with CIM sessions that are configured to use DCOM. We saw in Chapter 2 how to create the WinRM listeners using PowerShell and also using Group Policy Objects. If a target system does not have the appropriate listeners configured, the configuration enactment process using the Start-DscCofiguration cmdlet results in a WinRM error (see Figure 10-2).

```
PS C:\> Start-DscConfiguration -Wait -Verbose -Path .\DemoConfig
VERBOSE: Perform operation 'Invoke CimMethod' with following parameters, ''methodName' = SendConfigurationApp
ly,'className' = MSFT_DSCLocalConfigurationManager,'namespaceName' = root/Microsoft/Windows/DesiredStateConfi
guration'.
The client cannot connect to the destination specified in the request. Verify that the service on the
destination is running and is accepting requests. Consult the logs and documentation for the WS-Management
service running on the destination, most commonly IIS or WinRM. If the destination is the WinRM service,
run the following command on the destination to analyze and configure the WinRM service: "winrm
quickconfig".
    + CategoryInfo          : ConnectionError: (root/Microsoft/...gurationManager:String) [], CimException
    + FullyQualifiedErrorId : HRESULT 0x80338012
    + PSComputerName        : WS8R2-1

VERBOSE: Operation 'Invoke CimMethod' complete.
VERBOSE: Time taken for configuration job to complete is 3.072 seconds
```

Figure 10-2. *Error when pushing configuration to a system with no WinRM configuration*

You can use the Get-Service cmdlet to verify if the remote system has WinRM service in running state. If the service is running but you still can't push the configuration, check if WinRM listeners are available on the target system, by running the Test-WsMan cmdlet. If this cmdlet results in the same error as shown in Figure 10-2, you have to create the WinRM listeners, as shown in Chapter 2. If the Test-WsMan cmdlet output includes an error code 2150859046, you will have to add firewall exceptions for the WinRM port numbers being used. On systems with Windows 8 or later and Windows Server 2012 or later, the firewall rules can be managed using the cmdlets in the NetSecurity module. That said, in an Active Directory (AD) domain environment, I recommend that you use Group Policy Objects to deploy WinRM configuration on the target systems. This ensures that there is a consistent method to configure the WinRM settings on all the domain-joined systems.

Yet another common issue beginners face with WinRM-based remote connectivity is with the usage of the IP address of the target system as an argument to the -ComputerName parameter of the Start-DscCofiguration cmdlet. Although not a common practice, when we test-drive new features, we end up using IP addresses in place of computer names. DSC configuration scripts do not complain when you use an IP address as the Node identifier. Here is an example:

```
Configuration DemoConfig {
    Node 192.168.100.106 {
        Environment TestEnv {
            Name  = 'TestVar'
            Value = 'TestVarValue'
            Ensure = "Present"
        }
    }
}
```

You can run this configuration to generate the MOF file and use the Start-DscConfiguration cmdlet to push the configuration to a target system. However, the enact process would result in an error when the target system is in default WinRM configuration. This is shown in Figure 10-3.

```
PS C:\> Start-DscConfiguration -Wait -Verbose -Path .\DemoConfig -Force
VERBOSE: Perform operation 'Invoke CimMethod' with following parameters, ''methodName' = SendConfigurationApp
ly,'className' = MSFT_DSCLocalConfigurationManager,'namespaceName' = root/Microsoft/Windows/DesiredStateConfi
guration'.
The WinRM client cannot process the request. Default authentication may be used with an IP address under
the following conditions: the transport is HTTPS or the destination is in the TrustedHosts list, and
explicit credentials are provided. Use winrm.cmd to configure TrustedHosts. Note that computers in the
TrustedHosts list might not be authenticated. For more information on how to set TrustedHosts run the
following command: winrm help config.
    + CategoryInfo          : ConnectionError: (root/Microsoft/...gurationManager:String) [], CimException
    + FullyQualifiedErrorId : HRESULT 0x803381bb
    + PSComputerName        : 192.168.100.106

VERBOSE: Operation 'Invoke CimMethod' complete.
VERBOSE: Time taken for configuration job to complete is 0.047 seconds
```

Figure 10-3. *Error when using IP address as a Node identifier*

In the default WinRM configuration, using IP addresses is not allowed, unless HTTPS transport is used. As the message in Figure 10-3 suggests, we need to add the IP address of the system from which the Start-DscConfiguration cmdlet is run as a trusted host in the target system's WinRM configuration. For step-by-step instructions on how to do this, refer to the about_Remote_Troubleshooting topic.

■ **Note** You can use Windows Remote Management logs in the event viewer, to analyze WinRM related issues. For much lower level issues with WinRM, you can use the cmdlets in the PSDiagnostics module.

Errors with Pending Configuration

At times, applying configuration on a target system might fail for many reasons. For example, when using the Push mode, if the target system crashes and reboots while the configuration enactment process is still in progress, it leaves the pending.mof in the C:\Windows\System32\Configuration folder, indicating that the last configuration push is not complete. Now, if we try to push the same configuration again, you will see an error that there is a pending configuration. This is shown in Figure 10-4.

```
PS C:\> Start-DscConfiguration -Wait -Verbose -Path .\DemoConfig
VERBOSE: Perform operation 'Invoke CimMethod' with following parameters, ''methodName' = SendConfigurationApp
ly,'className' = MSFT_DSCLocalConfigurationManager,'namespaceName' = root/Microsoft/Windows/DesiredStateConfi
guration'.
VERBOSE: An LCM method call arrived from computer DEMO-AD with user sid S-1-5-21-3906674661-2793090968-249130
2047-500.
VERBOSE: [WS8R2-1]: LCM:  [ Start  Set      ]
VERBOSE: [WS8R2-1]: LCM:  [ End    Set      ]
An old configuration is still pending. Please wait for the pending configuration to finish. If the problem
persists, execute Start-DSCConfiguration command with -Force parameter.
    + CategoryInfo          : ResourceExists: (root/Microsoft/...gurationManager:String) [], CimException
    + FullyQualifiedErrorId : MI RESULT 11
    + PSComputerName        : WS8R2-1

VERBOSE: Operation 'Invoke CimMethod' complete.
VERBOSE: Time taken for configuration job to complete is 0.105 seconds
```

Figure 10-4. *Error with a pending configuration*

As shown in Figure 10-4, the error can be resolved by using the -Force parameter with the Start-DscConfiguration cmdlet. If this still doesn't solve the problem, you can manually delete the pending.mof on the target system, to be able to push the configuration again.

As in the case of pushing a configuration using the Start-DscConfiguration cmdlet, the Restore-DscConfiguration cmdlet will also fail, with the same error message shown in Figure 10-4. This is because restoring configuration involves applying previous.mof, if present. However, the solution shown in the error message won't be applicable to the Restore-DscConfiguration cmdlet. If you find yourself in such a scenario, the only way you can restore the previous configuration is to manually delete pending.mof from the target system and then run the Restore-DscConfiguration cmdlet.

DSC Engine Cache

The DSC engine cache is used to cache DSC resources on the target system. While this improves performance during a configuration enactment process, this can be quite annoying when developing and testing custom DSC resources. With the DSC engine cache, newer versions of DSC resources won't be loaded. Let us see a quick example to understand this better. The following code snippet shows the contents of a custom DSC resource:

```
function Get-TargetResource
{
    param
    (
        [Parameter(Mandatory)]
        $dummy
    )
    return @{dummy = Test-Path "${env:SystemDrive}\Process.txt" -ErrorAction SilentlyContinue}
}

function Set-TargetResource
{
    param
    (
        [Parameter(Mandatory)]
        $dummy
    )
    Get-Process -Name svchost | Out-File "${env:SystemDrive}\Process.txt"
}

function Test-TargetResource
{
    param
    (
        [Parameter(Mandatory)]
        $dummy
    )
    return $false
}
```

The preceding custom resource is very trivial. The Set-TargetResource function is just writing a text file that contains the output from the Get-Process cmdlet. In this function, I have hard-coded the process name as svchost.

■ **Note** For using the preceding sample code as a DSC resource, you'll require an MOF file and the complete DSC resource nested module. You can get it from the DSCDeepDive.zip given as a part of this chapter's source code, located in the Source Code/Download area of the Apress web site (www.apress.com).

Let us create a configuration script containing this custom resource and enact it. The result from this configuration enactment is shown in Figure 10-5.

```
Configuration DemoConfig {
    Import-DscResource -ModuleName DSCDeepdive
    Node localhost {
        TestDscCache DscCache {
            dummy = "Dummy Value"
        }
    }
}

DemoConfig

Start-DscConfiguration -Verbose -Wait -Path .\DemoConfig
```

```
PS C:\> cat .\Process.txt

Handles  NPM(K)    PM(K)     WS(K) VM(M)    CPU(s)     Id ProcessName
-------  ------    -----     ----- -----    ------     -- -----------
   1353      47    23196     36736   138 1,130.06      92 svchost
    498      26     6628     12852    86    24.17      428 svchost
    623      37     9780     19124  1254     5.13      636 svchost
    471      14     4936     11508    45     6.45      812 svchost
    413      18     4072      8172    32    38.50      856 svchost
    989     120    22432     39712   467 5,200.83      992 svchost
    357      33     8976     10376    53     0.38     1104 svchost
    107      10     3220      7332    41     0.05     1508 svchost
    159      14     4644      8548    47     0.11     1952 svchost
    893      31    44084     54440   215   107.36     2520 svchost
    486      26    11844     15976   863   122.52     2544 svchost
    269      17     2912      8084    51    45.75     2560 svchost
    111      10      980      4200    21     0.03     2624 svchost
```

Figure 10-5. *Process output written by the DSC resource*

All is well. Let us now modify the DSC resource, to add the process name as a variable. This is a simple change.

```
$svcName = "system"
function Get-TargetResource
{
    param
    (
        [Parameter(Mandatory)]
        $dummy
    )
    return @{dummy = Test-Path "${env:SystemDrive}\Process.txt" -ErrorAction SilentlyContinue}
}
```

```
function Set-TargetResource
{
    param
    (
        [Parameter(Mandatory)]
        $dummy
    )
    Get-Process -Name $svcName | Out-File "${env:SystemDrive}\Process.txt"
}

function Test-TargetResource
{
    param
    (
        [Parameter(Mandatory)]
        $dummy
    )
    return $false
}
```

The only change in the resource module is the addition of the $svcName variable and its usage in the Set-TargetResource function. As the variable value is set to system, if I enact the configuration again using the Start-DscConfiguration cmdlet, as shown in the preceding code, I expect the output in $env:SystemDrive\ Process.txt to contain system process details. However, that won't be the case here, as indicated in Figure 10-6.

```
PS C:\> cat .\Process.txt

Handles  NPM(K)    PM(K)     WS(K) VM(M)    CPU(s)     Id ProcessName
-------  ------    -----     ----- -----    ------     -- -----------
   1360      47    22216     35636   139  1,132.75     92 svchost
    496      26     6628     12840    86     24.22    428 svchost
    619      37     9788     19496  1254      5.25    636 svchost
    471      14     4936     11508    45      6.47    812 svchost
    415      18     4060      8120    32     38.73    856 svchost
    983     119    22536     39820   466  5,212.64    992 svchost
    359      32     8976     10376    53      0.38   1104 svchost
    107      10     3168      7320    40      0.05   1508 svchost
    159      14     4644      8544    47      0.11   1952 svchost
    896      31    44992     59204   215    108.63   2520 svchost
    486      25    11556     15852   862    122.53   2544 svchost
    269      17     2912      8084    51     45.94   2560 svchost
    111      10      980      4200    21      0.03   2624 svchost
```

Figure 10-6. *Process output after resource module change*

The reason for the output shown in Figure 10-6 is the DSC engine cache. In our example, especially, the DSC engine fails to load the changes made to the resource module.

In the current implementation, the only way that this issue can be resolved is to kill the WMI processing hosting the DSC provider. The following code example shows how this is performed.

```
Stop-Process -Name WmiPrvSE
```

After this step, we can reenact the configuration, using the `Start-DscConfiguration` cmdlet, and we will see that the changes made to the resource module are reflected in the output.

Summary

Working with a new technology can be quite intimidating at times, especially when there is little or no help to be found. When deploying and using such new technology, it is always possible to bump against the most common problems. Having a ready-made solution to such problems will not only help you adopt the new technology but allow you to learn the technology better. There are, of course, several ways to troubleshoot an issue. This chapter identified some of the most common problems and provided solutions to them. As I mentioned, this is not a complete list. So, when you need more help in troubleshooting or debugging a problem, don't forget that you have DSC event logs. In Chapter 8, you saw how to group event logs into DSC operations and use that information. That knowledge should come in handy when you need it.

CHAPTER 11

DSC—From the Field

Desired State Configuration (DSC) is relatively new. It was released as a part of Windows Management Framework 4.0, and many people have started exploring this for production use, and some have even deployed it in production. So far in this book, you have learned, from the very basics to some of the most common issues that you might face, how to use or implement DSC. As with the list of common DSC issues and solutions presented in Chapter 10, it will be helpful to learn a few tips and tricks about the real-world use of DSC. This knowledge will be quite helpful in making effective use of DSC in production environments.

In this chapter, we will discuss some real-world scenarios, such as cross-domain configuration management with DSC, tips that make better use of DSC API, and best practices to follow when writing custom DSC resources and configuration scripts. The sections in this chapter are unrelated, and you can use this chapter as a reference for different topics that are covered in the book. It is not necessary to follow every section from beginning to end.

DSC for Cross-Domain Configuration Management

Most of the examples we have seen in this book assume that you have a single Active Directory (AD) domain environment. In an AD domain environment, Common Information Model (CIM) cmdlets and the DSC PowerShell cmdlets that depend on CIM work without any additional configuration or input. But not so in a multi-domain environment or in an environment in which both domain- and workgroup-joined systems have to be managed. The latter is not a common occurrence, but multi-domain environments are very common in large enterprises. In this section, we will see what you need to know to perform cross-domain configuration management using DSC.

As we understand, DSC depends on CIM, and CIM uses the WS-Management (WSMan) protocol for remote connectivity. Within a single AD domain, to connect to a remote computer using WSMan, we just have to be a part of the local administrators group on the remote computer. We don't have to explicitly authenticate by using administrator credentials. Of course, there are ways to create constrained endpoints and provide non-administrators access to remote computers over WSMan. For now, let us limit our discussion to the default WSMan configuration.

In the default configuration, the use of CIM cmdlets to connect to a target system in an AD domain different from the local system results in an error. Let us see this using an example.

```
Configuration CrossDomainConfig {
    Node WSR2-4 {
        WindowsProcess ProcessDemo {
            Path = "Notepad.exe"
            Arguments = ""
            Ensure = "Present"
        }
    }
}

CrossDomainConfig
```

In the preceding example, the target system specified as the Node identifier is a part of the second domain of my demo lab. There is no trust configured between the default and the second domain that I have in my setup. Let us enact this configuration and see what happens (see Figure 11-1).

```
PS C:\> Start-DscConfiguration -Wait -Verbose -Path .\CrossDomainConfig
VERBOSE: Perform operation 'Invoke CimMethod' with following parameters, ''methodName' = SendConfigurationApp
ly,'className' = MSFT_DSCLocalConfigurationManager,'namespaceName' = root/Microsoft/Windows/DesiredStateConfi
guration'.
WinRM cannot process the request. The following error occurred while using Kerberos authentication: Cannot
find the computer WSR2-4. Verify that the computer exists on the network and that the name provided is
spelled correctly.
    + CategoryInfo          : NotSpecified: (root/Microsoft/...gurationManager:String) [], CimException
    + FullyQualifiedErrorId : HRESULT 0x80070035
    + PSComputerName        : WSR2-4

VERBOSE: Operation 'Invoke CimMethod' complete.
VERBOSE: Time taken for configuration job to complete is 0.229 seconds
```

Figure 11-1. *Error when target system is external to the AD domain*

As seen in Figure 11-1, pushing configuration to a target system in a different AD domain results in a WinRM error. There are multiple ways to work around this.

Using Credentials

The Start-DscConfiguration cmdlet has a -Credential parameter that can be used to provide credentials to authenticate to the WinRM service on the target system. This is the first method by which to perform cross-domain configuration management. It is shown in Figure 11-2.

```
PS C:\> $cred = (Get-Credential)
cmdlet Get-Credential at command pipeline position 1
Supply values for the following parameters:

PS C:\> Start-DscConfiguration -Wait -Verbose -Path .\CrossDomainConfig -Credential $cred
VERBOSE: Perform operation 'Invoke CimMethod' with following parameters, ''methodName' = SendConfigurationApp
ly,'className' = MSFT_DSCLocalConfigurationManager,'namespaceName' = root/Microsoft/Windows/DesiredStateConfi
guration'.
VERBOSE: An LCM method call arrived from computer WSR2-1 with user sid S-1-5-21-2822971449-1330478472-1314077
324-500.
VERBOSE: [WSR2-4]: LCM:  [ Start  Set      ]
VERBOSE: [WSR2-4]: LCM:  [ Start  Resource ]  [[WindowsProcess]ProcessDemo]
VERBOSE: [WSR2-4]: LCM:  [ Start  Test     ]  [[WindowsProcess]ProcessDemo]
VERBOSE: [WSR2-4]: LCM:  [ End    Test     ]  [[WindowsProcess]ProcessDemo]   in 11.5000 seconds.
VERBOSE: [WSR2-4]: LCM:  [ Start  Set      ]  [[WindowsProcess]ProcessDemo]
VERBOSE: [WSR2-4]:                           [[WindowsProcess]ProcessDemo] Process matching path 'C:\Windows
\system32\Notepad.exe' started
VERBOSE: [WSR2-4]: LCM:  [ End    Set      ]  [[WindowsProcess]ProcessDemo]   in 0.7660 seconds.
VERBOSE: [WSR2-4]: LCM:  [ End    Resource ]  [[WindowsProcess]ProcessDemo]
VERBOSE: [WSR2-4]: LCM:  [ End    Set      ]
VERBOSE: [WSR2-4]: LCM:  [ End    Set      ]      in  18.8750 seconds.
```

Figure 11-2. *Connecting to a target system using credentials*

Using Domain Trusts

The most common and most recommended method for cross-domain connectivity is to use domain trust relationships.

Using a trust relationship between multiple domains enables users in one domain to be authenticated by domain controllers in another domain. There are different types of trust relationships. For more information on this, you can refer to http://technet.microsoft.com/en-us/library/cc775736(v=ws.10).aspx. For the purpose of demonstration, I have created a two-way forest trust between two different AD forests that I have in the lab infrastructure.

Note   The steps to create a trust relationship are outside the scope of this book. You can refer to
`http://technet.microsoft.com/en-us/library/cc780479(v=ws.10).aspx` for additional information on this.

Apart from the two-way trust, you must also make the domain administrators group of the local domain a member of the local administrators group on all target systems in the second domain. Once you complete this configuration, you can push configuration to a target system in another domain, without explicitly passing credentials, using the `Start-DscConfiguration` cmdlet.

Configuration Management As API

We understand that Desired State Configuration (DSC) is a management platform unlike the other players in the configuration management (CM) space. By management platform, we understand that DSC provides an application programming interface (API) that can be used as a part of existing configuration management processes. It is not necessary that you use the PowerShell cmdlets provided as a part of the DSC feature, to manage configuration on the target systems. In Chapter 4, when discussing Local Configuration Manager (LCM), we saw a list of Common Information Model (CIM) methods in the `MSFT_DscLocalConfigurationManager` class and how they map into the cmdlets in the `PSDesiredStateConfiguration` module. As we saw there, not all CIM methods have a corresponding cmdlet. These CIM methods can be used by the in-house CM tools or any other CM frameworks available on the market today.

In this section, we will see a few examples of how these CIM methods can be used, and some tricks that we can build on. I suggest that you look at the MSDN documentation for these CIM methods, before we go further. You can find this documentation at `http://msdn.microsoft.com/en-us/library/dn469253(v=vs.85).aspx`.

As you see in the CIM method's documentation, most of the methods take `ConfigurationData` as a parameter. When calling such CIM methods, we need to pass the contents configuration MOF file as a byte array. So, before we look at how to call these CIM methods directly, let us look at how we can convert the configuration MOF to a byte array representation.

Although the following sections show calling these CIM methods in PowerShell, you can use any programming or scripting language that supports invoking WSMan methods.

Configuration MOF to Byte Array

Most of the CIM methods in the `MSFT_DscLocalConfigurationManager` class take the configuration Managed Object Format (MOF) contents as a byte array. Since DSC PowerShell cmdlets use CIM and CIM uses WS-Management (WSMan), the way we construct this byte array depends on whether we are calling the method locally or sending the configuration data to a remote system. Depending on where the target is, we need to pad a few more bytes to the configuration data byte array. The following function explains how to do this.

```
Function Get-ByteArry {
    param (
        [string]$ConfigurationMof,
        [switch]$Remote
    )
    $configurationData = Get-Content -Path $ConfigurationMof -Encoding Byte -ReadCount 0
     if ($local) {
        $buffSize = 0
        $totalSize = [System.BitConverter]::GetBytes($configurationData.Length + 4 + $buffSize)
        $configurationData = $totalSize + $configurationData
    }
    return $configurationData
}
```

In the preceding function, I have used a -Remote switch parameter to indicate whether the target for the configuration is a remote system or the local system. If it is the local system, we don't need the additional bytes in the WSMan payload. Therefore, if the target is a remote system, we add the additional bytes, as required. This function returns a byte array representation of the configuration MOF file provided as an input. In the subsequent section, we will see how this byte array representation can be used with some of the CIM methods in the MSFT_DscLocalConfigurationManager class.

GetConfiguration

We have seen the Get-DscConfiguration cmdlet and its functionality. We understand that this cmdlet returns the current state of the resource from the target systems. Remember: The current state need not be the desired state. This cmdlet calls the GetConfiguration CIM method, and by default, if no configuration data byte array is provided as an input, the contents of the current.mof are used for getting the current state of the resources. This is the reason you see an error message that says no current configuration exists, when you use the Get-DscConfiguration cmdlet on a target system that never received any configuration using DSC. So, here is a trick. What if you want to find out the current state of a specific resource before you enact any configuration on to the target system? For example, let us say we want to check whether or not a specific file exists on a remote system, but we don't really want to create it. Here is how we do that:

```
Configuration DemoConfig {
    Node Test {
        File FileDemo {
            DestinationPath = "C:\Windows\System32\Drivers\Etc\Hosts.backup"
            Contents = ""
            Ensure = "Present"
        }
    }
}

$mof = DemoConfig
```

In the preceding configuration script, we have specified the path to a Hosts.backup file. In addition, we are generating the MOF file and storing that file object in a variable called $mof. Now, let us see how we can use the GetConfiguration CIM method to determine what the current state of this resource is. Remember: We are not enacting this; we are simply querying for the current state of the resource.

```
$configurationData = Get-ByteArry $mof.FullName
$result = Invoke-CimMethod -ComputerName WSR2-1 -Namespace root/Microsoft/Windows/
DesiredStateConfiguration -ClassName MSFT_DSCLocalConfigurationManager -MethodName GetConfiguration
-Arguments @{ConfigurationData = $configurationData}
```

In the preceding example, I am using the Get-ByteArray function we created at the beginning of this section. This is used to create the byte array representation of the MOF file that we just generated. The $result variable is used to store the objects returned by the GetConfiguration CIM method. This method returns an array of the current state for all resources present in the MOF file. Because we have only one resource in the MOF file, $result[0] should give us the current state of the file resource. The ItemValue property of each object in this array contains the actual state of the object.

As we see in Figure 11-3, the current state of the resource tells us that the Hosts.backup file does not exist on the requested path. This method can be quite useful when all you want to do is verify the current state of a resource, without enacting the configuration.

```
PS C:\> $result[0].ItemValue


Attributes      :
Checksum        :
Contents        :
CreatedDate     :
Credential      :
DestinationPath : C:\Windows\System32\Drivers\Etc\Hosts.backup
Ensure          : absent
Force           :
MatchSource     :
ModifiedDate    :
Recurse         :
Size            :
SourcePath      :
SubItems        :
Type            :
PSComputerName  : WSR2-1
```

Figure 11-3. *Getting the current state of the resource*

SendConfiguration

The SendConfiguration CIM method can be used to send the configuration MOF to the target system. The target system stores the configuration MOF as pending.mof and does not enact the configuration. This method has no related PowerShell cmdlet in the PSDesiredStateConfiguration module. This method takes the byte array representation of the configuration MOF as one of the input parameters.

```
Invoke-CimMethod -ComputerName WSR2-1 -Namespace root/Microsoft/Windows/DesiredStateConfiguration
-ClassName MSFT_DSCLocalConfigurationManager -MethodName SendConfiguration -Arguments
@{ConfigurationData = $configurationData; Force = $true}
```

The preceding example stores the byte array representation of the configuration MOF as pending.mof. We cannot use this method when the target system already has a pending configuration. This can be worked around by using the Force parameter. Also, the Force parameter comes in handy when you want to push configuration to a target system that is configured as a pull client.

```
Invoke-CimMethod -ComputerName WSR2-1 -Namespace root/Microsoft/Windows/DesiredStateConfiguration
-ClassName MSFT_DSCLocalConfigurationManager -MethodName SendConfiguration -Arguments
@{ConfigurationData = $configurationData; Force = $true}
```

ApplyConfiguration

In the preceding section, using the SendConfiguration method, we created a pending.mof file on the target system. We can use the ApplyConfiguration method to enact that configuration on the target system. This method does not take any parameters and always looks for a pending.mof that can be applied. In addition, this method has no related cmdlet in the PSDesiredStateConfiguration module. Here is an example of calling this method:

```
Invoke-CimMethod -ComputerName WSR2-1 -Namespace root/Microsoft/Windows/DesiredStateConfiguration
-ClassName MSFT_DSCLocalConfigurationManager -MethodName ApplyConfiguration
```

As simple as that! If you have been following the examples in the related section so far, you can run the GetConfiguration CIM method to see if the current state of the resource is on the target system. Remember: By applying configuration in the preceding example, we created a current.mof on the target system. Therefore, there is no need to send the configuration MOF as a byte array.

The result from GetConfiguration with no ConfigurationData input is shown in Figure 11-4. Contrast this with the output shown in Figure 11-3. Once a resource is found on the target system, whether in a desired state or not, some additional details about the resource configuration appear in the current state.

```
PS C:\> $result[0].ItemValue


Attributes       : {archive}
Checksum         :
Contents         :
CreatedDate      : 7/14/2014 2:34:11 PM
Credential       :
DestinationPath  : C:\Windows\System32\Drivers\Etc\Hosts.backup
Ensure           : present
Force            :
MatchSource      :
ModifiedDate     : 7/14/2014 2:34:11 PM
Recurse          :
Size             : 0
SourcePath       :
SubItems         :
Type             : file
PSComputerName   : WSR2-1
```

Figure 11-4. Resource current state, after applying the configuration

SendApplyConfiguration

In the preceding examples, we first sent the configuration, using the SendConfiguration CIM method, and then applied it, using the ApplyConfiguration CIM method. Using the SendApplyConfiguration method, it is possible to combine these two steps, and this is what the Start-DscConfiguration cmdlet calls when pushing configuration to a target system. So, we have to pass the configuration MOF as a byte array to this method.

```
$configurationData = Get-ByteArry $mof.FullName
Invoke-CimMethod -ComputerName WSR2-1 -Namespace root/Microsoft/Windows/DesiredStateConfiguration
-ClassName MSFT_DSCLocalConfigurationManager -MethodName SendConfigurationApply -Arguments
@{ConfigurationData = $configurationData; Force = $true}
```

As with the SendConfiguration method, the Force parameter can be used to force push configuration to a system that already has a pending configuration or a target system that is a pull client.

TestConfiguration

While the GetConfiguration method gives the current state of each resource in the configuration MOF, the TestConfiguration method tells us if the target system is in a desired state. This method is called by the Test-DscConfiguration cmdlet. If you look at this method's documentation, it has the ConfigurationData parameter, but that has not been implemented in the first release of DSC. In the current implementation, this method takes the current.mof and checks whether or not each resource in that MOF is in a desired state. In the current release, this method returns the InDesiredState property, as a part of the output that has a value set to True or False, indicating whether the target system is in a desired state or not (see Figure 11-5).

```
Invoke-CimMethod -ComputerName WSR2-1,WC7-1,WC81-1,WS8R2-1 -Namespace root/Microsoft/Windows/
DesiredStateConfiguration -ClassName MSFT_DSCLocalConfigurationManager -MethodName TestConfiguration
| Select PSComputerName, InDesiredState
```

```
PSComputerName InDesiredState
-------------- --------------
WC7-1                    True
WSR2-1                   True
WC81-1                   True
WS8R2-1                  True
```

Figure 11-5. *Testing target systems using* TestConfiguration

As shown in Figure 11-5 and the code example, we are only selecting the InDesiredState property from the TestConfiguration output. There is another property, called ResourceId, but it has not been implemented in the current release of DSC.

RollBack

Once we enact the configuration, we understand from our earlier discussion that the applied configuration gets stored as a current.mof, and any existing configuration gets stored as a previous.mof. When this method is called, the previous.mof gets enacted on the target system, overwriting the current configuration. We can use the Restore-DscConfiguration cmdlet to perform the same function as the RollBack CIM method. The Rollback method, per the MSDN documentation, has a ConfigurationNumber parameter. However, in the current implementation, this parameter is not implemented. The following example shows how this method can be invoked:

```
Invoke-CimMethod -ComputerName WSR2-1 -Namespace root/Microsoft/Windows/DesiredStateConfiguration
-ClassName MSFT_DSCLocalConfigurationManager -MethodName Rollback
```

PerformRequiredConfigurationChecks

We have seen in Chapter 9 that changing the initial Local Configuration Manager (LCM) meta-configuration or configuring the target system as a pull client will create two scheduled tasks: Consistency and DSCRestartBootTask. If you look at the action defined in these scheduled tasks, you will notice that they call the PerformRequiredConfigurationChecks CIM method in the MSFT_DscLocalConfigurationManager class (see Figure 11-6).

```
Get-ScheduledTask -TaskName Consistency, DSCRestartBootTask |
Select TaskName, @{Name="Action";Expression={[regex]::Matches($_.Actions.Arguments,
'(?<=")[^"]*(?=")')}} | Format-List


TaskName : Consistency
Action   : Invoke-CimMethod -Namespace root/Microsoft/Windows/DesiredStateConfiguration -Cl
           MSFT_DSCLocalConfigurationManager -Method PerformRequiredConfigurationChecks -Arguments @{Flags
           = [System.UInt32]1}

TaskName : DSCRestartBootTask
Action   : Invoke-CimMethod -Namespace root/Microsoft/Windows/DesiredStateConfiguration -ClassName
           MSFT_DSCLocalConfigurationManager -MethodName PerformRequiredConfigurationChecks -Arg @{Flags =
           [System.UInt32]2 }
```

Figure 11-6. *Scheduled task definitions to invoke DSC CIM methods*

As shown in Figure 11-6, the Invoke-CimMethod cmdlet is used to call the PerformRequiredConfigurationChecks method with the Flags parameter. This parameter takes Regular (1), Reboot (2), and Bootstrap (3) as the valid arguments and invokes the consistency engine, and we have already discussed what happens when a consistency check gets invoked. In the current implementation, flags 1 and 2 have no difference. They just invoke the consistency engine. Flag 3, apart from starting a consistency check, creates the scheduled tasks, if they don't exist. Because these scheduled tasks do not exist by default, this method can be used as a mechanism to create the tasks.

```
Invoke-CimMethod -Namespace root/Microsoft/Windows/DesiredStateConfiguration `
    -ClassName MSFT_DSCLocalConfigurationManager -MethodName PerformRequiredConfigurationChecks
    -Arg @{Flags = [System.UInt32]3 }
```

Also, by using any of these flags, we can make sure that the target system checks the current state of the configuration and then takes action, based on the value of the ConfigurationMode setting. If the target system is a pull client, and the pull server has an updated configuration, invoking this method will make LCM download the updated configuration and enact the same. So, in a Pull configuration, when you want the target system to receive the updated configuration immediately, instead of waiting for the consistency task interval, you can invoke the PerformRequiredConfigurationChecks method with any flags.

As in the case of the methods we have seen so far, the LCM meta-configuration can be employed, too, using the CIM methods. The GetMetaConfiguration and SendMetaConfigurationApply methods are used for this purpose. Using the knowledge you have gained so far, try invoking these two methods.

Expert Tips

As I said at the beginning of this chapter, Desired State Configuration (DSC) is fairly recent, and few have explored it completely. In fact, DSC is still evolving and is expected to change with the next few releases. There will be corner-case issues and questions that you may have. So, this section provides a list of expert tips that are useful to know.

PowerShell Profile and Customization

In Chapter 2, we looked at how we can use PowerShell profile scripts to customize the PowerShell environment. While this helps with many aspects, some of the customizations might actually conflict with the way DSC functions. Steven Murawski, one of the early adopters and a DSC expert, discovered that changing the output field separator variable, using a profile or in the PowerShell session, can have adverse effects when generating configuration Managed Object Format (MOF) files.

Here is an example. The output field separator in PowerShell is represented by a variable called $OFS. This variable is not set by default, but a space character is used as the output separator. But, when it is set, and you try to convert a collection such as an array to a string, you will see that the value specified in $OFS gets used as an output separator. Let us see this in action (see Figure 11-7).

```
PS C:\> $array = 'Item1','Item2'

PS C:\> [String]$array
Item1 Item2

PS C:\> $OFS=';'

PS C:\> [String]$array
Item1;Item2
```

Figure 11-7. *Output field seperator in PowerShell*

Now, how is this related to DSC? If you look into the DSC PowerShell module, there are places where an array gets converted to a string format, especially when generating an MOF document from a configuration script. Let us try this. Go ahead and open PowerShell ISE and set $OFS to any arbitrary value you like. Then, write a simple configuration document and try to generate an MOF using the configuration command in the script. Figure 11-8 shows what I see.

```
Write-NodeMOFFile : Invalid MOF definition for node 'Localhost': Exception calling "ValidateInstanceText"
with "1" argument(s): "Syntax error:
 At line:11, char:1
 Buffer:
D = "[File]TestFile";
;^Ensure
"
At C:\Windows\system32\WindowsPowerShell\v1.0\Modules\PSDesiredStateConfiguration\PSDesiredStateConfiguratio
n.psm1:1425 char:17
+                 Write-NodeMOFFile $name $mofNode $Script:NodeInstanceAliases[$mo ...
+                 ~~~~~~~~~~~~~~~~~~~~~~~~~~~~~~~~~~~~~~~~~~~~~~~~~~~~~~~~~~~~~~~~~~~
    + CategoryInfo          : InvalidOperation: (:) [Write-Error], InvalidOperationException
    + FullyQualifiedErrorId : InvalidMOFDefinition,Write-NodeMOFFile


    Directory: C:\Demo
```

Figure 11-8. *Errors when generating an MOF with* $OFS *set to* ';'

As we see in Figure 11-8, the MOF generation fails. If you look at the fourth line of the error message, you will understand how the value of $OFS is affecting the MOF generation. In my example, I use a semicolon as the value for $OFS.

So, when you can't figure out what is going wrong with your configuration script or MOF generation, start your PowerShell session without a profile script and validate the configuration again.

Avoid Multiple Configuration Scripts

When creating configuration scripts for systems in your environment, always look to create incremental configurations. This means you use the same configuration document and put any additional resource configurations into the same. Be aware of removing any resource configuration sections completely, without actually performing a configuration removal from the target system. Take a look at the following example.

```
Configuration DemoConfig {
    Node localhost {
        File DemoFile {
            DestinationPath = "C:\Scripts\Temp.txt"
            Contents = ""
            Ensure = "Present"
        }

        WindowsProcess DemoProcess {
            Path = "Notepad.exe"
            Arguments = ""
            Ensure = "Present"
        }
    }
}
```

What we see in the preceding example is a simple configuration. It will configure File and WindowsProcess resources accordingly on the target system. Now, imagine you remove the DemoFile resource section completely, regenerate the MOF, and reenact the configuration. What do you expect should happen to the empty text file we created at C:\Scripts? It won't get deleted. In fact, DSC won't even know that the file C:\Scripts\Temp.txt was created using DSC configuration scripts. In addition, it will never appear as a DSC configured resource when you monitor DSC configurations. For example, subsequent Get-DscConfiguration runs will only list the current state of the DemoProcess resource. This is by design. We already know that DSC tracks the current configuration using a current.mof on the target system, and if a previously configured resource is no longer present in the current.mof, DSC will never know about it. To avoid such scenarios, you should always use a single configuration script or employ composite resources when you think the configuration script is too long.

When you want to remove a resource configuration completely from the configuration script, first decide if you really need that resource configured on the target system. If not, use DSC to first remove resource configuration and then eventually remove that resource configuration from the script. So, going back to the example, if my intention is to remove the empty text file, I should first set the Ensure property to Absent. Then, in the subsequent revisions of the script, I can remove the DemoFile section completely.

Version Control and Backups

The scenario that we discussed in the preceding section can result from human error too. When you lose a configuration script or unintentionally make an irreversible change to the script that was enacted on a target system, you may not be able to regenerate the same again, unless you have a backup. So, this is where version-controlling the configuration scripts will help. In the case of DSC, you should put under version control the configuration scripts and any custom DSC resource modules you develop.

A second level of protection is to back up the version-controlled repository of configuration scripts and custom resource modules. This helps in recovering the content when the version control is not available. It is not necessary to protect the generated MOF files under version control or back up any MOF files. The reason is that these MOF files can be regenerated anytime, using the most recent configuration script but not vice versa.

If you are using OData-based Pull services, you can optionally deploy a software load balancer for the HTTP or HTTPS services, such as Windows Network Load Balancing (NLB), to provide highly available Pull services. While the Pull service is essential for pull clients to keep the configuration up to date, providing high availability for the Pull services is not critical. As long as you have protected the configuration scripts and custom DSC resources, the Pull services can be rebuilt with very little effort.

Automatic and Environment Variables in Configuration Script

When writing configuration script, try and avoid referencing automatic and environmental variables in a resource configuration. For example, take a look at the following:

```
Configuration DemoConfig {
    Node WSR2-1 {
        File DemoFile {
            DestinationPath = $env:SystemDrive
            SourcePath = "\\Server1\Data$\Packges"
            Type = "Directory"
            Recurse = $true
        }
    }
}

DemoConfig
```

The preceding example is technically correct. But, look at the value of the DestinationPath property. I have specified it as $env:SystemDrive. Now, if you look at the generated MOF file for this configuration, you will notice that this environment variable gets expanded to its value on the system where the MOF is generated.

```
/*
@TargetNode='WSR2-1'
@GeneratedBy=Administrator
@GenerationDate=08/15/2014 12:35:54
@GenerationHost=DEMO-AD
*/

instance of MSFT_FileDirectoryConfiguration as $MSFT_FileDirectoryConfiguration1ref
{
ResourceID = "[File]DemoFile";
 Type = "Directory";
 SourceInfo = "::3::9::File";
 DestinationPath = "C:";
 ModuleName = "PSDesiredStateConfiguration";
 Recurse = True;
 ModuleVersion = "1.0";
 SourcePath = "\\\\Server1\\Data$\\Packges";

};
```

```
instance of OMI_ConfigurationDocument
{
 Version="1.0.0";
 Author="Administrator";
 GenerationDate="08/15/2014 12:35:54";
 GenerationHost="DEMO-AD";
};
```

This is perfectly fine if your intention is to use the values of environment variables from the local system. To be specific, in our example, the value of $env:SystemDrive is C:. Although your intention is to copy the contents of SourcePath to $env:SystemDrive, this may not happen, as the variable gets expanded to a local drive letter, which may or may not exist on the target system.

Therefore, it is best to avoid using the PowerShell automatic and environment variables in a configuration script, unless you intend to use the values of those variables from the system on which the MOF is being generated.

Summary

This chapter concludes our Desired State Configuration (DSC) journey of discovery. Deploying any new technology in the real world is different from using or testing it in a development or lab setup. When you deploy DSC in a real production environment, additional configuration may be required for DSC to function, as it depends on other technologies, such as Common Information Model (CIM) and Windows Remote Management (WinRM) technologies. Configuration management is also not a new thing in enterprise data centers. IT managers have been using configuration management (CM) tools to manage applications and infrastructure. With this in mind, DSC provides a configuration management platform and application programming interface (API) that can be used by any existing CM framework or tool set, to manage Windows systems easily. This chapter demonstrated a few examples of that. Finally, all that hard work you put into creating configuration scripts and custom DSC resources must be properly protected. This is where the need for version-controlling and regular backup protection plays a role.

APPENDIX A

DSC Community Resources

For many system and IT administrators managing a mix of Windows and Linux/Unix-based environments, small or big, configuration management and preventing configuration drift is an essential task. Desired State Configuration (DSC) is built into the Windows operating system with the release of Windows Server 2012 R2, and Microsoft is working on enabling DSC for Linux or Unix environments. With these exciting changes in the IT data center management landscape, the community has been quick to adopt DSC and extend the resources to configure different elements in the IT ecosystem. With the official release of Windows Management Framework 4.0 and 5.0, there has been only a smaller subset of DSC resource modules. These resources are meant to cover some of the basic configurable entities in an operating system. We saw some of them in Chapter 5. DSC provides a framework to author custom DSC resources. If you already have the expertise to write PowerShell script modules, as was covered in Chapter 9, it is very easy to convert that skill to writing a DSC resource module. Several enthusiasts from the PowerShell community have built such custom DSC resource modules for configuring different entities in their IT environment, and they are sharing their work with the rest of the community.

To support the community and extend the number of DSC resources, the Windows PowerShell team released several DSC resource kits. The total number of DSC resource modules in the DSC resource kit is staggering and is continuing to grow. There are not only resource modules but also helper modules that enable creating a template for custom DSC resources and debugging the configuration enactment process when using DSC.

In this appendix, we will look at an overview of some of the community DSC resources and a few DSC resource kit modules released by the Windows PowerShell team. In the earlier chapters, we did several configuration changes to build the DSC infrastructure manually, for example, creating an OData-based Pull service and so on. I mentioned in Chapter 7 that there is a simple method to do that, using the community resources. Also, when talking about authoring custom DSC resources, I warned that you have to be careful when authoring Managed Object Format (MOF) files. The DSC resource designer module makes it very easy to generate templates for DSC resources. In addition, we spent quite a bit of time examining different event logs and methods to debug DSC resources, in Chapters 8 and 10. The DSC diagnostics module in the resource kit makes it seamless to query event logs and get the right debugging information. We will look at these in detail in this appendix.

The DSC Community

The Windows PowerShell community, like any other active technical community, is very strong and has members who are experts in several other technologies, not just PowerShell. PowerShell is the glue. Each person in this community has a specific need when it comes to using PowerShell in their daily lives. With the release of Desired State Configuration (DSC), the community started to look at writing DSC resources and helping one another in doing more with DSC. For example, PowerShell.org began an initiative to host community-built custom DSC resources, and any that were updated to Microsoft provided resources as a GitHub repository. You can access it at https://github.com/PowerShellOrg/DSC. This is a public repository that accepts contributions from any community member. So, if you have your own custom DSC resources and want to share them with the rest of the community, this is the place where you can publish all that. Steven Murawski, a Windows PowerShell MVP and an expert in all things related to DSC, manages this repository. He is the author of all StackExchange DSC resources in this GitHub repository. There are many other DSC experts who help others get answers to their DSC-related questions, either through technical forums and/or their own blogs.

As I mentioned, the PowerShell.org repository has a mix of DSC resource modules and other helper modules, from both the community and the PowerShell team resource kits, so I won't provide details of the modules here. Instead, we will look at some of the modules in the official Microsoft DSC resource kit.

Windows PowerShell DSC Resource Kit

Soon after the release of WMF 4.0, the Windows PowerShell team started releasing several waves of DSC resource kits. At the time of this writing, wave 4 is the current release and has more than 50 PowerShell modules. These modules cover a breadth of features and applications, such as basic computer management, Azure virtual machines, Active Directory, SQL Availability Groups, Hyper-V Virtual Machine configurations, and so on. You can download these modules from the TechNet gallery at http://gallery.technet.microsoft.com/DSC-Resource-Kit-All-c449312d.

I encourage you to read the documentation accessible from the preceding link, to get a complete overview of the available modules in the resource kit. The modules in the resource kit are packaged as nested PowerShell modules. Therefore, once you download the zip file at the preceding link, you should extract it to the $env:ProgramFiles\WindowsPowerShell\Modules folder. Each resource kit module begins with the letter *x*, to indicate that it is an experimental resource module.

■ **Note**   There is no official support for any of these modules. You can, however, report issues and seek help through Microsoft Connect and several other technical online forums.

There are two types of modules in this resource kit release. The first type is a PowerShell script module that complements the functionality of DSC. For example, the xDscDiagnostics, xDscResourceDesigner, and xPSDesiredStateConfiguration modules are PowerShell Script modules that are not DSC resources. You can see these modules in the output of the Get-Module cmdlet when the -ListAvailable switch parameter is used.

The second type of modules in the resource kit are DSC resource modules written as PowerShell script modules. We can use the Get-DscResource cmdlet to obtain a list of all these resource modules. This list is too exhaustive to fit in a single screenshot, but I recommend that you run this command and verify whether or not the DSC resource modules are listed.

It is impossible in this book to write about each of these modules. Therefore, I have chosen to showcase three modules that I use often when working with DSC. The following sections describe these modules and how some of the examples shown in earlier chapters can be executed in an easier way, with the help of these or custom DSC resources. Let us begin.

DSC Resource Designer

We have seen in Chapter 9 what it takes to create a custom DSC resource. We have to create a schema Managed Object Format (MOF) with a specific syntax, a PowerShell module script that uses special semantics, and finally, a PowerShell module data file that describes the module. Each of these files has to be validated, so that they don't have any errors and don't fail when someone attempts to load them as DSC resources. For someone who has no knowledge of writing a schema MOF file, it will be hard to understand what qualifiers to use and so on. So, to make this process easy, and to create a skeleton for a custom DSC resource, the PowerShell team included what is called a DSC resource designer in the resource kit. What the resource designer can't help you with is the logic for the Get, Set, and Test-TargetResource functions of the DSC resource module.

You can access a list of cmdlets in this module by using the Get-Command cmdlet. This is shown in Figure A-1.

```
Get-Command -Module xDscResourceDesigner
```

```
CommandType       Name                             ModuleName
-----------       ----                             ----------
Function          Import-xDscSchema                xDSCResourceDesigner
Function          New-xDscResource                 xDSCResourceDesigner
Function          New-xDscResourceProperty         xDSCResourceDesigner
Function          Test-xDscResource                xDSCResourceDesigner
Function          Test-xDscSchema                  xDSCResourceDesigner
Function          Update-xDscResource              xDSCResourceDesigner
```

Figure A-1. *Cmdlets in the DSC resource designer module*

To understand how to use this module, and for demonstration purposes, let us create a skeleton for the HostsFile resource that we built in Chapter 9.

Defining Resource Properties

The HostsFile resource has only three attributes: IPAddress, HostName, and Ensure. The Ensure property is a value map that takes Present or Absent as valid values. Let us explore how to define these properties. We use the New-xDscResourceProperty cmdlet for this.

```
$HostName = New-xDscResourceProperty -Name HostName -Type String -Attribute Key
$IPAddress = New-xDscResourceProperty -Name IPAddress -Type String -Attribute Key
$Ensure = New-xDscResourceProperty -Name Ensure -Type String -Attribute Write -ValidateSet
  Present, Absent
```

In the preceding code, we are creating the required properties. The -Name parameter is used to specify the name of the resource property, and the -Attribute parameter defines the attribute qualifier that must be used for the property. For the HostsFile resource, both HostName and IPAddress are key properties. The preceding code creates the properties and stores them in the variables specified.

Creating DSC Resources

The next step will be to generate the resource files. This can be done using the New-xDscResource cmdlet for this. The -Name parameter of this cmdlet is used to specify the name of the resource. -Path is used to specify the path on which the module files have to be created, and the resource properties are specified using the -Property parameter.

```
New-xDscResource -Name HostsFile -Property $HostName, $IPAddress, $Ensure -Path
'C:\Program Files\WindowsPowerShell\Modules\HostsFile'
```

As shown in Figure A-2, the New-xDscResource cmdlet generates the folder structure. Note that the folder structure created is similar to how we package DSC resources nested modules.

```
Directory: C:\Program Files\WindowsPowerShell\Modules

Mode                LastWriteTime     Length Name
----                -------------     ------ ----
d----         6/11/2014   2:46 PM            HostsFile


Directory: C:\Program Files\WindowsPowerShell\Modules\HostsFile

Mode                LastWriteTime     Length Name
----                -------------     ------ ----
d----         6/11/2014   2:46 PM            DSCResources


Directory: C:\Program Files\WindowsPowerShell\Modules\HostsFile\DSCResources

Mode                LastWriteTime     Length Name
----                -------------     ------ ----
d----         6/11/2014   2:46 PM            HostsFile
```

Figure A-2. *Folders created by the New-xDscResource cmdlet*

This cmdlet also creates the .psm1 and schema MOF files for the resource. This is shown in Figure A-3.

```
PS C:\> dir 'C:\Program Files\WindowsPowerShell\Modules\HostsFile\DSCResources\HostsFile'

    Directory: C:\Program Files\WindowsPowerShell\Modules\HostsFile\DSCResources\HostsFile

Mode                LastWriteTime     Length Name
----                -------------     ------ ----
-a---         6/11/2014   2:46 PM       3438 HostsFile.psm1
-a---         6/11/2014   2:46 PM        472 HostsFile.schema.mof
```

Figure A-3. *.psm1 and MOF files generated by the resource designer*

Once the MOF file is generated, we can validate the schema, using the Test-xDscSchema cmdlet. This cmdlet returns a Boolean value based on the schema validity.

```
Test-xDscSchema -Path 'C:\Program Files\WindowsPowerShell\Modules\HostsFile\DSCResources\HostsFile\
HostsFile.schema.mof'
```

If the DSC resource schema is valid, we can go ahead and edit the .psm1 file and add the necessary logic so that the resource is built to perform the required configurations. Once the module is built, you can use the New-ModuleManifest cmdlet to create a PowerShell module manifest file for this custom DSC resource. We have seen examples of this in Chapter 9. The xDscResourceDesigner module provides the Update-xDscResource cmdlet, in case you have to add any new properties to the DSC resource. The hosts file in Windows also takes comments for each host file entry. So, try creating this new property and updating the resource schema and .psm1 file, using the Update-xDscResource cmdlet.

DSC Diagnostics

The DSC diagnostics module in the DSC resource kit is my all-time favorite. For me, this tops the list of most useful modules in the resource kit. The cmdlets in this module help diagnose errors in DSC. This module has three cmdlets, as shown in Figure A-4.

```
PS C:\> Get-Command -Module xDscDiagnostics

CommandType      Name                            ModuleName
-----------      ----                            ----------
Function         Get-xDscOperation               xDscDiagnostics
Function         Trace-xDscOperation             xDscDiagnostics
Function         Update-xDscEventLogStatus       xDscDiagnostics
```

Figure A-4. *Cmdlets in the xDscDiagnostics module*

We looked at querying DSC event logs, including the analytics and debug logs, in Chapter 8. We used the wecutil.exe command-line tool to enable the analytic and debug event logs. The Update-xDscEventLogStatus cmdlet in the xDscDiagnostics module helps us enable or disable the Analytic and Debug event log channels. For example, the following command can be used to enable the Analytic event log channel for DSC:

```
Update-xDscEventLogStatus -Channel Analytic -Status Enabled
```

You can use the -ComputerName parameter to specify the target system in which you have to enable or disable these event log channels. We did a lot of heavy lifting to understand and group the event logs for any given DSC operation. While discussing the event logs, we have defined DSC operations for a complete sequence of events that occur when DSC performs the configuration enacting process. So, to that extent, the Get-xDscOperation cmdlet gets a list of all DSC operations performed on a given target system. For example, the following command gives a list of all DSC operations from a remote system called WSR2-2 (see Figure A-5).

```
Get-xDscOperation -ComputerName WSR2-2
```

```
ComputerName  SequenceId TimeCreated          Result   JobID                                   AllEvents
------------  ---------- -----------          ------   -----                                   ---------
WSR2-2        1          6/11/2014 4:56:47 PM Failure  826996e9-0528-4df4-ac3b-10589b7cb09c    {@{Message...
WSR2-2        2          6/11/2014 4:40:43 PM Failure  0b2a4f53-73e9-4256-8bd4-938a05422fb7    {@{Message...
WSR2-2        3          6/11/2014 4:25:17 PM Failure  23dbe546-e368-43fe-b2b5-58ad106a2b47    {@{Message...
WSR2-2        4          6/11/2014 3:41:56 PM Failure  53365b76-377d-447d-9cd5-91268b99b315    {@{Message...
WSR2-2        5          6/11/2014 3:27:25 PM Failure  9752c7db-4afe-4801-8ded-e3606492dcbc    {@{Message...
WSR2-2        6          6/11/2014 3:11:07 PM Failure  700d67fc-4517-4392-8f4d-fac2cac6954c    {@{Message...
WSR2-2        7          6/11/2014 2:10:52 PM Failure  bfe518b8-43b6-4b6f-b0cf-ec5dc15b378e    {@{Message...
WSR2-2        8          6/11/2014 1:26:14 PM Failure  85964fa1-a8fe-437a-95bf-7d19c25ef40a    {@{Message...
WSR2-2        9          6/11/2014 1:10:35 PM Failure  c43d05a8-76b0-4e5e-aad8-3ac2596150e2    {@{Message...
WSR2-2        10         6/11/2014 12:55:41 PM Failure 702fa81b-c5a7-48eb-8e54-c6d7a2e3d37e    {@{Message...
```

Figure A-5. *List of all DSC operations from a remote system*

The JobId property, shown in Figure A-5, uniquely identifies each DSC operation. The SequenceId property is added to the Get-xDscOperation cmdlet, to make tracing the events within the DSC operation easier. We can use the Trace-xDscOperation cmdlet to delve into a specific DSC operation and understand why it failed or to determine the exact sequence of events during the DSC operation.

```
Trace-xDscOperation -SequenceId 2 -ComputerName WSR2-2
```

As shown in Figure A-6, the Trace-xDscOperation cmdlet shows all the events in chronological order, leading to either successful completion or failure of the DSC operation.

```
ComputerName    EventType     TimeCreated           Message
------------    ---------     -----------           -------
WSR2-2          OPERATIONAL   6/11/2014 4:40:42 PM  Configuration is sent from computer NULL by user sid S-...
WSR2-2          OPERATIONAL   6/11/2014 4:40:43 PM  Attempting to get the action from pull server using Dow...
WSR2-2          OPERATIONAL   6/11/2014 4:40:43 PM  WebDownloadManager for configuration e86549dc-7a5f-45b6...
WSR2-2          OPERATIONAL   6/11/2014 4:40:43 PM  WebDownloadManager for configuration e86549dc-7a5f-45b6...
WSR2-2          OPERATIONAL   6/11/2014 4:40:43 PM  WebDownloadManager processed certificate: [Subject]...
WSR2-2          OPERATIONAL   6/11/2014 4:40:43 PM  WebDownloadManager for configuration e86549dc-7a5f-45b6...
WSR2-2          OPERATIONAL   6/11/2014 4:40:43 PM  Successfully got the action GetConfiguration from pull ...
WSR2-2          ERROR         6/11/2014 4:40:43 PM  Failed to delete the current configuration file
WSR2-2          OPERATIONAL   6/11/2014 4:40:43 PM  Attempting to get the configuration from pull server us...
WSR2-2          OPERATIONAL   6/11/2014 4:40:43 PM  WebDownloadManager for configuration e86549dc-7a5f-45b6...
WSR2-2          OPERATIONAL   6/11/2014 4:40:43 PM  Attempting to get the configuration e86549dc-7a5f-45b6-...
WSR2-2          OPERATIONAL   6/11/2014 4:40:43 PM  WebDownloadManager processed certificate: [Subject]...
WSR2-2          OPERATIONAL   6/11/2014 4:40:43 PM  WebDownloadManager for configuration e86549dc-7a5f-45b6...
WSR2-2          OPERATIONAL   6/11/2014 4:40:43 PM  WebDownloadManager for configuration e86549dc-7a5f-45b6...
WSR2-2          OPERATIONAL   6/11/2014 4:40:43 PM  The checksum validation for configuration e86549dc-7a5f...
WSR2-2          OPERATIONAL   6/11/2014 4:40:43 PM  The checksum validation for configuration C:\Windows\TE...
WSR2-2          OPERATIONAL   6/11/2014 4:40:43 PM  Skipping pulling module PSDesiredStateConfiguration wit...
WSR2-2          OPERATIONAL   6/11/2014 4:40:43 PM  Skipping pulling of modules since all modules specified...
WSR2-2          OPERATIONAL   6/11/2014 4:40:43 PM  Successfully got the configuration from pull server usi...
WSR2-2          ANALYTIC      6/11/2014 4:40:43 PM  Applying configuration from C:\Windows\System32\Configu...
WSR2-2          ANALYTIC      6/11/2014 4:40:43 PM  Deleting file from C:\Windows\System32\Configuration\Pe...
WSR2-2          ERROR         6/11/2014 4:40:43 PM  This event indicates that failure happens when LCM is t...
```

Figure A-6. *Event trace from a DSC operation*

This module in the resource kit is very handy when troubleshooting the DSC configuration enacting process, but be aware that the volume of analytic and debug events can be quite high, based on how often the DSC consistency engine runs. So, it is recommended that analytic and debug logs be disabled when not required.

DSC Service Resource

In Chapter 6, we looked at how we can configure HTTP- or HTTPS-based Pull service endpoints using PowerShell commands. We can convert them into a reusable function or module to help us configure Pull services, on an as-needed basis. However, the resource kit contains a DSC resource called xDSCWebService in the xPSDesiredStateConfiguration nested module that helps deploy OData-based DSC Pull services, using a configuration script similar to any other DSC resource. When we looked at the examples in Chapter 6, we assumed that we were working on a fresh install of OS with no IIS web sites already present, and so on. However, this may not always be the case. To ensure that we do not overwrite any existing configuration or delete any existing endpoints, it is mandatory that we have these validations and error-handling in our scripts. With the xDscWebService resource, we get all this ready-made.

Let us look at a few examples using this resource. We will start by creating an HTTP Pull service endpoint.

```
Configuration DscWebService
{
    param
    (
        [string[]]$NodeName = 'localhost',

        [ValidateNotNullOrEmpty()]
        [string] $certificateThumbPrint
    )
    Import-DSCResource -ModuleName xPSDesiredStateConfiguration
```

```
    Node $NodeName
    {
        WindowsFeature DSCServiceFeature
        {
            Ensure = "Present"
            Name   = "DSC-Service"
        }

        xDscWebService PSDSCPullServer
        {
            Ensure                 = "Present"
            EndpointName           = "PSDSCPullServer"
            Port                   = 8080
            PhysicalPath           = "$env:SystemDrive\inetpub\wwwroot\PSDSCPullServer"
            CertificateThumbPrint  = $certificateThumbPrint
            ModulePath             = "$env:PROGRAMFILES\WindowsPowerShell\DscService\Modules"
            ConfigurationPath      = "$env:PROGRAMFILES\WindowsPowerShell\DscService\Configuration"
            State                  = "Started"
            DependsOn              = "[WindowsFeature]DSCServiceFeature"
        }
    }
}
```

```
DscWebService -certificateThumbPrint AllowUnencryptedTraffic
```

This is it. The preceding configuration document generates the MOF file required to perform the DSC Pull service configuration on the local system. We can either use Push or Pull mode to complete the enactment process.

If you look at the preceding example, we are taking a certificate thumbprint as an input to the configuration command. With this type of parameterization, we can use the same configuration command to deploy an HTTPS-based Pull service endpoint. So, assuming that you have a certificate thumbprint to use for the web server, the following command is all you have to execute:

```
DscWebService -certificateThumbPrint A5056E6456B44C505E6144275EA9C9E5EB044537
```

When using the DSC Service feature in WMF 4.0 and later, we can take advantage of the compliance server endpoint to query the compliance status of all pull clients. We looked at this in Chapter 8 and saw an example that configures the compliance server endpoint. The following example shows how this can be done with the xDscWebService DSC resource.

```
Configuration DscWebService
{
    param
    (
        [string[]]$NodeName = 'localhost',

        [ValidateNotNullOrEmpty()]
        [string] $certificateThumbPrint
    )
```

```
Import-DSCResource -ModuleName xPSDesiredStateConfiguration
Node $NodeName
{
    WindowsFeature DSCServiceFeature
    {
        Ensure = "Present"
        Name   = "DSC-Service"
    }

    WindowsFeature WinAuth
    {
        Ensure = "Present"
        Name   = "web-Windows-Auth"
    }

    xDscWebService PSDSCComplianceServer
    {
        Ensure                = "Present"
        EndpointName          = "PSDSCComplianceServer"
        Port                  = 9080
        PhysicalPath          = "$env:SystemDrive\inetpub\wwwroot\PSDSCComplianceServer"
        CertificateThumbPrint = $certificateThumbPrint
        State                 = "Started"
        IsComplianceServer    = $true
        DependsOn             = @("[WindowsFeature]DSCServiceFeature","[WindowsFeature]WinAuth",
                                    "[xDSCWebService]PSDSCPullServer")
    }
  }
}

DscWebService -certificateThumbPrint AllowUnencryptedTraffic
```

You can simply enact the MOF file generated from this configuration script, using your favorite method of configuration delivery. See how simple things are with a custom resource for configuring the Pull services? There are many such custom DSC resources in the resource kit. I encourage you to take a look at each one of them to understand how they work and use them as needed. If not a direct benefit, looking at the code behind each of those resources will certainly help when you start writing your own resources.

Summary

Desired State Configuration (DSC) is a new kid on the block, and there are many people in the PowerShell community looking at and using it in production. The DSC platform makes it easy to write custom resources, and quite a few community DSC resources have already been written and shared publicly. The Windows PowerShell team is supporting the community by releasing DSC resource kit waves that not only include DSC resources but many other helper modules that extend DSC functionality. We have not looked at each of those resources in this appendix. I encourage you both to delve into the available resources and share your custom DSC resources, to help other community members looking for help.

■ ■ ■

WMF 5.0 and DSC for Linux

Desired State Configuration (DSC) is in its early stages of evolution. This is a feature built into the operating system (OS), starting from Windows Server 2012 R2 and Windows 8.1. It is available for down-level operating systems, such as Windows 7 and Windows Server 2008 R2, and Windows Server 2012, as Windows Management Framework 4.0. As with any other software release, while providing a great start, some features of DSC have limitations. Windows Management Framework 5.0 will address some of these limitations, while enhancing the overall DSC functionality. At the time of writing, the WMF 5.0 preview was available for Windows Server 2012 R2 and Windows 8.1 operating systems.

While working on enhancing the DSC functionality on the Windows OS, Microsoft is also working at extending this standards-based configuration management platform to Linux and Unix operating systems. DSC for Linux is available in open source and free.

In this appendix, we will explore some of the changes and enhancements to DSC on Windows and look at how to deploy and use DSC for Linux. Note that these two components are still in the early stages of development, and the content in this chapter may or may not be applicable upon the final release. Also, any subsequent changes to WMF 5.0 and DSC for Linux may void the content of this chapter. This is provided as early guidance, and I recommend that you refer to any available documentation regarding these releases.

Windows Management Framework 5.0

At the time of writing, Windows Management Framework 5.0 was available as a preview download for Windows Server 2012 R2 and Windows 8.1 operating systems. You can download this preview from www.microsoft.com/en-us/download/details.aspx?id=42936. Follow the WMF 4.0 installation procedure shown in Chapter 1, for installing WMF 5.0 too.

WMF 5.0 includes more than just changes or enhancements to DSC. But because our focus is DSC, let us look at the changes to DSC in this preview release.

Credential Property of Archive Resource

In WMF 4.0, the built-in Archive resource did not have a Credential property. So, it was not possible to extract zip archives directly from a network share, unless the target system was given permission to access the share. This is solved in the WMF 5.0 preview. The updated Archive resource includes a Credential property. Here is a quick example of using the Credential property. This is not different from how we use the Credential property of other resources.

```
$ConfigurationData = @{
    AllNodes = @(
        @{
            NodeName="WSR2-1"
            PSDscAllowPlainTextPassword=$true
        }
    )
}

Configuration ArchiveDemo {
    param (
        [Parameter(Mandatory]
        [ValidateNotNullOrEmpty()]
        [String]$Path,

        [Parameter(Mandatory)]
        [PSCredential]$Credential,

        [Parameter(Mandatory)]
        [String]$Destination
    )

    Node $AllNodes.NodeName {
        Archive ArchiveDemo {
            Path = $Path
            Destination = $Destination
            Credential = $Credential
        }
    }
}

ArchiveDemo -ConfigurationData $configurationData -Path "\\Demo-AD\Scripts\Resources.zip"
-Credential (Get-Credential) -Destination "${env:ProgramFiles}\WindowsPowerShell\Modules"
```

In the preceding example, we are using a plain text password. Remember that the right way of using credentials in DSC is to encrypt those credentials using certificates.

Multiple Attributes in the File Resource

In Chapter 4, when looking at the built-in File resource, we saw the limitation imposed by the Attributes property. It was not possible to specify multiple attributes. WMF 5.0 enhanced the File resource, to support multiple attributes.

```
Configuration FileDemo {
    Node WSR2-1 {
        File FileDemo {
            DestinationPath = 'C:\Scripts\test.dll'
            Attributes = System','Hidden'
        }'
    }
}
```

Installing Packages from an HTTPS Location

In WMF 4.0, we could install MSI and EXE packages from an HTTP location. However, there was no support for HTTPS-based URLs. This is fixed in WMF 5.0.

```
Configuration PackageDemo {
    Node localhost {
        Package PackageDemo {
            Path = 'https://psmag.blob.core.windows.net/downloads/7z920-x64.msi'
            Name = '7-Zip 9.20 (x64 edition)'
            ProductId = '23170F69-40C1-2702-0920-000001000000'
        }
    }
}
```

PackageDemo

The package resource includes one more change as well. In WMF 4.0, the product ID specified in the resource configuration does not get validated until the package installment is complete. This results in an error toward the end of the enact process and leaves the system in an inconsistent state when a wrong product ID is specified. To fix this, the updated package resource in WMF 5.0 preview includes a pre-validation for the product ID. This is applicable only for MSI packages. Before enacting the configuration, the package resource reads the MSI and compares that to the value of the ProductId property. Any mismatch prevents the package installation.

Changes to Test-DscConfiguration

We have seen and discussed that the Test-DscConfiguration returns only a Boolean value, indicating whether or not the target system is in the desired state. This was not very helpful, because it won't really tell us why the system is not in the desired state or which resource is not in the desired state. This is changing in the WMF 5.0 preview. At least, the change is an indication that we would be able to see which resource is or is not in the desired state. To get this information, we have to use the -Detailed switch parameter (see Figure B-1).

```
PS C:\> Test-DscConfiguration -Detailed

ResourceID                                                              InDesiredState
----------                                                              --------------
{[File]FileDemo}                                                                 False
```

Figure B-1. *Test-DscConfiguration changes in the WMF 5.0 preview*

The ResourceID property in the output provides the list of resources that are a part of the configuration. In the preview release, this is just a string and does not include any more details.

DebugMode in Meta-configuration

In Chapter 10, we looked at some common problems, and one such problem was updated resources not loading on the target system. This was due to resource caching in DSC. In WMF 4.0, the only way to overcome this was to restart the WMI host process. In WMF 5.0, the LCM meta-configuration is updated to include a new property called DebugMode.

Using this property, we can disable the resource caching functionality in DSC, and we can use the configuration script to update the LCM meta-configuration. We have seen several examples of this, and here is one more that shows updating DebugMode:

```
Configuration LCMConfig {
    Node Localhost {
        LocalConfigurationManager
        {
            DebugMode = $true
        }
    }
}
```

```
LCMConfig
```

Once you have the LCM meta-configuration changed, as shown in the preceding example, you can try the configuration scripts we discussed in Chapter 10, to observe the difference the DebugMode feature enables.

DSC for Linux

DSC for Linux is an open source initiative to bring a standards-based configuration management platform to Linux and Unix operating systems. Microsoft is working with the Open Group to build an Open Management Infrastructure that can be used as a Common Information Model (CIM) server on Linux-based platforms.

At the time of writing, a few Linux OS variants have been validated, but if you are a Linux expert, you may be able to get DSC running on any Linux OS variant. This is available as a CTP release and can be downloaded from https://github.com/MSFTOSSMgmt/WPSDSCLinux. At the moment, this requires multiple steps to get DSC running on Linux platforms. This includes compiling OMI and DSC libraries and configuring the same. For demonstration purposes, I have used a CentOS system with Internet connectivity.

Installing and Configuring DSC for Linux

We use the Yum repository to install the required prerequisites. I will not go into the details of each, but they should be clear from the package names. These commands have to be run as root user. In the following set of commands, I have added a -y switch to avoid the prompt:

```
yum -y groupinstall 'Development Tools'
yum -y install pam-devel
yum -y install openssl-devel
yum -y install python
yum -y install python-devel
```

Once the prerequisite installment is complete, we must download and install the OMI server. This can be directly downloaded from the Open Group web site, and the supported version is 1.0.8.

```
mkdir /root/downloads
cd /root/downloads

wget https://collaboration.opengroup.org/omi/documents/30532/omi-1.0.8.tar.gz
tar -xvf omi-1.0.8.tar.gz
```

```
cd omi-1.0.8
./configure | tee /tmp/omi-configure.txt
make | tee /tmp/omi-make.txt
make install | tee /tmp/omi-make-install.txt
```

The tee command with make and make install commands will help us capture the output from the make process for any analysis later. The preceding set of commands build and install the OMI server.

Once the OMI server installation is complete, we can download and install DSC for Linux from the GitHub site.

```
cd /root/downloads

wget https://github.com/MSFTOSSMgmt/WPSDSCLinux/releases/download/v1.0.0-CTP/PSDSCLinux.tar.gz
tar -xvf PSDSCLinux.tar.gz
cd dsc/
mv * /root/downloads/

cd /root/downloads
make | tee /tmp/dsc-make.txt
make reg | tee /tmp/dsc-make-reg.txt
```

We now have the OMI server and DSC LCM built. We can start the OMI server so that the access to DSC LCM is enabled.

```
OMI_HOME=/opt/omi-1.0.8
/opt/omi-1.0.8/bin/omiserver -d
```

The preceding commands set the $OMI_HOME variable in the shell and start the OMI server. At this moment, you should be able to create a CIM session to connect to these Linux systems. This is it. We have DSC for Linux configured and listening at port number 5985. At the moment, you can test the connectivity to the Linux system, using the Get-CimInstance cmdlet on a Windows system. You should be able to use root username and password for providing credentials required for the connectivity.

DSC Resources for Linux

The built-in DSC resources for Linux are different from those available on the Windows OS. At the moment, there are five DSC resources for Linux. These resource modules are a part of the DSC build that is compiled and installed on the Linux system. These resources are identified with an *nx* prefix.

- nxFile: Used to manage files on Linux systems

- nxUser: Used to manage user account on Linux systems

- nxGroup: Used to manage groups on Linux systems

- nxScript: Used to execute arbitrary shell scripts on Linux systems

- nxService: Used to manage services/daemons on Linux systems

At the time of writing, custom DSC resources for Linux could only be written as Management Infrastructure providers and required knowledge of C or C++. This is outside the scope of this book, and also, there is no guidance available at the moment on the semantics for developing these resources.

Enacting Configuration

As we understand from the knowledge gained so far, to generate a Managed Object Format (MOF) file from a configuration script, we would require the resource schema available on the system on which we are generating the MOF file. At the time of writing, there was no method available on Linux systems to generate the configuration MOF files. So, to be able to generate an MOF file for Linux configuration, we have to copy the Linux DSC resources' schema files to a Windows system. These schema files are available for download at https://github.com/MSFTOSSMgmt/WPSDSCLinux/releases/download/v1.0.0-CTP/nx-PSModule.zip. They have to be extracted to the %SystemRoot%\system32\WindowsPowerShell\v1.0\Modules folder on the Windows system.

Once you have the schema files copied, you can author configuration scripts for the Linux systems the same way you do for the Windows OS.

```
Configuration MyDSCDemo
{
    Import-DSCResource -Module nx
    Node DSC-Linux1 {
        nxFile myTestFile
        {
            Ensure = "Present"
            Type = "File"
            DestinationPath = "/tmp/dsctest"
            Contents="This is my DSC Test!"
        }
    }
}

MyDscDemo
```

We can generate the MOF file by running the MyDSCDemo configuration command and using the PowerShell cmdlets or CIM methods to push this configuration to a Linux system.

```
Start-DscConfiguration -Wait -Verbose -Path .\MyDSCDemo -Credential (Get-Credential)
```

We need to explicitly provide root credentials when pushing configuration to a Linux system. The current release of DSC for Linux does not support configuring LCM as a pull client. This functionality may come in a future release.

Once the configuration enactment is complete, we can use the cmdlets in the PSDesiredStateConfiguration PowerShell module to manage the Linux systems too.

Linux Configuration Store and Logs

On Windows systems with WMF 4.0 or 5.0, the configuration store is located in the C:\Windows\System32\Configuration folder. On Linux systems, this is located at /opt/omi-1.0.8/etc/dsc/configuration. As with Windows systems, this configuration store contains current.mof, backup.mof, previous.mof, and so on. The LCM meta-configuration gets stored at this location as MetaConfig.mof.

DSC on Linux systems store the log files at /opt/omi-1.0.8/var/log. The dsc.log file contains all messages related to the configuration enactment process, while omiserver.log contains any log messages from the OMI server process.

■ **Note** Any issues related to DSC for Linux can be submitted on GitHub at `https://github.com/MSFTOSSMgmt/` `WPSDSCLinux/issues`.

Summary

Microsoft is aiming to build standards-based, cross-platform configuration management that can be used to manage any compatible element in the data center. DSC for Linux is a step in that direction. In addition, DSC, as a platform itself, is still evolving. The WMF 5.0 preview includes several fixes and enhancements to the DSC platform, which will be improved further. There are also several device vendors adding OMI support to devices such as network switches and storage arrays. With this move, it becomes easy to manage almost every fabric in the data center, using the DSC platform.

Index

A

Active Directory (AD), 257–258
Active Directory Certificate Server, 166
AD. *See* Active Directory (AD)
AllowUnSecureConnection property, 197
American National Standards Institute
    Structured Query Language (ANSI SQL), 55
Application programming interfaces (API), 52
Archive resource, DSC
    computer account permission, 119
    configuration, 116
    enforcing, archive content change, 117
    LCM, 115, 118
    properties, 115
    unpacking archive, UNC path, 119–120
    zip archive, network share, 118
Arithmetic operators, 21–23
Assignment operators, 23–24

B

Building custom, DSC
    composite resources, 242–244
    configuration change, 237
    execution flow, 226–227
    Get-TargetResource
        Export-ModuleMember-Function, 234
        function, 233–234
        HostsFile resource, nested module, 235–236
        partial output, HostsFile resource, 235
    granularity, 242
    help content, 241–242
    HostsFile, 229
    InstanceName parameter,
        configuration command, 245–246
    packaging, resource modules, 228–229
    qualifiers, schema, 224–225

    resource development, 223–224
    resource module manifest, 227–228
    resource patterns, 237
    resource PowerShell module, 226
    Set-TargetResource, 232–233
    Test-TargetResource
        execution flow, 230
        function, 231–232
    Verbose and Debug messages, 238, 240
    writing, resource, 229
Built-in resources, DSC
    DependsOn property
        demonstration, 149
        multiple dependent resources,
            configuration script, 150
    exploring
        list, 113–114
        WMF 4.0, 114

C

CIM. *See* Common Information Model (CIM)
CIM cmdlets
    classes and instances, 52–55
    description, 52
    methods, 65
    module, 52
    remote systems, 66–68
    Win32 WMI classes in the root\wmi namespace, 53
    WSMan protocol, 257
    WQL, 55–58, 60–61, 63–65
CM. *See* Configuration management (CM) processes
Common Information Model (CIM)
    cmdlets (*see* CIM cmdlets)
    definition, 51
    MOF, 69–71, 73–74
    MSFT_DscLocalConfigurationManager class, 259
    windows management instrumentation (WMI), 51

Community resources, DSC
  designer module, 270–271
  diagnostics
    event trace, 273–274
    remote system, 273
    xDscDiagnostics module, 272–273
  New-xDscResource cmdlet, 271–272
  parameter, 271
  properties, 271
  psm1 and MOF files, 272
  service resource, 274–276
  Windows PowerShell community, 269
  Windows PowerShell DSC Resource Kit, 270
  Comparison operators, 24–25
Configuration management (CM) processes
  enactment, 207
  life cycle, 77–78
  monitoring and correction, 210
  target system configuration, 207–209
  target system meta-configuration, 210
  tools or frameworks, 259
Configuration scripts, DSC
  credentials (see Credentials)
  data parameter, 156
  extended configuration data, 159–160, 162–163
  nested configurations (see Nested configurations)
  reusable
    MOF file, 152
    parameters, 152–153
    string array, 153
  separating configuration data, 157–159
Consistency task interval, 203
Credentials
  encryption
    Active Directory Certificate
      Server/certificate authority, 166
    Get-Credential cmdlet, 168
    LCM, 169–170
    meta-configuration, 169
    MOF, 168–169
    PSDscAllowPlainTextPassword, property, 167
    Thumbprint, 167
  plain-text credentials, 163

■ D

Desired State Configuration (DSC)
  archive resource (see Archive resource, DSC)
  byte array, 259–260
  CIM (see Common information model (CIM))
  CM, 77–78, 259
  configuration reporting, 214
  conformance endpoint service
    metadata, 220
    NodeCompliant, 221–222
    Pull Service endpoint, 217–219

    status method, 219
    status method output properties, 219–220
  consistency checks, 210, 212
  continuous delivery process, 80
  credentials, 258
  cross-domain configuration management, 257–258
  delivery modes (see DSC configuration
    delivery modes)
  desktop management task force (DMTF), 43
  domain trusts, 258–259
  environment resource, 120–122
  event logs
    messages, 214
    operational logs, 212–213
    partial set, 213–214
  execution policy, 88–90
  expert tips, 264
  extended phases, configuration management, 79
  file resource (see File resource, DSC)
  GetConfiguration, 260–261
  Get-HotFix cmdlet, 83
  group resource, 126–128
  imperative vs. declarative syntax, 81–82
  KB2883200 download locations, 83
  log resource, 128–130
  management architecture (see DSC configuration
    management architecture)
  multiple configuration scripts, 266
  package resource (see Package resource, DSC)
  PowerShell Cmdlets, 215–216
  PowerShell profile and customization, 265
  registry resource, 136
  RollBack, 263–264
  script resource (see Script resource, DSC)
  SendApplyConfiguration, 262
  SendConfiguration, 261–262
  service resource, 142–144
  TestConfiguration, 263
  user resource, 144–146
  version control and backups, 266, 268
  WindowsFeature resource, 146–148
  WindowsProcess resource, 133–135
  WinRM (see Windows remote management
    (WinRM))
  WMF 5.0 (see Windows Management
    Framework (WMF) 5.0)
Download manager, 196
DownloadManagerName property, 196
DSC. See Desired State Configuration (DSC)
DSC configuration delivery modes
  Action and Module, 193
  CimSession parameter, 184
  cmdlet, 180
  ComputerName parameter, 184
  ConfigurationModeFrequency, 201
  Enhanced Key Usage (EKU), 190

HTTP/HTTPS endpoints, 190–191
jobName parameter, 181
parameters, 179–180
PathPullServer, 191
properties, 182
pull client configuration, 198–200
Pull mode, 186
PullServer, 188
pull service endpoint, 189, 192
pushing configuration, 184
Push mode, 179
refresh mode frequency, 200–201
script resource, 181
SiteID variable, 190
ThrottleLimit parameter, 183
Windows PowerShell, 187
WinRM error, 183
XML output, 193
DSC configuration management architecture
authoring
configuration script, 98–99, 101–102
description, 91–92
PowerShell module
(*see* DSC PowerShell module)
Pull mode, 104
Push mode, 104
resources, 96–97
requirements, 103
WebSiteConfig, 93
enactment
LCM, 105–109
Pull mode, 110–111
Push mode, 109–110
staging and delivery, 103
DSC PowerShell module
commands, 94
configuration keyword, 95–96
Node keyword, 96

E

Environment resource, DSC
configuration, path variable, 121–122
creation, 121
properties, 120

F

File resource, DSC
"Archive Resource" section, 126
attributes property, 125
configuration, 125
empty file, creation, 123–124
empty folder, creation, 124
properties, 123

G

GetConfiguration method, 209
Globally Unique Identifier (GUID), 130
Group resource, DSC
adding group members, 128
DSC, creation, 127
members property, 128
properties, 126
GUID. *See* Globally Unique Identifier (GUID)

H

HTTP endpoints, 197
HTTPS WinRM listeners
configuration, 47
creation, 45
force parameter, 45
Get-ChildItem cmdlet, 49
Listener_1084132640, 46
localhost container, 46
new-WSManInstance command execution, 49
new-WSManSessionOption cmdlet, 50
non-default port numbers, 48
port number, 47–48
PowerShell, 46
PowerShell certificate, 49
properties, 47
remote system, 50
retrieving certificate thumbprint, 49
self-signed SSL certificate, 48
Set-Item cmdlet, 47
SSL parameter, 48
successful creation, 49
testing, 45

I, J, K

Integrated Scripting Environment (ISE), 9–10
ISE. *See* Integrated Scripting Environment (ISE)

L

LCM. *See* Local Configuration Manager (LCM)
Linux, DSC
configuration store and logs, 282
installing and configuring, 280–281
resources, 281
Local Configuration Manager (LCM)
CIM methods, 106, 259
default settings, 108
GUID, 203–204
meta-configuration settings, 107, 109
MOF, 169–170
pull client configuration, 194

Local Configuration Manager (LCM) (*cont.*)
 UNC path, access, 118
 zip archive, 115
Logical operators, 26
Log resource, DSC
 messages, event log, 129
 properties, 128
Looping, PowerShell
 Break statement, 32
 Continue Statement, 32
 Do Statement, 31
 ForEach Statement, 30
 For statement, 30
 While statement, 31

■ M

Managed object format (MOF)
 comments, 72
 compiler directives, 70
 compiling, 72–73
 definition, 69
 dynamic-link library (DLL) file, 69
 instance, 71
 qualifiers, 70
 type declarations, 71
 Win32_CurrentTime, 70
Meta characters, 58

■ N

Nested configurations
 data structure, 170–171
 Get-DscResource output, 172
 MOF, 174
 parameters, 172
NewGuid() method, 195

■ O

Operators
 arithmetic, 21–23
 assignment, 23–24
 comparison, 24–25
 logical, 26

■ P, Q

Package resource, DSC
 configuration failure, invalid package name, 133
 GUID, 130
 installation, 131
 properties, 130
 uninstalling package, 132

Plain-text credentials
 configuration data, 163, 165
 file resource, property, 164
 PSDscAllowPlainTextPassword, property, 165
PowerShell
 aliases, 33
 arrays, 26–27
 branching, 29–30
 cmdlet parameters, 14
 commands, 11–12
 console, 7–8
 custom objects, 28
 description, 3
 distributed automation engine, 5
 downloading and installing WMF 4.0, 6
 environment, 40
 flow control, 28
 functions, 37
 Get-Help cmdlet, 12–13
 Get-Member cmdlet, 13
 hash tables, 27
 installation, 5
 ISE, 9–10
 looping (*see* Looping, PowerShell)
 modules
  discovering, 38
  importing, 39
  writing, 39–40
 named parameters, 14
 New-Object cmdlet, 28
 object-based shell, 4
 operators (*see* Operators)
 pipeline, 33–34
 positional parameters, 15
 scripting languages, 5
 scripts
  execution policies, 34–35
  writing and executing, 35–37
 switch parameters, 15
 variables (*see* Variables, PowerShell)
 version table, 6
PowerShell Cmdlets
 CimSession parameter, 216
 configuration, 216
 current implementation, 216
 REST, 216
 Test-DscConfiguration, 215
 testing, 215
PowerShell execution policy, 88–90
PreviousInstance property, 64
PSDesiredStateConfiguration, 94–95
PSDscAllowPlainTextPassword, 165, 167
Pull client configuration settings, 194, 198
Pull clients and pull server, 197

R

RefreshFrequencyMins property, 201
Refresh mode frequency, 200–201
Registry resource, DSC
    key and value creation, 136–137
    properties, 136
Remote procedure calls (RPC), 51
Representative state transfer (REST), 216
REST. *See* Representative state transfer (REST)

S

Script resource, DSC
    Boolean value, 138–139
    Get-DscConfiguration, 140
    MOF schema, 141
    output, Get-DscConfiguration, 142
    properties, 138
    TestScript and SetScript usage, 140
Server Message Block (SMB), 194
Service resource, DSC
    AudioSrv, 143
    properties, 143
Simple object access protocol (SOAP), 43
SMB Pull mode, 198

T

TargetInstance property, 64
ThrottleLimit parameter, 183
Troubleshooting, DSC
    custom resources, 249
    engine cache, 252–254
    pending configuration, error, 251–252
    WinRM issues, 249–251
    WMF 4.0, 247–249

U

User resource, DSC
    creation, 145
    properties, 144–145

V

Variables, PowerShell
    automatic, 19
    cmdlets, 18
    environment, 20–21
    names, 16–17
    New-Variable cmdlet, 18
    preference, 20
    string, 17

W, X, Y, Z

Web-Based Enterprise Management (WBEM)
    technologies, 51
WindowsFeature resource, DSC
    AD domain services installation, 147
    DSC messages, reboot, 147
    .NET framework 3.5, external source, 148
    properties, 146
Windows Management Framework (WMF) 4.0
    configuration, 247–248
    WMI, 248–249
Windows Management Framework (WMF) 5.0
    credential property, archive resource, 277–278
    DebugMode, meta-configuration, 279–280
    enacting configuration, 282
    Linux, 280–282
    multiple attributes, file resource, 278
    packages, HTTPS location, 279
    Test-DscConfiguration, 279
Windows Management
    Instrumentation (WMI), 51, 248–249
Windows PowerShell. *See* PowerShell
WindowsProcess resource, DSC
    properties, 133–134
    starting process, DSC, 135
    termination, arguments, 135
Windows Remote Management (WinRM)
    configuration, Group Policy, 87
    Group Policy Management Editor, 85–86
    inbound rules, 87
    listeners, Group Policy, 84, 86, 88
    service status, 44
    settings, 88
    WS-management, 43
    WSMan Cmdlets, 44–51
WinRM. *See* Windows Remote Management (WinRM)
WMF 4.0. *See* Windows Management
    Framework (WMF) 4.0
WMF 5.0. *See* Windows Management
    Framework (WMF) 5.0
WMI. *See* Window Management Instrumentation (WMI)
WMI query language (WQL)
    ANSI SQL, 55
    keywords, 55–56
    operators, 56
    queries
        AND condition with PreviousInstance, 65
        error, subscripting to non-event class, 62
        event classes in root\cimv2 namespace, 62–63
        $Event variable, 60–61
        event subscription and
          script block execution, 59
        exploring the $Event variable, 60

WMI query language (WQL) (*cont.*)
    extrinsic events and timer events, 65
    filtering windows processes, multiple process, 58
    filtering windows process objects, 57
    handlecount, 58
    InstanceModificationEvent, 63
    intrinsic events, 63
    LIKE keyword, 57
    message from event subscription, 62
    meta character, 58
    Register-CimIndicationEvent cmdlet, 61
    subset of properties, 57
    TargetInstance and PreviousInstance, 64
    testing event, 64
    types, 59
WQL. *See* WMI query language (WQL)
WS-management (WSMan) cmdlets
    accessing management information, 50–51
    communication error without listeners, 44
    HTTPS WinRM listeners, 45–50
    powershell 4.0, 44
    remote system communication, 44

Get the eBook for only $10!

Now you can take the weightless companion with you anywhere, anytime. Your purchase of this book entitles you to 3 electronic versions for only $10.

This Apress title will prove so indispensible that you'll want to carry it with you everywhere, which is why we are offering the eBook in 3 formats for only $10 if you have already purchased the print book.

Convenient and fully searchable, the PDF version enables you to easily find and copy code—or perform examples by quickly toggling between instructions and applications. The MOBI format is ideal for your Kindle, while the ePUB can be utilized on a variety of mobile devices.

Go to www.apress.com/promo/tendollars to purchase your companion eBook.

Apress®
THE EXPERT'S VOICE™